The
BRAZILIAN EMPIRE
Myths and Histories

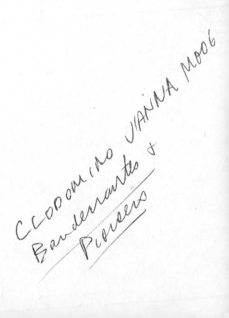

Jose Bonifacio on slavery.
42

CLODOMIRO VIANNA MOOG
Bandenrantes &
Pioneers

The

BRAZILIAN EMPIRE
Myths and Histories

———————

EMILIA VIOTTI DA COSTA

The Dorsey Press
Chicago, Illinois 60604

The Dorsey Press edition published April 1988.
This book is being printed with permission of the
University of Chicago Press.

Library of Congress Cataloging-in-Publication Data

Costa, Emília Viotti da.
    The Brazilian empire.

    Rev. translation of: Da monarquia á república.
    Reprint. Originally published: Chicago: University
of Chicago Press, 1985.
    Bibliography: p.
    Includes index.
    1. Brazil—Politics and government—1822-1889.
2. Brazil—Politics and government—1889-1930.
3. Brazil—Economic conditions—19th century.
4. Brazil—Social conditions—19th century.
5. Elite (Social sciences)—Brazil—History—19th
century. 6. Liberalism—Brazil—History—19th century.
I. Title.
[F2535.C6713   1988]   981'.04   88-7001
ISBN 0-256-06239-0 (pbk.)

Printed in the United States of America

1 2 3 4 5 6 7 8 9 0 ML 5 4 3 2 1 0 9 8

For Flora, Lucia, and Ulisses

CONTENTS

ILLUSTRATIONS

CHRONOLOGY

June 1763   José Bonifácio de Andrada e Silva is born.

1776   Adam Smith publishes *The Wealth of Nations*.

1789   Inconfidência Mineira.

1792   A conspiracy is uncovered in Rio de Janeiro.

1798   Bahia conspiracy.

1808   Napoleon's troops invade Portugal and the Court moves to Brazil.
Prince João opens Brazilian ports to all nations.

1814   Congress of Vienna abolishes the slave trade south of the equator.

1815   Brazil becomes a kingdom united to Portugal.

1817   Revolution in Pernambuco.

1819   José Bonifácio returns to Brazil.

1820   Oporto revolution.

1821   João VI returns to Portugal.
Prince Pedro becomes regent.

1821–22   Several acts of the Portuguese Côrtes limit Brazil's autonomy.

January 1822   Disobeying the Côrtes' order to return to Portugal, Prince Pedro announces he will stay in the colony.

June 1822   Prince Pedro calls the National Convention.

7 September 1822   Prince Pedro, now Emperor Pedro I of Brazil, proclaims Brazilian independence.

1823   The emperor dissolves the National Convention.

1824   The emperor grants a constitutional charter.
Confederação do Equador.

1825   José Bonifácio publishes his *Representação à Assembléia Geral Constituinte e Legislativa do Império do Brasil Sobre a Escravatura*.

1826   The emperor reopens the legislature.

1831   Unrest in Rio de Janeiro and other port cities.

7 April 1831   Pedro I abdicates in favor of his son.

June 1831   The regency government creates a national guard.

August 1831   José Bonifácio is officially recognized as the prince's tutor.

November 1831   Law freeing slaves entering Brazil.

1832   Enactment of the Judicial Code.

1833–35   José Bonifácio is tried and acquitted.

1834   Ato Adicional to the constitution.

1835–45   Revolution in Rio Grande do Sul (Farrapos).

1837–38   Unrest in several provinces of the North and Northeast (Cabanos e Balaios).

1838   José Bonifácio's death.

1840   Law interpreting the Ato Adicional. Prince Pedro is granted majority and rules as Pedro II.

November 1841   Law reestablishing the Council of State.

December 1841   Reform of the Criminal Code.

1842   Revolution in São Paulo and Minas.

1848   Revolution in Pernambuco (Praieira).

1850   Land Law.

Law establishing measures to repress the slave trade.

1851–55   Construction of the first Brazilian railroad.

1853–57   Marquis of Paraná cabinet (Conciliação).

1865   Beginning of the Paraguayan War.

1868   Political crisis triggered by the fall of the Zacarias de Góes e Vasconcelos cabinet.

1869   Liberal party manifesto.

1870   Republican party manifesto.

Construction of telegraphic lines linking North and South.

End of the Paraguayan War.

1871   Free Birth law.

Adoption of the metric system.

1872   First general census of Brazil's population.

1872–74   Conflict between Church and State.

1873   Republican convention in Itú (São Paulo).

1877   Opening of the railroad between São Paulo and Rio.

1878   Agriculture Congress in Rio.

Agriculture Congress in Pernambuco.

1881   Law establishing direct elections.

1883–84   Slavery abolished in Amazonas and Ceará.

1885   Law emancipating slaves sixty years old and older, known as Saraiva-Cotegipe Law.

13 May 1888   Abolition of slavery.

June 1889   Viscount of Ouro Preto cabinet.

15 November 1889   Proclamation of the republic.

PREFACE

In 1893, four years after the creation of the Brazilian republic, Sylvio Romero, the most important literary critic in Brazil in the nineteenth century, complained with some bitterness that the new regime was incapable of transforming the nation into a free and democratic society. The fault, he thought, lay with the Brazilian elites, which he described as an "aristocracy of money . . . the most vicious and bastard of all aristocracies." The Brazilian masses, he wrote, had been condemned to a permanent state of political and social infancy. Some years later, after the republic had been in existence for two decades, he lamented again that ignorance and poverty were still the omnipresent facts of life in Brazil. Sylvio Romero's struggle for a freer and more democratic society continues to be the struggle of many Brazilians today. For them, as for him, the problems Brazilians face must be understood historically. They have their roots in the Brazilian empire. That empire, along with some of its more or less permanent legacies, is the subject of these essays.

This book is a revision and adaptation for American readers of a book I published in Brazil a few years ago. It contains a number of closely related essays on the history of Brazil in the nineteenth century and is the cumulative result of a project I have developed over a period of many years. Versions of some of the chapters were published at various times and places. But each of them was born out of the same intellectual concern: to come to a clear understanding of the Brazilian elites from the beginning of the nineteenth century to the fall of the empire in 1889. What came out of the process of revision is a new book. I dropped some historiographical essays I thought would be of limited interest to an American audience, expanded others, and rewrote all of them.

After living in the United States for several years I have become even more aware of the role myths have in the shaping of history, both as it is experienced by the participants and as it is recalled by historians. And it is not by chance that this book is entitled *The Brazilian Empire: Myths and Histories*.

When I started writing these essays I had several questions in mind. Why in a country that was so rich in material resources was there so much poverty? How could we explain the extraordinary contrasts between areas that were very modern and highly developed and others that still seem to live in the past? Why did elites who called themselves "liberals" lead the country twice to authoritarian regimes? Did the Brazilian people accept the oppressive condition in which they lived? I could only begin to answer these questions after I understood the nineteenth-century sources of our economic dependence and political culture and practices.

Since World War II it has become fashionable among Brazilian historians to analyze historical processes more as the outcome of large, impersonal, and involuntary forces than as the result of decisions by individuals and groups. Historians have seen Brazilian history as a product of capitalist development in a peripheral nation, and Brazilian politics and ideologies as its inevitable result. It is true that the position Brazil has had in the international market has defined the limits and possibilities of its development. This can never be overstressed. But this approach often loses sight of the effects political struggles and choices have had on economic and social development. And, what is more important, by depicting the elites as victims of a history over which they have no control, we tend to forget both the margin of choice and the degree of responsibility they had for the conditions they bequeathed to the republic.

In this book I have assumed that, within the constraints imposed by Brazil's peripheral position in the international market, the Brazilian elites participated more or less deliberately in the creation of political, economic, and social structures that defined the contours of Brazilian history in the nineteenth and twentieth centuries. From this perspective, I have analyzed the formation of the Brazilian elite at the time of independence—its ideological and institutional options; its internal conflicts; conflicts with other social groups, and the eventual emergence of a new power bloc at the end of the empire. And since I believe it is impossible to understand ruling classes without understanding those they rule, I have devoted special attention to slaves and sharecroppers, two groups who, although excluded from the political system during the empire, helped to shape its history. As a result, although this book is not a survey of the history of the Brazilian empire, I hope, the reader will have a reasonably comprehensive view of Brazilian society in the nineteenth century.

The translation of these essays and their adaptation for the American public were not easy tasks. After trying to work with one translator or another, I decided to do it myself. I soon discovered that the task was more difficult than it seemed at first. Language is etiquette. Different academic traditions express themselves in different languages. What is acceptable in one may not be acceptable in another. Besides there are words that cannot be translated because the experience they signify is lacking. How to translate, for example, the word *bacharel* or the word *sertão*? How to translate experiences that are similar but not identical? Should I call the Brazilian Câmara dos Deputados, Chamber of Deputies, as it is usually called in books about Brazil? Or should I call it House of Representatives, an expression with which Americans are more familiar? Should I use the words *fazendeiros* instead of "planters" and *colonos* instead of "colonists" when referring to immigrants working on plantations? What about measures of weight such as *arrobas*, *alqueires*, and others? If I crowded the text with Brazilian words, would I not be imposing an unnecessary burden on the reader?

But these were minor difficulties. The real problem was how to convert a Brazilian prose that is more suggestive than precise, full of long sentences, often written in the passive voice (the voice of the oppressed, who never feel they are making history) into the short and assertive sentences of American style? How to do that without losing the nuances, the interconnections, and the notion of process?

The problem was not only one of translation, a problem of words and styles. It also had to do with historiographical traditions. We seldom stop to think how much the things we consider worth studying, the questions we ask, and the methods we choose are shaped by the academic traditions we belong to, by the myths of our societies, by our social and political consciousness, and by the audience we address. We also tend to forget that we usually speak to an audience with whom we share more or less the same assumptions, the same codes, and the same anxieties and perplexities, an audience capable of attributing meaning to the points of silence in our text. But when we move from one country to another, we have to do much more than translate words: we have to translate our experience.

Like many other Brazilians of my generation, I followed with great interest the debate over Marxism opened by its foes and friends. Like most of them I was critical of reductionist explanations and the reification of historical categories, so typical in earlier Marxist historiography. I wanted to define more clearly the role of human subjectivity and to understand better the way ideologies work. I felt the need to stress the relative autonomy of the artistic, ideological, and political instances. And I was troubled by traditional notions of class and class consciousness which seem not to account for the variety and even contradictory nature of class experience. Most of all I was concerned with bringing dialectic back into what had become a linear and mechanistic approach.

These and many other problems which had occupied my mind and the minds of others with whom I worked in Brazil were not part of the mainstream academic tradition in the United States. In fact, most Americans either ignored these issues or looked upon them with suspicion. In translating my essays into English I was conscious of all these difficulties. But I held to a conviction that only an honest dialogue between scholars coming from different traditions can save us all from the dangers of dogmatism and political mythology. I hope the reader will find the result worthwhile.

I want to thank all those who helped me at different times to translate these essays, particularly Julie Graham, Barbara Weinstein, Florencia Mallon, and Michael Hall. A special word of gratitude goes to Marie Claire Van Leunen, who, while she was editing this manuscript, taught me many lessons in style and who, with her enthusiasm and sensitivity, gave me confidence in my capacity to write in English. Most of all my recognition goes to R. J. Wilson, who endured with admirable patience hours of endless debates over the meaning of things I wanted to say and who by his intelligent criticism much improved my text. The secretaries at Yale University, particularly Mary Whitney, who typed and retyped this manuscript many times rendered me an inestimable service. And it was the warm support of my students at Yale University that made me feel that my effort was worthwhile. My thanks also go to Charles Blitzer and the National Humanities Center and its staff. Stealing a few weeks from my fellowship, I was able finally to finish this manuscript. My final words go to all those who over the years have helped me to make the difficult transition from one culture to another.

INTRODUCTION

In the past twenty years there has been a clear shift in historical studies. Political and institutional histories have lagged as young scholars have turned their attention to the study of economic and social history. Equipped with new quantitative techniques, they have measured family size, demographic changes, and levels of production and exchange. In the process, they have neglected the elites who had been the traditional center of attention and have turned to the oppressed: slaves, workers, peasants, women, Indians, blacks. This shift has added immensely to our knowledge. New material has been uncovered and new interpretations have been born.

There is, however, a risk in these kinds of studies. They usualy give us a fragmented picture of the society and often make us lost sight of the interconnections among economic, social, political, and ideological institutions and structures. More important, they make us forget that in modern societies, even more than in the past, politics is at the center of human life. This centrality of politics is a result of both the incorporation of increasing numbers of people into the market economy and the overwhelming presence of the modern state in the lives of people. As a consequence of these two processes, which are intimately related, political decisions have come to affect economic and social life in ways never seen before. The life of a peasant in some lost village in the backland, the labor conditions of a worker in a factory, a woman's status in a society, the opportunities denied or opened to a black person, all depend not only on their own struggles or on the cold logic of the market, but also on decisions taken by those in power. It is impossible to understand the history of the powerless without understanding the history of the powerful. (And, of course, the reverse is also true.) History from the bottom up can be as meaningless as history from the top down. What I am proposing here is not to reestablish an old-fashioned, elitist political and institutional history, but to conceive one in which politics (although keeping its relative autonomy, since one cannot reduce politics to a mere epiphenomenon) is seen in connection with other aspects of human life. This book is an attempt to do that by examining some critical and decisive moments in the formation of the Brazilian elites in the nineteenth century.

I am interested in the ways elites are formed and act over time. When I talk about elites I am thinking about a variety of social groups: plantation owners, merchants, intellectuals, bureaucrats, clergymen, and military men—although not all those who belong to these groups can be considered members of the elites, since not all are in positions of power. Members of the elites share some common notions about the world and are tied to each other by different institutional arrangements. They consolidate their power by controlling the state apparatus and by exerting other forms of social control to subordinate different social groups. Ideologies are an integral part of this process, and intellectuals have an important role to play within it. So are the political and legal systems. In their attempt to establish a hegemonic position in the society, however, elites meet with more or less resistance from other social groups. The forms and degree of resistance they meet help to shape their identity and set limits to their power. Elites are also often divided by internal conflicts, conflicts between those directly in power and those who are not, conflicts between different economic or interest groups. Such conflicts echo in the political arena. The way these conflicts are solved or not depends in part on the nature of the political system. When conflicts cannot be resolved within existing political structures, those in power may try to change the political system. If they fail, they either resort to force to secure their position or they will be overthrown by those groups that are challenging their dominance. Those were the alternatives the Brazilian elites had to face at the end of the nineteenth century.

An essential part of the task of understanding the empire is to explain the relative stability of the monarchical system (1822–89). Part of the explanation lies in the fact that economic and social structures did not undergo fundamental change during the seven decades of the empire. The Brazilian economy continued to be based on the export of tropical products, and Brazilian elites could agree about fundamental issues. They also created an army and a national guard to put down resistance. But, more important, the elites were able to maintain a system of clientele and patronage efficient enough to disguise racial and class tensions. Looking backward in the twentieth century, Brazilian elites could even boast of the stability of the empire and contrast it to the instability experienced in other Latin American nations. They could also celebrate the apparent "racial democracy" they had created—in such happy contrast to the history of racial prejudice and conflict in the United States. But behind the pretension of social and racial harmony lay a reality of oppression and marginalization for millions of Brazilians who were never allowed to participate actively in the economic and political systems. The amiable posture of the Brazilian elite and their benign liberal rhetoric masked their authoritarian and antidemocratic purposes and their inability to accept and institutionalize social conflict or to cope creatively with any form of opposition.

The Brazilian elites that took power in 1822 were made up of planters, merchants, and their clients. Linked to the export-import economy, they were interested in maintaining traditional agrarian structures of production based on slave labor and the latifundio. They opposed attempts to promote industrial development and resisted British pressure to abolish the slave trade, continuing to use Africans as the primary source of labor. Though brought up in the tradition of the Enlightenment, they purged liberalism of its most radical features and shaped for their own use a basically conservative and antidemocratic ideology.

The presence in Brazil of the heir of the House of Bragança made it possible to achieve independence in 1822 without resorting to popular mobilization. Once in power the elites organized an electoral system based on income qualification, which excluded the great majority of the population; from the electorate. They also created a strongly centralized political system that placed *municípios* under the control of provincial governments and provinces under the direct supervision of the central government. Following the colonial tradition, they subordinated the Church to the State, made Catholicism a state religion, and denied citizenship to non-Catholics; though, in a concession to the Enlightenment, they authorized the private practice of other religions. Adorned with titles of nobility generously distributed by the emperor, they monopolized positions in the Parliament, the Council of State, and the ministries. Lifetime appointments to the Senate and Council of State, along with the system of clientele and patronage, helped perpetuate the elites' power, creating a true oligarchy during the Second Empire.

In 1822 the elites opted for a monarchical regime and supported the prince, but once independence was achieved they began to compete with Pedro I for control of the nation, a contest they won in 1831, when the emperor abdicated his crown in favor of his five-year-old son. During the following years those in power confronted the opposition of radical liberals who rebelled in different parts of the country. The opposition came from people who resented centralization and demanded a federation. Some of them proposed gradual abolition of slavery and nationalization of commerce, and even suggested the expropriation of unproductive estates. Among them were artisans and small merchants whose lives had become difficult because of growing foreign competition. They found support among doctors, lawyers, journalists, and other urban professionals—who for one reason or another did not have direct connections with those in power—and among the urban population of free blacks and mulattos badly hurt by inflation, especially by increases in food prices. All these frustrated groups, including some mercenary soldiers who had found themselves without jobs when they returned from the Cisplatina War, constituted a threat to the ruling classes, who responded to the threat with violence and repression. The Ato Adicional (1834), which increased the autonomy of the provinces, was the last concession the political elites made to the radical groups. After that, Brazilian elites became increasingly conservative, trying, in the words of one of their spokesmen, "to stop the revolutionary coach." With this purpose the government created the National Guard, a police force controlled by the propertied classes interested in maintaining the status quo. At the same time, the army received orders to repress the revolts that had broken out in different provinces—a task it performed with great success.

Through such means, the political oligarchy had consolidated its position by the middle of the century and set itself to promote the development of the economic infrastructure. This was made possible not only by a flow of capital coming from the outside (whether as direct investments or loans) but also by capital accumulated in the export and import sectors. A new generation of politicians took power and governed the nation under the benevolent tutelage of Pedro II, whose majority had been anticipated in 1840 to allow him to become emperor at the age of fifteen. The dissenters of the earlier period disappeared from the political scene, some swept away by foreign competition, others co-opted by the system. The career of Tôrres Homem, an important political figure of the empire, is typical: in his youth he was an active member of the opposition and author of the radical pamphlet *Libélo do Povo*, but later he became a member of the Council of State, a senator, and a minister of the empire. Very similar were the political careers of Antonio Carlos de Andrada e Silva, Bernardo de Vasconcelos, Diogo Feijó, and others who moved from liberal to conservative positions.

In fact, at different times in their history, the Brazilian elites used liberalism for different purposes, interpreting it in a more radical or a

more conservative fashion, according to their convenience. Before independence, liberalism provided a rationale for those who fought to
emancipate the country from colonial domination. During the First
Empire (1822–31), the elites used liberalism as an ideological weapon
in their struggle against royal absolutism and as a tool in the demoli-
tion of the remaining colonial institutions. In both these cases, liberalism had a revolutionary function. But when the time came for the
elites to create new institutions, they gave up their revolutionary rhetoric and adopted a more conservative position. And in 1831, when
those in power confronted the radical demands of other groups, they
became even more conservative. By the middle of the century, differences between Liberals and Conservatives became less relevant, and it
was momentarily possible to form a cabinet integrating members of
both parties. After a ten-year truce, Liberals and Conservatives again
opposed each other, taking turns in power. But, in spite of their pro-
grammatic differences, they often tended to agree on fundamental issues at least until about 1870, when the relative unity among the elites
broke down again, leading finally to the fall of the monarchy.

The survival in the empire of the system of patronage, whose roots
can be found in the colonial period, had important consequences. It
impeded the creation of a stable and competent bureaucracy. For the
elite, the bureaucracy was a matrix of patronage; for the beneficiaries
of this patronage, positions in the government were sinecures. From
either perspective, that of the patron or that of the client, the system
depended on the caprices of politics. Patronage permeated not only administration but the entire political system. Political careers depended
on patronage. Political struggles were struggles between clienteles, and
voters were committed to their personal loyalties rather than to political programs.

As in many other countries, capitalism in Brazil grew within a web
of patronage. But, contrary to what happened in other areas, it did not
destroy the foundations of patronage. This explains why in Brazil the
ethic of patronage coexisted in permanent tension with the ethic of
capitalism. Throughout the empire the bourgeois gentilhomme typical
of the Brazilian elite, avid both for profits and titles of nobility, was
ambivalent about the bourgeois ethic and its corollary, liberalism. The
capitalist ethos, with its cult of individual freedom, emphasis on thrift
and work, praise of the "self-made man," and worship of equality,
made little sense in a society where work was done by slaves, human
relationships were defined in terms of reciprocal obligation, social mobility depended on patronage, and the protocol of favor prevailed over

the competitive ethic. But liberal ideals continued to function as uto-
pias for all those groups that felt oppressed by patronage.

The system of clientele and patronage had other, less perceptible
effects. Through patronage, middle- and lower-class individuals could
find a place within the elites. Typical of this process is the rise of the
bacharel (holder of an academic degree, a term for an intellectual or
professional in nineteenth-century Brazil). Bound to the elites by family relations, friendship, or clientele, the *bacharel* often became their
spokesman. In the second half of the nineteenth century, however, the
example of intellectuals abroad, the relative expansion of the internal
market, and the growing number of cultural institutions made it possible for the Brazilian *bacharel* to cultivate dreams of independence
and autonomy. He enthusiastically adopted new ideas, gave support to
dissenting political movements, and presented himself as the emissary
of progress, a progress he defined in European terms, but wanted fil-
tered through tradition. He converted himself into the spokesman for
the people. Yet, even then, he did not oppose the elites; he compromised. He never trusted the people: he spoke for them, but he seldom
spoke to them. As a result, he allied with the most progressive sectors
of the oligarchy, participating in reformist movements such as the campaigns for electoral reform, abolition, and a republican regime. Like
the *bacharéis*, the new urban groups, even the industrialists, did not
take a truly independent political stand. Equally co-opted, with a few
exceptions, were the mulattos and blacks who succeeded, thanks to
patronage, in becoming lawyers, writers, journalists, engineers, or
politicians. All these groups, which theoretically could have become
the main agents of change, assimilated the life-style and aspirations of
the traditional elites. No wonder the reforms they proposed had limited consequences.

Sure of their positions, controlling social mobility, and imbued with
a hierarchical conception of the world that ratified social inequalities and postulated reciprocal obligations, the Brazilian elites did not
resort to open racial discrimination and segregation—particularly
since blacks and mulattos were "naturally" segregated in a socio-
economic system offering limited possibilities. And blacks like the novelist Machado de Assis, the poet Cruz e Souza, and the engineer André
Rebouças, who were incorporated into the elites, automatically acquired the status of whites and were forced to accommodate to the
protocols of patronage.

Through the manipulation of patronage, the Brazilian elites reinforced their hegemony and secured political stability. But even more

important than the patronage system for the stabilization of the regime was the expansion, throughout this period, of the export economy, a result of the increasing demand for tropical products in the international market. Yet, in the long run, economic development would have contradictory results. While it conferred stability on the regime by strengthening the traditional agrarian economy, it also stimulated urbanization, the slow but still significant expansion of the internal market, and capital accumulation. Economic growth, generating new opportunities, led to splits within the elites, who did not benefit equally from this process. The debates in the Chamber of Deputies and the Senate about land and labor policies were the first symptoms of a conflict between different sectors of the elites, a conflict that would deepen during the second half of the century. The abolitionist campaign would reveal even more clearly the growing tensions among different sectors of the elites and between them and the masses.

The growth of coffee plantations in Minas, Rio de Janeiro, and São Paulo created two interdependent problems: the recruitment of manpower and the regulation of landownership. The planters in frontier areas, more in need of labor, worried about the interruption of the slave trade, something that by the beginning of the 1840s seemed inevitable. Hoping to solve their problem by importing Europan labor, they wanted the government to subsidize immigration and they proposed legislation that would make it difficult for the newly arrived immigrants to acquire land, thus forcing them to work on plantations. Their view of the role the immigrants should play in Brazil was not, however, shared by other groups. Planters who were well supplied with slaves and intellectuals who saw Brazil through European lenses both regarded immigrants as civilizing agents rather than as mere substitutes for slaves. Thus they opposed plans to subsidize immigration for the purpose of bringing cheap labor to the plantations. They argued instead for the creation of independent immigrant settlements and supported legislation that favored the distribution of land to immigrants.

The first attempts to use immigrants on coffee plantations culminated in bitter confrontations between planters and immigrants. Most planters concluded from these early experiments that slave labor was more productive than free labor—or at least more manageable—and they continued to use slaves, buying them in areas of declining productivity. In the second half of the century, however, new opportunities for investment in railroads, banks, manufacturers, and urban facilities made investment of capital in slaves less attractive. At the same time, improvements in the processing of coffee, sugar, and jerked beef, as well as the expansion of the means of transportation, allowed some rationalization of the methods of production. This made the use of free labor more viable than it had been before, and sometimes even more productive than slave labor. Abolitionist pressures also contributed to the devaluation of slaves, as did the promulgation of emancipation laws and the growing unrest among slaves. Confronting what seemed to be an inevitable process leading to abolition, the planters in the most productive coffee areas turned again to immigrants as a possible source of labor. Once sectors of the upper classes had come to accept abolition, slavery could be peacefully abolished by an act of Parliament. Abolition liberated whites from the burden of their slaves and abandoned the freedmen to their own devices.

By this time, the political system organized in 1822 seemed unsatisfactory to the social groups linked to the most dynamic sectors of the economy. Many people throughout the country did not feel that they had adequate representation in the government. This feeling was particularly strong among the coffee planters of the frontier areas and an increasing number of individual's belonging to the urban middle classes. The Republican party, founded in 1870, recruited most of its followers from these two groups.

During the last two decades of the empire, Republicans and abolitionists adopted a political style symptomatic of the changes occurring in the economic and social structure. For the first time politics was brought to the streets and politicians talked to the urban masses in public meetings. But in spite of these rhetorical attempts to incorporate the common man into politics, the monarchy was overthrown the same way independence had been achieved: without mass mobilization. The new Republican government would be born out of a military coup. Republicans preferred to adopt a conspiratorial strategy rather than a revolutionary one, which would inevitably have involved mass participation. The army appeared to them the ideal instrument to overthrow the regime. Since the Paraguayan war, many officers had felt increasingly hostile to the monarchy. They had become convinced that the imperial elites were corrupt and that it was the task of the military to save the nation. Thus nothing could have been more natural than an alliance between the military and the Republican party, an alliance which led to the fall of the empire in 1889.

Predictably, the new regime they created did not represent a real rupture with the past. They did replace the monarchy with a republican system, introduce a more decentralized administration, and adopt universal suffrage. But a predominantly export-oriented economy, the monopoly of the means of production by a few, electoral fraud, and the system of patronage, all outlived the empire. And with them survived the myths the Brazilian elites had about themselves. To create a real democracy was a task left to future generations.

+/ of change 1884

SUGAR, COFFEE
AND RUBBER
PRODUCTION

Sugar

Coffee

Rubber

THE BRAZILIAN EMPIRE

I   INDEPENDENCE
The Building of a Nation

We have grown so accustomed to studying history within national boundaries that we often fail to perceive the larger forces that shape our lives. But when we look beyond those limits and see similar processes occurring elsewhere, we recognize that to understand fully the history of one country we must place it within a larger picture.

Brazil's independence was not an isolated event. After centuries of colonial domination the European colonies of the New World, one after another (with the exception of a few odd cases) won their political autonomy within a period of fifty years, starting with the American Revolution. Before we can explain this wholesale collapse of the traditional colonial system, we have to ask some questions. How did the colonial system work? What interests did it serve? Who benefited from it, both in the colonies and in the mother countries? What sort of ideology provided its rationale? Only after we answer such questions will we be able to understand the processes that led to its destruction. This, however, will not be enough to explain the many forms the struggle for independence took in different countries, its different pace and results. For that we do have to look at internal circumstances: the character of the groups that fought for and against independence in each country; the fortuitous appearance of different types of leaders; the different degrees of mass mobilization; the relationships among different segments of the colonial elites or between them and the masses. We also have to deal with the ever present and always imponderable accidents of hitsory and with human actions that are inexplicable and idiosyncratic. But even then it is important to remember that in the lives of those who fought to liberate their countries pulsed the rhythms of the larger world. It is this complex dialectic between a generalized colonial crisis and the particular events which led many

Abridged and revised edition of the article "The Political Emancipation of Brazil" in A. J. R. Russell-Wood, ed., *From Colony to Nation: Essays on the Independence of Brazil* (Baltimore, 1975), 43–88.

Brazilians to struggle for independence that we want to grasp in this essay.

Europe's discovery and exploitation of the New World was related to the creation of the modern centralized and absolutist state and the concomitant development of a powerful class of merchants, who associated themselves with the Crown in exploiting the colonies. Colonial policies reflected the alliance between mercantile groups and the state. The Crown was interested in expanding its domain and increasing its wealth, but it did not have the economic resources to undertake this enterprise alone. Kings had to rely on merchants and bankers to supply the means for the colonial venture. Merchants, on the other hand, needed the support of the Crown to secure a monopoly of the markets—a prerequisite for accumulation of capital at this stage of capitalist development. During the first two centuries of the colonial era, the limited size of the markets—both colonial and international—and the enormous risks involved in overseas trade made it imperative to adopt a system of monopolies and privileges that would restrict competition and guarantee profit. The colonists were forbidden to trade with other nations and were forced to export their products through the mother country, from which they had to import what they needed. This system initially satisfied the aims both of the vested interests in the mother country and of colonial groups linked to the export and import trade.

But the colonial system, organized according to the logic of commercial capital and the interests of the Crown, was threatened when the expansion of the market, the development of industrial capitalism, the growth of the European bourgeoisie, and the crisis of the absolutist state made such restrictions on trade and production inoperative and undermined the assumptions of mercantilist theory. The extraordinary increase of production in the eighteenth century was incompatible with closed markets and with privileges and monopolies that inhibited trade. These constraints were viewed by many as obstacles to large-scale production and to the expansion of commercial relations.

As one might expect, the transition from mercantilism to free trade took place earliest in regions where industrial capitalism had first matured. In England, by 1776, Adam Smith had already criticized mercantilist principles and condemned the system of monopolies and privileges.[1] He recommended free trade and asserted that free labor was superior to slave labor. An even more radical position was adopted by the Frenchman Jean-Baptiste Say. In an economic treatise published in 1803 Say argued that the colonies were a burden to the mother country, since the mother country had not only to maintain a colonial army and a colonial bureaucracy but to invest capital in the construction of public buildings; worse still, the mother country was obliged to buy inferior and costly products from its colonies when it could obtain superior goods at better prices in other parts of the world.[2] Reinforcing his argument, Say used convincing figures to show that France paid more for the sugar it bought from its colonies than it would pay to buy it from Great Britain. And while Say demonstrated how inconvenient the colonial system was to the metropolis, Raynal and others showed that it was also disadvantageous to the colonies.

These criticisms helped to undermine the theoretical basis of the traditional colonial system. Condemned in theory and outmoded in practice, the system which had lasted for three centuries was ready to collapse in the second half of the eighteenth century. Two circumstances, however, conspired to keep it functioning: first, both in the colony and in the mother country there were still several groups interested in its survival; and second, industrial capitalism did not progress everywhere. Thus while in England industrialization was opening the way to economic theories based on free trade and free labor, in Portugal and Spain, countries marginal to the Industrial Revolution, traditional mercantilist theories still enjoyed great prestige.

The crisis of the colonial system coincided also with the crisis of absolutist forms of government. The critique of the ancien regime, the new doctrines of social contract and natural rights, the cult of freedom and equality before the law, the commitment to representative forms of government—all these liberal dogmas that characterize the new credo served to challenge traditional forms of power and social organization in both Europe and the New World. These revolutionary ideological tools, forged in Europe during the period that culminated in the French Revolution, supplied the colonists with additional reasons for revolt and with arguments to justify their rebellion.

So the foundations of the traditional colonial system were shaken by several pressures at the end of the eighteenth century. In Europe, the alliance between the commercial bourgeoisie and the Crown, which had given rise to traditional colonial policies, was undermined by important changes in economic, political, and social life: the emergence of a bourgeoisie linked to industrialization, which aimed at new economic policies; the development of ideologies that sought to destroy the theoretical basis of the absolutist state; and the expansion of the international market, which increased the demand for colonial products and made the monopoly system inoperative. While these transformations occurred in Europe, in the colonies the increase in population, the growth of production, the expansion of the internal markets, and most of all, the new opportunities offered by the international market made the restrictions imposed by the mother country intolerable. An increasing number of colonists became resentful of colonial policies, jealous of their own resources, and aware of their own identities.

It is true that colonial policies, particularly the system of monopolies and privileges, had always created conflicts. There had been numerous clashes in the international arena between those who had the monopoly on commerce in the New World and those who were excluded. The French and Dutch occupation of parts of Brazil in the sixteenth and seventeenth centuries, the attacks of pirates and corsairs, and the increase in smuggling along the coast were all expressions of the struggle against Portuguese monopolies. Internally, monopolies and privileges had been the subject of complaints and rebellions since the sixteenth century.[3] The colonial period was punctuated by confrontations between producers and merchants, between merchants and bureaucrats, and between one merchant and another. In Brazil, these conflicts were expressed in uprisings like the Mascates in Pernambuco,[4] the Beckman rebellion in Maranhão,[5] and the revolts in the mining areas during the first half of the eighteenth century (Emboabas, Felipe dos Santos).[6] But throughout the early centuries of the colonial period the conflicts were seen as clashes between subjects of the same kingdom. And the colonists saw the king as mediator between the disputants. In the late eighteenth century, however, the conflicts gained a new dimension. Most colonists no longer perceived the colonial pact as a contract between brothers; they had come to see it as a unilateral arrangement to the advantage of the Crown and its protégés.

That the traditional colonial system had become obsolete was something neither the Crown nor the colonists perceived immediately. The Crown was conscious only of gold smuggling, fiscal evasions, losses to the royal treasury, contraband, and the colonists' continual transgression of the law. The colonists, on the other hand, rebelled against particular institutions or measures taken by the Crown—increases in taxes, restrictions on free communication between the provinces, the exploitative nature of certain monopolies, the inefficiency of the courts, the corruption and arbitrariness of the Crown's officials, and discrimination against subjects born in the colony.

Gradually, however, colonial uprisings and the violent repression that followed them revealed the fundamental antagonism between the interests of the colony and those of the mother country. The colonists, who at the beginning had considered themselves the Portuguese of Brazil, perceived more and more clearly that their interests were linked to

Brazil rather than Portugal. And their struggles, which at first had seemed to be conflicts between subjects of the same king, began to be perceived as struggles between colonists and the mother country. Since the colonists identified the interests of the Crown with those of the mother country, their anticolonialism led them to criticize the indiscriminate power of the king and to stress the sovereignty of the people. It was for these reasons and within this contest that colonists became receptive to liberal ideas.

In eighteenth-century Brazil, Rousseau, Montesquieu, Raynal, and even more radical authors like Mably were eagerly read by the intellectual elite in spite of censorship.[7] But even more important than these books to the spread of revolutionary ideas were the American and French revolutions. Resenting colonial domination and royal absolutism, the colonists found in the two revolutions a model to be followed. In the last two decades of the eighteenth century the tensions undermining the colonial system were expressed in a series of conspiracies inspired by the new revolutionary ideology.

Among the books confiscated from Luis Vieira, a priest involved in the conspiracy of 1789 in Minas (Inconfidência Mineira), were copies of Montesquieu, D'Alembert, Turgot, Raynal, and Mably. Tiradentes, one of the leaders of the same conspiracy, was charged by Portuguese authorities with an attempt to translate a French edition of the United States' Constitution. Others who were arrested and tried in 1789 were accused of having praised the American Revolution or of following the "French party."[8] Some years later, in 1792, when a conspiracy was discovered in Rio, the men arrested were accused of plotting a rebellion to establish a "democratic, free, and independent government."[9] They were clearly influenced by what were known at the time as "the abominable French principles." When a group was arrested for conspiracy in Bahía in 1798, one of the leaders was charged with inciting others to "become French" so they could live in equality and abundance.[10] "To become French" meant to adopt the revolutionary ideas that France exported to the world.

The inquiry set up by the count of Rezende, then viceroy, to investigate the conspiracy of 1792 revealed some of the "sinful thoughts" circulating in public places as well as private houses where some individuals were inveighing against religion and the divine power of kings in "scandalous and impious speeches." According to the inquiry these men denied the existence of miracles and declared that kings had received power from men rather than God. They openly asserted that if the Bible had given kings power to punish their vassals, it had also given vassals the power to punish their kings. The suspects said that men were born free and could claim their freedom at any time. And they argued as well that the laws in France were fair and should be adopted in Brazil. Some had gone so far as to hope that the French would conquer Rio de Janeiro. In the opinion of the authorities in charge of the investigation, the revolutionaries should be severely punished since they had tried "to seduce the rustic and ignorant people and to alienate them from their legitimate and natural sovereign."[11]

But neither arrests nor threats of exile or death could stop the revolutionary process. Censorship proved a vain attempt to limit the dissemination of ideas that challenged the existing order. Equally useless were the harsh punishments that came down upon the rebels. Books continued to arrive in the country and students who traveled abroad to study in Portugal or France brought home new ideas. They gathered in private houses or on street corners, in literary and scientific academies or in secret societies to discuss the books they had read, to comment on the things they had seen, and to talk about their dreams. Revolutionary ideas passed from person to person and, in spite of violent repression, the "abominable French principles" continued to inspire new uprisings. As late as 1817, a group of rebels in Pernambuco still perceived the French constitutions of 1791, 1793, and 1795 as models to be followed. And one of the leaders of the rebellion, Cruz Cabugá, decorated the walls of his house with portraits of French and American revolutionary heroes. In a symbolic gesture the revolutionaries of 1817 abandoned traditional protocol—instead of addressing each other as *Vossa Mercê* (Your Honor) or *Senhor* (Sir), they followed the example of French revolutionaries and used the expressions *vós* (you) and *patriota* (patriot).[12]

By that time, however, the French Revolution belonged to history and the atmosphere in Europe had changed. After the Restoration, European governments interested in sweeping away the effects of the French Revolution had adopted counterrevolutionary policies. The Holy Alliance cautiously watched over Europe, ready to suppress any uprising. Crimes committed during the revolution had turned many people against revolutionary ideas and inclined them to reformist and conservative programs. But some who lived in Brazil in the early nineteenth century had continued to be stubbornly loyal to the ideals of the French Revolution. Although they had become more conservative and more afraid of mass movements, they had not given up their dreams of independence.

Imbued with revolutionary ideas, the Brazilian elites who conspired for independence in the late eighteenth century had created quite a number of secret societies. The Conjuração Bahiana, a conspiracy discovered in 1798 in Bahía, followed upon the creation in 1797 of a Masonic lodge: Os Cavaleiros da Luz (the Knights of the Light). Some of the men arrested in Pernambuco in 1817 were members of secret societies, and in 1818, John VI was informed that many important people in Rio de Janeiro—royal functionaries, merchants, planters, lawyers, professors, and priests—had connections with the Masonry. They constituted a powerful group and stoutly resisted the king's attempt to close their lodges. In 1821 they played an important role in politics and were ready to lead the movement for independence.[13]

Although the influence of secret societies and liberal ideas on the revolutionary conspiracies is undeniable, one should not overestimate their importance. They seem to have played an important role only in 1821–22 and even then only a small minority belonged to secret societies. And only a few members of the elite were familiar with European authors, whom they read with more enthusiasm than judgement.[14] The common man remained unmoved by theoretical speculation though he could be stirred by references to the "French principles," "pátria," and "freedom," expressions which seemed to have a magic effect upon the urban masses.

In addition to illiteracy, political indifference, and the deficient system of communication—all of which created obstacles to the spread of liberal ideas among the population—the very nature of these ideas imposed limits on their dissemination in Brazil (see chap. 3). In Europe, liberalism had originally been a bourgeois ideology, an instrument in the struggle against the absolute power of kings, the privileges of the nobility, and the feudal institutions that inhibited economic development. But in Brazil, liberalism became the ideology of rural oligarchies, which found in the new ideas arguments they could use against the mother country. These men were primarily concerned with eliminating colonial institutions that restricted the landowners and merchants—the two most powerful groups in colonial society. When they struggled for freedom and equality, they were actually fighting to eliminate monopolies and privileges that benefited the mother country and to liberate themselves from commercial restrictions that forced Brazilians to buy and sell products through Portugal. Thus, during this period, liberalism in Brazil expressed the oligarchies' desire for independence from the impositions of the Portuguese Crown. The oligarchies, however, were not willing to abandon their traditional control over land and labor, nor did they want to change the traditional system of production. This led them to purge liberalism of its most radical tendencies.

The elites' commitment to slavery constituted a major obstacle to their full acceptance and implementation of liberal ideas. Since the eighteenth century, those who nurtured dreams of independence and conspired against the Portuguese government had confronted the problem of slavery. Serious talk of revolution was often stopped short by the fear of a slave rebellion. The revolutionary leaders were with few exceptions elitists and racists. But where would they find support for a conspiracy for independence if not among the blacks and mulattos who formed the majority of the Brazilian population? How would they control the masses of slaves and freedmen in a revolutionary situation? Should slaves be granted freedom? All of these questions were raised by the leaders of the Inconfidencia Mineira in 1789 [15] and again in 1798 by some participants in the Conjuração Bahiana. The uneasiness of the white leaders in the face of the masses is most visible in the Conjuração Bahiana. Although most of the conspirators arrested in Bahia were mulattos and blacks—some free, some still enslaved—Cipriano Barata, a middle-class white and one of the heads of the conspiracy, wrote a letter to a friend advising him to "beware of this rabble of blacks and mulattos." Later, the leaders of the 1817 revolution in Pernambuco, anxious to gain the slaveowners' support, issued a proclamation to reassure them about their slaves: "Patriots," read the proclamation, "your property rights, even those that offend the ideal of justice, are sacred. The government will find the means to diminish the evil [slavery], but will not stop it by force." [16]

Their distrust of the masses, their fear of a slave rebellion, and their desire to preserve the slave system led the elites to repudiate democratic procedures and to avoid mass mobilization. In 1821, those who struggled for independence sought the regent's support, hoping to gain independence without social turmoil. Considering the revolutionaries' commitment to slavery and their intention to exclude the majority of the population from the electoral process, their manifestos in favor of representative government, their speeches about the sovereignty of the people, and their designation of freedom and equality as inalienable human rights can only sound false and empty to modern ears.

Another peculiarity of Brazilian liberals during this period was their conciliatory attitude toward the Church and religion. In 1817 placards appeared in Recife showing such slogans as "Long live the country," "Long live the Virgin," "Long live the Catholic religion," and "Death to the aristocrats." These and the cheers to revolution and religion that could be heard in the streets suggest the revolutionaries' commitment to the Church and Catholicism. The participation of numerous priests in the conspiracy reinforces the impression. So many clergymen joined the 1817 rebellion in Pernambuco that the uprising came to be known as the Revolution of Priests. [17] When they were brought to trial, some priests were charged with using their churches to propagate subversive ideas. Others were accused of being Masons and of actively cooperating with the rebels. And certain churchmen, like the famous Friar Canéca, appeared in the court records as guerilla leaders.

At first glance, it might seem difficult to explain the revolutionary tendency of the Brazilian clergy and their sympathetic attitude toward Freemasonry, which in Europe was the bulwark of the struggle against the Church. A closer analysis of the relationship between Church and State in Brazil reveals that the right of patronage granted by the pope to the Portuguese kings was the source of the clergy's hostility toward the system and explains their commitment to liberal ideas. As a consequence the anticlericalism and the secular tendencies typical of European liberalism were not to be found in Brazil at this point. Equally atypical was the role nationalist ideas played in Brazil. While in most European revolutions of the nineteenth century, liberal and nationalist ideas were closely associated in Brazil nationalist ideas found a less propitious ground. Nothing in the economic structure of the country furthered contact among the provinces. The internal market was insignificant, since most goods were shipped abroad and the communications network that linked the provinces was precarious and underdeveloped. Thus the conditions that led to national integration and inspired nationalist ideas in Europe were lacking in Brazil. It is not surprising, then, that most of the revolutionary movements before 1822 had a regional character and failed to develop national goals. The *inconfidentes* of 1789 talked about uniting Minas and São Paulo. The conspiracies of 1792 in Rio and 1798 in Bahía never spread beyond the limits of the two urban centers. The revolution of 1817 in Pernambuco, which followed a more ambitious plan, still recruited supporters only in a few northeastern provinces. And even in 1821, one year before the proclamation of independence, Brazilian representatives to the Portuguese Côrtes still made a point of presenting themselves as delegates from their provinces rather than from the colony.[18] Because of these centripetal tendencies, many leaders of the 1822 movement feared that Brazil would follow the example of the Spanish colonies and split into several states after independence. So generalized was this opinion that in Portugal in 1822, plans to recolonize Brazil counted on the country's lack of unity.[19] The maintenance of Brazil's territorial integrity after independence, then, cannot be attributed to a strong nationalist ideology; Brazilian elites simply recognized that the only way to assure the independent status of the nation was to eschew secession.

If there were no powerful nationalist ideas to promote national integration, there were definite and unifying anti-Portuguese tendencies in

Brazil at the end of the colonial period. In spite of the fact that many Portuguese participated in the conspiracies and fought for independence, the majority of the revolutionaries were native Brazilians. And hostility against the mother country often expressed itself as hostility against the Portuguese. Even more curious, considering the underlying "racism" of the elite groups, is the fact that attacks against the Portuguese were sometimes voiced as racial antagonism between blacks and whites; in the words of a revolutionary in 1789, "We will soon throw out of Brazil these little whites from the mother country who wish to take over our land." [20] In a memoir written in 1817, a conspicuous royalist observed that the "rabble" of mulattos, blacks, and the like, seduced by the word freedom, was not royalist and should be under constant surveillance. His impression was not unfounded; blacks and mulattos had several times expressed their animosity toward the Portuguese and white Brazilians and had shown their willingness to support revolutions. One year after independence, in an uprising in Pernambuco, the crowd still sang: [21]

> Portuguese and whites
> all are destined to meet their doom
> because only pardos and blacks
> will inhabit the country.

Lower-class blacks and mulattos saw independence as a step toward eliminating the racial discrimination that prohibited their appointment to administrative positions, barred their access to the University of Coimbra, and made the higher church positions inaccessible to them. Equal opportunity for all without regard to race or color was their primary aspiration. They also hoped to abolish class differences that separated men into rich and poor. And in liberalism they found the arguments they needed to justify their hopes. To these people the fight for independence was first of all a battle against whites and their privileges. As one of them put it, they would all be rich when privileges would be abolished and merit became the only criterion for promotion. [22]

While the masses expressed their hostility against the Portuguese in racial terms, the white elite in general expressed fear of blacks and mulattos and would have endorsed the words of Carneiro de Campos, a high official in the administration, who wrote that "slaves and free coloreds were congenital enemies of the white man."

In spite of their mutual distrust and different goals, they joined together in their conspiracies and fought side by side for independence in the name of liberal ideals. [23]

Most of the *inconfidentes* of 1789, for example, were landowners or high bureaucrats. But among them there were others of modest origins, petty functionaries, soldiers, muleteers, artisans, and servants. And two completely different groups participated in the Bahian conspiracy of 1798. The first was composed of "men of property and standing" educated in the Enlightenment tradition. The second group included slaves, freedmen, blacks, and mulattos recruited among the urban population, tailors, shoemakers, masons, hairdressers, soldiers, and peddlers.

The same combination of upper- and lower-class people characterizes the 1817 revolution in Pernambuco. Again the leaders were merchants, landowners, and royal functionaries from important families. At their trial, these men defended themselves by arguing that they could not have conspired against the government: they belonged to "the first and highest nobility of Pernambuco, and had been raised to respect the hierarchy of classes and orders."[24] Their lawyer argued that these members of the elite had been forced to concede to the irresistible pressure of the masses. To present the elites as victims of mass rebellion was merely an expedient of the defense, but there is no doubt that in 1817, as in previous conspiracies, the common people had gladly joined with the revolutionary elite. The enthusiasm for "this damned freedom"—as counterrevolutionary documents called it—had spread among the urban masses of blacks and mulattos, although they seemed always more titillated by the idea of equality.

The behavior of the urban masses during the revolution of 1817 scandalized members of the elite who had not been carried away by revolutionary ideas. One of them, Cardoso, wrote to a friend that the "half-castes, mulattos, and creoles had become so daring that they declared all men equal, and boasted that they themselves would marry only white women of the best stock." Pharmacists, surgeons, and bloodletters gave themselves airs, and barbers refused to shave Cardoso, claiming that they were occupied in the service of their country. To his horror, Cardoso was forced to shave himself. Worse yet, the half-castes were familiar and disrespectful in manner. As he wrote to his friend, "You Grace would not permit a half-caste to come up to you, hat on his head, and clapping you on the shoulder address you: 'Well met, patriot, how are you? How about giving me a smoke, or taking some of mine?' Such was the offer one of Brederodes' slaves made to Crown Judge Afonso! Fortunately," Cardoso concluded with evident satisfaction, "the half-caste received his well-deserved punishment. He has already been awarded five hundred lashes."[25] Like many other conservatives, Cardoso was horrified to see Domingos José Martins, a well-established man and a leader of the 1817 revolution, walking arm in arm with members of the lower classes.

Before independence, the class and racial conflict latent in Brazilian society could often be disguised among the revolutionary ranks. Everyone was fighting for the same cause—to emancipate the colony from the mother country. Liberal formulas were at this stage sufficiently vague and abstract to encompass different aspirations and to create an illusory sense of unity. Besides, there were other mechanisms soothing class and racial tensions. People belonging to the lower classes—whites, blacks, or mulattos—were frequently linked to members of the elites through the system of clientele and patronage. And if patronage did not actually eliminate the lines of color and class, it did create an appearance of comaraderie and reciprocity that obscured social distinctions.

In spite of the mechanisms that contributed to solidarity among the revolutionaries, their goals, as we have seen, were often different if not contradictory. Slaves aimed at emancipation; free blacks and mulattos hoped to abolish racial discrimination and gain equality; upper-class white farmers and merchants wanted above all to free themselves from restrictions imposed by the mother country but were not inclined to emancipate their slaves or to make fundamental concessions to the poor. These contradictory interests came into open conflict after independence; earlier, different groups struggled side by side against the Portuguese government.

Until the beginning of the nineteenth century, every conspiracy failed. Those in Minas (1789), Rio de Janeiro (1792), and Bahía (1798) never progressed beyond the stage of plots and intrigues. The rebels were severely punished, the leaders condemned to death or exile. And the majority of the population remained indifferent to the events. In spite of growing discontent, nothing seemed to indicate that Portuguese control over Brazil would soon come to an end. One incident, however, accelerated the historical process—the invasion of the Iberian Peninsula by French troops and the consequent transfer of the Portuguese court to Brazil.

The location of the government center in the colony imposed fundamental changes on colonial policies. Brazilian ports were opened to all nations in 1808; Brazil became a kingdom united with Portugal in 1815; and new institutions were created to satisfy the needs of the imperial government. All these measures benefited the colony and hurt the mother country. And the most harmful measure of all, from the point of view of Portugal, was the adoption of free trade policies and the elimination of the commercial monopolies the Portuguese had formerly enjoyed.

Until 1808 the bulk of Portuguese trade was conducted with Brazil. Portugal was the distributor of colonial products in Europe and of European manufactures in Brazil. Outfitters, sailors, royal functionaries, and merchants all benefited from colonial trade.[26] This profitable system broke down when Brazilian ports were opened. Worse yet, once in Brazil João VI granted preferential tariffs to England as compensation for the English help against the French. The Portuguese king tried to counteract the unpopular effects of his policies by granting his Portuguese subjects several privileges.[27] He favored products transported in Portuguese ships as well as products that came from Portugal or the Portuguese empire. But this was of little use since Portuguese producers and merchants were not capable of competing in a free market. They could survive only as long as the system of monopolies and privileges was maintained. Without solving the problems of the Portuguese, the protective measures taken by the king aroused dissatisfaction among foreign merchants and Brazilians. Trying to satisfy conflicting interest groups, the king incurred the resentment of all.

Portuguese living in the mother country were particularly discontented. The economic crisis had not affected the mercantile groups alone. Both the manufacturing and the agricultural sectors were severely hurt. Other countries that had modernized industrial and agricultural production were producing more at lower prices, while Portugal had not kept pace with modernization of the methods of production. The Portuguese, however, could not perceive the real reasons behind the economic depression. They believed that it derived exclusively from the relative autonomy the colony had gained, and they hoped that with the king's return to Portugal the concessions that had been made to the colony would be cancelled and the traditional system of monopolies and privileges reestablished. They did not foresee the resistance of the colonists or the opposition of foreign merchants who were benefiting from the present situation.[28]

In hopes of convincing the king to reestablish the traditional system, a great number of pamphlets were distributed in Portugal and Brazil. They argued that free trade had caused the destruction of crafts and internal commece in Portugal and Brazil.[29] It had damaged the merchant marine and impoverished the local population while benefiting foreigners. A pamphlet published in 1822 under the title *Reflections about the need to promote the Union of the States that constitute the United Kingdom of Portugal, Brazil, and Algarves in the four parts of the World*[30] asserted that the practice of importing manufactures from other countries had damaged the Luzo-Brazilian economy. Wealth was flowing to other countries while Brazilians and Portuguese wer increasingly impoverished. In his *General Ideas about the Brazi'*

Revolution and Its Consequences,[31] published in Lisbon in 1823, Francisco Sierra y Mariscal denounced the exploitative nature of British commerce and argued that the treaty of 1810 with England had been detrimental to Brazil and Portugal. As a consequence of the treaty, Brazil was importing everything from England—shoes, clothes, furniture, even ornate coffins. He concluded that one had more to fear from an English businessman than from all the British artillery.

Not everybody agreed with this opinion. Many pamphlets were written in Brazil from the opposite point of view to demonstrate the advantages of free trade and the disadvantages of mercantilist policies that tied Brazil to the mother country, inhibiting commerce and production and benefiting only a few privileged groups.[32]

The conflict between these two points of view—one favoring a return to the system of monopolies and privileges, the other supporting free trade—made it increasingly hard for the king to rule his kingdom. Tollenare, a traveler in Brazil between 1816 and 1818, pointed out the difficulty of being at the same time king of Portugal and king of Brazil, two nations whose interests were clearly contradictory: "One cannot live without monopolies," he said, "while the progress of the other requires their suppression." Thus the king could not please anyone; resentments accumulated on both sides of the Atlantic.[33]

In Brazil, economic expansion after 1808 made the obsolescence of traditional institutions even more apparent. And in spite of censorship, publications denouncing the inefficiency of those institutions appeared one after another. Their main argument can be summarized in the words of Hipólito da Costa. In 1817, he wrote in the *Correio Braziliense,* a newspaper published in London, that a country on its way to becoming a great and civilized nation could not continue to endure a military government and colonial institutions that had been established when Brazilian settlements were mere garrison posts. Da Costa's opinion was corroborated by many travelers who visited the country in the first two decades of the nineteenth century.[34] The colonists were obviously unhappy with the government. And the more they complained, the more discontented they became. They felt more alienated from and more eager to introduce changes in the administration. It is true that João VI had taken halting steps in that direction, but he had not gone as far as Brazilians wanted. The revolution of 1817 in Pernambuco was a symptom of these tensions. Repression could stop it but could not remove the causes of dissatisfaction. At any time revolutionary discontent could surface again, as it did in 1820, when the revolutionary tide that swept Europe reached Brazil.

In January of that year, Spain was shaken by a liberal revolution and

João VI hastily pressed several new laws intended to favor Portuguese merchants. He hoped with these measures to secure their support and to avoid repeating in Portugal the events in Spain. But in August 1820, there was an uprising in the city of Oporto. The revolutionaries demanded a constitution and the king's immediate return to Portugal.

These events had great repercussions in Brazil. Many people manifested their sympathy with the constitutionalist revolution. Portuguese and Brazilians, merchants and plantation owners, royal functionaries and military men supported the revolution for a variety of often contradictory reasons and with predictably incompatible goals. Portuguese merchants, who identified themselves with the interests of the mother country, supported the constitutionalist revolution in the hope that the king would be forced by the Côrtes to reestablish the colonial pact. They had the support of most military men and royal functionaries who were eager to return to Portugal. Plantation owners, foreign merchants, and all the others, Portuguese or Brazilian, who had benefited from free trade, as well as royal functionaries and military men who had invested money in Brazil or had established links with Brazilian families, saw the revolution as a liberal movement that would put an end to absolutism and sweep away the remaining monopolies and privileges. They believed that a constitutional government would give them the opportunity to express their own interests in the Côrtes. And they hoped to consolidate the privileges they had gained since the Portuguese court had arrived in Brazil.

The contradiction between the two groups passed unnoticed at the beginning. But it soon became clear that the revolution, which had started in Portugal as a liberal revolution, now had as its main objective the annullment of liberal concessions made by João VI to Brazil. This realization, however, was several months in coming. Meanwhile a number of revolutionary juntas were formed. On 20 February 1821 a military pronunciamento was followed by street demonstrations in Rio de Janeiro. The main purpose of the demonstrations was to force the king to accept the demands of the Portuguese Côrtes. João VI agreed to swear allegiance to a still-to-be-written constitution and ordered the municipal councils in Brazil to do the same. He called for the election of Brazilian representatives to the Côrtes and decided, much against his will, to return to Portugal, where a hostile and demanding convention awaited him. In April he left Brazil, leaving his son Pedro as regent.[35]

While the events in Rio echoed in the capital cities of the provinces, mobilizing the urban masses, the rural population remained passive and indifferent. A French traveler who visited São Paulo at that time was surprised to learn that the creation of a revolutionary junta in the capital had not generated any enthusiasm in the backlands. The only thing the Paulistas in those areas seemed to care about was freedom of commerce.[36] They believed that the reestablishment of the colonial system would hurt their interests since they would have to lower their prices. Paulistas in the backlands did not seem very interested in political discussion. Most of them were loyal to the monarch, whom they considered the supreme arbiter of their lives. When asked to comment on the incidents in Rio, they would blame the uprisings on foreigners. The cultivated traveler could not hide his amazement in the face of such passivity and ignorance. It appeared to him that most Brazilians had no coherent political views and no knowledge of governmental procedures. If they did come into conflict, it was seldom for ideological reasons. Their "political" disputes had to do with rivalries between families, competition between towns, personal sympathies and antipathies, "or other petty motives." And the masses seemed to ask "like the donkey in the story, 'Won't I have to carry the packsaddle all my life?'"[37]

The traveler's perceptions were very close to be truth. In Ceará, for example, when town councils were ordered to swear allegiance to the Portuguese constitution, the very word "constitution" aroused a great debate. Some people maintained that "'constitution' was a new form of government which would harm the sovereign, hence an impiety and an attack on religion." Others, who looked on any decree as a plot against the poor, held the view that "'constitution' was an attempt to curtail the freedom of the masses" and alleged there was a scheme afoot to throw the poor into captivity. Most astonishing of all, there were those for whom "'constitution' was a palpable entity to which they attributed a terrifying perversity." Ignoring the meaning of their actions, most people did what the local chiefs told them to do. In the city of Crato no oath of allegiance was taken to the constitution because the local political leader, Capitão-Mór José Pereira Filgueiras, refused to allow it. In the nearby township of Jardim, however, the oath was taken without the slightest hesitation because the vicar Antonio Manuel supported the constitution.[38]

While the majority of the population was unconcerned with politics, a minority was determined to benefit from the political crisis, which had given them an opportunity to be heard in the Portuguese Côrtes. But they were quickly disappointed. The measures taken by the Côrtes soon revealed that the Portuguese intended not only to restrict free trade and reestablish the old monopolies and privileges, but also to limit the colony's administrative autonomy. It was also clear that the Côrtes were not willing to accept any compromise. The Brazilian delegates were greatly outnumbered by the Portuguese; only 50 of the appointed 75 had arrived in Portugal, out of a total of 205 delegates. They could do nothing to protect the colony's interests. Given these circumstances, the only sensible response was rebellion.

Leaflets denouncing the "recolonizing" intentions of the Côrtes and encouraging the people to support the cause of independence were posted around the city of Rio.[39] From many parts of the country came petitions calling on the regent to disobey the Côrtes. As early as October 1821, verses were posted in the streets suggesting to the prince that being Pedro the First in Brazil now was better than waiting to be Pedro the Fourth in Portugal. Proclamations announced that separation from Portugal was inevitable and accused the Côrtes of attempting to recolonize Brazil. In a letter dated 18 December 1821, the prince told his father that the decrees of the Côrtes had so profoundly shocked Brazilians and foreigners living in Brazil that people were openly voicing their displeasure in the streets, saying "If to have a constitution can bring us nothing but trouble, then to hell with it. We must keep the prince from leaving." Rumor had it that if Pedro left Brazil, the British and the Americans would help Brazilians establish their independence.

It was clear that the measures taken by the Côrtes—the last of which was an order for the prince to return to Portugal—had made it impossible for the Brazilian elites to reach the compromise they had hoped for at the beginning. They had dreamed of creating a dual monarchy, a system that would respect Brazilian autonomy, yet keep the two countries united (see chap. 2). But the decrees abolishing administrative autonomy and limiting free trade had made this solution impossible. There was no alternative left to the Brazilian elites but to resist the orders. And the best way to minimize the effect of such disobedience on Portugal was to have the regent on their side. Even more important, with the prince's support they could hope to achieve political autonomy without mass mobilization.

On 9 January 1822, in response to a request from the Municipal Council of Rio de Janeiro, the prince announced that he would remain in Brazil. This was not, however, a declaration of independence. His communication was received with cheers for the union of Portugal and Brazil, which seemed to indicate a lingering hope that an agreement could be reached.

While he waited to hear from Portugal, the prince surrounded himself with the most prestigious men in the colony, men known for their loyalty to the monarchical system and for their administrative skills. (Among them was José Bonifácio de Andrada e Silva, who became his main advisor.) These men had not in fact given up the idea of a united

Brazil and Portugal, and they hoped that the prince's intransigence would force the Côrtes to back down. Their expectations appear totally unrealistic today to anyone who knows how vital it was for most members of the Côrtes to reestablish the traditional colonial system, but they seemed more reasonable at that time. After all, the Portuguese revolution had been made in the name of liberal principles, and the contradictions that lurked in the heart of the revolution were not yet clearly perceived. Brazilians knew that there were still some men in the Portuguese king's entourage who would advise him to adopt liberal policies toward Brazil. And they trusted that the king himself would support his son. Confident of finding support in Portugal, the Brazilian political elite could expect the Côrtes to reverse its decisions. This explains why on 23 May 1822, just a few months before independence was formally proclaimed, the Municipal Council of Rio de Janeiro petitioned the prince to call a national convention that would "consider the conditions under which Brazil could remain united with Portugal."[40] It also explains why the prince defined the primary objectives of the Luzo-Brazilian Convention as the establishment of guidelines both for independence and for "Brazil's union with other parts of the great Portuguese family." Meanwhile, in Portugal, the Brazilian Committee on the Constitution suggested to the Côrtes a dual monarchy, with two parliaments, a regent, and an independent Brazilian court system.

The plan to keep Brazil and Portugal united and at the same time insure Brazil's administrative autonomy—a plan very dear to the Brazilian elite—proved unworkable.[41] Recognition of the colony's autonomy would inevitably imply free trade, something that the Côrtes could not agree to. Thus the events in Rio could only provoke outrage in Portugal. The conflict had reached the point of no return. The Côrtes again ordered the prince to return to Portugal immediately and sent troops to Brazil to maintain order.

But since February 1822, the prince had prohibited the landing of Portuguese troops. And shortly afterwards, in response to the open show of disapproval his decision had aroused among Portuguese troops in Rio, he ordered them to leave for Portugal. In May 1822 he ruled that no decrees originating in the Côrtes could be enforced in Brazil without his approval. And when the naval squadron with orders to escort him to Lisbon arrived in Brazil, it was forbidden to enter the harbor of Rio de Janeiro, unless its commander agreed to obey the prince's orders. Less than three weeks later, the squadron returned to Portugal, leaving behind some six hundred men who had sworn loyalty to the regent. On 13 May 1822, the Municipal Council of Rio de Janeiro granted the prince the title "Perpetual Defender of Brazil." And in June, the Conselho de Procuradores, which the prince had created, recommended that he call a national convention. He accepted their suggestion immediately.

A ruling of 19 June 1822 established eligibility requirements for the electorate.[42] It gave the ballot to any male citizen, married or single, who was over twenty years of age and was not living with his parents. But it excluded from suffrage those whose income came from wage labor, with the exception of clerks in commercial firms, high-ranking employees of the royal household, and administrators of rural plantations and factories. It also denied the vote to members of religious orders, foreigners not yet naturalized, and criminals. Such legislation deprived the masses of the right to choose their representatives and gave all political power to the elites.

After convoking the national convention the prince took the advice of José Bonifácio and passed several decrees that furthered the cause of independence. On 21 June 1822, the government stipulated that any person appointed to a civil service job had to swear to support Brazilian independence. On 1 August, the prince decreed that Portuguese troops trying to land in Brazil would be regarded as enemies. Some days later he ordered the provincial governments to prevent anybody appointed by the Portuguese government from taking office.

That same month the prince addressed a manifesto to the nation and another to the "friendly nations." Both manifestos sounded like declarations of independence. But in both the prince still stressed his intention to maintain the unity of the empire. To Brazil he said that the constitution to be drawn up by the Brazilian national convention would recognize João VI, his father, as king. To Brazil's allies he declared the political independence of Brazil "salva a devida e decorosa união com Portugal" (respecting the union with Portugal).[43]

On 2 September 1822, the prince's wife Leopoldina presided over a meeting of the Council of State in Rio while the prince was traveling in São Paulo. She informed the councilors that the Côrtes intended to send troops to Brazil because it considered the regent and his advisors traitors and enemies of the Crown. It became clear then that the prince had only two options: to obey the Côrtes and return to Portugal in disgrace or to formalize Brazilian independence and remain in Brazil as king. José Bonifáio wrote to him: "From Portugal we can expect only enslavement and horror. Come back and make a decision; irresolution and temperate measure cannot help. In view of this merciless enemy, one moment lost is a disgrace."[44] Recognizing the inevitable, Pedro proclaimed Brazilian independence on 7 September

1822, while he was still in São Paulo. Once independence had been formally proclaimed, it was too late to back down. All the efforts of the Portuguese government to reverse the situation were frustrated. One after another, Portuguese attempts to get European support for their recolonizing project failed. The position of the British government was a decisive factor in consolidating Brazil's independence. Canning, the British minister, made it clear at his first meeting with the Portuguese foreign minister that Britain would not tolerate European military intervention in the New World. Any such action would force His Majesty to recognize the independence of the colony in question. Great Britain's strong position discouraged Portuguese plans to reconquer Brazil. England would later serve as mediator in Brazil's diplomatic efforts to obtain formal recognition of independence from Portugal.[45]

After independence, the government fell into the hands of an elite of planters, merchants, and high functionaries, many of whom later received titles of nobility for their services to the crown.[46] Typical among them was Manuel Jacinto Nogueira da Gama, later marquis of Baependí. He had been a teacher at the Royal Naval Academy in Lisbon and inspector of the gunpowder factories in Brazil. Following independence, he became a representative to the National Convention in 1823, a senator for Minas Gerais in 1826, and president of the Senate, minister of Finance, and a member of the Council of State during the empire. Estevão de Rezende, another member of the political elite,

FIG. 1. Prince Pedro acclaimed emperor of Brazil

FIG. 2. Pedro Américo, a Brazilian painter, depicts Prince Pedro proclaiming Brazilian independence.

was made a baron in 1825, count in 1826, and marquis of Valença in 1845. He had been born in Minas Gerais in 1777; his father was from a Portuguese noble family, his mother from a wealthy family in Minas. He married the daughter of a rich Portuguese nobleman who lived in São Paulo. Like many other members of the Brazilian elite, he had graduated in law at the University of Coimbra and had started his bureaucratic career as a judge in Portugal. In 1810, he was back in Brazil, where he continued as a judge for a while; in 1816 he was appointed supervisor of the diamond mnes of Sêrro Frio (Minas Gerais). He also occupied an important position in the court of Bahía and later in the court of Rio. After independence, Rezende was elected a representative to the Chamber of Deputies and became a senator and member of the Council of State after 1827.

Another important man in the government was Joaquim Pereira do Faro, who was born a Portuguese and had made his fortune in commerce. He became a knight of the Imperial House and the Order of Christ as well as baron of Rio Bonito. His son, the second baron of Rio Bonito, was a planter and a businessman like his father. His grandson would be an important planter in the coffee areas; his daughter became the baroness of São Clemente, one of the most elegant women during the empire. Belarmino Siqueira, later baron of São Gonçalo, was very infuential at the time of independence. In the biographical dictionaries of the time, he appears as a planter and "capitalist." He was also a member of the Chamber of Deputies, a commander of the National Guard in Niteroi, and president of the Rural Mortgage Bank. Jose Egídio Álvares de Almeida, later baron and marquis of Santo

Amaro, was born in Bahía in 1787 to a noble family. Before independence, he was secretary to João VI and counselor of the Treasury. In 1823, he was elected to represent the province of Rio de Janeiro at the National Convention. He served as ambassador to England and France and eventually became a member of the Council of State as well as a senator. Maciel da Costa, later viscount and marquis of Queluz, was born in Mariana, Minas Gerais, in 1763. He studied in Coimbra and returned to Brazil, where he was elected to the National Convention. Later he was a representative in the Chamber of Deputies and then became a senator and a member of the Council of State. Twice during the empire Maciel da Costa was appointed to the ministry and was chosen president of the province of Bahía. He married into the Werneck family, important coffee planters in Vassouras.

But the most important politician of this period was Joaquim Carneiro de Campos, later marquis of Caravelas. Born in Bahía in 1768, the son of a businessman, he graduated in theology and law at the University of Coimbra. On his return to Brazil in 1808, he was immediately appointed to an administrative position. In 1818, he became a counselor to João VI. After independence, he was elected to the National Convention and on several occasions served as minister. And he, like the others, was a member of the Council of State. When the first emperor of Brazil resigned in 1831, Carneiro de Campos was made regent.

There were many others who had similar careers and who received titles of nobility: the viscount and marquis of Nazareth, the barons of São João Marcos, Itapoca, Jacutinga, Pindamonhangaba, the viscount of Macaé, count of Rio Pardo and the marquises of Taubaté, Cantagalo, Quixeramobim, and Jacarepaguá. Most of these men, who were responsible for the organization of the nation after independence, were over fifty years old in 1822. A few had been born in Portugal, but most were natives of Brazil. Many had studied in Coimbra and had occupied important administrative positions before independence. Others were plantation owners and merchants. They were very often related to each other. After independence they occupied important positions in the government and became a typical oligarchy, holding office in the Council of State, the Senate, and the Chamber of Deputies. They also served as presidents of the provinces and ministers of state.

These men were interested in maintaining the traditional structure of production based on the large estate, slavery, and the export of "colonial" products, and they opposed any attempts at industrialization. Although they had been raised in the Enlightenment tradition and had adopted liberal ideas, they were clearly antidemocratic. When they organized the electoral system, they deliberately excluded the masses from the electorate, or made them puppets of the local bosses, adopting income qualifications for suffrage and establishing a system of indirect elections. To qualify as a voter in the primary elections, one had to have an annual income of 100$000 from real estate, industry, commerce, or a profession. To be an elector, one needed an income of 200$000. To be a representative, one had to have an income of 400$000, and 800$000 was the lower limit for a senator. That the situation did not benefit most of the populace was clear, to Saint Hilaire, among others. Comparing the events in Brazil to those in France at the time of the French Revolution, he observed that the majority of people in France had profited from their revolution. In Brazil, however, he remarked, "all the abuses in the past issued from a powerful group of men, the same men that led the revolution." All they cared about was diminishing the power of the king and increasing their own.[47]

Like Saint Hilaire, many travelers noticed a contradiction between the liberal theoretical framework adopted by the Brazilian elite and its actual practice. The elites were not disturbed by this contradiction. Throughout the empire politicians continued to use the rhetoric of liberalism in their sonorous speeches to the Chamber of Deputies and the Senate. And the intellectual elite created an ideology that hid the contradictions inherent in the system.

Brazil's independence had been won by the classes interested in preserving traditional economic and social structures. Their sole objective had been to destroy the colonial system only insofar as it restricted commecial opportunities and administrative autonomy. Brazil as an independent nation would continue to have a colonial economy, but would pass from dependence on Portugal to dependence on Great Britain. The face of liberalism raised by the elites disguised the misery and servitude of most people living in Brazil. To achieve the complete emancipation of the nation, to integrate the majority of the population into the political and economic system—these were tasks left to future generations.

2 JOSÉ BONIFÁCIO DE ANDRADA E SILVA
A Brazilian Founding Father

Every class, caste, and social group has its heroes and myths. Men search the past for characters and events that can be used to symbolize the dominant values of their social group. Indeed, once they are fully elaborated, myths and heroes can actually determine people's sense of social and historical reality. And when social structures and values change, myths and symbols change, too. Heroes and myths that can no longer satisfy social needs lose their old meanings. When social tensions break into open confrontation between different classes, there is a surge of iconoclasm. Traditional myths and heroes are either destroyed or subjected to a process of wholesale reinterpretation that adapts them to the new situation. At the same time, new images and symbols appear, novel constructs that synthesize new aspirations, a fresh inventory of ideological instruments for those who struggle for power.

The mythic heroes who captivated the imagination of primitive men, the saints and knights who peopled medieval ballad and chronicles, the kings and nobles who loomed so large in the consciousness of the ancien regime—all these have been more or less replaced in our age by nation builders. The triumph of the national state brought forth a collection of myths and heroes that could galvanize men's consciousness of their national identity. In the Americas, the "forgers of nationality," the men who fought for their countries' independence—Bolivar, Miranda, San Martin, Washington, and Jefferson—came to be seen as heroes. Again and again, in one country after another, what once had been crime became the highest virtue. Words and deeds that had been punishable by death in the colonial period quickly became memorable and heroic. In 1789, Tiradentes was a *pérfido* and was condemned to death for his horrendous crime—participating in a conspiracy to emancipate Brazil from the yoke of the mother country. After independence, he was transformed into a blessed memory. In 1817, the slogans of the rebels of Pernambuco—"Viva a Pátrià" and "Viva a Liberade"—

were condemned by authorities as the ultimate treason, but historians who later looked back through the lens of nationalism interpreted the same slogans as affirmations of patriotism.

In 1822, José Bonifácio de Andrada e Silva could only be regarded by Portuguese authorities as a dangerous enemy, because of his participation in the succession of events that culminated in Brazilian independence. To all the partisans of the Portuguese, José Bonifácio was infamous and his supporters were "perfidious satraps."[1] But like so many other "infamous" men, he was consecrated by historians as a national hero—even as the principal national hero, the father of his country.

In the figure of this national patriarch, reality and the hero, the man and the myth, are so blended and confounded that it is difficult to evaluate objectively the actual role he played in the movement toward independence. Myth has beclouded reality. From their primers, schoolchildren learn to worship him even before they have any idea of pátria—much less any idea of history. Historians often struggle in partisan ways to get behind the myth. Some of them even promote a dark legend of José Bonifácio that either minimizes his actual importance or subverts his heroic status by replacing him with an alternative hero figure, a Pedro I, a Gonçalves Ledo, a Princess Leopoldina.[2]

Neither the worshipful gaze of the schoolchildren nor the equally partisan stare of those who debate who the *real* hero of independence was is a useful view for the modern historian. His task is neither to elevate nor to denigrate, but to analyze the relationships between a real historical individual and the larger structures that shape him and are in turn shaped by him. One of the primary tasks of historians is to reduce myths and heroes to their actual proportions. But this does not mean that legends can be simply forgotten. Instead, they have to be confronted and examined as products of specific social needs and realities. Otherwise the historian will be trapped in the legend's web.

The image of José Bonifácio as the patriarch of independence was forged in the heat of political struggle. The necessity of defending their point of view, and of consolidating his position as the head of the new government—in a word, of legitimizing the new regime—led Bonifácio's supporters to present him to the public as father of his country, pilot of independence, and patriarch. These expressions had already begun to circulate in 1822, when he was a member of the ministry of Pedro I. Shortly after the proclamation of independence, when José Bonifácio resigned from the ministry, petitions and pamphlets began to appear urging his return to the government. One petition, presented to the Municipal Council of Rio de Janeiro, referred to him and his brothers as the "sole anchor of the new empire."[3] In the press, the same process was already under way. Eloquent panegyrics appeared in the *Tamoio*, a Rio newspaper edited by Menezes de Drumond, a close friend and political ally of Jose Bonifácio's family, the Andradas. Early in August 1822, the *Tamoio* described him as a "good son, good father, good husband, good brother, good relative, good friend"—all this in addition to being the man who had consolidated independence. A little later, the same newspaper described José Bonifácio and his brothers as savants known and celebrated by civilized Europe—and this was a mere ornament to the essential fact: they had brought happiness and independence to Brazil and had founded a new empire, vast and rich. According to this same editorial, José Bonifácio had been the first to labor against the vicious Portuguese Côrtes, the first to suggest the proclamation of Brazilian independence; he had also beaten down both the Portuguese loyalists in Brazil and that other dangerous faction, the republicans who were demanding that the prince regent be shipped back to Portugal.[4]

"Patriarca da Independencia," the title conferred on José Bonifácio, appeared in various other publications of the period. In 1832, ten years after the resignation of the emperor, he was accused by the regency government of plotting the reestablishment of the monarch. Cândido Japi-Assú, who took charge of his defense, invoked the already potent image of the hero's identification with independence, using the standard phrases: "Pai da Pátria" and "Patriarca da Independencia." Under such rhetorical banners, José Bonifácio passed into history. José da Silva Lisboa, the author of one of the earliest histories of the period, proclaimed in 1835 that impartial history would confer on José Bonifácio the title Savior of Brazil.[5] It appeared, then, that independence was the outcome of deliberate efforts by José Bonifácio and the young prince, with José Bonifácio cast in the primary role of planner and instigator.

There was no shortage, even at this early stage, of other, opposing versions of José Bonifácio's personality and significance. Born out of political rivalry and personal hostility, developed by his host of adversaries, these versions saw in José Bonifácio just one minister among several, or an extreme conservative, or a man who was simply arbitrary, vain, and capricious. Diatribes against José Bonifácio and his policies appeared frequently in the opposition press, *Correio do Rio de Janeiro*, *Revérbero Constitucional*, and *Malagueta*, reproving him for his aristocratic attitudes and his opposition to representative government and a constitutional convention. His critics accused him of being consistently averse to the idea of independence, and of persecuting the more liberal elements that desired a broadening of civil liberties. The most violent criticism of José Bonifácio appeared in 1832 and 1833, when in the Chamber of Deputies, the Senate, and the press, his enemies actually set out to destroy his political stature and reputation.

In one form or another, the heroic and the dark legends—both created at the time of the events themselves—were incorporated into history. And this incorporation came during a time when historians typically engaged in a very limited kind of characterological analysis, looking primarily at the motives and the personal quarrels of a few political leaders, as though the process of history were merely the outcome of conscious personal choices made by a handful of men. And so historians joined in the fray, endorsing one or another version of José Bonifácio, depending on their own personal sympathies and antipathies.

An analysis of José Bonifácio's personal life within the context of social and political struggle at the time of independence may enable us to transcend the limits of the subjective chronicles, to understand more clearly the process of independence, and so redefine in more objective terms José Bonifácio's actual role in the movement.

José Bonifácio was born 13 June 1763, into one of the richest families of Santos. His father was a royal functionary and was listed in the 1765 census as the second richest man in the city. It is difficult to say exactly how his fortune was accumulated, but it is possible to make some reasonable guesses. He had begun his career as a colonel in the Auxiliary Dragoons of the São Paulo military district. He then served, successively, as supervisor for the mines of Paranapanema, secretary to the commission of the Royal Patrimony, and treasurer for the Royal Patrimony. In the census of 1765, José Bonifácio's father was listed as a merchant in Santos. Living in the port, he probably benefited from the rapid increases in the export trade. Money and the circle of well-placed acquaintances he had developed as a royal official allowed him to pass on to his sons an important status in the colony. Three of them, José Bonifácio, Martim Franscisco, and Antonio Carlos, eventually occupied high posts in the government. The three oldest boys also studied at the University of Coimbra in Portugal. Before he enrolled there at the age of twenty-one, José Bonifácio had completed a classical preparatory course with Friar Manuel da Ressureição. Like other candidates for the university, he had to learn something of French, rhetoric, metaphysics, and logic. At sixteen, like many other boys his age, he was composing little poems governed by the rigid rules of Latin pastoral, a tradition he later repudiated.

Coimbra was an important institution for the Brazilian elite—and also for its numerous clientele. There was no university in Brazil as yet, so in the course of the eighteenth century about seventeen hundred young Brazilians were trained at Coimbra. From São Paulo had come, like José Bonifácio, Bartolomeo Lourenço de Gusmão, Alexandre de Gusmão, Pedro Taques d'Almeida, Matias Aires, João Caldeira Brant, Tomás Antonio Pizarro e Araujo, Antonio Rodrigues Veloso de Oliveira, Diogo de Toledo Lara, Francisco José Lacerda de Almeida, José Arouche de Toledo Rendon, and many others.[6] After graduating from Coimbra, such young men had become outstanding figures in Brazilian culture and politics. They occupied important administrative and political posts and joined the colonial "republic of letters." Most of the elite that, after independence, became responsible for creating the institutions of independent nationality were graduates of Coimbra—an important fact for understanding their political performance and their ideology.

Some years before José Bonifácio enrolled at Coimbra, the university had passed through an important transformation. As part of his attempt to remodel Portugal along the bourgeois lines that had become current in other European countries, the marquis of Pombal had decided to reform the university. He wanted to liberate the curriculum from the obscurities and routines of classicism, to introduce the most modern methods and concepts of enlightened empiricism, and to emancipate the institution from Jesuit control. The reform involved a new emphasis on science and a condemnation of traditional methods of teaching as "merely theoretical and bookish." To replace the old School of Arts, its new School of Philosophy was formed to promote work in philosophy and natural science. It was in this new school that José Bonifácio enrolled some years later.

But it was not Pombal's reformed and enlightened university that José Bonifácio attended. By the time he reached Coimbra, Pombal had fallen into disgrace, and a full-scale counter-Enlightenment was under way. Pombal's ideas had seemed too advanced to an archaic and sanctimonious Portugal and, with his fall, several reactionary measures had been taken. The *alvará* of 5 February 1778 ordered the confiscation of numerous books of "pernicious doctrines," books that threatened to corrupt the "good habits" of society and were contrary both to "Catholic religion and public peace." Many teachers were put on trial for reading French authors—Rousseau in particular—and the university's rector, Francisco de Lemos, was dismissed. His replacement was the Principal of the Lisbon Church, whose stated mission was to quench the "revolutionary ardor which the young brought to the study of books of erroneous doctrine."

This alternation between reform and repression created heightened sensitivity among students to the backwardness of Portuguese policy. In 1785, an anonymous satirical poem, *The Kingdom of Stupidity*, impiously castigated the teachers and courses at Coimbras.[7] The poem is usually attributed to a Brazilian student, Francisco de Melo Franco, and some scholars believe that José Bonifácio had a hand in it. *The Kingdom of Stupidity* recalled, with considerable bitterness and no less mordacity, that Pombal's reforms had brought a few professors to the university who were worthy of their titles. But now it would take a most perspicacious eye to pick them out—"so complete is the reign of Stupidity." As for law students—and both Franco and José Bonifácio were among them—they were taught only "pedantry, vanity, and indisposition to learning, powdered over by the four lies of the Roman Law." They learned nothing of modern legislation, international law, politics, or commerce, nothing, in short, that might conceivably be useful to them or to society. The poem also lamented Portuguese backwardness in comparison to the progress being made in other countries: the arbitrariness of the nobility, the improprieties of the clergy, the fanaticism, credulity, and ignorance of the people in general, and Portugal's resultant victimization by foreigners:

> Miserable nation! that faithfully
> Opens its treasures to foreigners
> For cheap cloth, for buckles and baubles,
> For other immense nothings.

It was in this university, however, this "kingdom of stupidity" from which Pombal's reforms had not been able to sweep tradition and formalism, that José Bonifácio had his first encounter with the authors of the Enlightenment and deepened his acquaintance with the classics. He was an indefatigable reader and did not limit himself to what was taught in his courses. His notes, scattered today in different Brazilian archives, his poetry, and his letters are full of references to Rousseau, Voltaire, Montesquieu, Locke, Pope, Virgil, Horace, and Camões. He became, despite the official reaction at the university, an adept of the Enlightenment, and its intellectual habits would appear again, years later, in his political theories.

Although he continued to write poetry, José Bonifácio became increasingly preoccupied with science, especially the infant discipline of mineralogy. With the aid of the duke of Lafões, he obtained a grant to

travel to other European countries—a journey which somehow pro-
longed itself into ten years. During this decade, he attended lectures in
chemistry by such masters as Fourcroy, Lavoisier, and Jussieu; he visited the most important mining centers in Europe; and he traveled in-
cessantly through France, Germany, Austria, Hungary, Sweden, Nor-
way, and Denmark. What met the eye of his acquaintances in this
period was the young scientist, the mineralogist; he gave no hint that
twenty years later he would play such an important role in the emancipation of a Portuguese colony several thousand miles away.

Despite his specialization in mineralogy, José Bonifácio kept up his
more general interests—like any model figure of the Enlightenment.
He continued to read history, philosophy, and literature, and he remained generally sensitive to the meanings of politics and social movements. When he visited France in 1791, he was pained by what he
viewed as the excesses of the revolution. He had already developed a
habit of mind that would remain strong all his life. He distrusted the
masses and any revolutionary movement that involved mass mobilization. Among his own Enlightenment masters, he was always much
more comfortable with Montesquieu and Voltaire than with Rousseau. His irreverence in matters of religion and his lack of sympathy
for democratic regimes were reminiscent of Voltaire's. In the simplest
terms, José Bonifácio would be a liberal, but never a democrat. His social and political ideas were, at bottom, very much like those of Melo
Franco, his fellow-student at Coimbra and a disciple of Condillac,
Helvetius, and Cabanis, for whom "the license of great freedom" was
as pernicious as any despotism. From Voltaire's *Essay on Human In-
equality*, no doubt, had come Melo Franco's conviction that there was
no way to rid human societies of extremes of poverty and wealth [8]—an
idea to which José Bonifácio could subscribe with little or no hesitation.

When José Bonifácio ended his ten-year period of wandering study,
he returned to Portugal and began to display all the signs of a permanently established life. He acquired a wife, the Irish woman Narcisa
Emília O'Leary. And he began to accumulate positions: professor of
mineralogy at Coimbra, supervisor of the mines of the kingdom, ad-
ministrator of the coal mines in Buarcos and of the iron foundries of
Figueró dos Vinhos and of Avelar. He was also director of the labora-
tory of the Royal Mint. He supervised the attempt at reforestation
along the shore and was superintendent of public works at Coimbra,
where he had charge of setting up sewage and water systems.

This astonishing variety of positions no doubt resulted in part from
the varieties of expertise he brought back to Portugal from his decade
of study and travel in the more sophisticated countries to the north.

But he also owed them to the powerful Portuguese tradition of patronage. (José Bonifácio was a close friend of high officials in the government such as the count of Linhares, who was one of King João VI's ministers). Until he was fifty-six, the man who later would be considered the head of Brazil's independence was perfectly adjusted to both his administrative and his social life in Portugal. He also kept up a more generalized identification with all that was most sophisticated in Europe at large. He continued to study and published numerous articles in various European scientific and technical journals.[9] He acted out the Enlightenment ideal of universality by keeping up a lively interest in a great variety of topics like history, literature, philosophy, and political economy.[10] All in all, his intellectual life, his administrative work, and his social connections blended harmoniously, and the whole seemed rounded, complete, and comfortable.

José Bonifácio repaid Portugal for his secure and satisfying life there with military courage and skill. In 1808, when the Napoleonic invasion of Portugal forced the king to flee to Brazil, José Bonifácio stayed behind to fight. He joined the Corps of Academic Volunteers and participated in several actions, first as a major, then as a lieutenant-colonel, and finally as commandante. He also served in the army secret service and helped with the manufacture of weapons and the erection of fortifications. His manifest patriotism, his diverse skills and his personal courage won praise from the government. To all intents and purposes, he was simply a good Portuguese, loyal to the king and to the country.

Ironically, José Bonifácio's patriotic services coincided with a marked shift in the nature of the colonial relationship between Portugal and Brazil. After Napoleon's defeat, for reasons few Portuguese could fathom, João VI remained in Brazil and granted new privileges to the Brazilians; this irritated many people in Portugal, especially those with commercial ties to the colony. The Portuguese hoped that by forcing the king to return to Portugal they would reestablish their lost monopolies and privileges.

The irritations and hopes of the Portuguese were mirrored by a reverse set of irritations and hopes in the colony.[11] In 1817, Brazilian rebels organized a revolution whose purpose was to resolve the growing contradictions of the colonial system by declaring Brazil an independent republic. The news of this unsuccessful revolt and the repression that followed—a repression that spared his brother Antonio Carlos, one of the rebels—could only inspire in José Bonifácio a wish to go back to Brazil. He requested permission to return home. In October 1818, the permission was granted. José Bonifácio lingered until the following June, when he finally announced his decision to the Academy of Sciences: he would go to the "new Portugal." As the phrase suggests, he did not think of himself as leaving Portugal at all; he still regarded Brazil as a natural extension of the realm—"new," yes, but still "Portugal." [12]

José Bonifácio returned to Brazil with an extensive cargo; his own fifty-six years of life and experience, an astonishing record of service to the Crown, a remarkable library of some six thousand volumes—all this plus a wife and a daughter. The wife, according to his estimate of her, was not blessed by nature with a cool mind or strong nerves. But she had had nerve and coolness enough to accept the daughter—who was not her own. [13]

When he reached Brazil, José Bonifácio made one important decision, to settle at Santos, his birthplace, away from the political intrigues and complexities of the Court at Rio. In fact, science seemed to attract his energies more than politics. In 1820, he traveled with his brother Martin Francisco throughout São Paulo, taking copious notes of his observations—notes he later published under the title *Memória Econômica e Metalúrgica*. [14] José Bonifácio next published another scientific study, on the Brazilian salt mines, but it was not long before he abandoned his scientific studies and became deeply involved in politics: in August 1820, he was appointed a counselor of the Crown.

His appointment as counselor coincided with a profound change in the political situation. In January 1820, Spain was shaken by a liberal revolution. In August a revolution broke out in the important Portuguese commercial center of Oporto and quickly spread to other parts of the country. The revolutionaries organized a parliament, the Côrtes, and demanded a constitution and the return of the king to Portugal.

When the news of the Portuguese revolution reached Brazil, there were many demonstrations celebrating the revolution. In February 1821 a crowd of people gathered on the streets of Rio de Janeiro to demand that the king accept the stipulations of the Côrtes. Royal troops joined the crowd, and the king was forced to promise to accept a constitution still to be written by the Côrtes. He also agreed to call an election of Brazilian representatives to the Côrtes and to return home, leaving his son Pedro behind as a regent. Meanwhile new governments (*juntas administrativas*) were formed in each capital city.

In 1821 the "people" of the province of São Paulo were called to select the members of a provisional government. José Bonifácio was chosen a member of the *junta governativa*, in which he sat side by side with representatives of the different classes—as they were then called—

the military, the commercial, the literary, the pedagogical, and the agrarian.

With his characteristic energy and enthusiasm, José Bonifácio immediately set to work to draft a set of instructions for the delegates that São Paulo, like the other Brazilian provinces, was sending to the Portuguese Côrtes. These instructions were subscribed to by all the members of the junta.[15] As an initial premise the document endorsed the notion of a united kingdom so long as the colony had representation in the Côrtes. José Bonifácio and his colleagues insisted that the relative autonomy achieved during the king's residence in Brazil be maintained. They proposed the creation in Brazil of an executive government and demanded that Portuguese and Brazilian citizens of the united kingdom enjoy the same political and civil rights "so far as the diversity of customs, territory, and actual conditions may permit."

The São Paulo instructions also revealed José Bonifácio's Enlightenment views. He recommended the establishment of a university for Brazil and a general upgrading of the school system. He proposed the construction of a new national capital in the backlands which would promote the settlement of what Brazilians called the *sertão*. The instructions also stressed the importance of furthering immigration, protecting native tribes and emancipating slaves. To rationalize the processes of settlement, José Bonifácio also recommended the revocation of royal land grants in cases where the land had not been actually cultivated.

At the time and from the perspective of São Paulo, the expectations that the Côrtes at Lisbon would see the wisdom of such principles and policies did not seem unrealistic. But it soon became quite clear that the Portuguese of Brazil and those of Portugal would never agree. José Bonifácio and most other members of the Brazilian elites (landowners, slave traders, senior members of the royal bureaucracy) had been lured by a vision they shared with other colonial elites: unity with the mother country but also substantial autonomy. But the uncompromising posture of the Côrtes forced José Bonifácio and all the others who thought as he did to abandon their dreams of unity and to fight, reluctantly, for independence.

Conscious of this inevitable outcome, the prince began to cast about for supporters among powerful men who had reputations as loyal monarchists, thus creating what amounted to a party. José Bonifácio was one of those recruited by the prince. When he went to Rio to present to the prince a document expressing the dismay of São Paulo at the recent actions of the Côrtes, he was invited by the prince to become his chief advisor, exercising in effect the powers of a prime minister.

José Bonifácio assumed his new duties at a critical moment. Three groups were contending for control of a very fluid situation. The first was composed mainly of Portuguese merchants living in Brazil who were anxious to reestablish old trading privileges. They were joined by most of the Portuguese military officers and by some royal functionaries. Their program was, in most of its features, indistinguishable from that of the Côrtes. This group was concentrated in Rio and other port cities of the North and Northeast. A second faction united Brazilians and Portuguese men of property and standing, occupying positions in the government, involved in international trade, or presiding over large plantations. This faction aimed still for the dual monarchy but was willing to move toward independence if the situation required it.

The third faction, and the most radical, had already opted for independence. Most of the members of this group were linked to urban middle-class activities. Among them there were pharmacists, journalists, lawyers, doctors, teachers, merchants, artisans, field grade officers in the army, and priests. They dreamed of reorganizing Brazil to fit the republican patterns that had apparently triumphed in other American countries. This third faction lost prestige and momentum as soon as it seemed possible to achieve independence with the help of the prince. Many of the members of the republican faction, in fact, deserted it as soon as the regent announced his intention to remain in Brazil—among them, Antonio Carlos, José Bonifácio's brother, the ex-revolutionary of 1817, who now felt at ease with the idea of a monarchical revolution.

José Bonifácio apparently had always been a monarchist. Nothing could be more natural for him than to join the monarchical party, where he found himself allied with powerful landowners and slaveholders and with men who held high offices in the government. Like his associates, he feared what he always defined as the excesses of popular liberty and he mistrusted democratic solutions. As he once wrote, with characteristic vehemence, "I never was, and never will be, a pure royalist, but I will never enlist under the ragged banner of the dirty and chaotic Democracy. . . . My constitution is not theirs, and I will be everything they want me to be, so long as I do not have to be what they are: neither *corcunda* [the popular name of the party of the King], nor *descamisado* [the popular label pinned on democratic political movements]." [16]

José Bonifácio's formulation of his position as a man of the center inevitably would make him the object of opposition from both radicals and conservatives. In 1822, however, his position was still confortable;

the potential menace of the Côrtes and of the Portuguese faction in Brazil forced all those interested in Brazilian autonomy to rally around the prince and José Bonifácio. It was only after independence that the precariousness of José Bonifácio's effort to define a tenable center became evident. In February 1822, he was still very much the master of the situation. As the prince-regent's minister, he forbade the landing of Portuguese troops in Brazil and ordered all those already in the country to leave. A few months later, he formally declared that no laws enacted by the Côrtes would be enforced in Brazil until they had been approved by the regent.

In various ways, José Bonifácio set out to give substance to such decrees and to solidify the regent's position. When some provinces in the Northeast failed to share Rio's enthusiasm for the decisions of the regent and his minister, José Bonifácio sent emissaries there to court the local elite's support for the cause of independence. He also hired the French general Labatut to organize a revolutionary army against any Portuguese troops who defied the order to leave Brazil. Bonifácio signed a petition to the regent asking for a national convention—a request the regent answered in June 1822.[17] But José Bonifácio did not want a convention that was democratically constituted. He wanted a set of procedures that would ensure the control of politics by men of culture and honor, *sábios e honrados*. (Rumors soon spread that he had actually threatened to "hang the constitutionalists in Constitution Square," rumors that would eventually help alienate any radical support he might have had at the outset.)

Forced by circumstances, José Bonifácio and the regent moved toward independence. The actions taken by the regent and his minister were treated in Portugal as a declaration of war. José Bonifácio and his brothers—the Andradas, as they were called—were declared traitors. Thus the same José Bonifácio who had served the Portuguese Crown for so long and with such loyalty found himself on the leading edge of a movement that seemed inevitably to carry the former Portuguese colony toward independence.

With characteristic energy and decision, José Bonifácio devoted himself to the task of eliminating opposition. He persecuted the loyalist Portuguese party and the liberals—whom he called demagogues and anarchists—any time members of either faction overstepped the limits he defined as reasonable. For these purposes, he increased the number of secret police and ordered them to seize the publications and arrest the journalists of the opposition. He also created a special court, modeled on courts martial, to judge the "crimes" of the press. Such measures obviously alienated even further the radical groups, who responded with more intense attacks in the press and intrigues with the prince against José Bonifácio.

While he attempted to put down opposition at home, José Bonifácio set about the intricate task of establishing relations with foreign governments. He appointed representatives to London, Paris, Washington, and Buenos Aires, with instructions to assure those governments that their rights and interests would be respected. He was confident that Brazil would get the support, or at least the neutrality, of Austria, a nation that had agreed at the Congress of Vienna to join the Holy Alliance to suppress revolutions both in Europe and America. The regent's wife, the Princess Leopoldina, was, after all, the daughter of the Austrian emperor, and José Bonifácio was confident she would be able to persuade her father to keep Austria neutral. With the Austrian ambassador, meanwhile, he played a curious game. He assured the Austrian that the Portuguese monarch was secure in Brazil, and at the same time threatened to form a league of American countries to protect their independence. The ambassador dutifully informed Vienna that Monsieur Andrada was committed to such a league, which would then adopt the Chinese system and close American ports to any European power that did not accept the fact of independence.[18]

José Bonifácio's threat of an American league was more than a diplomatic trick, though it was that, too. He really did dream of creating a federation of American nations. To this end, he had already instructed the Brazilian representative in Buenos Aires to discuss the advantage of an alliance with Argentina, Brazil, and other American nations.[19] In a daring speech to the British attaché, José Bonifácio declared that Brazil wanted peace with other nations, of course, but would never tolerate any outside interference in its internal affairs.

To the modern eye, José Bonifácio's vision of autonomy looks naive. How could he or anyone else close Brazil's ports when the whole economy depended on foreign markets? How could he avoid foreign interference in Brazil's internal affairs when most manufactured goods came from England? But José Bonifácio was a child of the Enlightenment. He believed that men make history. He believed in the efficacy of declaring whatever was "self-evidently right." It was in such belief that he advised the prince, in September 1822, to proclaim independence.[20]

The proclamation of 7 September 1822 began a new period in José Bonifácio's life. With independence came an intensified campaign by his opponents and enemies. And they had a powerful ally, the future marquise de Santos, with whom the emperor was having an affair. From the outset, the minister and the marquise had been hostile to-

Pedro I

ward one another, and she now became a center of opposition intrigue. Another focal point was the Grand Orient Masonic Lodge, where José Bonifácio's enemies, who made the prince grand master of the lodge, gathered regularly. José Bonifácio distrusted the Masons and created what he hoped would be a countervailing secret order, the Apostolado, made up of those members of the elite most committed to "maintaining order" and restraining the "excesses of the masses." He set out to defeat the radical factions led by Gonçalves Ledo and Januário da Cunha Barbosa.[21] Despite the relatively democratic tone of their political rhetoric, however, these men did not in fact have enough popular support to fend off José Bonifácio and the Apostolado. Only when the radicals could temporarily gain the support of the prince could they win. At one point, for example, when José Bonifácio had actually brought charges against a number of the members of the radical faction, Ledo was able to persuade Pedro to have the charges dismissed. Such reversals bitterly disappointed José Bonifácio, and he wasted little time expressing his resentment. On the eve of the acclamation of Pedro as the emperor of Brazil, Gonçalves Ledo and his associates were hissed and stoned as they left the Senate. The assault was attributed to José Bonifácio and the Apostolado. Their connection with the incident was never proven, but some days later the minister did threaten Ledo with dire consequences if he continued his opposition. José Bonifácio also ordered the opposition paper, the *Correio do Rio de Janeiro*, to cease publication, and told its editor, Soares Lisboa, to leave the country. And the unkindest cut of all, José Bonifácio persuaded the emperor to allow him to close the Grand Orient Lodge.

After the first shock, the "radical" opposition regrouped and convinced the emperor to reopen the Grand Orient and to reverse the order for Soares Lisboa's deportation. Offended, José Bonifácio resigned and was followed quickly by his brother, Martin Francisco, also a member of the ministry. The Andradas' supporters now mounted public demonstrations demanding their restoration to power. Manifestos and proclamations appeared in the streets of Rio, depicting the Andradas as victims of a conspiracy of radicals. From several provinces came letters supporting José Bonifácio and his brother.

The opposition characterized the conflict as one between liberalism, republicanism, and democracy, on one side, and José Bonifácio, a conservative servant of the emperor and the government, on the other. In fact, the ideological divisions were by no means clear. Ledo was more liberal than José Bonifácio with respect to the mechanics of the electoral system, but their disagreement involved only direct versus indirect elections. Ledo was no democrat, a fact made quite clear by a

series of articles he published in the *Revérbero Constitucional*. At one
point, for example, he wrote that "Brazil, having adopted the prince,
has adopted the safest course: [it would] enjoy the benefits of freedom
without the commotions of democracy" (a point of view to which José
Bonifácio could have subscribed without hesitation). And Ledo was no
more republican than he was democratic. He wanted only to limit the
monarchy by subordinating it to the Parliament. Later, in fact, Ledo
and his followers were attacked for their conservatism by a group of
democratic radicals.[22]

However inaccurate they were, however distorted by the passions of
the day, the images of José Bonifácio and Ledo that emerged from the
struggle for political power were to endure and become points of departure for historians long after the events of the 1820s. Over and over
again, Ledo and his groups have been pictured as republicans, liberals,
and democrats; José Bonifácio has appeared as the loyal supporter of
the principle of monarchy. José Bonifácio's own behavior ratified the
portrait of Ledo, since the minister seemed to be genuinely convinced
of the radicalism of his enemies. Thus when he rejoined the ministry,
once more sure of the emperor's support, he immediately ordered arrests, investigations, and deportations of opponents like Ledo, Januário
da Cunha Barbosa, Clemente Pereira, and Pereira de Nóbrega.[23]

In his new assault on the "radical faction," José Bonifácio had the
support once more of the Apostolado. In fact, the narrow sector of the
elite represented by that society and the uncertain support of the Crown
had become the keys to political power for José Bonifácio. The difficulty was that José Bonifácio—the European scientist and bureaucrat,
the man of the Enlightenment—had a social and economic program
that was, by the standards of the day, progressive. Yet he was allied
with, and in some ways the hostage of, the most conservative elements
in Brazilian society—"servile aristocrats," as they were called by Friar
Canéca, an ex-revolutionary of 1817 who was later arrested for his
participation in the rebellion of 1824, the Confederação do Equador.
Most important, there was a fundamental contradiction between José
Bonifácio's conservative political program and his progressive social
and economic program. He might count on the support of the elite for
one, but not for the other. In fact, his social policies would eventually
bring him into direct conflict with his only supporters, and he would
find himself a man in exile. It was this contradiction and its consequences that the contemporary image of José Bonifácio overlooked
and that later historians have failed to understand; their failure, in
turn, helped to perpetuate both the heroic myth and the dark legend of
José Bonifácio.

The mixture of political conservatism and economic and social progressivism was not the private eccentricity of José Bonifácio. It was, in fact, quite common in men of the Enlightenment. What was peculiar was José Bonifácio's position as the ally of an elite that was basically conservative in both political and socioeconomic matters. José Bonifácio was to fall victim to the contradiction of liberal practice in Brazil, where an ideology that was essentially bourgeois in its origins had been transformed into an instrument of slaveowners.

In his thirty years as a European intellectual and bureaucrat, José Bonifácio had assimilated the ideology of the European bourgeoisie. His criticism of the unproductive large estate, his preference for free labor and his condemnation of slavery, his sympathy for mechanization—all these ideas had come out of the Enlightenment. And he had developed other faiths, too, just as typical of the European bourgeois: anticlericalism, a commitment to education (even for females) as a means of social change, an aversion to titles of nobility, and an abhorrence for "absolutism" in all its forms. Like many of his contemporaries in Europe and America, he thought of the head of state as a combination of enlightened despot and constitutional ruler but *never* as a popular leader whose power rested on mass support.

Throughout his life, José Bonifácio consistently maintained the elitist view of practical politics that his ideology entailed and instinctively sought to define a workable center position against both republican and absolutists. When he came to believe the emperor was drifting toward absolutism in 1823, he responded with the same forceful opposition he had earlier directed at Ledo and Barbosa, those dangerous "democrats." Like any child of the Enlightenment, he praised "liberty" in prose and verse: "Liberty is a good that men ought to lose only with their blood."[24] And in order to protect freedom, he conceived a constitutional system modeled on Great Britain's parliamentary system, although he carefully cautioned himself that institutions could not simply be transferred intact from one nation to another, but would have to be adjusted to the particular realities of each society.[25]

The difficulty was precisely that Brazilian realities, as José Bonifácio perceived them, seemed to defeat any possibility of constitutional government. He once confided to the Austrian attaché that he doubted whether Brazil contained a hundred men capable of being discerning and responsible members of the Parliament. He remarked, with considerable malice, that he regretted he could not recruit legislators in Austria or Switzerland, as he had done with soldiers.[26] How, he wondered, could a constitutional monarch govern a country divided into provinces isolated from each other, with different habits and prejudices and with heterogeneous and scattered populations?[27] How could an impoverished people, ruined by slavery and by wars, support the luxury of a proper court or a nobility without its own financial resources?[28] Still, despite such reservations, José Bonifácio persisted in his belief that constitutional monarchy was the only acceptable form of government in the long run.

Like many of his contemporaries, José Bonifácio was committed to a belief in "the progress of the human spirit." But this belief, too, had to confront what he perceived as the difficulties of the actual situation. He was in favor of gradual reforms, so long as they took account of the realities of time and circumstance.[29] But he opposed radical commitments to abstract principles. In the National Convention, he criticized men who wanted to act on metaphysical principles without considering the limits of human nature. This lack, he thought, had been the great error of the French Revolution; it was this commitment to abstract principles that led men to perpetrate horrible crimes and to rip apart constitutions almost as soon as they were written. The same kind of dedication to principle, he believed, had caused bloodshed in Spain and Portugal. "We want a constitution," he said, "that will give us the freedom we are capable of—that freedom that makes for the happiness of the State, and not the kind of freedom that lasts some moments and is the beginning and end of terrible disorder."[30] He was deaf to the argument that the tragedy in France had actually resulted from the struggle of the privileged to survive, rather than from the reforms of those who aimed at freedom. Nor was he moved by those who accused him of supporting despotism in Brazil rather than serving the interests of the people who had elected him. In any case, he soon would prove he was not a simple absolutist: he would break with the emperor because he had, in José Bonifácio's judgment, abused the constitution.

José Bonifácio's political program allied him closely with the rural oligarchies, who shared his goal of constitutional monarchy. (The only disagreement he had with these supporters was that they wanted the Crown made subordinate to the legislature; like a good royal bureaucrat, José Bonifácio wanted the legislature to be subordinate to the Crown.) His economic and social program, however, was consonant with that of the extreme liberals he so relentlessly persecuted. José Bonifácio never endorsed the revolutionary methods or the democratic purposes of the radical newspapers of the 1820s and 1830s, such as Nova Luz Brasileira and O Jurujuba dos Farroupilhas. Yet his opinions on several subjects coincided precisely with theirs: his criticism of the unproductive character of the large estates, his condemnation of slavery, his attacks on the privileges of the nobility, and his opposition to commercial treaties that benefited foreigners. Like the radicals, José Bonifácio despised titles of nobility. But it was his own supporters who most ardently coveted such titles; in fact, most of the fellows of the Apostolado were granted titles by the emperor. They were inevitably uneasy with a leader who ridiculed the Brazilian "aristocracy" for its "servility," "ignorance," and "sordid interests," who not only ridiculed them but also actually refused the title he was offered by the emperor. José Bonifácio was blessed, or cursed, with a caustic and mordant wit, and he turned it often on his elite supporters. A few years after independence, in exile in France, he wrote, "Who would imagine that in the present circumstance the Great Duck [the emperor] would lay so many eggs at once: nineteen viscounts, twenty barons. . . ." And in the same acid tone, he chastised the government for granting titles to people who were utterly without qualification, like Domitília, whose only service to the state was as the mistress of the emperor.[31]

José Bonifácio's aversion to titles of nobility and his sarcasm were irritating to the Brazilian elites, but they were more disturbed by his plans for the gradual abolition of slavery and his projects for reforming the landowning system. In the instructions to the Paulista representatives to the Portuguese Côrtes, he had already pleaded for legislation to improve the living conditions of slaves and to promote emancipation, which would transform "immoral and brutish individuals into active citizens." He did add that all this should be done circumspectly, so as not to trigger slave rebellions; but this caution was not enough to allay the fears of men whose wealth was based on slaves. To almost every member of the landed elite, José Bonifácio's program for replacing slavery with a system of free labor seemed quite visionary. Not even his own example of using immigrant labor on his farm in Santos convinced his opponents that the scheme could work. But he was committed to emancipation, and he wrote a memorandum on the subject to be presented to the National Convention (his *Representação à Assembléia Geral Constituinte e Legislativa do Império do Brasil sôbre a Escravatura*, printed in Paris in 1825).

Echoing the Encyclopedists, José Bonifácio wrote that civil society had as its first role social justice and as its main goal human happiness. What right had any man, he asked, "to steal another man's freedom and, even worse, to steal the freedom of his children and his children's children?" One might argue, he acknowledged, that to emancipate slaves would be an attack on property. "But do not have any illusions, Sirs," he replied, "property was created for the common good, and how can it be good for the slave to lose all his natural rights and to be converted from a person into a thing. . . . It is not the rights of property you want to defend, but the rights of violence. . . . Men cannot be things; thus they cannot be property."[32] Slavery, since it violated the first principles of civil polity, inevitably corrupted the societies in which it existed. Because of slavery, work was not valued, families were disorganized, and religion corrupted. In a typically racist vein, José Bonifácio remarked that blacks had contaminated whites with vices and immorality. Thus, emancipating slaves was really emancipating whites from the evils of slavery. He also pointed to the paradox of a nation like Brazil, which adopted a liberal constitution but still enslaved half of its people.

On more pragmatic grounds, he tried to convince the slaveowners that if they correctly evaluated the costs of buying and maintaining slaves, they would realize that free labor was really more productive than slave labor. To this practical argument, he joined an equally practical expectation: the introduction of machinery that could facilitate the transition from slave to free labor, not only without loss but with actual gains in productivity.

But no matter how theoretically correct he believed his position to be, José Bonifácio had to recognize that it would be difficult to abolish slavery because of the entrenched opposition of a powerful interest. So he suggested a gradual approach. First, the traffic in slaves should be abolished over a period of four or five years. Then legislation should ameliorate the living conditions of the existing slaves. Slaveowners should be prohibited from manumitting slaves when they were old, sick, and in need of support; husbands, wives, and children should not be separated by sale; slaves should have access to legal assistance; childhood and pregnancy should be protected by law.

Even such ameliorative proposals were totally unacceptable to the Brazilian elite. Only a few isolated individuals such as Maciel da Costa and José Eloy Pessoa da Silva,[33] representatives of the Brazilian intelligentsia identified, like José Bonifácio, with the Enlightenment, subscribed to his program. The rest, the landowners and the merchants who were dependent on slave labor or interested in the slave trade, were either deaf or hostile to arguments against slavery. They were equally indifferent or opposed to José Bonifácio's proposals for the mechanization of agriculture and the rationalization of production. The easiest way to increase production, it seemed clear to the planters, was to acquire more land and more slaves, not to alter the system of production itself.

In any case, José Bonifácio never even had a chance to present his memorandum because the emperor dissolved the National Convention before it had accomplished its tasks. Years afterward, Joaquim Nabuco, the leader of the abolitionist faction in Parliament, suggested that José Bonifácio's ideas on slavery had triggered the opposition that eventually forced him to leave the government.[34] There is no direct evidence to support Nabuco's opinion, but two months after José Bonifácio resigned, the government did in one sense legitimize the slave trade by creating a tax on imported Africans. The decree was signed by the minister Manuel Jacinto Nogueira da Gama, the future marquis of Baependí; he was himself an important landholder and slaveowner and the son-in-law of Bras Carneiro Leão, one of the wealthiest men of Rio; his brother José Inácio Nogueira da Gama was one of the greatest planters of Rio do Peixe. The presence of such men in the government lends credence to Nabuco's interpretation. José Bonifácio's views on slavery could not help troubling his relationship with the landholding elite.

The same men who had originally supported José Bonifácio because of his political conservatism would later oppose him, not only because he was against slavery but also for several other reasons. In his "Instruções" of 1822, he had proposed that undeveloped land grants revert to the state. This reform would have left original grantees with only one square *légua* from each undeveloped grant, and even this they could keep only on condition that they immediately begin to cultivate it. The grants that reverted to the state should, he proposed, be sold, and the income used to promote colonization. He also suggested that immigrants, Indians, free blacks, and mulattos be given small plots of land to cultivate for themselves. In José Bonifácio's mind, there was nothing radical about such proposals. They had come directly from the colonial tradition of land legislation that had attempted to inhibit the monopolization of land by a few great proprietors.[35] But colonial legal restrictions had been evaded in various ways, and at the time of independence there were men who controlled vast, undeveloped tracts. Thus, although José Bonifácio could legitimately regard his program as restoration rather than innovation, in practice the proposals *were* radical and could only provoke violent opposition.

In his opposition to slavery and his program for the redistribution of land, José Bonifácio sided with the radical liberals against the conservatives. He was also on the liberal side in matters of religion. A disciple of Voltaire, he maintained a consistent irreverence, which shocked and offended pious Catholics. How could they not be scandalized when José Bonifácio commented that Catholicism was a religion more suited to despotism than to constitutional government? Or when he proclaimed that a religion which "stimulates idleness and considers celibacy a virtue" was poisonous to Brazil? Because of his ideas on religion, José Bonifácio took sides in the National Convention with men such as Muniz Tavares, Custódio Dias, and Carneiro de Campos, who favored religious freedom. Once more, he found himself opposing some of his habitual supporters—Azeredo Coutinho, for example, who wanted to establish Catholicism as the state religion.[36]

José Bonifácio again offended his original constituency on the issue of foreign loans and commercial treaties. He condemned all the loans and treaties as being harmful to Brazil. To the French attaché in Rio, he declared that the treaties of friendship and commerce between Brazil and the European powers were foolish actions, which he would not have allowed if he had been in the government at the time they were signed. And, commenting on Brazil's promise to pay Portugal 2,000,000 pounds as a compensation for independence, José Bonifácio wrote from exile, "At least our independence is recognized, though our national sovereignty has been kicked in the stomach. I do not know if it will die or recover. Everything depends on the Tatambas"—his sarcastic nickname for the Brazilian elite.[37]

José Bonifácio's situation thus became increasingly difficult. He could not accept the radicals' political program; his social and economic proposals angered the conservative elite. His only recourse seemed to be to rely increasingly on the emperor, to whom he gave, at first, unconditional support. He defended the emperor in the National Convention when many members were offended by what they regarded as an unwarranted assertion of prerogative: the emperor's remark that he hoped the constitution would have his "imperial approval." But soon José Bonifácio would alienate even the emperor. He had first threatened to resign but was persuaded by Pedro I to remain in the ministry. A second time he did resign but was recalled by the emperor. Finally on 15 July 1823 he resigned and was not asked to return.

The catalytic issues in the final crisis of José Bonifácio's career as minister had been two decrees dated November and December 1822. In the first, José Bonifácio had canceled all benefits and privileges enjoyed in Brazil by people who lived in Portugal. The second had expropriated the property of Portuguese subjects. Both measures encountered severe opposition. They attacked the interests of a large Portuguese constituency, which was connected by ties of marriage and interest to the Brazilian elites and therefore had much influence with the emperor himself. The *Malagueta*, an opposition newspaper edited by L. C. May, claimed that the impact of the decrees was to drive thousands of substantial citizens—and their capital—out of Brazil. About

4,600 people, the *Malagueta* claimed, had left the country "with fear and funds."[38] These two aggressive and unpopular decrees were more than José Bonifácio's already precarious political position could survive, and his resignation followed in a matter of months. After resigning, he continued to be politically active, but as a member of the opposition.

During the second half of 1823, a conflict between the elites and the Crown that had been brewing since the opening of the National Convention grew in intensity. Among the politicians, there was a general feeling of malaise, especially after a counterrevolution in Portugal restored João VI and put an end to the political power of the Côrtes. After the coup, the Portuguese government had sent emissaries to Brazil to try to convince Pedro I to accept a reunion of the two monarchies. The Portuguese merchants still living in Brazil were naturally excited by the prospect that Brazil might be returned to colonial status and that they might thus regain their old privileges. But if the idea pleased Portuguese merchants, it distressed not only Brazilians but also foreign merchants, who feared they would lose the control over trade that they had held since 1808. The possibility that the status quo ante might be restored increased tension between the Brazilian legislature and the Crown. The emperor became suspect, since he was the potential vehicle for the reestablishment of the united kingdom.

It was in this setting that the debate over whether the emperor ought to have the right to veto parliamentary acts took place. The emperor claimed the right of absolute veto, and the opposition denied it. Opposition newspapers attacked the emperor; the military garrison at Rio entered the debate with a pronunciamento in favor of the veto. The situation was tense enough to prompt the emperor's supporters to toy with the idea of dissolving the National Convention altogether—a coup they were ready to justify as "saving" Brazil's institutions from "demagogues and anarchists." As so often happens in moments of great and complex political tension, a small incident triggered the crisis. Some Portuguese officers, offended by articles published in the newspaper *Sentinela* under the pseudonym Brasileiro Resoluto, assaulted (apparently by mistake) the pharmacist David Côrte Real. The incident caused a sensation in the convention. Several speeches condemned the military and the Crown to the enthusiastic applause of excited galleries. Several ministers resigned in protest, and to replace them the emperor appointed men who did not have the support of the legislature. At the same time, units of the Rio garrison appeared on the streets, in a gesture of armed support for the emperor. The minister of the interior was summoned before the convention to explain the government's policy. But on 12 November 1823, the emperor dissolved the convention.[39]

Many representatives were arrested as they left the building where the convention had been meeting. Montezuma went to jail, with José Joaquim da Rocha, the priest Belchior Pinheiro, and two Andrada brothers, Martin Francisco and Antonio Carlos. José Bonifácio had left the convention earlier, and he was arrested at home, then jailed with the others. Some days later, he was deported; the patriarch of Brazilian independence was in exile.

For five years, José Bonifácio lived in southern France, near Bordeaux. Like many other exiles he went back to his books. He worked on translations of Virgil and Pindar. He revised and collected his own earlier poetry, which he later published under the pen name Américo Elísio.[40] He spent hour after hour on letters, all punctuated with biting expressions, profanity, irreverent political remarks, and emotional outbursts about his own loneliness and distress at being so far from his "bestial province." He spared no one. He jibed at the emperor with rude but clever nicknames: "the Imperial Child," "the Little Rascal," "Pedro Malazartes," "the Great Duck." João VI of Portugal, to whom José Bonifácio had once dedicated poetry, became "John the Ass." The Brazilian aristocrats came in for their share of pungent nicknaming— the Tatambas—as did the Portuguese, who José Bonifácio thought had been at the bottom of a conspiracy against him and whom he rewarded with the names *pés de chumbo* ("lead feet") and *corcundas* ("hunchbacks").

Still, in the midst of classical literature, poetry, and bitter letters, José Bonifácio found time to follow with care the bloody events of 1824 (Confederação do Equador) and the conflicts between the emperor and the new legislature established in 1826. The reopening of Parliament made it more likely that José Bonifácio could return to Brazil. He lobbied toward this end in an active and extensive correspondence with his friends, arguing that he had been arrested and deported "without crime and without sentence."[41] In 1829, he was finally allowed to return home. He arrived in Brazil a man of sixty, in deep sorrow over the death of his wife, who had died on the voyage. He decided to retire to Paquetá Island, in Rio de Janeiro Bay, a refuge accessible only by boat. Even there, however, José Bonifácio was not beyond the reach of politicians—nor immune to the political urge. The situation, always tense, was once again critical. The news of the revolution of 1830 in France set off deep resonances in Brazil. The liberals, unhappy with the emperor's assertions of his prerogatives, were excited by the deposition of the authoritarian Charles X in France. In fact, their animosity toward the emperor had been increasing since 1826. The military defeats of Brazilian troops in the Cisplatina and the rebellion of the mercenary soldiers in 1828 had weakened the emperor's prestige. The situation was made more critical by a jump in food prices—always a focal point for urban discontent.

In such a setting, a small event could once more trigger a crisis. A well-known liberal journalist, Líbero Badaró, was murdered in São Paulo. The murder provided the occasion for several demonstrations against the government in both São Paulo and Rio. In an attempt to recover prestige, the emperor decided to travel to Minas, where he had been received so warmly on a similar journey in 1822. This time, however, he was met with cold formality. When he returned to Rio, the Portuguese mounted a public demonstration of support, but the opposition took to the streets too. Inevitably, the two groups fell into a violent confrontation. The emperor's situation had become untenable. He decided to abdicate in favor of his son, a five-year-old child, and to leave for Portugal—where his daughter's right of succession was being challenged by his brother, Prince Miguel.

In a moving letter to José Bonifácio, his ex-minister and the man whom he had sent into exile, the emperor now requested "still another proof of friendship": Would José Bonifácio take up the post of tutor to his children? José Bonifácio had apparently forgotten his resentment, and did not deny his emperor this last favor. Once again, he was called on to play an important role at a moment of national crisis. But this time, his task was more difficult. He was older, and he had ranged against him not only old enemies but new ones who envied his restoration to prestige. In Parliament, these opponents argued that the emperor did not have the right to make such an important appointment without consulting with the legislature. In fact, the Chamber of Deputies formally annulled the emperor's decision, but the Senate confirmed José Bonifácio as royal tutor and by this means asserted the power to control his performance in the post.[42]

After Pedro's abdication, men took power who had a record of opposition to the Crown, men who in their own day had been "radicals." But once in power, they became more moderate and drew criticism from new radical factions. In the shadow of the Crown, the moderates consolidated their power. It would be years before the young prince could have any real voice in politics, so the men who controlled Parliament controlled, in effect, the whole government. But they had to face the opposition of radicals on one side and *restauradores* on the other. The proponents of restoration schemed more or less quietly for the emperor's return, whereas the "radical" opposition was more aggressive and staged several uprisings during early years of the regency, all of which were quickly and severely repressed.

As royal tutor, José Bonifácio became the target of political intrigue. The moderates feared that he would become the center of a conspiracy to bring the emperor back to Brazil. The more the government feared counterrevolution, the more it became convinced that José Bonifácio was the instrument of the restorationists. Bernardo de Vasconcelos, Feijó, and Evaristo da Veiga attacked him violently in both Parliament and the press. Finally, they formally accused him of plotting against the government. In a report to the Chamber of Deputies on 10 May 1832, Feijó pointed out that the headquarters of the restoration movement was Boa Vista, where José Bonifácio resided. Several members of the Chamber suggested that José Bonifácio be removed from his position as tutor. This proposal was passed by the Chamber, 45 to 31, and was defeated in the Senate by a margin of only one vote.

José Bonifácio's position became increasingly difficult as his enemies subjected him to relentless public criticism. His smallest gestures became subjects of controversy; his habitually irreverent language, for example, and his negligence in matters of etiquette and protocol were constantly criticized. He was also charged with carelessness for the loose way he was rearing the future emperor. Some of the accusations and criticisms were pure fiction, others had some grounding in reality. José Bonifácio had always despised the pretentiousness and artificiality of the manners of the improvised Brazilian courtiers. In an undated note, he wrote, "nothing bores me more than seeing hypocritical faces and hearing monotonous, pompous, and erudite conversations." At another point, he described himself as a man who liked a small group of select people, who abhorred crowds, a man deliberately free in his speech but intrinsically modest. "Etiquette bores me," he wrote, "and when I am sure of myself I do not care about what other people will say." [43] This self-image both reflected and shaped his actual behavior. He did seem to take pleasure in shocking his audience with witty and often scandalous remarks. The number of his enemies could only be multiplied by the operation of his tongue. Of the three regents appointed by Parliament to govern the nation after the abdication, he said, "Two are blockheads and one is a rascal." No wonder these same regents were ready to promote a merciless campaign against him, a campaign that infuriated the old Andrada and made him even more sarcastic and insolent. To a priest who was sent by the government to sound out his willingness to resign as tutor, José Bonifácio replied, "Tell those scoundrels that I will only concede by force!" [44] His words

1831.

1822.

1816.

1808.

J.B. Debret del.

Lith. de Thierry Frères Succ.ʳ de Engelmann & C.ᶦᵉ

AMÉLIORATIONS PROGRESSIVES DU PALAIS DE S.ᵗ CHRISTOPHE,

(Quinta de Boa Vista), depuis 1808, jusqu'en 1831.

FIG. 3. Quinta da Boa Vista architectural changes

were prophetic. In fact, his enemies had only to wait for an adequate pretext to depose him, and sooner or later they were bound to find one. In December 1833, the Military Society, a stronghold of the ultra-conservatives, posted a portrait strongly resembling the ex-emperor. It was stoned from the street, and new rumors about the restoration of the emperor were spread. This tiny crisis gave the government all the excuse it required, and José Bonifácio was suspended.

The old man attempted to resist. He wrote to the minister of the empire, the cabinet minister responsible for internal affairs and thus for José Bonifácio's function as tutor, that the arrangement under which he tutored the prince was a private one between himself and the emperor, and no business of the government. But, whatever the logic of his position, he was forced out. Troops were sent and his house was surrounded. But still he refused to step aside. The soldiers had to invade his house and remove him forcibly. The government wanted more than an end to José Bonifácio's brief career as royal tutor, however, and charged him with conspiracy. During the ensuing trial, nothing was proved against him. With the same haughtiness and arrogance that had characterized his whole life, he refused at first even to retain a lawyer. Persecution, exile, old age, and the disease which now sapped his strength—all taken together had not weakened his enormous pride. He would have no lawyer, he said, because he had committed no chargeable offense, and if it became absolutely necessary to stage a defense, then he would accept any honest counsel who volunteered for the task.[45] Cândido Japi-Assú did offer to defend José Bonifácio, and the old man agreed; but the presiding judge refused to accept the arrangement, ruling that he had already sacrificed his right to counsel. Cândido Japi-Assú, in the end, published the speech he had prepared for the court in José Bonifácio's defense, a speech in which he celebrated José Bonifácio as the patriarch of independence and a statesman of the empire.[46]

The trial dragged on from December 1833 to March 1835, when José Bonifácio was unanimously absolved by the court. More than two thousand people applauded the reading of the verdict. But justice had come too late. Broken by age, disease, and disappointments, José Bonifácio would spend the last three years of his life among his books and notes at Paquetá, working on essays that politics had never allowed him to finish. As his illness worsened, he was forced to make a pilgrimage to Niterói in search of medical assistance. He died there on 6 April 1838, in his seventy-fifth year.

During the last years of his life, he had watched the ruling moderate faction become increasingly conservative. Their last liberal gesture had been the Ato Adicional (Additional Act), which amended the constitution by granting greater autonomy to the provincial governments. The elections of 1836 brought to power a group of politicians led by Bernardo de Vasconcelos and Honório Hermeto, whose real constituency was the great landowners and their clienteles.

José Bonifácio had also witnessed the defeat of his political and economic programs. He had dreamt of constitutional monarchy, but what he saw in power was a strong oligarchy—something he had always feared. He had struggled against the concentration of land in the hands of a minority, but what he had to watch was the growth of large estates in the new coffee areas. He had fought for the interruption of the slave trade and the gradual emancipation of those already enslaved, but the law of 1831 prohibiting the slave trade had been systematically disregarded, and thousands of Africans were being smuggled into the country every year. José Bonifácio had tried to promote European immigration, but he saw instead the failure of settlements that could not survive in a country where the internal market was simply too narrow to support them. He had disapproved of the commercial treaties and the loans that made Brazil dependent on foreign nations and merchants, but he had seen the treaties with England renewed and new loans contracted. He had, on the whole, wanted to modernize Brazil, but to preserve what he thought were some precious customs and traditions,[47] thus preventing the country from becoming an artificial copy of England or France; the reality he had to face in the last years of life was one in which British products controlled the Brazilian market, and British and French manners and mores were the models followed by the Brazilian elites. Finally, José Bonifácio had abhorred titles of nobility and had consistently despised the improvised Brazilian "aristocracy"; what he saw around him, in the end, was a nation under the control of a multiplying crowd of barons, counts, and marquises.

José Bonifácio's disappointments and the failure of his ideas and programs were the result of the success of groups he had actually supported at the beginning of his political career—as the only alternative to factions he had perceived as radical and democratic. A member of the Brazilian elite by birth, an enlightened bourgeois by conviction, a bureaucrat by profession, an intellectual by talent and training, José Bonifácio was trapped in his own contradictions. He was too progressive to be trusted by the elites but not progressive enough to trust the masses. Right at the time of independence he was an adequate political instrument for the elites, but he soon became superfluous and inconvenient and was ostracized by his erstwhile supporters.

History, which condemned José Bonifácio because of his contradictions, ultimately absolved him because of the same contradictions; he was worshiped by later generations of Brazilians who could appreciate his social and economic progressivism and forgive or forget his political conservatism. Twice arrested, once sent into exile, charged, tried, and absolved, José Bonifácio entered history as the Patriarca of Brazilian independence. The "dark legend" forged by his political adversaries gradually receded as José Bonifácio's ideas began to gain momentum in Brazilian society. The traditional economy and its social arrangements gradually changed under the impact of capitalist development. Slavery was abolished and immigration became the preferred solution to the problem of labor. Abolitionists found in José Bonifácio a precursor and an object of praise. They re-edited his memoir on slavery and celebrated him as a pioneer abolitionist. Positivists, an important group in the second half of the century, approved of his aversion to metaphysical principles and identified themselves with his reformist and antirevolutionary approach to social problems; they worshiped him as a national hero. Men of the empire and the republic, anxious to reconcile order and progress, found in José Bonifácio an attractive model of the patriarch as politically conservative, hostile to the "excesses" of democracy and the dangers of "unrestrained freedom." But, paradoxically, the same José Bonifácio who had disliked so much that "dirty and chaotic democracy," was also worshiped by the nationalists and "democrats" of the twentieth century, who could admire him for his projects of agrarian reform and his efforts toward slave emancipation. One of his twentieth-century biographers summed up José Bonifácio as a "nationalist, republican, and man of the left." [48]

   Despite the efforts of academic historians to reduce the image of José Bonifácio to reasonable and accurate proportions, his legend has remained intact at its center. The myth of Brazilian nationality still places him at the core of the national experience. As a symbol of aspirations for independence, José Bonifácio will probably continue to be revered as a hero as long as nationalist ideas and passions remain alive.

3 LIBERALISM
Theory and Practice

The first task of the men who took power after independence was to replace colonial institutions with others more adequate for a newly independent nation. They were not inexperienced men, confronting for the first time problems of politics and administration. In fact, most were like José Bonifácio—men over fifty, with impressive records of public service—men who had served the Portuguese Crown in many capacities during the colonial period and were well prepared to do their job.

Among those who sat in the National Convention were many priests—something to be expected in a country where the Church had had the monopoly of culture and churchmen had played an important role in administration. Others were public functionaries or professionals—lawyers, doctors, teachers—most of whom had received their degrees at the University of Coimbra or some other university in Europe, since there was no university in Brazil. There were also merchants and plantation owners. But whatever their social origin or professional affiliation, the delegates to the National Convention were linked by family or clientele to the export-import groups and represented an elite closely tied to agriculture and trade. It was according to the interests of these groups that they organized the nation.

Attributing the instability of other Latin American countries to their republican form of government, the Brazilian ruling classes had adopted in 1822 a constitutional monarchy with which they had hoped to create unity and political stability. Haunted by the specters of the French Revolution and the Haitian rebellion, they had a deep suspicion of both monarchical absolutism and revolutionary upheavals and were determined to curtail the power of the emperor and to keep the masses under control. In European liberalism they found their main source of inspiration.

Brazilian liberalism, however, can only be understood by reference

An abbreviated version of this essay was published in Emília Viotti da Costa, *Da Monarquia à República* (São Paulo, 1977), 109–26.

to Brazilian reality. Brazilian liberals imported liberal principles and political formulas but tailored them to their own needs. And since the same words may mean different things at different times, we have to go beyond a formal analysis of liberal discourse and relate liberal rhetoric to liberal practice in order to define the specificity of Brazilian liberalism.[1]

In Europe, liberalism was originally a bourgeois ideology, intimately related to the development of capitalism and the crisis of the seigneurial world. Liberal notions were born out of the struggles of the bourgeoisie against the abuses of royal authority, the privileges of the clergy and the nobility, the monopolies that inhibited production, and traditional obstacles to free circulation, free trade, and free labor. In their struggle against absolutism, liberals defended the theory of social contract, stressed the sovereignty of the people and the supremacy of the law, fought for the division of powers and for representative forms of government. To destroy corporate privilege, they made freedom, equality before the law, and the right to property universal rights of men. And to the traditional regulations that inhibited production and trade they opposed free trade and free labor. Although rooted in an expanding capitalist economy and in the experience of the bourgeoisie, the liberal message was universal enough to appeal to other social groups that, for one reason or another, felt oppressed by institutions of the ancien re-

FIG. 4. Fazenda do Secretário in Vassouras

gime. Thus, liberalism served the English bourgeoisie to strengthen its position in the government, the Russian nobility to fight the czar, and the French "populace" to send the nobles to the guillotine.

At different times during the nineteenth century, liberal ideas were used by different people with different purposes. But wherever liberals took power their main challenge was to translate their theory into practice. And everywhere in this process liberalism lost its original revolutionary meaning. Rights defined as universal became the privilege of a minority, the minority of those with property and power. And everywhere economic and social structures set the limits of liberalism and the conditions for its critique.

It is impossible to analyze here all the contradictions involved in this process. For our purpose it is enough to remember that the critique of liberalism appeared in Europe in the first half of the nineteenth century, when it became clear that an oligarchy of capital was replacing the oligarchy of birth. The first attacks on liberalism came from the stronghold of traditional privileged groups, the second from the ranks of the working class.

In Brazil the main supporters of liberalism were, as we have seen, men whose interests were related to the export-import economy. Many of them owned large tracts of land and slaves and were interested in keeping the traditional structures of production while freeing themselves from the grip of the mother country. The economic and social structures Brazilian elites wanted to maintain meant the survival of a clientele and patronage system and of traditional values which represented the very essence of what European liberals were fighting against. Finding a way to deal with this contradiction (between liberalism and slavery and patronage) was the greatest challenge Brazilian liberals had to face. Liberal discourse and liberal practice in Brazil revealed this permanent tension.

The colonial status of Brazilian economy, Brazil's peripheral position in the international market, the system of clientele and patronage, the use of slave labor, and the delayed Industrial Revolution—which happened in Brazil only in the twentieth century—all those circumstances combined gave to Brazilian liberalism its specificity, defined its issues and contradictions, and set the limits for its criticism. In other words, liberal theory and liberal practice in nineteenth-century Brazil can be explained by the peculiarities of the Brazilian bourgeoisie and by the absence of the two other classes which in Europe were the bourgeoisie's necessary point of reference, the aristocracy and the proletariat.

Contrary to what has sometimes been suggested,[2] the Brazilian elite's commitment to liberal notions was not a mere gesture of cultural mimicry, an expression of a colonial and peripheral culture subordinated to European ideas and to the European market. Liberalism was not just a fancy of the Brazilian elites and liberal slogans were not just badges they used to mark their "civilized" status, although for some people it may have been just that. For most people, however, liberal ideas were ideological weapons to reach some very specific political and economic goals.

Initially liberal ideas were an instrument of the Brazilian colonial elites in their struggle against the mother country. In this early stage liberals were politically revolutionary and socially conservative. Their struggle—a struggle which in Europe was against royal absolutism—in Brazil was primarily a struggle against the colonial system. Freedom, equality, sovereignty of the people, self-government, free trade—all those high-sounding words and phrases so dear to European liberals—had specific connotations in Brazil. To fight for freedom and equality meant to fight against Portuguese monopolies and privileges and against the restrictions Portugal imposed on production and circulation. To fight for freedom of expression meant to fight for the right to criticize the colonial pact. To fight for the sovereignty of the people was to fight for a government independent from the arbitrary favors and impositions of the Portuguese Crown.[3]

Liberal notions also appealed to slaves, who dreamed of emancipation, and to the urban lower classes, who hoped to abolish privileges that wealth had created and the Portuguese government had legitimized. Thus the conflicts of interest that opposed one class to another could be temporarily hidden behind what seemed to be an all-encompassing utopia, and the elites' goals could be presented as the goals of all. This momentary illusion, however, would soon be dispelled. That the elites and the masses had opposite goals became clear at the time of the first conspiracies for independence, when the aspirations to equality and freedom on the part of blacks and mulattos, enslaved or free, were met with indifference if not hostility by the elites. The most pathetic instance of the confusions and deceptions engendered by liberal rhetoric occurred in 1821, when slaves, hearing rumors that a constitution was about to be enacted, gathered in large numbers in Ouro Preto and surrounding areas to celebrate their long-awaited freedom. They soon learned that their celebration was premature.[4] With the exception of a few odd individuals, the Brazilian elite was not prepared to abolish slavery and did not perceive any incompatibility between liberalism and slavery. Some even suggested that the constitution include a paragraph saying that the "contract" between slaves and masters would be respected! But those who finally wrote the constitution preferred another type of fiction. When the Constitutional Charter was granted by the emperor in 1824, there was no mention of slaves, and although Article 179 of the Constitutional Charter defined freedom and equality as inalienable rights of men, millions of blacks continued to be enslaved.

The Brazilian elites' expectations and the limits of their liberalism were expressed in the manifesto addressed by the regent to the Brazilian people in 1 August 1822, a manifesto apparently written by Gonçalves Ledo, a man perceived by his contemporaries as an authentic liberal and a leading figure in the movement for independence. It started by accusing the Portuguese Côrtes of trying to reestablish the Portuguese monopoly over Brazil by closing the Brazilian ports to foreigners, of plotting to emancipate slaves and to arm them against their masters, and of destroying Brazilian agriculture and industry, and of reducing the Brazilian people to the situation of pupils and colonists. After those virulent attacks on the Côrtes, the manifesto laid down a liberal program promising legislation adequate to local circumstances, honest judges that would put an end to the trickeries of the Portuguese Courts of Justice, a criminal code dictated by "reason and humanity" to replace the "bloody and absurd existing laws," and a system of taxation that would respect "the sweatings of agriculture, the labors of industry, the hazards of navigation, and freedom of commerce," and that would "facilitate investment and circulation of assets." To those who cultivated science and letters, "abhorred and despised by despotism, the stimulant of hypocrisy and imposture," it promised freedom and "a liberal education" for the citizens of all classes.[5]

The proclamation of independence a month later brought to an end the heroic age of liberalism. From that moment on liberals confronted the difficult tasks of converting ideals into realities. They had reached their first and most important goal: to emancipate the colony from the mother country. Their second goal was to secure control of the nation for themselves. In their struggle to assert their hegemony they met not only with the emperor's opposition but also with the hostility of the masses.

The conflict between the emperor and the Brazilian elites broke out in the first meeting of the National Convention. The gap between the convention and the emperor only grew with the passing of time. The liberal opposition was relentless in its attacks against the emperor. It criticized his favoritism toward the Portuguese, condemned the lack of freedom of the press and protested against the arrest of political dissidents by the government. Those who tried in the National Convention to speak in favor of the emperor were vehemently rebuked by their peers. The tension increased during discussions of the procedures to be adopted for the appointment of provincial governments and became even more serious when some representatives suggested that the ministers be put under the direct control of the legislature. This threat to his powers did not please the emperor, who became even more irritated when some recommended that the army also be put under legislative control. The last straw on this already critical relation came during the debates about the emperor's right to veto—a right most liberals wanted to reduce to a minimum and a few went as far as to deny altogether. The conflict between the elites and the emperor ended momentarily with his victory in 1823, when he sent troops to dissolve the National Convention and ordered the arrest of several representatives, sending some into exile.[6]

In contrast with this behavior, typical of an absolutist king, the emperor himself granted a Constitutional Charter the year after. This gesture was an attempt to reconcile his interests with those of the Brazilian elites. The charter followed closely the project drafted by the National Convention and the Council of State, but, as one might expect, reinforced the emperor's powers. According to the charter, he was responsible for the implementation of the legislation approved by the Parliament and for the appointment and promotion of high personnel in the civil, military, and ecclesiastical bureaucracy. He also had the final word in the distribution of resources among the different administrative branches and could grant titles of nobility and other personal benefits in reward for services to the Crown. Following the colonial tradition of royal patronage he had the right to give or deny permission for the implementation of papal bulls. In addition to his executive prerogatives, the emperor enjoyed others issuing from what was called the moderating power by which he could choose his ministers independent from the Parliament, and adjourn, prorogue or dismiss the Chamber, calling for new elections. He could also appoint the members of the Council of State and choose the senators from among the three candidates who received the most votes in a senatorial election.

If the 1824 Constitutional Charter gave considerable power to the emperor, it also created conditions for the formation of a powerful oligarchy. Senators were appointed for life and since the age requirement for the senate was forty, they could stay in power for many years. At the end of the empire, five senators could boast of having been in the Senate for over forty years. Besides, senators were often chosen to be members of the Council of State (a body created to advise the monarch), members of cabinets and heads of political parties. During the First and Second Empires 40 percent of the senators received titles of nobility. Together with the councillors of state (who were also appointed for life) they constituted a powerful group, envied and respected. Since their support was often decisive for obtaining a loan from a bank, a position in the bureaucracy, a government pension, approval for a joint stock company, or the success of a political career, they created a large clientele.[7]

Second in rank, but sometimes as powerful, were the members of the Chamber of Deputies. Although elected for a period of only four years, they often managed to be reelected for several legislatures and were appointed to important administrative positions. Many found in the Chamber an easy road to the Senate and to the Council of State. Like the senators and councillors of state the deputies belonged to a political network of clientele and patronage which they used to their own advantage and to the advantage of their friends and clients.

What gave exceptional powers to these politicians, particularly to the members of the Council of State, was the excessive centralization of the Brazilian political system that subordinated the provinces to the central government, municipal governments to the provinces and placed the judiciary, the church, the army, and the business community at the mercy of the politicians. The central government controlled tariffs on imports and exports, the distribution of unoccupied lands, banks, railroads and stock companies, and decided on labor policies and loans. Until 1881 no liability company could be created without permission of the Council of State. The central government was not only the regulator but the protector of native and foreign enterprises, authorizing or prohibiting their functioning, providing subsidies, guaranteeing interests, establishing priorities, giving tax exemptions. Although liberal in its inspiration and phraseology, the Constitutional Charter consolidated a system of patronage that dated from the colonial period.[8] It also gave to Catholicism the status of a national religion, prohibiting the public worship of other denominations and giving the Catholic church the right to control birth and marriage registers and cemeteries.

Another peculiarity of the 1824 charter was to include an article reproducing almost word by word the Declaration of the Rights of Men issued in France in 1789. There were, however, a few curious but very revealing omissions. The article that in the original French version read, "The nation is the source of all sovereignty; no individual or body of men can be entitled by any authority which does not expressly derive from it," was dropped. Also lacking was Article VI: "The law is an expression of the will of the community." And in Article II, "The goal of all political association is the preservation of the natural and

not laissez-faire

imprescriptible rights of men and these rights are liberty, property, security, and resistance to oppression," the last four words were sup-
pressed. These omissions may be explained by the fact that this was
a charter granted by an emperor, not a constitution written by the
"representatives of the nation." But they expressed as well the antidemocratic tendencies of the Brazilian elites.

During the debates in the National Convention and many times
after it became clear that the Brazilian elites were profoundly antidemocratic. Most representatives would have endorsed the words of
Henriques de Resende, an ex-revolutionary of 1817, a man who, in
spite of his revolutionary and republican traditions declared himself in
the National Convention to be "an enemy of democracy."[9] It is not surprising that men who so emphatically expressed their hostility toward
democracy would choose an electoral system based on indirect elections and income qualification, denying suffrage to most of the Brazilian
population. Throughout the First and Second Empire, the electoral
system would be controlled by a minority. In spite of several electoral
reforms (1846, 1855, 1862, 1876, and 1881), the electors continued
until the fall of the empire to represent between 1.5 and 2 percent of
the total population. Such a small number of people could be easily
manipulated.

In spite of the effort to accommodate liberalism to Brazilian realities, the gap was obvious, particularly to those like Saint Hilaire who
traveled in the country at that time.[10] The Brazilian constitution stressed
the equality of all before the law and guaranteed individual freedom.
But the majority of the population remained enslaved and excluded
from citizenship. The constitution protected the right of property. But
most of the rural population (when they were not enslaved) lived as
tenants on land they could not own. The constitution secured freedom
of thought and speech. But throughout the First Empire and the regency many people lost their lives for believing in the constitution. The
law established measures to protect the individual and to guarantee
the inviolability of the home. It endorsed the principle that nobody
could be arrested unless charges were brought, and it stipulated that
no one could be sentenced except by the relevant authority and in accordance with the terms of the law. But for a few mil reis, anyone could
hire a *capanga* to kill an enemy. The autonomy of the judiciary was
guaranteed by law, but in fact the courts were instruments of the upper
classes. The constitution abolished torture, but the slavemaster was
the supreme judge on his plantation, and in the slave quarters stocks,
manacles, whips, and fetters continued to be used throughout the
nineteenth century. The constitution abolished legal discrimination

Theory & Practice of Const.

and guaranteed to all the right to be appointed to any position on the basis of merit and talent. But the bonds of blood, friendship, and godparenthood, typical of the patronage system, always prevailed over the criteria of merit and competence.

Politics, in those circumstances, was more a matter of family arrangements and family rivalries than ideology. Elections were controlled by local bosses who through a system of clientele and patronage were able to deliver votes to their favorite candidates. Their support carried an obligation of reciprocity. Thus behind the liberal facade, pesonal influence, personal loyalties, and reciprocal favors were the real ingredients of power. Political rhetoric was subordinated to the opinion of those few who controlled the electorate. From time to time an aspiring politician tried to make a career by raising issues which might sound too radical to the ears of the ruling classes. But if by some chance he found a place in the Chamber of Deputies, he would moderate his radicalism.[11] Those who persisted in their radical stances were condemned to political ostracism. This situation changed only in the last decade of the Second Empire, when economic growth and the emergence of new groups of interests created new constituencies. But even then, because of the constraints of the electoral law, the great majority of the Brazilian population continued to be denied suffrage and politicians continued to depend mainly on elite support.

Although the political, social, and economic structures were conducive to the creation of a political oligarchy, its consolidation was the product of struggles that lasted for more than two decades after independence. During these years three factions struggled for power: one more conservative, favoring centralization and initially supporting the emperor; another more liberal, intending to increase the power of Parliament; and a third, more democratic, supporting decentralization, universal suffrage, and nationalization of trade. The first episode in a long series of confrontations among those different groups and between the elites and the emperor was triggered by the dissolution of the National Convention in 1823, and the granting of the Constitutional Charter in 1824. Several uprisings occurred then in the North and the Northeast (Confederação do Equador) where the local elites, fearing the loss of their political autonomy and resenting their subordination to the central government in Rio, rebelled. The insurgency of these local elites created an occasion for other social groups to express their discontent. The rebels raised the banner of federalism and criticized the excessive power the Constitutional Charter had granted to the emperor.[12] One of their most eloquent spokesmen was Frei Canéca. In his newspaper the *Typhis Pernambucano*,[13] Canéca argued that Brazil's conditions, its size, the variety of its resources and inhabitants, were more compatible with a federation than with a centralized government. He also condemned the appointments of senators for life and the creation of a nobility. The moderating power seemed to him "a Machiavellian invention," a "master key to oppression." The provincial councils created by the charter to govern the provinces were in his opinion nothing but "ghosts to deceive the people." Most of all, he questioned the emperor's right to grant a Constitutional Charter usurping the people's rights to express their sovereign will through their representatives in the National Convention.

Canéca's critique exemplifies liberal rhetoric at this juncture. In the name of those issues people rose in Ceará, Pernambuco, Paraíba, Rio Grande do Norte, and Alagoas. The Confederação do Equador was put down by troops and the heads of the rebellion, including Frei Canéca, were condemned to death.

Repression and punishment, however, did not put an end to the issues raised by the revolutionaries of 1824. The conflict between the emperor and the elites, the central government and the provinces, the national and local elites, had not been solved. When the Chamber of Deputies met in 1826, the conflicts surfaced again, now aggravated by the divergencies within the elites themselves. The organization of the educational system, land legislation, abolition of the slave trade, freedom of the press, naturalization of foreigners, military recruitment, freedom of worship, the organization of provincial and municipal councils, the composition of the judiciary—these were the issues that divided the representatives into two opposing groups: one more liberal, the other more conservative. Liberals were in favor of a system of education free from religious control, of land legislation that would lead to the breaking down of the monopoly of land by a few. They opposed military recruitment, supported freedom of worship, favored decentralization, and provincial and municipal autonomy. Conservatives were on the opposite side of the spectrum. But although it is possible to identify these two positions by reference to ideal models of what was to be a conservative or what was to be a liberal, in reality it is impossible to find total consistency in any particular individual or group. There were men like José Bonifácio, liberal in their approach to social and economic programs but conservative in regard to political organization. And there were others who were conservative in matters of economy but politically liberal. In the Parliament, however, the predominant tone was conservative.

Whether they were liberal or conservative, the Brazilian political elites grew increasingly hostile to the emperor, who was finally forced to abdicate in 1831 in favor of his five-year-old son.

The regency brought to power men like Bernardo de Vasconcelos and Evaristo da Veiga, who during the First Empire had earned reputations as authentic liberals mainly because of their attacks against the emperor and their efforts to replace traditional colonial institutions with others more compatible with the new nation. But in regard to democracy their position was not different from that of José Bonifácio, whom they had always perceived as an entrenched conservative. Like him, they despised the masses and wanted to deny them political participation.

Evaristo da Veiga's newspaper, Aurora Fluminense, is one of the best sources for the study of their thought, "No extremism of any sort. To implement the Constitution is the liberals' main task." That was the newspaper's slogan. A constitutional monarchy with limited participation was its ideal.[14] Before the emperor's abdication, Evaristo da Veiga sided with the liberal opposition and devoted the pages of his newspaper to attacking both the republicans and the absolutists. Facing the rising tide of popular demands, Evaristo da Veiga become increasingly conservative after the emperor's abdication. Through his newspaper he accused the radical liberals of instigating "class struggle" and "racial hatred" and of seeking to discredit those who (like him) were committed to order and "wanted to avoid a violent confrontation between proprietors and the have-nots."[15] Veiga, like many others who passed from the opposition to government, found himself on the defensive. A man of the center, he felt challenged by those who conspired to bring the emperor back, but even more by those who wanted to put liberal ideas at the service of the masses. "I fear today more the rabble's courtesans," he wrote, "than those who hang on the monarch's cape."[16]

The shift from the center toward a conservative position characteristic of Evaristo da Veiga is also typical of Bernardo Pereira de Vasconcelos, another famous liberal politician of this period.[17] Like many other liberals he started by charging the emperor with favoring men of aristocratic origins and disregarding the constitution, which asserted the equality of all and prohibited any distinctions not based on merit.[18] Consistently with his liberal views, he condemned interference in the economy and insisted that private initiative was always more intelligent than that of the government.[19] In the Chamber of Deputies he opposed protectionist policies favoring local industries and spoke of the need to keep a "religious respect for freedom and property."[20] His struggle in favor of the abolition of colonial institutions, his criticism of royal despotism and of aristocratic power and privileges, his opposition to state intervention in the economy, his religious respect for freedom and property defined the nature of the elites' liberalism during this period. But like other liberals during the regency he became increasingly conservative. On the eve of the emperor's abdication, Vasconcelos was a popular leader, a spokesman for the people, acclaimed by the masses. Ten years later, his house was stoned by the people. The hero of the masses had come to be seen as their enemy.

Replying to those who accused him of having betrayed his liberal principles, Vasconcelos told the Chamber of Deputies in 1838: "I was a liberal when freedom was everyone's aspiration but did not exist in practice. Then, power was all and I was a liberal. Today, however, the country's situation is different. Democratic principles have won everything and have compromised much. Society once threatened by power is now threatened by disorder and anarchy. I want to serve it now as I served it in the past. That is why I have moved backwards. I am not a deserter. I do not abandon the cause I defended when it was in danger . . . I leave it now when its triumph is so certain that it risks being excessive."[21] Vasconcelos's words were greeted with vigorous applause. Among those who welcomed his speech were Antonio Carlos de Andrada e Silva and José Clemente Pereira, two of his former political adversaries. These men who in the past had struggled against each other had been brought together by their fear of the masses.

Apologizing for his change of political opinion, Antonio Carlos would say, "I asked everyone to examine his conscience. Didn't we all change our opinion?" A participant in the 1817 republican revolution, converted to a monarchist in 1822, an opponent of the emperor in 1823, accused in 1831 of conspiring to bring him back, Antonio Carlos had good reasons to speak about change of opinions. But he was not the only one to have changed his mind or to feel threatened by the radical liberals' demands.

Two newspapers of this period, O Jurujuba dos Farroupilhas and Nova Luz Brasileira, exemplify the radical liberals' position in the 1830s. To judge by the content of these and other radical newspapers, their constituency was the urban petite-bourgeoisie: small merchants, artisans, pharmacists, soldiers, schoolteachers, and the like, men who had been particularly hurt by economic and social change and often showed their discontent by rioting in the big cities. Their radicalism reminds us of the radicalism of the French sans culottes. Their flamboyant radical rhetoric frequently expressed a desire to rehabilitate old institutions and to resist change. But in this attempt they waged a merciless attack on the Brazilian elites and the institutions these elites had created.[22]

Radical liberals criticized the commercial treaties benefiting foreign merchants, particularly the English, who had acquired the monopoly of trade to the detriment of the local merchants and artisans. Using a strong nationalist language, they went as far as to suggest the revocation of those treaties.[23] They attacked the "aristocrats" whom they saw as responsible for the unpopular economic policies and supporters of absolutist regimes. In one of its articles *Nova Luz Brasileira* proposed that the right to vote be denied to the aristocrats, "hypocritical and ambitious people that only find reason in the rich capitalists and the powerful men, however ill-intentioned and dishonest those might be."[24] It went even further, suggesting that the assets of several well-known personalities such as the Barão do Rio da Prata, Vilela Barbosa, Baependi, and all the councillors of state, be expropriated.[25] Following the same line, the *O Jurujuba dos Farroupilhas*, another radical newspaper published in Rio de Janeiro, criticized the despicable aristocrats who sold the country and its freedom to Europe.[26] Believing that the aristocrats' source of power was their ownership of large tracts of land, the editor of *Nova Luz* engaged in a campaign for agrarian reform, proposing the expropriation of all unused land. With this proposal he hoped to put an end to what he called Brazilian "feudalism." *Nova Luz* also condemned slavery and racial discrimination and asked for the immediate emancipation of slaves—with the condition, however, that they continued to be bound to the land for a period of thirty years. Like many other radical liberals of this period, the editor of *Nova Luz* also opposed political and administrative centralization and favored "a democratic federation according to the North American model." Yet, in spite of his admiration for the United States he did not seem to have any appreciation for its republican form of government and continued to consider constitutional monarchy the ideal form.

The radicals' democratic claims and their critique of the elites were sometimes couched in traditional Christian rhetoric. "The ragged, honest people are those that please the Lord," wrote *O Jurujuba* in one of its editorials. "When the Redeemer came to the world, He chose his disciples and apostles among them, despising the evil capitalists, of whom He said it was easier for a camel to pass through the eye of a needle than for a rich man to enter heaven."

Viewing anarchy as "an ephemeral evil that ordinarily brings greater good," and history as "a struggle between the powerful and the powerless," radical liberals incited the people to rise against those who deceived them and betrayed the nation. At the same time, they appealed to the soldiers to join the people in "their struggle for their rights" and to fight for "a government of the people and by the people."[27]

These appeals to the soldiers were not mere rhetorical devices. In fact, at that time, many soldiers—mostly mercenaries returning from the Cisplatina on the southern frontier—were crowding into the city of Rio de Janeiro and joining the masses in their complaints against increasing food prices and an overflow of counterfeit money. Indeed, in July 1831 a crowd rioted in the capital demanding the dissolution of the Chamber of Deputies and the organization of a constitutional assembly to decide the future of the country.

While the soldiers answered the radicals' appeals, their officers sided with the government and organized a battalion of "volunteers" praised by the *Aurora Fluminense* as *Os Bravos da Pátria* ("the Fatherland's Warriors"). This battalion succeeded in putting down the uprising, bringing to an end what the elites' newspapers called the "ferocious *oklocracy*."

In other parts of the country, radical groups that rose up were also defeated by government troops. Revolutionary leaders were arrested, many soldiers were dismissed and the standing army was reduced. To strengthen its position the central government created instead a National Guard. Diogo Feijó, then minister of justice, ordered Rio de Janeiro's police chief to distribute arms to businessmen interested in keeping the order as well as to three thousand citizens qualified to be electors—in other words, men who had an annual income of 200$000 or more. This was the beginning of the National Guard, which in the hands of the government later became an important political tool with which to threaten the opposition.[28]

Commenting on the measures taken by the regency, *Matraca dos Farroupilhas*, another radical newspaper, wrote that "the one time popular and revolutionary priest Feijó had become the capitalist's hero."[29] Like Bernardo de Vasconcelos, Evaristo da Veiga, Andrada e Silva, and many others, the ultraliberal Feijó had found himself in a position increasingly conservative. After the repression he made an astonishing declaration. He said that the Brazilians were by nature an orderly people, respectful of the Constitution, and aspiring only to enjoy their rights and their freedom, a statement that although denied over and over again by the facts, became part of the set of beliefs that together with the myth of racial democracy and the benevolence of the Brazilian elites, constituted the core of their social mythology until the twentieth century.

In spite of Feijó's repressive measures and optimistic remarks, the struggle between the radical liberals and the moderate liberals-becoming-conservatives was not over in 1831. Although severely repressed, the radicals were not completely defeated. Their demands for decentralization found echo in the Chamber of Deputies and two steps were taken in that direction; the Judicial Code of 1832 and the Additional Act of 1834. The code gave local justices of the peace criminal jurisdiction and provided that the prosecutor, the municipal judge, and the judge of orphans—all of whom had formerly been appointed by the central government—were now to be selected from a list supplied by the Municipal Council. The code also gave ample powers to the jury. The Additional Act to the constitution was approved in 1834, as a concession to radical pressures. Radicals had demanded municipal autonomy, suppression of the Council of State, renewal of one-third of the Senate every four years, creation of provincial assemblies, and separation of provincial revenues from the national revenue. The Additional Act to the constitution did abolish the Council of State, transformed the provincial councils into provincial legislatures and separated provincial from national revenues. But it kept senatorial privileges intact, including appointment for life and maintained municipal governments subordinated to the provincial government. The president of each province was to be appointed by the central government.

To a certain point the Judicial Code and the Additional Act to the Constitution represented a victory for the radicals. Yet, as soon as they were approved, they were criticized by those who feared that local autonomy would mean a blow to their power and who were anxious to withdraw the concessions they had made under pressure. The persistent climate of insurrection in different parts of the country only solidified their decision. The 1836 elections—when less than six thousand out of more than three million people voted—brought victory to the conservatives and marked the beginning of what was called the *Regresso*.

By that time the development of coffee plantations in the surroundings of Rio de Janeiro had strengthened the conservatives' parliamentary basis. Coffee planters had established an alliance with sugar plantation owners from the Brazilian northeast, and, together with the export and import groups, they had succeeded in acquiring control over the central government. Meanwhile the growth of imports had undermined even further the position of the small merchants and local craftsmen who had supplied the grass roots for the radical movements in Rio and other port cities.

In 1840 hoping that the coronation of the second emperor would bring peace to the nation, Parliament decided to grant to the fourteen-year-old prince the right to rule. Simultaneously it approved several conservative laws reinforcing the power of the central government. According to the new legislation the municipal judge and the judge of orphans as well as the prosecutors were once more to be appointed by the government. The justices of the peace continued to be elected but lost several of their powers to the police and to appointed judges. Juries' jurisdiction was reduced, while more power was given to the judges appointed by the government. The same conservative mood inspired changes in the organization of the National Guard. Here, too, elected officers were replaced by officers appointed by the government. The National Guard, rather than serving primarily the interests of local elites, became an instrument of the central government. Finally, the Council of State and the moderating power, suspended during the minority of the emperor, were reestablished. All these measures represented a step back in relation to the Judicial Code and the Additional Act, giving the central government and the national elites more power than they had ever had.[30]

Contrary to the elites' expectations, however, the ascension of Pedro II to the throne in 1840 did not pacify the country. For more than ten years the nation continued to be shaken by uprisings in different regions. A revolutionary wave swept the North and the Northeast between 1837 and 1848 (Sabinada, Balaiada, Cabanagem), and between 1835 and 1845 the southernmost province, the Rio Grande do Sul, was torn by civil war (Farrapos). In 1842 there were insurrections in Minas Gerais and São Paulo, and in 1848 it was the turn of Pernambuco (Praieira). All these revolutionary movements were indicative of the resistance the national elites had to overcome to establish their hegemony.[31]

From 1831 to 1848 radical liberal rhetoric was used by the revolutionary leaders to justify their rebellion. In Pernambuco the revolutionaries' political vocabulary showed some socialist overtones, echoing Fourier, Lacordaire, and Louis Blanc. But the predominant tone was liberal. Federalism, universal suffrage, freedom of speech, the guarantee of individual rights, abolition of the moderating power, separation of powers, abolition of the draft, nationalization of commerce, and agrarian reform were the themes that appeared over and over again in the radical press. The liberal discourse expressed many different and sometimes even conflicting aspirations. Most of those who joined the revolutions, however, did not do so for ideological reasons. They were moved by immediate and concrete concerns. Local elites protested against the loss of their power and the inroads the central government made into their communities, replacing traditionally elected authorities with others appointed by the government, collecting taxes, intervening in the elections, and controlling private initiative. Native artisans and merchants protested against the increasing monopolization of trade by foreigners favored by commercial treaties. Peasants and urban masses reacted against military conscription and protested against the increase in food prices. Soldiers rioted because their salaries were not paid. Class and racial conflicts, tensions between the poor and the rich, between foreigners and natives or between blacks and whites, reluctance on the part of traditional elites to submit themselves to the central government, competition for power at the regional level between different segments of the elites, all these reasons mixed together were behind the uprisings that kept the imperial government on permanent alert for a period of almost twenty years after the abdication of Pedro I. Often the lines of conflict were difficult to trace because they were blurred by confusing networks of patronage.

During those years two political parties emerged from the struggles: the Liberals and the Conservatives. In theory, at least, these parties had two different programs, and indeed during the early years of the regency, Liberals and Conservatives spoke different languages and seemed to be battling for different causes. Liberals were federalists, favored local autonomy, demanded the abolition of the moderating power and the Council of State, opposed the appointment of senators for life and government interference in the economy, supported free trade, religious freedom, and freedom of expression. They advocated the principle "the king reigns but does not rule." The Conservatives defended centralization, the moderating power, the Council of State, tenure in the Senate, Catholicism as the official religion, and the principle that the king reigns *and* rules.[32]

But the appearance of political differences did not go very deep. During the regency, fear of the radical liberals had brought Liberals and Conservatives together, making their differences less and less relevant. Once the revolutionary movements had been repressed and the state apparatus reinforced, Liberals and Conservatives even participated in the same cabinets. This cooperation between the two parties, known as the *conciliação*, started in 1852 and lasted about ten years. By then Liberal and Conservative had become mere labels, and it became proverbial that there was nothing more similar to a Liberal than a Conservative. Once in power Liberals forgot the demands they had made while in the opposition, Conservatives in power implemented reforms Liberals had pressured for. Nor could party labels and platforms contain individual politicians. Within the Liberal party there were entrenched conservatives, and among the members of the Conservative party there were some politicians whose views were more liberal than those of the self-advertised Liberals. Ferreira Vianna, for example, was an important figure in the Conservative party. He occupied a position in the Chamber of Deputies in several legislatures between 1869 and 1889 and liked to present himself as a conservative man—"a man," he once said jokingly, "who liked to have the pitcher always in the same place so that he could find it in the middle of the night." But in spite of all his publicized conservatism, Ferreira Vianna was a great critic of the emperor's powers, opposed state intervention in the economy, and favored local and provincial autonomy.[33] All these issues belonged in the platform of the Liberal party. On the other hand, Zacarias de Góes, one of the leading figures in the Liberal party and the author of a famous book *Da Natureza e dos Limites do Poder Moderador* (On the Nature and Limits of the Moderating Power), in which he developed the thesis "the king reigns but does not rule," was one of the most eloquent supporters of the Church in a conflict between the bishops and the government in 1874. Together with his conservative political adversary Ferreira Vianna, the liberal Zacarias de Góes acted as the bishops' lawyer during their trial, defending them from the charges made by the Conservative cabinet headed by the Barão do Rio Branco, the bishops' main opponent.[34]

To find Liberals supporting conservative causes or Conservatives defending liberal proposals was not uncommon, particularly when the issues were of major significance and highly controversial, like the religious question or the abolition of slavery. When a bill proposing the emancipation of the children born to slave mothers was discussed, there were Liberals and Conservatives on both sides. The same happened later, when another bill, proposing the emancipation of sixty-year-old slaves, was voted.[35] And when the Parliament debated the measures to be taken against the bishops who had disobeyed the constitution, which prohibited them from implementing papal bulls without the government's approval, some Liberals, like Nabuco, supported the Conservative cabinet, others like Zacarias de Góes sided with the bishops. There were also Conservatives on both sides. On none of these occasions was party discipline enforced.

Internal divisions within each party and the lack of coherent ideological commitment help to explain the great instability of the cabinets. During the 49 years of Pedro II's rule there were thirty-nine cabinets. Dissidents often supported the opposition party, throwing their own party out of power. As long as the elites agreed about the main policies to be followed the alternation of political parties did not make any fundamental difference.

In the last decades of the empire, however, with increasing economic and social differentiation and growing divergences between different segments of the elites, political party rotation became a more meaningful matter. Even then it was still possible for a Liberal like Martinho de Campos, the head of a cabinet that lasted only six months in 1882, to say in his inaugural speech: "Today we can say, with the late Visconde de Albuquerque, 'They are very similar, a Liberal and a Conservative, and I would add, even a Republican. They all seem to belong to the same family. We live very well together on the same boat and we do not have any conflicts of opinion.'"[36]

A few months later, Ferreira Vianna, commenting on the similarity between the two parties, remarked in his ironic style, bringing laughter in Parliament: "The opposition of today says what the opposition of yesterday used to say. The opposition of yesterday today in power, glorifies the same deeds it condemned yesterday!"[37]

Machado de Assis, the great novelist of the nineteenth century, described well this reality when he made the wife of one of his characters, whose party had been defeated, tell her husband to change sides and support his political adversaries: "You were with them as in a ball, where it is not necessary to have the same ideas to dance the same minuet."[38] It is no wonder that "farce," "comedy," "theater," and "dance" were words frequently used by politicians to describe their politics. "I am tired of acting in this political comedy," said Ferreira Vianna.[39] His words sounded remarkably similar to those of Sales Tôrres Homem, who in a letter to the Visconde de Ourem confessed: "I have lost my health and all my illusions. However, here am I, for the second time, in the cabinet, playing a role in this theater of chimeras."[40]

The similarity between the two parties, the family resemblance of which Martinho de Campos spoke, was a product of the similarity of their social basis. In the past, some historians identified the Liberal party with urban groups and the Conservative party with plantation owners. Others made the opposite correlations, perceiving links between the business community, the bureaucrats, and the Conservative party, with the Liberal party representing agrarian interests. Both were guesses, based on impressionistic evaluations (and probably not totally wrong since to be a Conservative or a Liberal did not necessarily mean anything very different). More recently, however, Murilo de Carvalho has arrived at the more careful conclusion that agrarian interests were equally represented in both parties. Merchants and bureaucrats were more numerous among the Conservatives and professionals among the Liberals.[41] Yet this last difference fades in the light of the fact that the Conservative party stayed in power longer (26 years as against 13) and had more opportunity to exert patronage. Since both Liberals and Conservatives spoke for the same social groups, it is not surprising that party affiliation was usually more a question of family and kinship than of ideology. And until the last two decades of the empire, political struggle was really little else than a struggle for power between factions under the leadership of prestigious families. This, of course, did not make political competition less intense, or electoral dispute less passionate. Quite the contrary. In fact, both parties resorted to all sorts of political maneuvers to remain in power and electoral fraud was rampant. The cabinets replaced provincial presidents and functionaries loyal to the opposition, created parishes where they had friends, and abolished them where they had enemies. They harassed rank-and-file opposition voters, threatening them with conscription, rewarded those who supported the cabinet with jobs, promotions, and sinecures; mobilized the National Guard to intimidate the opposition by forcing its voters to stay home on election day. When this failed, they resorted to violence. Opposition voters were often expelled from the churches where they were supposed to vote. Ballot boxes were stolen and reappeared filled with more votes than there were voters or with the ballots replaced by others.[42] But all this struggle for power had more to do with the competition between factions than with fundamental ideological conflicts.

In the last decade of the empire the political competition acquired new meaning. Economic and social change since the 1850s brought to the political arena new groups of interests making it impossible to keep the alliance between the two parties. The Conciliação was broken. While in the first half of the century liberals had become increasingly conservative, in the second half the movement went in the opposite direction. An increasing number of politicians left the Conservative party to join the Liberal party in the sixties. This was the case of Pedro de Araujo Lima, the Marquês de Olinda, Nabuco de Araujo, Zacarias de Góes e Vasconcelos, the Marquês de Paranaguá, Sinimbú, and Saraiva. Justifying his political conversion Nabuco de Araujo, who had been a great supporter of the Conciliação in the past, said he had become convinced that instead of fighting against the overwhelming stream of democracy the statesman should try to guide it, so that it would not be fatal to the nation. It was in this Tocquevillian spirit that Nabuco and other Conservative politicians who had joined the Liberal party, founded the Progressive League in 1864, committing themselves to a program of reform.[43] Then once again the voice of Liberals would be heard and their rhetoric regain prestige. Liberals dug out old themes that had been buried since the revolution of 1848 in Pernambuco and started talking about the people again. In their rhetoric the people appeared associated with other favorite words such as progress, reason, and science. The beginning of the Paraguayan War in 1864 forced the liberals to postpone their project. But in 1868, the replacement of a Liberal by a Conservative cabinet triggered a political crisis of large proportions culminating in a Liberal party manifesto calling for decentralization, the transformation of the Council of State into an exclusively administrative organ, abolition of tenure in the Senate, direct elections, extension of the right to vote to non-Catholics, autonomy of the judiciary, creation of a system of education independent of the state, secularization of cemeteries, religious freedom, and gradual emancipation of slaves. In spite of its reformist tone the manifesto did not satisfy the most radical groups in the Liberal party and they issued their own asking for the abolition of the moderating power, the National Guard, the Council of State and slavery. They also demanded direct elections, universal suffrage and elections for provincial governors and police chiefs. A few months later a group of politicians, some of whom were Liberal party dissidents, founded the Republican party. Their manifesto did not add much to the two already issued by the Liberals. It denounced that in Brazil "freedom of conscience was nullified by a privileged church; economic freedom supressed by a restrictive legislation; freedom of press subordinated to the discretion of government functionaries; freedom of association dependent on government's approval; freedom of education curtailed by arbitrary government inspection, and by official monopoly; individual freedom, subjected to arrest, to the draft, to the National Guard, was deprived even of the guarantees of the habeas corpus." [44] After repeating more or less the same demands Liberals had made, the Republican manifesto suggested that a National Convention be given powers to change the regime.

An analysis of these three documents reveals that except for the obvious difference between republicans and monarchists, they all had the same goals: to undermine the structures of power that supported traditional oligarchies, to curtail government interference in the private sector, and to increase provincial autonomy. Only the radical faction within the Liberal party demanded immediate abolition of slavery.

The program of reform responded to growing feelings of dissatisfaction among several groups in the society. It appealed to the growing middle classes, particularly to the professionals and bureaucrats tired of the uncertainties of political patronage and to the thriving community of businessmen and industrialists oppressed by government regulations. It appealed to the military who during the Paraguayan War (1864–70) had become more cohesive and more conscious of the deficiencies of the army and more resentful of civilian "interference." It also appealed to a new generation of politicians for whom a program of reform could win an election. Intellectuals found in the reformist campaign new sources of inspiration and new constituencies. The reformist liberal program was also attractive to some regional elites, particularly in São Paulo, Pará, Pernambuco, and Rio Grande do Sul. Uneven economic growth and increasing competition for government subsidies, conflict of interests in relation to immigration policies, slavery, tariffs, and loans had made some sectors of the elite particularly aware of the disadvantages of centralization.

So universally recognized was the need for reform that even the Conservatives felt obliged to support them, particularly after the emperor himself came out publicly in their favor.[45] The Conservative cabinet of the Barão do Rio Branco (1871–75) took as its responsibility to promote some of those reforms. Considering their past history there is nothing surprising about Conservatives implementing Liberal reforms even though, as one might expect, they trimmed the proposals to make them more acceptable to their constituencies. More surprising is that when the Liberals took power in 1878 after ten years of political ostracism they did not accomplish many of the reforms they had battled for while in the opposition (reforms that the Conservatives themselves had not dared to carry on). When in 1889 the head of the last cabinet of the empire, the Liberal Visconde de Ouro Preto, presented his program to the Parliament,[46] many of the reforms he proposed were shockingly familiar; the limitation of the senators' terms, reduction of the Council of State to a mere administrative body, elections of municipal authorities, election of provincial presidents and vice-presidents from a list of those who had won the most votes in elections, universal suffrage, freedom of worship, reform of the system of education to further private initiative—all these suggestions, which had been in the platform of the Liberal party for at least twenty years, had never been put into practice because Liberal party politicians had been as reluctant as Conservatives to promote changes that in the long run would undermine their own sources of power and diminish their political authority. Only a minority in the Parliament did support the reforms. For many "Liberals" reform had been nothing but rhetoric.

The political elite's unwillingness to promote those reforms led in the end to the 1889 military coup that overthrew the monarchy. Pressured between the traditional elites, they wanted to displace the masses they did not trust (in spite of all their talk about the people), and unwilling to give up their patronage schemes, Brazilian Liberals had proved incapable of accomplishing the program of political reforms they had proposed. Ironically, it was only after the Republicans allied with the military to overthrow the monarchical regime that those reforms were implemented.

The failure of Brazilian Liberals to live up to the ideals of liberalism went much deeper than politics, however. It touched the heart of Brazilian social and cultural reality. Ideologically, the Liberals were committed to a program that if implemented would reduce the role of patronage in their world. But they functioned in that world as the creatures and the manipulators of patronage. And the unavoidable fact was that Brazilian society was saturated with both the practice and the ethic of patronage. All through the history of the empire, the Liberals, like the rest of the elite, had been basically conservative and antidemocratic. Their goal had always been to conciliate order and progress, the status quo with modernization. With the exception of the abolition of slavery, most of the reforms proposed by Liberals had been exclusively political and did not touch the economic and social structures. Nor did they increase popular political participation. Even the electoral reform of 1881 (which was greeted as a democratic conquest) did not lead to the expansion of the electorate. In fact, the total number of people voting diminished. The only effect the electoral reform had was to give more weight to the urban vote, since according to the 1881 law voters had to be literate—a requirement easier to satisfy in the cities. Nothing the Liberals had achieved touched the profound conflict between their supposed liberal values and the patronage system in which they lived and pursued their careers.

Because of the survival of traditional structures of production and of the system of clientele and patronage, liberal rhetoric in Brazil continued to be in conflict with the social and political practice. The typical bourgeois values usually associated with liberalism—commitment to work, thrift, reason, attachment to representative forms of government, respect for the law and the court system, individualism and self-reliance, belief in the universality of human rights—could hardly find confirmation in a slave society—a society that despised labor, cultivated leisure and ostentation, favored kinship, stressed individual dependency, openly promoted individuals on the basis of their personal relations rather than on their merit, institutionalized the arbitrary, made the exception the rule, and negated for most of the population basic human rights. Brazilian elites could not but be aware that in Brazil liberal theory did not have anything to do with the reality of the

1881 reform

lives of millions of people around them. But they could attribute this to Brazilian backwardness and could continue to imagine that in "civilized" nations liberal practice corresponded more closely to liberal theory. Thus while in Europe liberals who came to grips with the experience of the commune and were threatened by the masses were losing faith in bourgeois values which had inspired their liberalism, in Brazil, liberalism continued until the end of the empire to be a utopia, a promise to be fulfilled. Brazilians might question its practice, but not its premises. For them it was the practice that was wrong, not the theory.

It was the hope that the promise could be fulfilled that in the seventies was behind the criticism of the institutions, a criticism that expressed a naive belief in the redeeming qualities of progress, science, and reform. Disillusioned with the practice of liberalism in Brazil, many of the reformists of the seventies and eighties found in positivism their source of inspiration. In Comte they found support for their program aiming at reducing the state to a mere custodian of the social order and their desire to achieve progress and modernization without changing fundamentally the social structures. Comte's respect for civil liberties and his commitment to religious freedom, free association, freedom of opinion, and free enterprise could not but appeal to those who had endorsed the Liberal program in 1868 or the Republican manifesto of 1870. His notions about the family as the basic social unit were also pleasing to men who lived in a patriarchal society. Comte was even more appealing to them because of his critique of traditional elites and his deep respect for social hierarchy and social inequalities.

While liberalism continued to be a utopia for the elites, for the large majority of the Brazilian population trapped in the system of clientele and patronage, liberalism was nothing but empty rhetoric. As a consequence, for them liberalism did not have the masking effect that it did in other parts of the world. This ideological role was played by the ethic of patronage.

Establishing vertical relations between individuals from the dominant classes and those from below and defining their relations in terms of reciprocal favors, patronage helped to disguise (though not eliminate) class and racial tensions. Through patronage, talented individuals belonging to the lower classes were co-opted by the elites. Behind every self-made man there was always a patron to remind him that he would not have succeeded on his own. Within this system of clientele and patronage politicians and the state were not seen as representatives of the people but as their patrons, and individuals' rights appeared as personal concessions. The system of patronage based on personal loyalties and exchange of favors implied the subservience of the electorate to the local boss, the compliancy of the court system, the systematic disregard for the law, the legitimation of privilege.

The coexistence of the ethic of patronage with the liberal ethic reproduced at the ideological level the experience of people living in a society in which capitalism grew within a network of patronage. It also translated the contradictions of the bourgeois-gentilhomme, characteristic of the Brazilian elite—a man who lived in Brazil with his mind on Europe, "who had one eye on profit, the other on gentility"; who used slaves to produce for the international market; and who depended on traditional institutions to further capital accumulation.

The contradictions between the ethic of liberalism and the ethic of patronage made it possible for Brazilians to evaluate liberalism from the perspective of patronage and to evaluate patronage from the perspective of liberalism. The ethic of patronage uncovered the emptiness of liberal rhetoric. Liberal rhetoric exposed the violence and oppression of patronage. Nothing could define better the specificity of Brazilian liberalism than the words of Machado de Assis: "In Brazil political science finds a limit in the bullet of the henchman." [48]

4 LAND POLICIES
The Land Law, 1850, and the Homestead Act, 1862

Land and labor policies are always related, and both depend in turn on the stage of economic development. In the nineteenth century the expansion of markets and the concomitant development of capitalism caused a reevaluation of traditional land and labor policies in countries that were directly or indirectly affected by the process. Population growth, internal and international migration, improvements in transportation, the concentration of population in urban centers, the development of industry and the accumulation of capital—all these processes stimulated the integration of land and labor into the commercial and industrial economy. In many parts of the world there was an increase in the amount of land cultivated for commercial purposes and a related decrease in subsistence agriculture. In places where the land had been only partially exploited, the expansion of the market gave rise to more intensive use of land and labor, resulting very often in the expulsion of tenants and sharecroppers and in the expropriation of small properties and communal lands. Part of the population formerly dedicated to the traditional subsistence economy was absorbed as wage labor on commercial farms. Another part migrated to the cities. Where virgin land was available, new areas were put into use, increasing the demand for agricultural labor. As a result of this process, the meaning of land ownership changed and legislation controlling access to the land also changed.

The rhythms of change varied, however, from one country to another and from one area to another within a country, depending on the degree to which these areas were affected by the development of the commercial and industrial economy. A comparative study of the Homestead Act of 1862, which regulated land policy in the United States,[1] and the Brazilian Land Law of 1850[2] will allow us to analyze the relationship between labor and land policy in two countries where capitalism developed along different lines and led to opposite policies.

The land law enacted in Brazil in 1850 forbade the acquisition of public land through any means but purchase, putting to an end the traditional forms of acquiring land through squatting (*posses*) and grants from the Crown (*sesmarías*). Those who had obtained property illegally by squatting and those who had received grants but never legitimized their ownership were allowed to register and validate their titles after surveying their lands and paying taxes—but only if they had actually occupied and used the land. The size of the *posses* that could be legitimized was limited by the law; it could be no greater than the largest *sesmaría* in its district. The proceeds of public land sales and taxes on the registration of properties were to be used exclusively for surveying public lands and importing "free colonists." A bureaucratic service, the *Repartição Geral das Terras Públicas*, was created to control the public land and promote colonization.

The parliamentary debates on the law reveal a conflict between traditional and modern conceptions of landownership, a transition from a traditional view of land as the Crown's domain to a modern view of land as the public domain.[3] In the earlier period land was granted primarily as a reward for services to the Crown; later it became accessible only to those who could exploit it profitably or in other words, those who had capital. Thus land, which had been seen as a grant in itself, came to be a commodity; its ownership, which had essentially conferred social prestige, came to signify economic power. Changing attitudes toward land correspond to changing attitudes toward labor: from a commitment to slavery and certain forms of servitude to a commitment to free labor.

At the beginning of colonization, land was seen as part of the king's personal patrimony. In order to acquire a piece of land, one had to apply for a personal grant. The king's decision to concede the favor was based on his evaluation of the applicant, which involved considering his social status, personal qualities, and service to the Crown. Thus, the acquisition of land, though regulated by law, derived from the king's *arbitrium* and not from a right inherent in the supplicant. By the nineteenth century the concept had changed. Land had become the public domain, patrimony of the nation. According to the land law of 1850, the only way to acquire land was to buy it from the government, which would act as mediator between the public and the prospective proprietor. The personal relationship between king and applicant had given way to an impersonal transaction between state and buyer. No longer a personal gift conceded by the king according to an individual's personal qualities, land was a commodity that could be obtained by anyone with sufficient capital. When land was a royal grant, the king had the right to regulate its use and limit the size and number of grants received by each person. When land became merchandise, the individual who bought it made the decisions. The ownership of land always conferred social prestige, at first because it implied the Crown's recognition of the grantee's merits, then because it implied economic power. In the first case, then, economic power derived from social prestige while in the second case the reverse was true.

The transition from a traditional to a modern conception of land started in the sixteenth century with the onset of the commercial revolution and continued throughout the nineteenth century. The extent and rapidity of this transition depended on the degree to which a society was permeated by capitalist values. During the nineteenth century in Brazil the process accelerated primarily because of changes that occurred in economic and social structures in response to the expansion of the international market.

During the colonial period the theoretical positions outlined above were often blurred; in reality, contradictory attitudes toward land coexisted. Land was awarded to those who served the Crown, but at the same time the Crown required that it be granted only to men with the capital to exploit it. Land ownership meant social prestige but it also meant economic power. The ambiguities often found in concrete reality do not, however, invalidate the general theoretical framework, as we shall try to demonstrate.

Colonial Brazil was organized as a commercial enterprise, the product of an alliance of the merchant bourgeoisie and the Crown. This alliance was reflected in a land policy that embodied both feudal and mercantile conceptions of land. The original land legislation for the colony was derived from medieval Portuguese land policies. Agents of the Crown in the colony were entitled to grant land to all who wished to settle, according to their merits. Grants were considered personal favors and could not be inherited. Those to whom the land was granted had only the usufruct; ownership was reserved to the Crown.[4]

Very soon, however, land policy underwent certain modifications. The restrictions on inheritance were abolished when it became obvious that the Crown needed to attract settlers to the colony. By the middle of the sixteenth century, land policy had been redefined to reflect the growing mercantile concerns of the Crown. The turning point was the royal instruction given to the governor Tomé de Souza in 1548, on the occasion of his appointment as first governor general of Brazil. His instructions from the Crown directed that land for sugar mills be granted to anyone who could prove he had the resources to exploit and fortify it, that no more land be granted to anyone than he could use, and that grants be limited to one per person. In these prohibitions

colonial land grants

we can clearly see the Crown's intention to avoid concentrating land in the hands of a few, to avoid the establishment of a new feudal order in the colony. The intentions of the Crown in this respect were frustrated, however. Millowners tended to accumulate land not only to insure the supply of cane to their mills but because land granted social prestige. In order to extend their properties landowners resorted to several expedients, acquiring grants in the names of family members or friends. Thus they succeeded in accumulating land beyond their immediate production needs.

Because not all the land was utilized for commercial purposes the landowner could afford to maintain a number of tenants and sharecroppers who lived in the less fertile regions of his property, dedicating themselves to subsistence farming, hunting, fishing, and, occasionally, to working on the plantation. The practice of permitting tenants and sharecroppers to live on the plantation created a network of personal ties, with the landowner mediating between the tenants and sharecroppers and the Crown. The ownership of the land was the basis of his power. Since free men were not numerous enough to supply the manpower required by the plantation and since the natives proved "unfit" for plantation work, the landlord resorted to African slaves. His power over his slaves and over the free men living on the periphery of his estate conferred social prestige. Thus although profit was the mainspring of the economy, control over men and land was as important in defining a landowner's social status as in securing capital accumulation.

In the backlands, however—areas that had no commercial value— virgin land was available in large quantities; anyone who was able to fight the Indians and survive in the wilderness could secure a piece of land. During the colonial period, then, land could be acquired by squatting as well as by royal grant. (Of course, it could also be acquired by purchase, marriage, or inheritance.) But since the land belonged to the royal patrimony, squatting meant trespassing on royal property and could not be legitimized—except by the concession of a grant. The millowners, planters, and others involved in the commercial economy were interested in having rights to the land and would usually try to legitimize their *posses* by requesting land concessions in areas where they had already squatted. Squatting was more typical of the settler who was restricted to the subsistence economy because he did not have the capital to buy slaves, build mills, and join the commercial economy. Throughout the colonial period, the availability of large tracts of land made it possible for those who were unable to participate in the commercial economy to devote themselves to the subsistence economy as tenants, sharecroppers, or small proprietors. Though the colony was organized on a commercial basis from the sixteenth century on, the subsistence economy not only survived in the plantation areas but was typical of the rest of the country.

The system of social relations that emerged from this economic and social structure explains the survival of traditional conceptions of land. And the development of other sectors of the economy during the colonial period did not imply a fundamental change in the land and labor policies typical of the sugar cane areas. The general assumptions of the sixteenth century survived into the nineteenth.

At the time of independence in 1822, the grants policy of the colonial period was abolished, and until 1850, when the land law was enacted, squatting was the most common form of obtaining virgin land. This created an anarchical situation, since the rights of the squatters were not recognized by law. The *posses* resulting from squatting multiplied unchecked and the squatters accumulated great tracts of land whose limits were vaguely defined by geographic accidents: a river, a watershed, a slope. Although these properties had no legal status, they were bought and sold and written up in wills. The situation was aggravated by the expansion of plantations in response to the growing demand for colonial products in the international market. In the nineteenth century, coffee, which had never been important during the colonial period, supplanted sugar as the most important product in the Brazilian economy. New areas were occupied each year by the coffee planters, who felt acutely the need to legalize landownership and obtain labor, particularly because the traditional way of obtaining labor, the slave trade, was being threatened by steady opposition led by England.

The chaotic state of landownership and the problems of manpower forced the dynamic sectors of the Brazilian elite to reevaluate land and labor policies. The land law of 1850 expressed the concerns of these groups and represented an attempt to regulate landownership and the labor supply according to the new possibilities and needs of the time.

In 1842 the subject was discussed for the first time in the Council of State, and a bill formulated by the council was presented in the Chamber of Deputies the following year. The bill, inspired by Wakefield's theories, was based on the assumption that where access to land was easy, it would be impossible to get people to work on the plantations unless they were coerced by slavery. The only way to obtain free labor under these circumstances would be to create obstacles to landownership, so that the free worker, unable to get land, would be forced to work for others. Therefore the traditional means of access to the

land—squatting, tenancy, sharecropping—should be limited, and unused land should revert to the imperial government as public property
and then be sold at a price high enough to make it difficult for newcomers to buy. With the money accumulated from land sales the government could subsidize immigration, bringing Europeans to Brazil to
replace slaves on the plantations and solving the problem of manpower. The bill was designed to regulate the disposition of properties
that had been illegally acquired and at the same time to extend government control over land in general. A land tax based on the size of property was proposed, to encourage productive use of land and provide
revenues for subsidizing immigration.[5] An analysis of the arguments
for and against the bill clarifies the different conceptions of land and
labor that existed at the time.

Those who supported the bill pointed out that it would eliminate
the problems of excess land and scarce labor, which they saw as contributing to the deflation of land prices.[6] The sale of public land for a
relatively high price and the passage of the land tax would have several
positive consequences. First, by forcing new settlers to work for some
time on the plantations, it would give them the opportunity to adjust
to the new environment before they started their own enterprises. According to the bill's proponents, experience had shown that immigrants whose fares had been paid by a planter often left the plantation,
seduced by the prospect of property. Most of them had no capital,
could obtain no labor and, worst of all, lacked the experience necessary for living in the new environment. Knowing little about the soil,
the weather, and the crops, they were, in the words of one of the representatives, "dying in poverty in a country of abundance."[7] Thus the
traditional system, which allowed the immigrants to purchase land at
low prices or to obtain it by way of grants, was bad not only for the
landowner but also for the immigrants. Second, those who spoke for
the bill asserted that the sale of high-priced public lands would provide
the government with funds for promoting immigration. The increase
in land prices would also stimulate a more intensive and effective use
of land, putting an end to the unexploited big estate, which they considered one of the evils of the country.

One deputy emphasized that, as a result of the traditional system of
granting land (*sesmarías*), most land grants had not been surveyed or
exploited since, as he put it, the grantees wanted only to boast about
their land, not to cultivate it. Because of the gratuitous nature of land
grants and the ease with which titles were obtained, land did not represent wealth.[8] Those who did use the land were not concerned with
using it rationally. They lacked a spirit of innovation. They did not try

to diversify production, but cultivated one product until the soil was exhausted, then moved to other areas in search of virgin land. The increase in land prices, the legislators expected, would improve the system of production, making it more efficient, helping to eliminate monoculture, and forcing landlords to give up their routines and look for better methods.[9] The law would also put an end to another "vice" that corrupted the economy and society—the great numbers of tenants living on the fringes of the big estates at the expense of the landlord, working only two or three days a week and spending the rest of their time loafing, hunting, fishing, or sometimes even conspiring against the landowners.[10] By requiring that land be surveyed and titles registered, the law would legitimize property, ending the land quarrels that plagued society and making it easier to purchase and sell land.[11] The geographical programming of land sale would make it easier to create a system of highways and railroads, facilitating access to the market for more people.

Underlying all these particular arguments, the bill's supporters insisted, was the fact that the law would create conditions under which the planter could obtain free labor to replace slaves, whose supply was threatened by the imminent interruption of the slave trade. For them the new land policy was designed to help solve not only the problem of land but also the pressing problem of manpower. As one author correctly observed, what they really wanted was to force all land proprietors to pay for the costs of subsidizing free labor.[12]

Opposition to the bill came primarily from men who represented the less dynamic sectors of the economy. To them it seemed clear that the bill served the interests only of the planters of Rio, São Paulo, and Minas, the coffee land. Most of the opposition still believed that slavery was the best form of labor in a plantation society, and they were pessimistic about the possibility of replacing slaves with free immigrants. They were upset by the increasing interference of the central government in the life of the country and wanted to guarantee the independence of local authorities. Forbidding foreigners to acquire land, they said, was appropriate to a country like England, where the available land was insufficient to the needs of the population, but absurd in a country where most of the land was still to be occupied. Some of them, in fact, recommended the opposite policy: granting land to immigrants as a means of attracting them.[13] Their perspective on the question of immigration differed from that of the bill's supporters. For them it was a question not of supplying labor but of colonizing the country. They saw immigrants as agents of civilization, and the bill as it was conceived seemed designed to hinder the process of civilization.

The opposition also raised objections to the land tax. But then, even those who otherwise favored the bill were against the land tax. Opposition to the tax was so strong that it was eliminated from the final draft. Both sides were also critical of the plan to limit property size, but did not succeed in eliminating it completely from the law. Many opposed the requirement to survey the land, arguing that the country lacked experts to perform this task and that the process would be too costly, reducing the profitability of owning land.[14] But this feature, too, was retained in the law.

If we look closely at the bill and the arguments of those who supported it in the Chamber, it becomes obvious that the legislators wanted to foster the growth of the plantation system, which was fundamental to the Brazilian economy. They were willing to grant the government the power to control land and labor in order to insure the success of the plantation economy, but only for that reason. In relation to the land the government was seen not as a proprietor but as a representative of the people from whom it derived its power.

In accordance with modern ideas of profit and productivity the legislators took several steps to force the landowner to use his land more rationally. Aware of the need for a new type of labor to replace the slave, they resorted to immigration. And finally, since they assumed that immigrants to a country where land was available in large quantities might become landowners instead of working on plantations, they tried to make access to the land more difficult.

In the United States as in Brazil, land policy was linked to a certain conception of labor. But while the Brazilian law of 1850 made it difficult for free labor to obtain land, in the United States the Homestead Act of 1862 granted land to all who wished to settle. Using old arguments in favor of small property that were rooted in the historical experience of the early settlers and mobilizing new arguments derived from conditions created by nineteenth-century development, the Homestead Act reflected the impact of immigration, urbanization, industrialization, and capital accumulation on American society.

The bill was initially introduced in 1842 by southern representatives interested in westward expansion. But they soon dropped their support when it became clear that expansion toward the west would imply free labor. For the northerners and westerners who later supported the bill, free land, free soil, and free labor were inseparable concepts.[15] By 1860 the conflict between supporters and opponents of the act can be seen as an antagonism not only between two different conceptions of land and labor but also between the entrepreneur and the landlord, industrial capitalism and commercial capitalism.

Supporters of the Homestead Act used several arguments. They said the act would increase the number of independent farmers, putting an end to the undemocratic distribution of land. "It is not on the face of vast dominions but in the bosom of industry that the Father of mankind pours out the most precious fruits of the earth," said one representative,[16] expressing the feelings of those who thought the large estate was not a good system for exploiting the land. One representative in 1852 contrasted England and the United States. England's policy was to concentrate property in the hands of a few wealthy families, while in the United States the ideal was to distribute it among those who would cultivate it: "We desire to see them [the lands] owned and occupied by the lords of the soil, the sovereign people of this country. The British theory is that every acre of land in that country has its lord; and there is a regularly graduated dependence from the king down to the humblest tenant who tills the soil. The title descends from the Crown. Her policy is to preserve a pampered landed aristocracy, which policy is at war with the best interests of this country."[17] Ten years later, another congressman used almost identical language: "Instead of baronial possessions, let us facilitate the increase of independent homesteads. Let us keep the plow in the hands of the owner." And, he added, "In my judgment, the policy of applying the public lands in such a manner as to increase the number of independent farmers, of secure and independent homesteads, decentralizing and diffusing the wealth of the nation, is of the very first importance; vital, indeed, to the ultimate stability of the Republic."[18] For those who thought in such terms, the small homestead was the source of economic develoment and political stability, the concentration of land the source of social unrest.

Its supporters expected the Homestead Act to put an end to land speculation, which they believed to be responsible for the maintenance of large unexploited areas. According to them, the system of auctions, preemptions, and grants had always favored speculators at the expense of those who really wanted to work the land. The speculators' accumulation of large expanses of uncultivated land was contrary to the interests of the government. According to one representative the practice of selling large tracts to nonresidents and speculators had retarded the growth and improvement of the West more than anything else. The Homestead Act would bring the greatest possible amount of public land under actual cultivation.[19]

Granting land in homesteads would attract immigrants. Among the oppressed in Europe, there were milions "with strong arms and brave hearts"[20] who would gladly perform the task of cultivating the land but did not have the money to purchase it. And for those Americans who were in crowded urban slums, the act would create an opportunity to migrate west "before they become vicious" and make it possible for them to earn a living by honest industry.[21]

To those who argued against the bill because they considered government land a source of public credit, the supporters answered that the best form of credit was furnished by improved lands, lands owned by the people, not by wild lands held by the government.[22] In the opinion of one representative an acre of cultivated land was worth two acres uncultivated.[23] Another insisted, "There is no real wealth except the labor of men."[24] "What do you want of jurisdiction over trees and barren acres?" one of the bill's supporters asked members of the opposition. "It is men only that constitute the strength, power, and the glory of a State."[25] The supporters asserted that public credit was based upon general wealth and prosperity, which ultimately depended on the availability of labor. The occupation and exploitation of land would increase both production and consumption and consequently build up government revenues.

In short, the farmers who occupied the lands as a result of the Homestead Act would increase imports and exports; new employment would be created as a result of the expansion of the economy; and the effects of the farmers' labor would be felt throughout society.

The arguments of the opposition were weak. They feared that, instead of cultivating their landlords' property, tenants presently working in the Atlantic states would move to new areas, ruining the existing economy. Others feared that the poorhouses of Europe would be unlocked, pouring upon the United States thousands of undesirable immigrants and suggested that the act apply only to individuals born in America.[26] They argued as well that a free land policy would reduce land values and tried to prove that a policy of cheap land would damage the economy.[27]

The strongest argument against the bill rested on a pretext of unconstitutionality. Opponents claimed that the federal government did not have the right to distribute land. Rather, the states should decide the fate of public land. "Will you, at the expense of the rights of sovereignty and dignity of the State governments, induce the people of the United States to look up to this Federal Government as the only and sole dispensers (sic) of gifts and bounties?" asked one opponent of the bill.[28]

The opposition insisted that public lands constituted the basis of government credit and land sales the source of revenue. If this source disappeared, new taxes would have to be created or existing taxes increased. They complained about the increasing interference of the federal government in the economy in general, condemning the Act because it relied on the assumption that it was the government's duty to control labor and capital. Basing their arguments on classical liberal dogmas, they insisted that "men manage their own affairs better than Government can do it for them" and that the law of demand and supply directs the labor and pursuits of community.[29]

When the bill was passed in the house in 1862, 16 voted against it and 107 in favor. After many years of debate, the bill had passed without much opposition. Most of those who had opposed it—mainly southerners—had left the house because of the war. The passage of the bill was essentially an act of war. The Homestead Act had been a plank in the Republican platform and had faced the opposition of several Democrats. But the division of the House during the debates on the bill seemed to represent less a conflict between Republicans and Democrats than an opposition between two groups with different conceptions of land and labor. One group represented the point of view of land speculators and also of a great number of southerners interested in preserving the plantation system and slavery. The other represented those who were interested in populating the West and exploiting its resources with the help of small freeholders.

Some of the assumptions underlying the arguments of those who supported the act had roots in the colonial experience. Old myths served new purposes. The disruption of traditional social and economic structures by commercial and industrial development led many people to see the present as corrupt and to idealize the past, which they saw as the golden age of small property. The "myth of the garden" became a powerful ideological support of the Homestead Act.[30] The idea that small property represented a superior form of land use was associated with the idea of the dignity of labor and the notion that labor is the source of wealth and entitles a man to property. Ownership of land was seen as the ultimate source of all virtue. The yeoman was invoked as a symbol of frugality, morality, industry, and independence, and small property was considered the source of public morality, wealth, equality, and political stability. Some of these concepts were rooted in the Puritan ethic and in New England colonial agrarian society, but they became instrumental in the emerging competitive society of the mid-nineteenth century. The ideology expressed the desire to combine the best of two worlds—the virtues of small property with the benefits of industrial society.[31] What is more, it offered arguments to those interested in occupying and exploiting the West.

The need for expansion toward the west resulted from a complex set of processes: urbanization, industrialization, immigration, the accumulation of capital, and the expansion of the internal and international markets. In the eyes of the new entrepreneurial groups, the West was a fresh field for capital investment, a potential market for their manufactures, and a granary for the growing eastern cities and the expanding international market. Once investments were channeled toward the West—in the purchase of land and the construction of railroads, highways, and canals—and once new areas were populated, the investors and the new western settlers joined those who had supported the Homestead Act.

Virgin land was seen as a safety valve for the urban tensions that threatened the stability of this new industrial society, which periodically suffered economic depressions. In the increasingly competitive atmosphere the solution to the problems of urban poverty and unemployment seemed to be neither charity nor strikes but westward migration.[32] The nascent labor organizations and workingmen's parties made free land a political issue. To most easterners free labor and free land seemed a panacea for the ills of their society.

The occupation of the West by small freeholders would tip the political balance in favor of the antislavery states. Thus the Homestead Act found support also among those who opposed slavery, especially in the late fifties and early sixties, when the hostilities between the slaveowners and the rest of the country were approaching a climax. The entrepreneurs argued the superiority of the farming freeholder over the slaveowner. In the eyes of the eastern bourgeoisie, the most cherished values of the free labor system—social mobility, economic development, and political democracy—were violated on the plantation. The plantation economy seemed stagnant and the society hierarchical and aristocratic. Labor was demoralized by slavery. Leisure, laziness, ostentation, and routine existed in the place of hard work, industry, and frugality. In sum, the Homestead Act would create a society in which bourgeois values could flourish.

Though the ideology that supported the Homestead Act stressed the superiority of the independent small farmer, the economy at this time seemed, ironically, to be going in the opposite direction. Mechanization, increasing dependence on credit and transportation, vulnerability to the oscillations of the market—all characteristics of the new commercial agriculture—made it difficult for the independent freeholder to survive. Lacking the capital to purchase agricultural equipment, scratching away at infertile lands far from transportation, many homesteaders were forced to abandon their farms and become tenants on the lands of speculators. Speculation in land did not stop after the

Homestead Act. In fact, the traditional system of auctions, cash sales, and preemption survived side by side with the new policy. The Desert Land Act, the Timber Culture Act, the Timber and Stone Act, the land grants to railroads and states, the Indian land policy, the acts granting warrants to ex-soldiers or their heirs, and the Agricultural College Act (which granted millions of acres to the states) facilitated the monopolization of land by speculators, undermining the principle of land for the landless that had inspired the Homestead Act.[33] The expectation that the Homestead Act would benefit the urban poor was not realized. A majority of those who received grants were either eastern farmers who decided to move west or immigrants.

To a certain extent the act, which resulted essentially from the Industrial Revolution, was incongruous with new trends in industrial society.[34] The expectations that gave rise to the "myth of the garden" were frustrated by new economic trends. "In some way," as one historian said, "the Homestead Act was not the lodestone of a new democratic age but the capstone of a vanished era."[35]

In the nineteenth century, then, new land policies in Brazil and in the United States resulted from economic expansion. The contradictory strategies adopted by the two countries reflected differences in social and economic trends.

In Brazil, because the export of tropical products in the international market was most profitable at the time of independence, the colonial system of production was maintained. But in the United States even before independence, the plantation was not the only important economic base. After independence, the plantation owners had to share power with other groups, who became increasingly strong as new forms of enterprise developed in the nineteenth century. The existence and expansion of an internal market and the availability of capital favored the development of industry. In 1848, there were 123,025 manufacturing establishments in the United States. Twenty years later the number had increased to 353,863. In Brazil in the 1870s the number was still only around 200! In the United States in 1851, there were 8,886 miles of railroad and by 1861 there were 31,286. In Brazil the first railroad was just being built. The number of banks in the United States increased from 85 in 1811 to 1,931 in 1860. In Brazil there were only a handful. The population of the United States grew from 5,486,000 in 1800 to 33,188,000 at the time of the Homestead Act, while in Brazil the population was 2,419,406 in 1808 and grew to 7,677,800 in 1854. Most significant was the difference in the number of immigrants who entered the two countries. From 1820 to 1861, over 5,000,000 people, mainly from Europe, came to the United States. Up to 1850, fewer than 50,000 immigrants had entered Brazil.

Economic diversification and population growth had the greatest effect on the northeastern part of the United States, causing dramatic changes in the social structure. The number of industrial workers increased from 957,059 in 1849 to 2,053,996 in 1869.[36] (It was only in the 1960s that the number of workers in Brazil reached this level.) The middle classes also expanded rapidly. Entrepreneurial groups became more powerful. They invested capital in banks and manufactures, in railroads and canals, in urban developments and insurance schemes. In a society with so many opportunities the bourgeois credo seemed to be justified. Meanwhile, in the South, the maintenance of the traditional economic structure led, as it did in Brazil, to the survival of a seigneurial mentality.

While the northeastern part of the United States was changing very rapidly, the colonial social structure survived in Brazil: slave labor, the patronage system, a predominantly rural population, small urban populations concentrated in the main ports—all these features of the traditional colonial society remained. The elites were fundamentally conservative. And the only important revolutionary uprisings of the period found support among the urban *petite bourgeoisie*—shopkeepers, artisans, soldiers, professionals—the Brazilian counterpart of the sans culottes. They opposed the landed aristocracy and favored abolishing the slave trade, eliminating the great estates through agrarian reform, and nationalizing commerce.[37] Aligned with them on these issues were those few intellectuals and bureaucrats who were influenced by the Enlightenment and who did not identify with the landed aristocracy.

Radical movements were repressed, and the few radical intellectuals and bureaucrats continued to publish their books without affecting public opinion. The nation was firmly controlled by groups linked to the export-import economy—landowners, merchants, slavetraders, and their clients. In this society, there was little room for the development of a bourgeois ideology. The concept of the dignity of labor, the belief in labor as the source of wealth, and the faith in social mobility seemed incongruous in a hierarchical society in which labor was identified with slavery and social mobility with patronage.

The Brazilian elites resembled in some ways the planters of the South, with the essential difference that they controlled the nation alone. They delayed the abolition of slavery as long as they could. The law prohibiting the slave trade, enacted in 1831 under pressure from the British, was not obeyed until 1850, when a new law was enacted again mainly because of British diplomacy. During this period coffee plantations were rapidly expanding. When the slave trade was abolished, the landowners, whose interests were linked to the developing areas, felt they had to resort to immigration as an alternative means of recruiting labor. It was not by chance that the Land Law of 1850 was enacted in the same year as the law that abolished the slave trade.

While the Brazilians were trying to make land acquisition difficult, most of the emerging groups in the northeastern part of the United States backed the Homestead Act.[38] But they did it for a variety of reasons. The financial groups thought that the settlement and development of the West would create new possibilities for investment. Manufacturers saw new markets. Merchants expected an increase in exports and imports. The urban middle classes—either because they resented present trends or because they regretted a paradise lost—saw in the Homestead Act the promise of a better life. Workers expected the act to stimulate migration toward the West, reducing the labor surplus in the cities. Once the issue of slavery had clearly divided the nation, many abolitionists would associate free labor with free land and support the Homestead Act for that reason. All these groups contributed, in different ways, to create an atmosphere favorable to the law. Opposition came essentially from land speculators and from southerners linked to the traditional economy and landownership, the same group who had originally suggested it.

The modernization of land policy had begun in the United States at the time of the American Revolution, when the sale of public lands became one way for the government to obtain revenue. The system had allowed speculators to amass great tracts of the best land. Others who did not have enough capital to buy land squatted on public land despite legal prohibitions. Very often those who had bought the land did not settle, and those who did settle were not able to buy it. The preemption laws had tried to legalize the situation of the squatters, granting them permission to buy the land they had occupied and exploited. Several local homestead acts had been enacted and many grants had been made to those who wanted to build roads or mines or engage in other development projects. But the best land had remained in the hands of the speculators. The Homestead Act meant to release productive land that had been only in the hands of a few.

In both the United States and Brazil the line separating those who supported land reform from those who were against it seems to have coincided with political party lines. The Conservatives tended to support the Land Law of 1850 in Brazil, while the Liberals opposed it.[39] In the United States the Republicans included the homestead policy in their platform, while the Democrats opposed it. But in both countries, politics seemed less relevant than economic and social motives. Conflicts on the issue of land reflected conflicts between the most dynamic, capitalist sectors of the economy and the most archaic.[40]

A study of the debates that preceded the enactment of the land law in each country reveals the ambiguities and contradictions that divided ruling groups torn between past and present. In the wake of modernization, conservatism and idealization of the past seem to have played a role as important as utopian dreaming. The participants very often perceived new realities in traditional ways. The trends of the present were not always clearly understood, and the expectations and purposes of those who contributed to the enactment of the laws were not completely realized. Both laws, resulting as they did from the confrontation of several opposed tendencies and representing the conflicting world views of several groups, lagged behind the concrete realities of their time.

5 SHARECROPPERS AND PLANTATION OWNERS
An Experiment with Free Labor

During the nineteenth century, the question of immigration became increasingly important in Brazil. Immigration policies were discussed in the press and debated in Parliament. Most people agreed that it was necessary to promote European immigration, but they often differed about goals and strategies.[1] Planters of the new frontier areas, fearing that the abolition of the slave trade would cut off their supply of labor, hoped that immigrants might substitute for slaves. Accordingly, they supported legislation that made it difficult for immigrants to acquire land, thus forcing them to work on plantations. Planters in the traditional areas already well supplied with slaves and intellectuals who saw Brazil from a European perspective viewed immigrants as civilizing agents. They favored the distribution of land to Europeans who could then create their own settlements (*núcleos coloniais*). Both systems—using immigrants as plantation workers and promoting *núcleos coloniais*—were tried in the coffee areas during the first half of the century and both failed.

Attempts to promote immigration to *núcleos coloniais* had begun even before independence. Under João VI, the government created several colonies of Germans, Swiss, and Azoreans with the purpose of increasing the Brazilian population. But most of these experiments were unsuccessful and reinforced the opposition to autonomous settlements for immigrants.

Opposition came essentially from landowning groups concerned with obtaining laborers for their own plantations. In their opinion, government funds should be used only for immigrants to work on existing plantations.

One spokesman for these groups in São Paulo was Nicoláu de Campos Vergueiro, future senator and minister, who later distinguished himself as a pioneer in the creation of immigrant sharecropping colonies. Vergueiro frequently criticized measures taken by the government to further the creation of *núcleos coloniais*. As early as

1827, long before he became involved in the sharecropping experiment, he opposed the imperial government's plan to import German immigrants into São Paulo and candidly pointed to the incompatibility of this type of colonization with the landowner's interests. If fertile land located near urban centers was granted to the colonists, it would greatly inconvenience those planters who intended such land for their own use. On the other hand, the land the planters could spare the colonists would be infertile, exhausted, located in the backlands, at a great distance from the markets, and unsuited to their needs. Foreign colonization at the government's expense, moreover, seemed to him excessively costly. Besides subsidizing the Atlantic crossing, the government was also obliged to build homes, construct roads, and sustain the colonists until they were able to produce enough for their own subsistence.

Despite such arguments, there were still those in Parliament who defended the government's policy of subsidizing large-scale immigration and making land available to immigrants. Concrete measures were, in fact, taken toward this end, with colonies in Espírito Santo, Rio de Janeiro, São Paulo, Santa Catarina, and Rio Grande do Sul. In 1828, the superintendency of foreign colonization sent 149 families and 72 individuals, or a total of 928 immigrants, to São Paulo. Of these, 417 went to Santo Amaro, 238 to Curitiba, 39 to Itanhaem, and 27 to Cubatão; the rest scattered. Between 1827 and 1837, the government settled nearly 1,200 immigrants in different parts of the province, but most of the immigrants found themselves in remote and inaccessible areas, far from market centers, and plagued by poor soil or dense forest cover. As a result, most of the colonies eventually disbanded, abandoning the parcels of land they had futilely attempted to cultivate. Those who stayed gradually sank into a miserable existence comparable to that of the native population.[2]

While the imperial government persisted—in spite of such failures—in its attempts to create *núcleos coloniais*, the provincial governments were also led to promote immigration, although for a different reason. They had always relied on slaves to perform public service jobs. But with the development of coffee plantations it had become difficult to find workers for road construction and maintenance, bridge repairs, and similar tasks. In 1836, the government engaged 27 immigrants and their families through the Society for the Promotion of Colonization in Rio de Janeiro and sent them to São Paulo to work on the road linking São Paulo to the port of Santos. Between 1837 and 1838, 227 individuals arrived in São Paulo; 56 were assigned to the government's iron works, the Fábrica de Ferro, and 88 to road service, the rest scattering themselves throughout the province.[3] Again in 1838 the president of the province of São Paulo sent for 100 European workers including stonecutters, masons, pavers, blacksmiths, carpenters, and two foremen to be employed in the construction and maintenance of the province's roads and bridges. As before, the immigrants reached their destination, but soon abandoned the jobs for which they had been engaged. In spite of these successive failures, another attempt along the same lines was made in 1855. Saraiva, then president of the province of São Paulo, acknowledging the difficulty of finding laborers for public works, provided for the hiring of 350 Europeans.

The provincial governments' use of contract immigrants was a minor and noncontroversial element in the Brazilian attempt to promote immigration. And the imperial government, which viewed the issue of immigration on a national scale, continued to insist on the formation of *núcleos coloniais*. Year after year, the central government urged the provincial presidents to support such ventures.[4] In 1855, the imperial government made it known that it was prepared to subsidize immigrants provided that they "promptly settle . . . on moderate-size parcels of land."[5] Provincial presidents (who were appointed by the imperial government rather than by the province themselves) tried to implement this policy, but very often met the opposition of the planters, and accommodated to their views. The president of São Paulo, for example, recognized that the land parcel system was the most attractive to the foreigner, but he argued that it would be impossible to divide up the large landholdings quickly enough to satisfy the needs of the immigrants.[6]

The central government policy became more consonant with the interest of the Paulista planters whenever Paulistas occupied important positions in the imperial government, as in 1847, when Vergueiro, a Paulista, was minister of justice and provisionally minister of the empire, or later, in 1885 and 1887, when two other Paulistas, Antonio Prado and Rodrigo Silva, successively occupied the post of minister of agriculture. In fact, one could say that the imperial government oscillated between two different policies—one of creating *núcleos coloniais*, the other of recruiting labor for plantations—depending upon the amount of power wielded by the western São Paulo planters in the government ministries.

It would be a mistake to imagine that all Paulista planters viewed the problem in the same way. There was a clear divergence in points of view between the planters of pioneering areas in the west, who were interested in immigrants as a labor supply, and those of the Paraiba Valley, well supplied with slaves, who often supported the creation of *núcleos coloniais.* One Paraibano spokesman, Lacerda Werneck, argued in articles in the *Jornal do Comércio* that the only way of attracting immigrants was to grant them small landholdings; in his opinion, it was flatly impossible to replace plantation slaves with immigrants.

Despite some favorable sentiment toward *núcleos coloniais*, serious obstacles hindered their development in São Paulo in the first half of the century. Every attempt made by the government seemed destined to fail. At the same time, nonsubsidized immigration never amounted to more than a trickle. European immigrants seemed to prefer other countries to Brazil, primarily because Brazil offered little economic opportunity. Until 1850, when the slave trade was abolished, slaves were abundant; they answered most of the needs of both the cities and the rural areas. During this period, coffee plantations were for the most part self-sufficient, producing practically everything they needed to function. And the urban population at this stage could be supplied with the plantations' surplus. It was thus impossible for small proprietors to participate successfully in the commercial economy. The immigrant who did not have capital enough to invest in a coffee plantation was condemned to cultivate the land for his subsistence only, finding no market for his produce or for his labor.

More important, however, were the obstacles the immigrants had to face in obtaining land. The confusing legislation that regulated land-ownership caused unending and costly disputes that no immigrant was prepared to face. And the expansion of coffee production made disputes over vacant lands even more bitter. The anarchical land policy also undermined confidence in property titles granted by the government.[7] At the beginning of Pedro II's reign, the confusion over titles was such that the imperial government felt obliged to consider legislation on the matter. Legal confusion alone, however, did not explain the problems encountered in procuring land for immigrants. The greatest obstacle was the concentration of the best lands in the hands of a few large proprietors, who could count on support from the legislature and judicial officials.

The law of 1850, though it was not implemented until 1854, sought to put an end to land speculation, but failed. After 1850, as before, the planters monopolized the best lands, leaving the remote and unproductive areas to the immigrants.[8] According to the French traveler Expilly, four-fifths of the land was in the hands of the great proprietors in 1865, while the government retained only one-fifth, which consisted of lands that either were far removed from rivers, roads, urban centers, and the coast or were exposed to Indian attacks.[9] Expilly's testimony is confirmed by other sources.

Land monopoly was a constant preoccupation for those concerned with stimulating the creation of *núcleos coloniais*. Many went so far as to suggest agrarian reform to replace plantation monoculture with small-scale holdings producing a variety of crops. Quintino Bocaiuva, advocating a tax on uncultivated land in 1868, argued that it would force the subdivision of the large estates and facilitate the formation of *núcleos coloniais*. In 1878, Henrique de Beaurepaire Rohan said that "the fragmentation of the large estates is, in effect, an indispensable condition for the development of our agriculture, and will be even more so once slavery becomes totally extinct." The Central Society for Immigration (Sociedade Central de Imigração), founded in 1883, campaigned for the subdivision of mortgaged or bank-controlled estates into parcels that could be purchased by immigrants or native farmers. Alfredo d'Escragnolle Taunay, an important member of the Sociedade Central, voiced criticisms of the latifundia system; he insisted that the existing landholding system was incompatible with small property and colonization and declared that "the monopolization of land, which leads to sterility and waste, is odious and the cause of great social ills." It was, he said, "shameful and disturbing that the large landowners, without accounting to society or paying a bit of tax for their greed," maintained uncultivated "enormous and extremely fertile regions," when cultivation could greatly enrich the public wealth and bring relief from misery to hundreds of thousands of men who asked only for "a little land with which to free themselves from poverty and to contribute to the nation's prosperity by their honest labor." [10] He lamented the fact that whenever the government needed lands, it could obtain them only over the opposition of the large landowners.

The representatives of the Sociedade Central, along with the other critics of the planters' land monopoly, were certainly correct in considering this monopoly a major impediment to the development of small holdings. In fact, the monopoly was so absolute in some areas that the government was left with no public lands whatever. In the 1850s, when the imperial government inquired into the availability of public land in the province of Rio de Janeiro, most of the *municípios* (counties) responded negatively. The others indicated the existence of infertile and inaccessible lands. Nova Friburgo, for example, informed the government of some small vacant stretches that had gone unclaimed because of their infertility and location in the highlands. Mangaratiba, another *município* in Rio de Janeiro, mentioned some lands already occupied by squatters, high up in the Angra dos Reis mountains. And Itaboraí replied that there were no public lands at all. [11]

The situation was even worse in Minas Gerais. There the origins of the problem dated back to the mining boom of the eighteenth century, when every square inch of land had come under dispute. By the nineteenth century the government had great difficulty finding vacant areas, succeeding only in the hinterlands near the Bahian frontier and near Espírito Santo. Most *municípios* responded negatively to the government inquiry on the availability of public lands. What was left unoccupied consisted of a few patches in the backland. The *município* of Ponte Nova, for example, reported some densely forested vacant land bordering Espírito Santo; Minas Novas reported only "vacant" Indian lands. These lands would be of little value to the colonists, since in areas like the Mucurí region, which bordered on Indian territory, there were frequent bloody encounters between the white population and the natives.[12] The situation was no different in other *municípios* in the coffee area. No good land was available, and when planters were willing to sell parcels of their property they charged exorbitant prices.

The government, lacking well-located public lands, was obliged either to settle the immigrants in unproductive and isolated areas or to use public funds to purchase good land. Under these circumstances a system of small landholding was impractical and the immigrant was inescapably condemned to either sharecropping or wage labor.

Besides these restraints on the development of colonization policies, there were other obstacles that hindered spontaneous immigration to Brazil as well. One of these was the more favorable atmosphere offered in the United States, which attracted most of the European immigrants of the nineteenth century. The United States was closer to Europe, which meant cheaper fares; it had better economic conditions and consequently greater opportunities for social mobility; it offered easier access to land, more or less familiar climatic conditions, freedom of worship, and a democratic political system. Thus, during the first half of the nineteenth century, the stream of European migrants flowed toward North America, particularly to those areas where slavery had been abolished. Even if all else had been equal, the more expensive fares to Brazil would have deterred many immigrants. In the 1850s, it cost less than six hundred francs for a family of five to sail from Europe to the United States, one thousand two hundred francs to sail to Brazil. With the money it cost to travel from Hamburg to Rio de Janeiro, the family could not only pay its fare to the United States, but also have enough left to buy a few acres of land.[13]

There was, in addition, a widespread prejudice in Europe against tropical areas. Potential migrants looked warily at a country where the heat and humidity were believed to undermine the health of white men and where epidemics did, in fact, rage. There were also religious restrictions to consider, since Catholicism was the official religion, and there was not even a civil register to certify the births, marriages, and deaths of non-Catholics.

In such a context, the first attempts to promote *núcleos coloniais*, or spontaneous immigration, were bound to be, if not total failures, at the very least disappointments, generating a great deal of pessimism about the future of immigration. The lack of success of these early attempts to develop immigrant settlements discouraged new initiatives and reinforced the arguments of those who viewed slavery as the only possible solution to the labor shortage.

By the middle of the century, however, no one could ignore the fact that slavery would at most be only an interim solution to Brazil's labor problems. And the threat of extinction that dangled over the slave trade after 1831, to say nothing of its actual abolition in the fifties, served to stimulate further immigration experiments in the coffee areas—the areas most in need of labor.

In 1848, the São Paulo Legislature's Committee on Industry and Commerce, recognizing the urgent need for labor in the province, suggested that the government be authorized to make an annual agreement with any individual or company, whether Brazilian or foreign, to transport two hundred colonists from Northern Europe. In 1852, the legislature authorized a yearly allotment of 25 *contos* for the advancement of colonization. The original plan, presented by Gabriel dos Santos, sought to establish financial assistance for the transportation of workers' families from Northern Europe to São Paulo. Immigrants would receive half the cost of transportation to the port of Santos in the form of an interest-free six-year loan. The plan, with a few modifications, was approved and incorporated into the 1853–54 provincial budget.[14] The intention was to transfer the responsibility for promoting immigration into private hands while the government limited its role to guaranteeing financial backing. A private firm under the direction of Nicoláu de Campos Vergueiro undertook the first systematic promotion of a new type of colonization, based on sharecropping, with the purpose of settling colonists on the plantations.[15]

Senator Vergueiro's first efforts in this direction had taken place as early as 1842, well before the slave trade was effectively abolished. In December of that year, he had introduced into São Paulo at his own expense a group of Portuguese immigrants. It was only a matter of months, however, before the group dispersed. He took up the task again a few years later and with a subsidy from the imperial government organized a society for the promotion of immigration. This time he turned to Germany and Switzerland, importing a group of colonists whom he settled on his plantation, Ibicaba, in 1847. During the years following, he tried in vain to get the subsidy renewed. But the political climate had changed, and the president of the Council of State responded evasively to his petitions, even accusing him of wanting to monopolize colonization.

Vergueiro did not give up and turned instead to the provincial government, from which he received a subsidy of 25 *contos* to import five hundred colonists per year. During the next two years, 1,039 colonists were introduced into São Paulo as a result of this contract, 594 in 1852 and 445 in 1853. By July 1854, Vergueiro's company had completed or even exceeded its contract.[16] A new contract was drawn up, the contractors agreeing to import a thousand colonists annually in exchange for an interest-free loan of 20 *contos* per year, to be returned to the provincial treasury within three years, and an annual subsidy of 1 : 500$000 per thousand colonists.

The apparently successful results obtained with immigrants at Ibicaba encouraged the Paulista planters of the west to follow Vergueiro's example. The need for an alternative source of labor had grown even more urgent with the expansion of coffee plantations and the cessation of the slave trade after 1850. Pressured by those who considered foreign colonization a possible alternative to slavery, the provincial administration continued to support enterprises of this sort.

In 1854, the provincial legislature granted 7 *contos* to several planters for the transportation of colonists. The following year the legislature received a petition from a group of planters in Taubaté, soliciting aid for the importation of four hundred colonists. In 1856, the legislature authorized the provincial government to guarantee the credit of Paulista planters in Europe for any transaction that furthered immigration. And in the same year, the legislature authorized a contract with the firm Theodor Wille and Company for the importation of immigrants and their distribution throughout the province.

Under normal circumstances, a male immigrant received a monetary advance to cover his and his family's transportation costs, plus additional funds until they could produce enough to support themselves. Each family was assigned a certain number of coffee trees to cultivate, harvest, and process. While the coffee plants were young, the family was permitted to cultivate food crops for their own subsistence between the rows of trees. Once this was no longer possible, they were usually allowed to plant their food crops in other areas indicated by the planter. Whenever there was enough surplus to be sold, the planter would receive half the profits. The colonist, in turn, would receive half the profits from the sale of the coffee he harvested, after deducting for processing, transport, middlemen, taxes, and other expenses. The planter charged 6 percent interest on the original sums granted to the colonist. The whole family was held responsible for the debt, and at least half of their annual profits went toward its repayment.

Aside from being obliged to cultivate and tend a certain number of coffee trees, the sharecropper also had to contribute, in proportion to the amount of coffee he delivered, whatever services were required to prepare the coffee beans for the market. He endured strict discipline, and if dissatisfied, he could not leave the plantation without first notifying the planter and paying off all his debts. In cases where the colonist and landowner were unable to come to an agreement, the local authorities intervened to decide the matter.

Occasionally these rules were slightly altered according to the dictates of experience, but the content of the contracts was not changed substantially. There were planters, for example, who charged 12 percent interest instead of 6; there were some who included a clause in their contracts requiring additional services or specifying the number of times the coffee row had to be weeded; there were others who held the colonist responsible for replacing any trees that died.

A considerable number of colonists were imported into São Paulo under the sharecropping system. Most of them came under the aegis of Vergueiro and Company and were settled primarily in the western zone of the province. The president of São Paulo, Saraiva, in his annual address for 1855, described the major colonies then in operation including those in Campinas, Constituição, Limeira, Rio Claro, Jundiaí, and Ubatuba.[17] The following year, Vice-President Antonio de Almeida recorded a total of 3,217 colonists, not including those in Ubatuba, for whom no information was available. His figures included one colony in São Sebastião, four in Jundiaí, four in Rio Claro, seven in Campinas, one in Constituição, two in Bragança, one in Paraibuna, five in Limeira, four in Ubatuba, and one in Taubaté. Noting the generally favorable disposition among planters toward establishing sharecropping colonies, he attributed it to the growing labor shortage and the apparent success of previous experiments along these lines. Almeida also voiced his hope for a steady increase in the number of such colonies.

The majority of the sharecropping settlements appeared between 1852 and 1854. During these years the Vergueiro firm continued to import colonists in large numbers and even extended its activities to other provinces. The importation of colonists became a business of considerable proportions. The usual procedure for a planter interested in using sharecroppers was to apply to a firm involved in colonization for a supply of laborers. But some, like Souza Queiroz, transported colonists from Europe on their own account. Although a number of firms were participating in this "trade" by the mid 1850s, the terms of the contracts always followed the outlines of the original contract conceived by Vergueiro.

On most of the plantations that used colonists, slave labor coexisted with the sharecropping colonies. The tasks of each group were strictly defined and separate. Only the colonists from Portugal and the Azores were able to adjust to working side by side with slaves.[18] Although slave labor continued to predominate, a number of estates did employ a large free labor force. In 1857, Luis Antonio de Souza Barros had 329 Germans and Swiss on his estate. João Elias Jordão had 180 foreign colonists on his plantation in Rio Claro, while in Campinas, Floriano Penteado had 96 German and Portuguese colonists. By 1857, there were over eight hundred immigrants residing on the Ibicaba plantation, the majority being German, Swiss, or Portuguese.[19]

Ibicaba, having the first and largest sharecropping colony in the province, had become somewhat symbolic of the progress of colonization in São Paulo. And it was there that the contradictions inherent in the new system first became apparent. Ibicaba sharecroppers were among the first to revolt.

The sharecropping experiment was still young when planters and colonists both began to voice their discontent. Many planters wished nothing more than to rid themselves of the colonists as soon as possible. Some even admitted that they preferred slave labor. Floriano Penteado, in an 1859 letter to the municipal judge of Campinas wrote: "I intend, from this time on, to dismantle my colony, and gradually substitute slaves for the free laborers."[20] Joaquim Camargo, too, took a pessimistic view of his experience with free labor; he saw no advantage in continuing with it and maintained that slave labor, despite certain defects, was preferable. In 1859, the provincial president, Fernandes Tôrres, observed that "the colonists who have recently arrived from Europe seem to have been more burdensome than profitable to the planters, since there is no other way to explain the planters' preference for spending enormous sums of money to acquire slaves at exorbitant prices."

Landowners who were less pessimistic about free labor's potential continued their experiment, although they preferred Portuguese immigrants to Germans and Swiss. "I have gained nothing from the Swiss and German colonists," wrote Vieira de Macedo to the vice-president of the province in 1857. "They do not tend to the coffee trees assigned them, leaving them in a state of complete neglect, and we lack the means with which to force them to comply, even partially, with their contractual obligations. Second, they perceive our agriculture as requiring little effort. I wish therefore to experiment with Portuguese immigrants, and if the results meet my expectations, I will import them in greater numbers."[21]

The majority of the sharecropping colonies proved to be failures, and this rather bleak record discouraged most planters from further experimentation. By the end of the decade, it was difficult to place colonists who had arrived under the auspices of the imperial government. Although notice of their arrival was inserted in the provincial press, it was almost impossible to find buyers for these contracts. The municipal judge of Campinas wrote to Fernandes Tôrres in July 1858 that not a single person had applied for the services of the newly arrived colonists, and concluded, "I doubt that any will appear, since the local planters in general are not well disposed toward colonization." Despite his pessimism, which reflected the general attitude on the colonization question at the time, an applicant for the immigrants did finally appear: the planter Joaquim do Amaral, who continued to experiment with free labor for many years and became one of its most ardent defenders.

But Amaral was an exception, since most planters involved in colonization at this point freely expressed their desire to be rid of their sharecroppers. They complained that the colonists were undisciplined, disorderly, violent, lazy, given to drink and vice, and reluctant to perform tasks not specified in their contracts. Furthermore, their productivity was low, with each family capable of tending from 1,500 to 2,000 coffee trees at most. (The average slave tended some 3,000 trees, sometimes 3,500.) As a result, their profits were too small to meet even the family's interest payments on debts owed to the planter. The planters complained that the colonists did not adapt to the arduous labor required for coffee cultivation. During the harvest they would ask for a greater number of trees, but afterward would refuse to perform those tasks necessary for the plants' proper maintenance. In addition, they refused to accept responsibility for the less productive trees and would even abandon them, thus damaging their productivity permanently. Colonists were totally careless during the harvest, haphazardly mixing green and ripe beans. And the worst were those colonists who deserted the plantations without repaying their debts.

Most planters accustomed to slave labor were not prepared to deal with the problems posed by a free labor force. When Cunha Morais, who owned an estate in Amparo, reprimanded his sharecroppers for picking green and ripe beans indiscriminately, they quit harvesting altogether, causing him to lose the entire crop. The relations between Morais and the colonists had become so tense that a representative from the imperial government had to intervene in order to right the situation. Similarly, Elias Leite, whose plantation was located near Constituição, lost all his colonists when they heard rumors that the government was about to grant them land. On account of these rumors, a new plantation containing approximately thirty thousand trees was ruined.[22]

The colonists were also dissatisfied, and they expressed their dissatisfaction in several ways, the most effective being refusal to work, which placed their employers in a desperate situation. The sharecroppers complained bitterly about their lot. They felt that the planters reserved the most productive trees for the slaves, while assigning them either the young plants whose output was too low to give sufficient compensation or the old and withered ones, which were equally unrewarding. The colonists also considered the system used to calculate the interest they owed and their share of profits to be dishonest. A further cause for complaint was the debt colonists incurred from the moment they left Europe, which only increased with passing time. They pointed out how paltry the sums advanced to them before the harvest were and that, left with no cash, they were forced to buy whatever they needed in the plantation store, where the price of provisions was higher than in the neighboring towns. They complained that the weights and measures used always operated in the landlord's favor. And they considered in unfair to have to share the profit from their food crops with the proprietors.

Sharecroppers were also irritated by problems arising from day-to-day contact with the planters. The colonists portrayed the planters as despots, who prohibited them from leaving the estates without express permission and forced them to perform services not specified in their contracts, like constructing and repairing roads or mending fences. The uncomfortable housing provided for colonists, often little better than slave quarters, was another cause of discontent. Among the list of complaints there were also problems of a religious nature, since marriage by writ was not legally recognized despite its being the only procedure available to non-Catholics. The same complications arose with newborn children: Protestant parents were forced to baptize them in the Catholic church in order to obtain some kind of birth certificate. The colonists also felt totally unprotected, with no one to resort to in case of conflict, since the local judicial system seemed rigged in the planters' favor. Overall they considered themselves exploited by the landowners and reduced to the condition of slaves.[23]

Accumulated resentments reached the boiling point on various occasions and generated a series of small uprisings. As early as 1853, Souza Barros had to request police intervention to suppress the disturbances spreading among his colonists. Similar incidents occurred in other parts of the province.[24] Most of these were minor, but the uprising that took place in February 1857 in Ibicaba, the estate that had pioneered the adoption of the sharecropping system, reached the dimensions of a major revolt. It provoked a series of inquiries, some sponsored by the imperial government and others by the provincial administration. Even the Swiss government sent a special emissary to investigate the situation.

Asked for possible resolutions of the existing conflicts, the planters suggested first of all the institution of methods to coerce the colonists into fulfilling their contractual obligations and to repress all signs of unrest—although they also mentioned the necessity of decreasing the debts burdening the colonists. In general, the suggestions presented by the planters involved more government financing, closer supervision, and more systematic police repression. The planters also mentioned the immigrants' need for "spiritual guidance" and recommended that evangelical ministers be brought to the area.[25]

"It is irrelevant to me whether the colonists are contracted for wage labor or sharecropping or even a certain sum for each *alqueire* of coffee beans harvested. In short, any system is fine provided that future colonists do not arrive so burdened with debts as those that came under the auspices of Vergueiro and company," wrote Floriano Penteado to Fernandes Tôrres in 1857. Expressing his views on the same matter, Souza Queiroz, another large coffee planter, wrote, "It would be very beneficial if the government would take upon itself the responsibility for paying the immigrants' passage, at least for those under ten years of age, since it is the families with young children who find it most difficult to repay their debts. I also consider it necessary," he continued, "to make legal provisions for Protestants and even to provide a minister who would periodically circulate among the colonists." When asked how he dealt with his colonists, he said that he tried to resolve difficulties with them by "withholding supplies." Another landowner who was consulted on the problems involved in sharecropping replied that the system would prove beneficial once the government guaranteed, through "adequate legislation," the rights of both landowners and colonists. He even proposed that a special judgeship be created and that an inspector general be appointed to visit the colonies regularly. He also suggested more police surveillance, to ensure order on the plantations.

These opinions were far from new. In 1854, even before he began to have problems with his sharecroppers, Souza Barros called attention to the need for provincial regulations that would oblige the colonists to fulfill the terms of their contracts. Vergueiro, who expressed his position on this matter on various occasions, pointed out the need for more police regulations and for a magistrate "nominated by the planters" to enforce them. He admitted that in the absence of such mechanisms of control he had attempted to remedy the situation with fines, arbitrations, and as a last resort, eviction of the colonist—a solution that was not viable if the colonist was in debt, since his departure would penalize the planter as well. Queiroz Telles, writing to the provincial vice-president in 1854, expressed his deep pessimism about the use of immigrants on coffee plantations. He said that he was pleased to have spent very little capital on the sharecropping experiment since his colonists would be incapable of repaying him, even if given ten years to do so. He remarked that he was not criticizing the people themselves, "for they are of excellent quality, but rather the enormous debt they bring with them, which makes them lose all hope of repaying even the original advance." And he declared categorically that "as long as immigration cannot be either spontaneous or less expensive, I am completely convinced that it would be better to lose our coffee plantations than to be dependent upon colonists." He concluded, "colonization is not feasible at the present time."[26]

A majority of the Paulista planters would have agreed with this remark, but they would not have endorsed his statement on the good quality of the immigrants. In fact, the cause most often cited as responsible for the failure of sharecropping was precisely the poor character of the colonists. In 1863, after the disturbances at Ibicaba and other estates had convinced most planters that sharecropping was a failure, Casimiro de Macedo, deputy to the provincial assembly, made an eloquent statement that summarized the general sentiment on the issue. "Foreign colonization has fallen into disrepute among us," he said,

and while I do not number myself among those who have no faith in colonization, I have little hope for this alternative at present, given the methods currently employed in our country to accomplish it. Foreign colonization met its worst enemy when the Chamber of Deputies voted a credit of six thousand *contos*[27] to aid its development. This measure, although promulgated with diametrically opposite intentions, excited the greed and cupidity of the speculators, and the result has been, as a rule, what we have observed: The nation's agriculture, instead of obtaining workers suitable for rural labor, has acquired the dregs of the Swiss and

German populations. Fugitives from the law, men of evil habits, men who only recently inhabited the jails of those countries, have been imported into Brazil under the title of colonists. And here we have watched them abandon the plantations in order to set up taverns along the highways. This is not the kind of colonization our nation needs.[28]

The colonist's "bad character" was actually accepted as a fundamental cause of the collapse of the sharecropping system in Brazil. Only rarely did some planter acknowledge that other circumstances were involved. Souza Barros, one of the planters most familiar with the situation, wrote in a letter to the provincial president that the sharecropping system could survive profitably only as long as the price of coffee remained high. He sought an additional explanation for the conflicts between planters and colonists. Besides the poor character of those who emigrated, there was also the planters' total ignorance as to the way to treat the colonists. "I treated them much too well," he said, "wishing to gain their loyalty through gratitude, but I deluded myself, and thus when I demanded that they work according to their contracts, they rebelled." Vergueiro, in a letter to Nabuco, then president of the province, remarked that the immigration business was controlled by the shippers and their agents. It was this fact that accounted for the poor quality of the colonists since the people in control cared only about securing "cargo" for their ships and collecting commissions in proportion to the number of people who embarked.[29]

Inferior recruitment methods, which brought "bad" colonists to the plantations, the onerous debts that burdened the colonists as a result of their transportation costs, the lack of disciplinary mechanisms to combat contract violations and disorder—such were the reasons forwarded by most planters to explain the system's failure. The basic faults of sharecropping—its coexistence with slave labor and the contradictions inherent in its structure, with planters and sharecroppers each trying to enlarge their profit at the expense of the other—escaped the planters' notice completely. They did not probe very deeply in their analysis of the system's collapse.

Some independent observers, such as government officials, consular agents, and foreign travelers, were more perceptive. Valdetaro, one of the envoys sent by the Brazilian government, reported in 1857 on the Ibicaba and Angélica colonies. His explanation of the colonies' failure focused on the adjustment crisis the immigrant underwent during his first year in Brazil, usually caused by diseases stemming from changes in climate and diet. He also mentioned the low productivity of recently arrived colonists caused by their ignorance of local agricultural practices. Further on in his report he wrote that the large number of young children accompanying the colonists was particularly burdensome because of high cost of ship passage. He granted that in some cases one could include the colonists' negligence or unwillingness to work among the factors responsible for the failure of the project. The Swiss immigrants, for the most part, were unfamiliar with agriculture and had emigrated for political reasons. In a later, more detailed report—and one which betrays a greater bias in favor of the planters, whose opinions he eventually had consulted—Valdetaro maintained that the principal reasons for the failure of the colonies were poor recruitment, the lack of mandatory inspection and proper judicial administration, and, finally, deficiencies in religious and educational assistance. He suggested that in view of the distrust engendered by the system of remuneration adopted by the planters, it would be best to pay the colonists a fixed amount for each *alqueire* of coffee, with rates determined beforehand, as was already being done on some plantations. Valdetaro had incorporated into his explanation most of the causes emphasized by the landowners.

The Swiss consul in Rio de Janeiro approached the issue from a very different angle. In a report sent in 1857 to the Federal Council of Switzerland, he severely criticized the situation awaiting the migrants. He complained, in fact, that the sums allotted by the Brazilian Parliament to finance colonization were being used to acquire white slaves instead of black ones. Analyzing the legislation regulating relations between colonists and planters, he showed that it allowed the landowner to evict a sick colonist while still obliging the colonist to repay his debts at the risk of imprisonment. In addition, he said, Protestants were shorn of all legal protection, and the bishop of Rio de Janeiro had declared their marriages illegal, their wives concubines, and their children illegitimate. He concluded that sharecropping was nothing more than a system of servitude and false promises and that the Brazilian government had neither the courage nor the power to suppress such abuses. In view of this, he suggested that the Swiss government follow the example of Germany by restricting emigration to Brazil.[30]

Von Tschudi, who traveled throughout Brazil during this crisis period and who visited a majority of the colonies with the object of gaining firsthand knowledge of the situation, primarily blamed the Vergueiro firm. According to Von Tschudi, the company was responsible for the ambiguities in the sharecroppers' contracts and was to be blamed for collecting undue additional fees and refusing to repay the money advanced by various Swiss communes to the colonists. But in his opinion, a large part of the responsibility also belonged personally to the planters, the administrators, the overseers, and even to the colonists themselves. He, too, criticized the Brazilian government for its inability to put an end to abuses and injustices or to enforce observance of the law.

The planters and the colonists understood their problems only superficially and in partisan ways. Even the outsiders who attempted to analyze the failure of the sharecropping system never really understood the fundamental problems and contradictions inherent in the system, and though they were relatively disinterested, their observations assimilated some of the partisan views of either planters or colonists. The system of sharecropping did not fail because of the planters' cupidity or because of corruption in the companies that recruited immigrants or even because of the poor character and inexperience of the immigrants themselves. The reasons for the failure lay much deeper, in the contradictory dynamics of the sharecropping system as it functioned in the coffee areas during this period. The landowners' original intention had been to create an effective substitute for slave labor on the coffee plantations. The solution they chose intended to reconcile the interests of the planters, accustomed to slave labor, with those of the colonists, who were eager to acquire property, improve their living conditions, and rise in the social scale. The result did not please either group. The planters felt they had been swindled. The colonists believed that they had been reduced to the condition of slaves. Thus they rebelled.

In fact, their interests were contradictory. The colonists refused to plant coffee trees; the clearing of forest, the preparation of land, and the long waiting period that precedes the trees' productive stage (usually four to six years for a good output) were too tiring and unprofitable. One proposed solution—planting cereal crops between the rows of coffee trees while they were still small—did not generate sufficient profit for most of the colonists. This could be a practical project only when the plantation was near an urban center where the sharecroppers could sell their surplus and when the planter was willing to forego his share of the crop. But rare was the planter who, like Joaquim do Amaral, would try to compensate the colonists to whom he assigned young, unproductive coffee trees by ignoring the contractual clause that required them to share half of any profits earned by the sale of foodstuffs.[31] Most often, the colonist found himself impeded in his attempts to cultivate even basic crops, since the landowners believed that this would result in a diversion of energy away from the coffee trees. They also feared that it would contribute to the colonist's premature emancipation. Once his debts were paid, the sharecropper would abandon the plantation in search of a better position, and the planter's problem of finding labor would begin all over again.

Another way to interest the sharecroppers in growing new trees would have been to grant them simultaneously an area that was producing at an optimum level. The planter's interests, however, dictated the exact opposite. It was most profitable to assign the least productive areas to the colonists, with whom he had to share the profits, and to reserve the best coffee trees for the slaves. Very few planters followed the lead of Queiroz Telles, who gave his colonists the most productive trees and his slaves the least productive.[32] The conflict of interest between planters and colonists made it impossible to reach any reasonable agreement.

Another factor that contributed to the increase in tension between colonists and landowners was the complicated system of accounts used to determine the colonists' share of the profits on coffee produced. The calculations used to ascertain the amount of profit were complex, involving deductions for processing, transport, taxes, and commissions. The colonists were unable to keep track of all these deductions and felt they had been cheated. They had come in search of a miraculous fortune and instead, after a long wait for the end of the harvest, received a pittance. Their first reaction was bewilderment, but bewilderment eventually gave way to rebellion.

Also contributing to this tense situation was the instability of the coffee harvest, whose wild fluctuations from one year to the next generated widespread insecurity. Von Tschudi mentions a thirteen-year-old tract of coffee trees that produced four and a half pounds of beans per tree one year and half a pound per tree the next. His testimony is confirmed by Davatz, who cites the case of one family that picked 1,450 *alqueires* one year, but in the following year was unable to harvest more than 170 *alqueires* from the very same tract.

Many other problems contributed to the colonists' disillusionment. Their lack of familiarity with the rural environment, the climate, and the local customs and the clause of the contract which made a family collectively responsible for the debts of a single member, a clause that was particularly annoying because of the artificial character of those "families," to which the Swiss authorities often attached unknown and undesirable individuals—all this contributed to the colonists' discontent and, ultimately, to the failure of the entire system. Disillusioned, the colonists abandoned the plantations as soon as possible. Some did not wait until they had met their financial obligations, but fled.

By 1855, there were seven hundred sharecroppers in Vergueiro's colony. Ten families had left to settle in Rio Claro, where they were able to buy land. Some headed for Campinas, where they set up small businesses. Still others went to Piracicaba and Moji-Mirim, hoping to buy land. A few, probably disappointed in their attempt to make a go of it on their own, joined agricultural colonies. This pattern repeated itself on every plantation, although at a slow rate, given the difficulties the colonist encountered in freeing himself from debt. One can assume that those who achieved this goal most rapidly did so because they had some savings when they arrived or because almost all the members of the family could work full time or because they had been located on plantations that offered exceptionally good conditions.[33]

The colonists' desire to get away from the colony as soon as possible gave this work force a mobile and unstable character to which the planters were not accustomed. They were particularly vulnerable to this instability because of the scarcity of labor. It was also difficult for the landowners to adjust to the exigencies of free labor. Over the years, slavery had produced attitudes and expectations that were inadequate to deal with free labor. "An elderly landowner who had prided himself since his childhood on whipping and chastising his slaves could hardly tolerate free labor and could at best develop a crippled sharecropping system," as Avé-Lallemant, a traveler in Brazil at the time, remarked. Equally important in explaining the failure of the system was the sharecroppers' resistance.

All these problems undeniably contributed to the collapse of share-cropping. Nevertheless, the fundamental cause of the failure of the sharecropping system resided in the structure of coffee production prevalent at the time. Coffee-growing required a large and permanent work force. The first few years of a new plantation were devoted to clearing and cultivating the land—tasks that could be both expensive and exhausting in the more heavily forested areas. The smaller plants would first be eliminated, and the undergrowth reduced with scythes and axes. Then came the hazardous task of burning and clearing the land. After the coffee trees were planted, it was necessary to watch the seedlings carefully since, once they had attained a certain height, they had to be cut off about a foot above the roots and transplanted. During the next phase, the soil had to be assiduously hoed to keep the trees safe from harmful weeds. This hoeing took place two, three, four, or even more times a year. The Baron Patí do Alferes recommended in his guide for plantation owners three annual hoeings,[34] while Souza Queiroz, in an 1852 contract written up in Hamburg, demanded that each colonist hoe the coffee rows at least five times a year, "if not more."[35] Sometimes the coffee trees would begin to bear fruit at the age of four, but the period of heaviest production usually came only after the sixth year. The period of optimum output, a long time in coming, was of short duration; most coffee trees would decline in productivity after fifteen or twenty years. Coffee trees over twenty years of age produced beans at half their previous rate. Moreover, the length of the peak period and the health of the coffee trees depended on the fertility of the soil.

Once the trees began to produce, the work increased. Harvesting had to be done manually and required great care and patience, particularly in regions where the coffee ripened irregularly and the worker had to select among green and ripe beans on the same tree. Once the coffee was harvested, it was sent to the local processing center. At this point, a whole new round of tasks began—drying, hulling, sorting—all of which required much effort. The time-consuming harvest, the tasks performed on the *terreiros* where the coffee beans dried, the hulling and packing of the product and, finally, its transportation to the ports demanded, at least until the 1850s, a huge and versatile labor force.

The scarcity of machinery made it impossible to economize on labor. When Von Tschudi toured São Paulo in the 1860s, he observed that hulling machines were beginning to appear in the western part of the province, but only the most important estates were able to afford them. In the Vassouras area of the Paraiba Valley, the most advanced machine used at the time was a heavy crushing mill (*engenho de pilões*), which removed the shell and hull of the beans.[36] Many plantations continued to operate solely with traditional methods. In these cases, the slaves would thrash the coffee beans with sticks or pound them in mortars. Occasionally, a *monjolo* (water mill) might be used.[37]

Transporting the product also required a large number of workers. Prior to the construction of railroads, planters relied on mule- and ox-carts, an extremely labor-intensive means of transportation, since the animals required constant care and had to be supervised and guided on long trips. Before mid-century, coffee plantations had to devote part of their labor force to the cultivation of subsistence crops—maize, rice, squash, yams, beans, sweet potatoes, and manioc. Pigs and fowls were also raised for consumption on the estate. Some workers had to be employed in maintaining roads, repairing bridges, and mending fences. Given all these activities, the work routine of the average coffee plantation would be incessant, lasting the entire year and requiring a large labor force capable of handling highly diverse assignments.

The inefficient methods of production and transport resulted in high production costs, which left only a small margin of profit, particularly when coffee prices were low. To guarantee the profitability of the

FIG. 5. The immigrant's dream, published in the *Revista Illustrada* in 1876

FIG. 6. Traveling in an oxcart

enterprise required a high degree of labor exploitation, which at the time was more compatible with slave labor than with free labor.

Conditions began to change after 1850—after the abolition of the slave trade—with the progressive utilization of machinery, the improvement of highways, and the construction of railroads, all of which cut labor needs and increased productivity. By 1883, Delden Laërne, who visited the Paulista coffee estates, wrote that on many of the plantations he visited the coffee beans were pounded, hulled, sorted, polished, sacked, and weighed mechanically, freeing a large number of hands for other tasks.[38]

With this rationalization of the work routine and higher degree of specialization, the labor problem took a different form. The changes in the level of productivity modified the relations of production, favoring free labor. This tendency was further encouraged by the rise in coffee prices on the international market. Thus, in the last decades of the nineteenth century, the coffee planter could afford to be a great deal more flexible about the type of labor he used.

As we have seen, however, only the vague outlines of these developments had appeared at the time of the first sharecropping experiment, and the costs of production remained high. Under such conditions, the sharecropping system was impractical, satisfying neither the colonists nor the planters.

In 1854, when Silveira da Mota discussed in the Paulista legislature the various hardships plaguing agriculture, among which he included the high cost of transportation and the onerous interest rates on loans, he was suddenly interrupted by José Fonseca, who exclaimed: "Our agriculture is going to disappear. The colonists take half the profits, the other half goes for transportation, and what is left for the poor Paulista?"[39] He was exaggerating—so much so that his remark provoked general hilarity among the deputies. But his outburst reflects a

FIG. 7. Grinding coffee

point of view that others expressed more moderately. Hércules Florence, who created a model sharecropping colony, said that the main
adversary of the sharecropping system in his region was the lack of a
highway linking Campinas and Santos. Florence believed that as long
as transport costs absorbed half of the coffee-growers' profits, colonists
and landowners alike would be dissatisfied and colonization would be
a failure. After deducting expenses for transportation, processing,
taxes, and commissions, only a small margin of profit was retained by
the heavily indebted sharecropper.[40]

When coffee sold at 4,400 *reis* (4$400) per *arroba*, the average ex-
penses amounted to 1,602 *reis*, distributed thus:

Cost of transporting one *arroba*	1$040 *reis*
Processing costs	$400 *reis*
Taxes	$030 *reis*
3 percent commission	$132 *reis*
Total	
	1$602 *reis*

Therefore, the net profit amounted to 2,798 *reis* per *arroba* (not
counting investment in labor, land, etc.). Converting one *arroba* into
three *alqueires*, as the colonists' contracts stipulated, the profit would
come to 932 *reis* per *alqueire*. Of this, 466 *reis* per *alqueire*, or 1,399
reis per *arroba*, would go to the colonist.[41] The majority of the colonists had an average of 1,500 to 2,000 coffee trees assigned to them,
which could produce, in a particularly good year, about 150 *arrobas*,
210$000 a year. This sum could do nothing but make the average
colonist's situation precarious at best. This quantitative evidence, which
reveals the uncertain situation of the colonists is confirmed by the material supplied by planters' testimony and government investigations.

The position of a colonist with a large family was particularly ten-
uous, for additional members did not always signify greater labor potential. A large number of young children, an average of three or four
under ten years of age, emigrated with their parents to Brazil. Only a
family with several grown children could take charge of more than
3,000 coffee trees. Many took care of less than half that number. The
only exception to be found—which is flagrantly at odds with the average—was Hércules Florence's "model" colony where two families,
nineteen individuals altogether, tended some 14,000 coffee trees, or
about 800 trees per person, including adults and children.

The experience of the average colonist, on the other hand, easily explains the difficulty he encountered in repaying his debts, which often
amounted to more than one *conto* (1:000$000). A good illustration

of this situation would be the dispute that took place between Luciano Teixeira Nogueira, a planter, and the colonists Gilberto Collet and others. Writing to the provincial president on this matter, the municipal judge noted that Collet had 1,500 trees under his care and seven persons in his family. At this time, Collet owed the landowner nearly two *contos* (2:000$000); part of it (1:454$683) was subject to an interest rate of 12 percent, the remainder to a rate of 6 percent. The portion subject to the higher rate reflected the costs of passage, while the remaining debts were contracted in the course of Collet's first year in Brazil. The municipal judge mentioned that the colonist's income from the previous year was probably less than 120$000, and the current year would not bring much more since a poor harvest was expected. Under the best conditions, the colonist would earn about 200$000, and the interest on his debts alone would cost him more than that. "How is the colonist supposed to purchase food, clothing, and medicine for his family and still meet the interest payments on his debts?" asked the judge. The situation of another colonist, while less serious, was also discouraging. He arrived on the plantation with his wife and son, owing about 600$000. After a year of work, his debts had risen to more than one *conto* (1:000$000). Given the low rate of profit, how could he possibly hope to repay his debts and the interest? The judge concluded by pointing out that the situation of many other sharecroppers was more or less the same and that he had in fact been overly optimistic in his evaluations. If one took both good and bad years into account, the sharecroppers' income would not be even half of what he had calculated.[42]

Numerous plantation records describe conditions in the colonies, giving information on the number of persons in each family, their age, the number of trees in their charge, their output production, and their income. Using these data, one can corroborate many sharecroppers' claims. From the report on Senator Souza Queiroz's colony, for example, we can extract some telling statistics:[43]

Family 1   6 persons, 2,000 trees, output: 500 *alqueires* of coffee, plus 300 *alqueires* of maize

Family 2   4 persons, 2,500 trees, 450 *alqueires* of coffee, 300 of maize, 20 of rice, 6 of beans

Family 3   7 persons (ages 50, 41, 17, 11, 10, 10, 5), 3,500 trees, 790 *alqueires* of coffee, 300 of maize, 25 of rice, 8 of beans

Family 4   6 persons (13 years or older), 3,000 trees, 415 *alqueires* of coffee, 300 of maize, 25 of rice, 8 of beans

Family 5   6 persons (ages 58, 51, 22, 19, 14, 13), 2,000 trees, 630 *alqueires* of coffee, 300 of maize, 20 of rice, 5 of beans

Family 6   6 persons (ages 48, 43, 13, 7, 5, 3), 3,000 trees, 480
              alqueires of coffee
Family 7   7 persons (ages 35, 45, 20, 18, 14, 7, 5), 3,000 trees,
              830 *alqueires* of coffee
Family 8   7 persons (ages 43, 44, 15, 14, 12, 6, 4), 3,500 trees,
              800 *alqueires* of coffee
Family 9   3 persons (ages 40, 35, 2), 1,500 trees, 235 *alqueires* of
              coffee
Family 10   6 persons (ages 63, 44, 14, 5, 2, and 4 months), 1,800
              trees, 415 *alqueires* of coffee
Family 11   5 persons (ages 56, 40, 14, 12, and 9) 3,000 trees, 300
              alqueires of coffee

. . . .

Family 24   6 persons (ages 56, 32, 10, 8, 6, 2), 1,800 trees, 390
              alqueires of coffee, 100 of maize, 10 of rice, 4 of beans
Family 25   6 persons (ages 38, 32, 10, 6, 4, 1), 1,000 trees, 220
              alqueires of coffee

. . . .

Family 57   6 persons (48, 28, 13, 11, 9, 7), 3,000 trees, 200 *al-
              queires* of coffee, 150 of maize, 10 of rice, 4 of beans

This list clearly demonstrates the difficult situation facing the majority of the colonists and the large number of dependents that each
family head had under his care. Most families tended between one and
three thousand coffee trees, and only a few with several older children
were able to take charge of a larger number. In any case, the output,
and thus the income, was insufficient. Those who produced an average
of 500 *alqueires*, which was the norm, would earn 233$000 per year
when coffee was selling at 4$400 per *arroba*. With debts often surpass-
ing one *conto* (1:000$000) plus annual interest charges, the colonist
would obviously have great difficulty in freeing himself from his debt.
Sharecropping became a sort of indentured servitude.

Statistics for Senator Vergueiro's colony show that in 1853 there
were 53 families owing a total of 16:765$145. In that year they deliv-
ered 18,186 *alqueires* of coffee, from which they earned a little more
than 8:000$000, (an average of 160$000 per family)—hardly enough
to allow them to make any headway on their debts, since they also had
to support themselves. And the situation was the same throughout the
province. Vieira de Macedo, reporting from Ubatuba in 1857, estimated that one of the families on his plantation owed 1:800$000.[44]

In 1865, G. H. Krug, the Swiss vice-consul, wrote to the president
of São Paulo to describe the state of decline in which he had found the
Ibicaba colony. Many of the colonists had fled, while others, lacking

any means of subsistence, lived in a state of misery, hunger, and near nakedness. They suffered corporal punishment at the hands of the overseer, who would have them arrested without bail, and who even went so far as to "put them in stocks and lock them away." He reported that colonists were unable to hire lawyers to defend them since the lawyers demanded an advance payment of 200$000—an amount no colonist could afford.[45] Another traveler, Expilly, calculated that a colonist would need at least ten years to free himself from the debts he owed, while Davatz, a leader of the Ibicaba revolt, who wrote a memoir about his life as a colonist, maintained that a colonist who owed 2:000$000 (two *contos*), which was the norm, was like a slave who needed that sum to purchase his manumission.

The various reverses and failures resulting from the sharecropping system temporarily undermined the immigration policy. The colonists' complaints reached European ears and dissolved the dreams of potential emigrants. And the inquiries had negative repercussions among foreign governments. As a consequence, a number of European nations either placed serious restrictions on or completely prohibited immigration to Brazil. Meanwhile the Paulista planters allowed the sharecropping contracts to expire without making any effort to renew them. Only rarely did anyone speak in favor of maintaining the system. Sharecropping, which in theory had seemed to be the ideal solution for the labor problem in the coffee region, had failed in practice and was discredited both at home and abroad.

In 1858, when the minister of empire, Teixeira de Macedo, issued a government decree guaranteeing the transportation costs of future colonists, almost all the planters who took advantage of this new provision used it to import immigrants from Portugal rather than from Switzerland or Germany. The Portuguese seem to have been the only people who adjusted to the routine the landowners imposed on their workers. They lived like slaves, plodding right alongside them, from sunup to sundown, following the overseer's orders. But even the Portuguese sharecropping experiments were not very successful.[46]

By 1860, there were still some 29 sharecropper colonies in São Paulo. By 1870, there were only 13.[47] And a report from the inspector general for lands and colonization dated 1877 observed that because of the judicial disputes generated by sharecropping contracts in the past, "they have now all but disappeared." In fact, planters had moved to new types of contracts.[48] In 1863, Manuel de Araujo Porto Alegre wrote that there were still some sharecropping contracts in force, but that the planters wanted nothing more to do with them.[49] An excellent example was João Elisário Monte Negro, one of the planters most ded-

icated to replacing slaves with free labor and an insistent advocate of
colonization with Portuguese immigrants. Despite his commitment he
declared, in 1868, that experience had demonstrated that the sharecropping system produced only discontent, complaints, revolts, protests from foreign consulates, bitter disputes, and denunciations in the
press. Contracts limited to specific tasks, in his opinion, would give
better results and might, in the course of time, prove to be a satisfac-
tory solution. But until these could be developed it seemed to him that
a wage labor system would be the most feasible alternative.[50]

Since it was to the landowner's advantage to reduce all labor expenses to a minimum, the planters came to prefer a system of compensation to sharing half the profits with their work force. Thus the majority of planters who retained colonists on their estates abandoned
the old sharecropping contracts, replacing them with either piecework or a wage system. In some cases, a fixed price was paid for each
alqueire of coffee picked; in others, a standard monthly payment was
established. Of these two alternatives, the first was preferred, with
most planters paying 400 *reis* ($400) per *alqueire*. Some landowners
also granted their workers some land on which to grow subsistence
crops, while other planters supplied provisions instead of land. In exchange, the colonist was obliged to render any service needed on the
plantation.[51]

By 1857, there were two different systems in operation on the Pal-
meiras plantation in Campinas, sharecropping and piecework, with
the latter paying 480 *reis* ($480) for each *alqueire* hoed, cultivated,
and harvested. The first type of contract applied exclusively to the
Swiss colonists; the second applied to the Portuguese. On the Pacheco
Chaves estate, Brazilians and Germans who had arrived after the ex-
piration of the sharecropping contracts began tending coffee trees either for a fixed price per task or on a fixed amount per year. By 1863,
the colonists on Lourenço Franco's estate in Limeira were receiving
400 *reis* ($400) per *alqueire* of coffee harvested and were obliged to
tend a certain number of trees.[52]

For the colonists, a payment of 400 *reis* ($400) per *alqueire* during
this period came to slightly less than they would have normally earned
under a sharecropping arrangement. According to the calculations
above, as sharecroppers they would have received $466 (466 *reis*)
when the price per *arroba* was 4$400. Thus, there was a difference of
66 *reis* on each *alqueire* in the landowner's favor. In 1887, the baron of
Parnaiba, in a report presented to the legislature comparing the new
system with the traditional sharecropping system, asserted that the latter was much more beneficial for the colonist than for the landowner.

But, in spite of this, the new system functioned better than the old since, up to a certain point, it protected the colonists from price fluctuations on the international market and made it possible to pay them before the coffee had been sold. Thus both the benefits and losses of speculation accrued to the landowners.

Wages paid to the colonists in the early years were extremely low—an essential condition for keeping an estate profitable. For example, at Nova Lousa, Monte Negro's colony, there were in 1875 over 90 Portuguese-born laborers who received 14$000 per month during the first year, and 18$000 per month from then on. They also received a house, communal meals, and medical treatment and had their clothing washed and mended. Evaluating the advantages of this system in comparison to sharecropping, Monte Negro said that the immigrant who entered into a wage labor agreement knew in advance how much he was going to earn and could not complain that he was deceived with

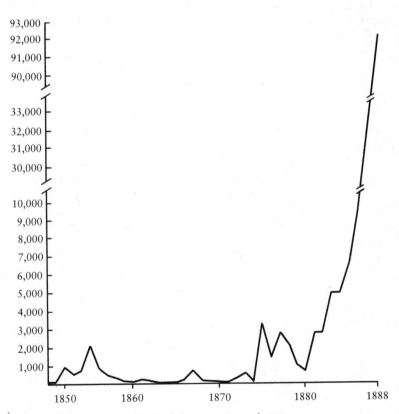

FIG. 8. Immigrants entering São Paulo between 1855 and 1888

false promises. It seemed to him that this system was more convenient for the planter. He remarked, however, that not many planters could afford the 18$000 per month.

Indeed, most of the coffee growers were neither inclined nor able to pay high wages. Low wages were not wholly a product of the landowner's greed, nor were they wholly the result of the small profit earned at a time when coffee prices were low and backward methods of production limited productivity. The persistence of slavery itself contributed to the debasement of wage labor. Low wages excluded those immigrants whose traditional standard of living was higher than such wages would permit. The possibility of transforming sharecroppers into wage laborers was small, especially when the colonists were Swiss and German. Only the Portuguese immigrants, accustomed to a lower standard of living, would accept such an arrangement at that time.

The failure of the sharecropping system reinforced the convictions of those who believed that slave labor was more appropriate to the plantations than free labor. Coffee planters bought the slaves they needed in areas of the country where the economy was in decline. It was only later, in the 1880s, when the abolition of slavery was imminent, that they again became interested in using immigrants and found in Italy the labor they needed. Between 1872 and 1885, 42,000 immigrants, predominantly Italian and Portuguese, entered São Paulo. In the two following years the province received 122,000. And in the decade that followed the abolition of slavery, more than 800,000 immigrants were brought to the area to replace slaves on the plantations.[53] Improvements in the means of production and transportation had made it more feasible and sometimes more convenient for the planter to use immigrants. Besides, after 1888 the abolition of slavery had left the planters with no alternative. Though the sharecropping system was never reestablished in its primitive form, the project of replacing slaves with immigrants, which had failed in the 1850s, would be a success by the turn of the century.[54]

6 MASTERS AND SLAVES
From Slave Labor to Free Labor

From the sixteenth to the nineteenth century the enslavement of Africans was the European solution to the problem of labor in the colonies of the New World where Indian labor proved unreliable. On the cotton plantations of the American South, in the sugar mills of the Antilles and Brazil, slaves constituted the principal labor force. Slavery was accepted as a legitimate institution and slave labor considered the ideal type of labor.

At the beginning of the nineteenth century, however, when the traditional colonial system collapsed and new techniques of control and exploitation replaced the old relationships between Europe and the New World, slavery came into question. In the European countries most affected by capital accumulation and economic growth, new groups tied to industrial capital began to condemn slavery. To some, the existence of millions of slaves in colonial areas seemed to contradict their fundamental liberal ideas—a moral outrage. To others, it seemed an obstacle to the expansion of markets for manufactured products. From this point on slavery, as a system, was doomed.

But slavery did not simply disappear overnight. The independence of the colonies in North and South America did not mean an abrupt change in prevailing economic structures. In many areas slavery survived as the preferred form of labor. In fact, with the disappearance of the old commercial monopolies that had tied the colonies to the mother countries and with the increasing demand for tropical products in European markets, plantation economies boomed and the slave trade increased.

The transition from slavery to free labor was a long and difficult process which varied from region to region according to local economic, social, political, and ideological conditions. In some parts of America, abolition was carried out peacefully by the parliaments. In others, it could only be won on the battlefield.

Though Brazil gained political autonomy in 1822, her traditional economic structure continued essentially unchanged. Some of the leaders of independence made conscious, if rather timid, attempts to pro-

mote national industries. But their projects died at birth. After independence, Brazilian markets were flooded with European manufactured
goods, especially British, favored by commercial treaties. In the Parliament, representatives of landowners and of merchants linked to the export economy stressed Brazil's agrarian vocation. They defended the
principles of free trade and opposed measures that would have protected industry. A classic statement of the liberal position was made by
Bernardo Pereira de Vasconcelos, one of the most eminent political figures of the First Empire and the regency. He said, "Government has no
authority to interfere actively and directly in the affairs of industry,
which needs no other guidance than that of private interest." In his
Letter to the Gentlemen Electors of the Province of Minas Gerais,
Vasconcelos opposed government aid to industries and argued that
Brazil should export what she could produce best—sugar, cotton, tobacco, cacao—and should receive in return the manufactured products she could not produce competitively. These ideas were to become
fundamental doctrines of the empire.

Controlled by representatives of the agrarian and mercantile groups,
Brazil remained bound to the traditional types of land use. All the features of colonial agriculture survived: an economy oriented toward the
international market, latifundia, slave labor, and backward systems of
production. Thus, although the country had become politically independent and new perspectives were opened to trade, traditional
economic and social structures remained fundamentally unchanged.
Slaves were everywhere: in the cane fields, at the sugar mills, in the
cotton fields, on cacao plantations, in the meat jerking plants of the
South, and on the new coffee estates opening in the Paraíba Valley. In
the countryside and in the city they continued to be the principal instruments of labor.

Meanwhile, the country was organized in the most fashionable political modes. In Parliament politicians recited the liberal credo and
debated the most modern theories of representative forms of government. The Constitution of 1824 included the formulas consecrated in
the Declaration of the Rights of Man. Individual liberties were assured. Privileges were abolished and all were made equal before the
law. Slavery was not mentioned in the text of the constitution, but, by
considering property an inalienable right, the constitution kept more
than a million people enslaved.

The contradiction between liberalism and slavery did not worry
most politicians. Few during those years denounced the evils of the
slave system or urged the abolition of the slave trade. And they were
mostly men who had been educated in Europe, who were well ac-

quainted with liberal thought and with the doctrines of the classical economists, and who condemned slavery from this perspective. Such was the case of Hipólito da Costa, a Brazilian living in London who stated in 1811 in the *Correio Braziliense* that slavery was contrary both to the laws of nature and to the moral inclinations of man.[1] Maciel da Costa in 1821, José Bonifácio in 1823, José Eloy Pessoa da Silva in 1826, and Burlamaque some years later also denounced the system as immoral and inefficient.[2] They argued that slave labor brought lower returns than free labor, retarded the process of industrialization, and cheapened the idea of work itself. Slavery, they argued, threatened national security, divided society into hostile groups, generated a regime of violence, degraded social customs, corrupted the family, and was responsible for the "bastardization" of the Portuguese race, a remark that reveals their racist bias. They also emphasized the ethical nature of the question, insisting that slavery violated natural law, the rules of morality, and the teachings of Christianity.

Neither the pessimistic picture they presented nor the eloquence with which they denounced the evils of slavery made much of an impression on the country as a whole. The slaveholding classes remained deaf to such arguments. Proposals for ending the slave trade and for gradual emancipation were systematically rejected. Not even the most advanced thinkers dared propose a drastic solution to the problem. Abolition, everyone agreed, would bring social chaos. Even José Bonifácio—who had gone as far as to say that the slaveholders were defending the right of force rather than the right of property—feared the consequences of immediate abolition. Instead, he proposed ending the trade within four or five years and suggested interim measures for protecting the slaves. But, as we have seen, despite their moderation, his plans did not win adherents during this period.

The best writings from these years are quite objective in analyzing the effects of slavery on society and the economy. Some even point out the ties between the colonial system and slavery. The most progressive propose freeing the newborn and establishing a definite schedule for emancipation. Yet all the authors of these proposals considered premature any radical measure that had not been previously prepared for by the replacement of slaves with free workers, and they all included provisions for compensating the slaveholders.

The arguments of these early writers foreshadow the reasoning of theorists and politicians who in the years to come closed ranks on behalf of abolition. From this point on, nothing essentially new was said about the evils of the slaveholding system or the incompatibility of Christian morality and slavery. The note of commiseration with the slaves intensified with the passage of time and the gradual measures suggested by emancipationists at the beginning of the century gave way to more drastic solutions urged by radical abolitionists. But the basic arguments against slavery did not change. What did change was the setting, the country as a whole. As a result of this change, words that before had little effect began to electrify audiences, mobilize the press, stir up crowds, and provoke heated parliamentary debates. After 1870, the slavery debate became one of the most impassioned of the Second Empire.

Those who wrote against slavery in the first half of the century had sought to demonstrate its drawbacks to the nation. As good children of the Enlightenment they had placed their confidence on the efficacy of knowledge and reason. They believed that they could obtain the abolition of slavery merely by informing public opinion. But they were mistaken. Socioeconomic realities at the time of independence nullified their efforts. Slavery continued for another fifty years and would be abolished only in 1888.

Shortly after independence there were 2,813,351 free inhabitants of Brazil and 1,147,515 slaves. The slaves were concentrated in the traditional sugar-growing areas of the Northeast and Bahía, the old gold-mining areas of Minas, and in Rio de Janeiro.[3] By that time the coffee plantations, then opening in the Paraiba Valley, were beginning to acquire substantial numbers of slaves. Brazil possessed vast areas of uninhabited land and her population was small and unevenly distributed. In order to mobilize the necessary labor force to bring land under cultivation, the coffee planters had to resort to African slaves. Ideologies and values expressed this reality. As in the colonial period, owning land and owning slaves were among the highest aspirations of the age. Land and slaves were signs of wealth and conferred social prestige. And most people still believe that slave labor was the only form of labor compatible with large-scale agriculture.[4]

Free labor, however, never disappeared completely. It had been associated with the plantations since the colonial period as a supplementary form of labor. To free laborers were given the most dangerous tasks—or those jobs at which slaves had proven to be inefficient. Clearing forests, accompanying mule trains, and supervising slaves were often freeman tasks.

Free workers formed part of the master's network of dependents and clients. They followed their master in his political battles and made up his private militia. On the sugar plantations sharecroppers often had a few slaves of their own and some livestock, but they did not own their own land. They grew cane in the plots assigned to them by the plantation owners, with whom they shared a percentage of the sugar produced. Sharecroppers usually cultivated the land without contractual guarantees and could be driven off at any time. This lack of guarantee of land use explains the precariousness of their living arrangements. They constructed provisional huts and fences and were always prepared to lose any improvements they had made. Tenants were in even worse conditions. Holding no land and living on whatever was assigned to them by the landowner, they were completely dependent on his benevolence and lived under his "paternalistic" protection. Tenants usually produced only enough for their own survival, occasionally providing additional labor for the plantation. On the coffee plantations the situation of the free workers was no better. Tenants were subject to the arbitrary whims of the owners and their living conditions were not different from those of the slaves. Sharecropper arrangements were exceptional in the coffee areas, where most of the work was done by slaves.[5]

Until mid-century, in the rural areas the slaves continued to be "the hands and feet of the master." Even in the cities slaves performed most of the crafts and household work. Some masters lived from the rental of their slaves, while others maintained large numbers working for fees. City slaves were involved in a great variety of activities. There were slave shoemakers, carpenters, tinsmiths, tailors, potters, street vendors, carriers, and masons. They went out in the morning to their work and returned in the evening to turn over their earnings to the master.[6]

Since slave labor predominated in both the countryside and the cities, slave trade continued despite international pressures to halt it. But while slavery continued to prevail in Brazil, it was being internationally proscribed. In Britain, the antislavery movement had gained momentum in the early nineteenth century and the slave trade to British colonies had been abolished in 1807. From this point on, the British government opposed slave trade. When the Portuguese court moved to Brazil in 1808, João VI had promised the British government that he would cooperate in the campaign against the trade and restrict the trading activities of his subjects to the African territories under his rule. After the Congress of Vienna (1814) had decided to end the slave trade north of the equator, Portuguese traders had been deprived of some of their traditional sources of supply, but they had continued to trade in other parts of Africa. And despite its pledges to terminate the trade at the earliest possible moment, the Portuguese government had taken no concrete action in that direction. After independence, the Brazilian government, needing British support, had endorsed the agree-

FIG. 9. Slaves departing to the fields

ments previously signed between Britain and Portugal and promised to prohibit the slave trade. In accord with these agreements, the government had issued a law in 1831 freeing all slaves arriving from outside the empire and imposing severe penalties on slave smugglers.[7]

The law, however, had proved ineffective. The government, in which the agrarian interests and the slave traders were well represented, had no real desire to displace them. Besides, the imperial authorities were powerless against the oligarchies who held political and administrative power in the provinces. The courts, controlled by the oligarchies, posed little threat to their interests. Those who administered the law were generally tied by family, friendship, or convenience to the dominant local groups, and even when this was not the case, judges and attorneys lacked sufficient independence to implement the law. Their jobs were jeopardized when they attempted to incriminate leading figures in the local society—men of social and political influence. Frequently, a single important family dominated a whole region. These families, large in themselves, could enlist support from a vast network of allies and clients. On the rare occasions when some local potentate was indicted in a trial for slave smuggling, no one dared to testify against him. And despite all the evidence presented by the prosecutor, the smuggler would inevitably be absolved by the jury. Thus the zeal of a few officials came up against the stout opposition of the slaveowners. The agents of the imperial government occasionally sent to investigate

reports of illegal slave trading saw their efforts frustrated, while slave
smuggling continued, protected by the connivance of the population.[8]

The development of coffee plantations in the decades that followed
independence could only stimulate the demand for labor. During those
earlier years Parliament was flooded with petitions calling for the re-
peal of the 1831 law. But although completely ineffective, the law was
kept. Neither British cruisers nor the Brazilian authorities managed to
put a stop to the action of the smugglers. The blacks they brought in,
though legally free after 1831, were still sold as slaves. Plantation owners and slave traders simply defied the law, resisted British pressures,
and disregarded Brazilian authorities. The slave trade continued after
1831 at an increasing rate. Between 1840 and 1850 an average of
30,000 to 40,000 blacks were smuggled into Brazil each year, under
the complaisant eyes of the Brazilian authorities.[9]

The British attempts to suppress contraband angered the Brazilians,
even more so because British subjects living in Brazil did not hesitate
to own slaves. This caused doubts about British philanthropy and
strengthened longstanding animosity toward Britain. In fact, since
1810 exceptional treaty provisions had favored English products.
Those provisions had been renewed in 1826. British products and
merchants had invaded the Brazilian market. These facts gave rise
to xenophobic sentiment, which surfaced in the various revolts that
troubled Brazil during this period. Brazilian hostility toward Britain
was ably exploited by those interested in maintaining the slave trade.
Craftily, they argued that to give in to British pressure would be to bow
before oppression. The question thus turned into one of national
honor. Tensions increased in 1842 when the Brazilian government approved a new tariff law increasing taxes on British products. It reached
its peak in 1845 after the British Parliament, apparently in retaliation,
voted a bill known in Brazil as the Aberdeen Bill, which not only authorized the seizure of any ship involved in the slave trade but stipulated that violators be considered pirates and tried in Admiralty courts.

From then on, British cruisers repeatedly violated Brazilian waters
in search of suspect ships. Such incursions, seen as attacks on national
sovereignty, created an uproar in the Brazilian Parliament and stirred
up the entire nation. The slave trade continued even more intensely
than before. From 1845 onward, more than 50,000 slaves a year were
smuggled into the country. It was in this climate of international tension and internal unrest that the Parliament began to reconsider earlier
proposals aimed at the suppression of the trade.

Brazilian public opinion was divided. Planters well supplied with
slaves or in debt from their purchases of slaves viewed the possible end-

ing of the trade rather calmly. They saw that such a measure might well raise the value of their property. Opposed to the abolition of the slave trade were the slave traders themselves and the planters in the frontier areas who could not yet count on a sufficient number of workers to cultivate their plantations. The question passed into the realm of partisan maneuvering as politicians realized its political importance. Finally, severe measures were taken against the slave smugglers in a law of 4 September 1850.[10] The authorities reinforced their vigilance and foreign slavers were expelled from the country. Contraband continued on a small scale for a few more years and finally ended once and for all.[11]

The ending of the trade doomed slavery because of the high rate of mortality among slaves. After the abolition of the trade planters recognized the need to improve the living conditions of the slaves and at the same time to consider other solutions for the problem of the labor force.

Before the suppression of the slave trade, the lives of slaves in rural areas had been quite precarious.[12] Their work day was long, often reaching sixteen or eighteen hours, including additional night work. They lived in wattle and daub huts thatched with palm leaves or *sapé* grass—generally windowless or equipped with barred windows. The slaves slept on mats spread over wooden platforms two and a half or three feet wide. They received at most two or three changes of clothing a year. Men wore pants and shirts of coarse cotton with a *surtum*—a sort of sleeveless jacket of rough cloth lined with baize. On the majority of plantations these clothes were replaced only once a year and slaves went around in rags. Municipal ordinances aimed at preventing their being seen dirty or half-naked in the streets of the towns imposed fees on careless slaveholders but they seem not to have had great success since they constantly had to be renewed. In any case, such measures did not extend to the plantations where the will of the master was law.

The slave diet did not vary: beans, gruel, manioc flour, from time to time a piece of jerked beef or salt pork, more rarely yams, cassava, pumpkins, or sweet potatoes. In the sugar-growing areas, molasses and white rum accompanied meals, and in the coffee regions, coffee. On the poorer plantations the diet was reduced to beans and a little manioc flour. Slaves often suffered from parasites, fevers, tuberculosis, and syphillis; they also were subject to the epidemics of smallpox, cholera, and yellow fever that periodically swept the country.

Medical treatment on the plantations was inadequate. Planters used medical manuals and also resorted to folk healers and curers who used

FIG. 10. Master's house and slave's quarters (*senzalas*)

magic and sorcery along with remedies made of herbs. With these they sought to cure everything from venereal diseases to snakebites. Both blacks and whites, slaves and masters commonly believed that saints provided protection against certain illnesses, and they invoked Santa Luzia, protectress of the eyes, Santa Ágata for the diseases of the chest, Santa Apolonia for toothaches, São Lázaro for leprosy, and São Tomé for worms. Medical science itself was not far removed, in the country-side, from the primitiveness of the folk healers. This was the age of miraculous remedies: of Leroy's Purgative to treat pneumonia, dysentery, dropsy, and poisoning. It was the time of purges and bleeding, of home remedies, of balsam and absinthe teas, of orange and elderberry blossoms, of guava and nettle leaves.

The religious hospitals, or *santas casas*, performed a substantial service for the planters, taking in their ill and disabled slaves. Still, old and invalid blacks, abandoned by their masters, could often be seen along the roads or begging in the towns, and frequent attempts to restrict such abuses—in both the local and national legislatures—met with little success. In 1854, in São Paulo, a provincial law provided that "any master who, having adequate means, abandons his leprous, insane, crippled, or incurably ill slaves, and who allows them to become beggars," should pay a fine of 30$000 and be obligated to care for them properly, support them, and clothe them. The legislature's efforts, however, were futile. Though Parliament complained and the press protested, throngs of old, sick, and hungry free blacks continued to be seen along the roads, begging alms from travelers or wandering on the streets of the cities. Since they were no longer of any value in the labor force, their maintenance constituted a burden that many masters were happy to dismiss.

In short, many factors contributed to the high mortality rates of the slave population: insufficient medical knowledge and primitive treatment, poor sanitary conditions in the slave quarters, inadequate diet and clothing, harsh working conditions, dust inhaled in the preparation of coffee, the heat of the furnaces in the sugar mills, and the bites of poisonous snakes and insects in the fields. But most of all, high mortality was due to the hazardous sanitary conditions in the country as a whole.

In the 1870s it was said, probably with some exaggeration, that if a planter bought a lot of one hundred healthy slaves, after three years he would find twenty-five of them, at best, still able to work. On the plantations there were always some slaves—perhaps as many as 10 or 20 percent—temporarily unable to work, and pessimistic observers estimated the working life of the labor force to be fifteen years. Planters often complained about the high infant mortality, which according to some reached more than 80 percent. It was common to say that it was easier to raise three or four white children than one black—a situation attributed to "the greater fragility of the black race." The owner of one of the largest sugar mills in the province of Rio de Janeiro, and one of the first to introduce steam-operated machines—a measure of her progressive spirit—told the English traveler Maria Graham that not even half of the blacks born on her plantation lived to the age of ten. The baron of Piabanha, a planter in Paraíba do Sul, in the province of Rio de Janeiro, confessed some years later that, despite good treatment and care, the number of his slaves declined about 5 percent a year.

Contrary to these pessimistic evaluations, recent research has demonstrated that mortality, although high, was not as high as planters said, and certainly not much higher than mortality among the free lower classes.[13] Measuring infant mortality in a coffee district, one author has arrived at the conclusion that it reached 470 per 1000. Of the 36,807 children registered as born to slave mothers between 1871 and 1887, 8,454 died, which gives an index of 229 per 1000. If mortality was not as high as planters said it was, certainly it was high enough to make the balance between birth and death negative. Mortality as well as fertility seems to have differed widely from one province to another. Attempts to measure fertility have resulted in figures that vary from

210 per 1000 in Rio Claro, to 61 per 1000 in Rio de Janeiro, 160 per 1000 in Rio Grande do Norte, and 150 per 1000 in São Paulo.

While fertility in Brazil was lower than in the United States, slave mortality in Brazil was apparently much higher. The higher rate of mortality has been attributed to the general health and epidemiologic conditions that prevailed in Brazil at the time. On the other hand, the lower fertility rate has been attributed to the imbalance between males and females and to the higher instability of the slave family in Brazil.

Indeed, during the nineteenth century, particularly in areas of new settlement, there were always fewer women than men. In some regions the proportion was as low as one to five. This difference—more striking before the interruption of the slave trade—tended to diminish after that, sometimes disappearing completely in areas of old settlement.

Throughout the nineteenth century, travelers, slaveowners, priests, politicians, and abolitionists, all talked about the "promiscuity" that reigned in the slave quarters. We could argue that the documents are inherently biased, that priests were overconcerned with moral problems, that puritan travelers went out of their way to make slavery look evil, that politicians were merely debating points, that abolitionists always exaggerated the corruptions of slavery, and that slaveowners were prejudiced against blacks. In fact, recent historiography seems to contradict the testimony of the contemporary. Perhaps influenced by recent trends in United States historiography, historians found that the monogamous family was not uncommon among Brazilian slaves. It is often difficult, however, to reconstitute the slave family because common law unions were not registered and slaves in Brazil as well as most of the lower class often did not marry. The census of 1872 counted only 9 percent of the total slave population as married, compared to 27.1 percent of the free population. The situation did not seem to improve very much as time passed. In 1888, only 10.6 percent of the slaves were listed as married, though an additional 2.2 percent of the slaves were enrolled as widows and widowers. The figures for the nation as a whole can be very misleading, since there were marked variations from region to region. In Pará and Santa Catarina, only 1 percent of the slave population was registered as married in 1888. In Minas the figure was 17 percent, in Bahía 4.5, and in São Paulo 22. The figures for the city of Rio de Janeiro are particularly striking. In a total slave population of 7,488, there were only 38 married slaves. These variations are difficult to explain. Demographic imbalance between male and female does not correlate to marriage rates as one might expect. São Paulo, for example, which showed a predominantly male population of 62,688 males for 44,641 females, was also the province with the highest proportion of married slaves, while in Pará and Rio, where the marriage rates were lower, the male-female ratio was nearly one to one. It seems, thus, that only when the demographic imbalance was acute, as in the case cited by Stanley Stein in Vassouras, where 77 percent of the slaves were men, might demographic factors have any bearing on marriage. Nor does the number of priests and churches correlate to the number of marriages. There were more married slaves on plantations than in the cities, where there were more churches.

It is thus difficult to make generalizations about the slave family that are valid for the country as a whole, and one should not dismiss too quickly the testimony of contemporaries when they commented that sexual freedom, which for them was licentious behavior or promiscuity, was common in the slave quarters. It is also difficult to dismiss the tales about how masters, overseers, or other free whites used their position of authority to have affairs with slave women. Although we cannot measure how widespread these practices were, it is impossible to deny that from these unions emerged a large mestizo population. These situations created problems that concerned not only jealous wives and pious missionaries but also zealous legislators. By the time of independence, unsuccessful attempts had been made by some politicians to put into law a measure requiring slaveholders to free a slave who gave birth to her master's child. Such a law would have required a public admission of the slaveowners' responsibility. The ambiguous situation of many planters, who kept their children, their siblings, and even their mothers enslaved, seemed to them to be preferable to public scandal. Only in 1871 did a judicial ruling following the Free Birth Law of that year hold that a slave mother owned by her own son would have preference under the newly created Emancipation Fund. But, oddly enough in this same period, an appeals court prohibited a master from selling his illegitimate children, requiring him to continue to keep the mother and children as his own slaves.

The legislation aimed at the protection of slaves was always of dubious effectiveness, especially in the countryside, where the master's authority went unchecked. In the plantation, he represented the church, the law, and the police. His dominion was unhindered and his will limited only by his own benevolence.

Nevertheless, cases of kindness and paternalism on the part of the masters and examples of loyalty on the part of the slaves could always be found. In Brazil as in the United States, many a woman of the slaveholding class maintained all her life and passed on to her children the affection she retained for the nursemaid who had raised her and watched her children grow up. Many sons of planters kept throughout their lives sentimental childhood memories of the old black who had initiated them into the arts of hunting and fishing and the mysteries of nature. More than a few young students, on the day of their graduation, freed black boyhood companions who had accompanied them as servants during their years in school.

The images of the devoted "Black Mammy," of the loyal "Old Black Joe," of the childhood mate—these are not just inventions of romantic literature or artificial constructs of the planter's mind. They were found in real life. But equally real was the vengeful slave who tried to kill his master or overseer, who burned the fields, who ran away, or who incited rebellion in the slave quarters. And the truth is that most of the slaves probably did not fit in either of these extreme and opposite categories. Pictures of the faithful slave and the benevolent master—pictures fixed in Brazilian literature and history—represent not so much the actual behavior of slaves and masters, but myths created by a slaveholding society to defend a system which that society regarded as indispensable. They affected people's behavior only as much as any other idealization does.

Too much has been said recently about the paternalism of the slave-owners.[15] Historians have argued that paternalism was more than just a myth—an actual practice regulating the relations between master and slaves—a means of social control. This opinion, however, seems questionable when contrasted with the overwhelming evidence suggesting the violence of the system. Masters may have resorted to rewards as well as to punishment; they may have tried to impose order and discipline by presenting themselves as father figures. But all this should not blind us to the ultimate violence of a system which made slaves the property of their masters—a property that could be bought and sold and whose fate depended on the master's whim.

The forms of ritual kinship (*compadrío*) and the paternalistic relationships that slaveholding society developed as mechanisms of accommodation and social control could not eliminate the barriers that separated the two opposing and irreconcilable worlds of the slave and the master. Racial prejudice always separated the owner from the owned. Most whites, even those who considered slavery an economic and political aberration, believed in the moral inferiority and political and social incapacity of the African race. Racial prejudice served to maintain and legitimize the distance between a world of privileges and rights and one of deprivation and duties.

Even if the slaveholders often rewarded good behavior by granting manumission or conferring to their most loyal slaves a position of prestige within the slave community, more often they resorted to threats or

punishments to keep up the rhythms of work, prevent escapes or revolts, and keep slaves obedient and submissive. Physical punishment
was universally accepted as a method of coercion, although society
disapproved of both the masters who were excessive in their punishments and the ones who were overly benevolent. Leniency and cruelty
were considered equally dangerous.

Religion was another means of social control. Since the colonial period, the Church had undertaken to reconcile the masters' financial
interests with the dictates of religion and philanthropy. Discipline on
the *fazendas*, according to one traveler in the mid-nineteenth century
(who did not include paternalism as one of the means of social control), had two forms: the whip and the confessional. Patience, resignation, and obedience were the cathechism the priests taught the slaves.
Some went as far as to say that blacks were "cursed" and constituted a
condemned race whose salvation depended on their serving whites pa-
tiently and with devotion. Others played the role of mediators between
masters and slaves, preaching moderation and benevolence to the masters and obedience to the slaves. But whatever the priests' role was,
most people believed that religion and the confessional were the best
antidotes to insurrections.

When rewards, admonition, and advice did not produce the desired
result, slaveholders resorted to punishment. The most common methods were the *palmatória*, the stocks, and various kinds of whips and
lashes. Rare, but not absent, were neck shackles, manacles, iron rings
for squeezing fingers, brass masks, and imprisonment. Whipping and
the *palmatória* were common disciplinary punishments, recognized
and authorized by law. Slaves were not alone: soldiers and sailors were
also whipped when they committed certain offenses, and children were
subjected to the *palmatória* in school. Sometimes lower-class free men
were also beaten when they displeased a slaveholder or failed to treat
him with "proper" respect. In the nineteenth century, social relations
were based on dominance and oppression; on the power of father over
son, of husband over wife, of master over slave, of the rich over the
poor. Physical violence was an integral part of most people's lives.

The harshest punishments were applied to slaves who committed
murder, led other slaves to run away, or instigated rebellions. A mur-
derer was condemned to death if the crime was carried out against the
planter or his family and to chain gangs or prison otherwise. Runaways
received three hundred lashes, administered over several days. For a
long time it was the custom to brand slaves with a hot iron. Even on
the eve of abolition, the newspapers carried advertisements of runaway
slaves who could be indentified by those brands. All these devices for

FIG. 11. A master punishing his slave with the *palmatória*

torture and punishment were in frequent use until the middle of the nineteenth century. Such practices declined thereafter, but the history of Brazilian slavery is replete with cases of death or permanent injury from excessive punishment, enough to make us doubt the paternalistic pretensions of the masters.

Various travelers in nineteenth-century Brazil praised the excellence of the legislation that sought to protect the slave. They forgot, however, that the effectiveness of a law always depends on compliance and enforcement. And it is difficult to believe that these laws were implemented when, as we have seen before, slaveowners often interfered with the action of the courts. Before the abolitionist campaign, the slave was always seen as guilty by the jury, while the master always seemed to be in the right. Thus, most of the time the law was ineffective in the defense of the slaves but quite effective on behalf of the slaveholders.

In spite of all the mechanisms conceived to keep the slave population submissive, the planters lived in perpetual fear of slave insurrection. At the least rumor, severe measures were taken to prevent an uprising. The news spread swiftly: troops were mobilized, slaveholders warned, suspects arrested and interrogated, and the guilty severely punished. Laws were enacted to strengthen security measures. Both municipal and provincial legislatures reinforced the legal provisions that limited the slaves' movements. In the towns, every slave found on the street after curfew without his master's authorization was arrested.

Slaves were prohibited from congregating in shops or public places, and they were forbidden to enter gambling houses or taverns. The sale of arms or poison to slaves was severely punished, as was the renting of rooms or houses to them. It was illegal to buy any merchandise from slaves, unless they showed authorization from their masters. This was intended to reduce thefts, but neither vigilance nor repressive measures worked. Masters constantly complained that roadside stores traded in goods stolen by the slaves.

Despite the rumors of insurrections that periodically alarmed the slaveholding class, large-scale revolts were rare in nineteenth-century Brazil. Some of those that did occur, however, were quite impressive. The most famous slave revolts of this period had a religious character and were provoked by Muslim blacks. They occurred in the cities, where communication among the insurgents was easier than in the country and the concentration of slaves from the same part of Africa was greater.[16] Those revolts took place principally in the Northeast, where many Muslim blacks were to be found. The Malê revolts in Alagoas (1815) and Bahía (1835) were of this type. In Minas Gerais a famous uprising occurred shortly before independence. Some 15,000 slaves assembled in Ouro Preto and another 6,000 in Sao João do Morro. They spoke of a constitution and freedom and spread the rumor that in Portugal a constitution had already been approved in which blacks had been made equal to whites. Revolts of such size, however, were rare in the coffee areas and only occasionally took on the frightening aspects of the one that broke out in Vassouras in 1838, when about three hundred slaves, mostly Haussás, rose in revolt and troops had to be summoned from Rio de Janeiro to suppress them.

The repressive mechanisms that slave society had developed against uprisings were usually quite effective, and when a revolt did break out, it was quickly put down by the police or the army. But even careful vigilance could not prevent slaves from escaping to the forests and raiding plantations and villages. Communities of runaway slaves, known as quilombos, had been widespread since the colonial period, and in the nineteenth century some became famous, such as Jabaquara in São Paulo and Gávea in Rio de Janeiro. Quilombos grew in importance during the final years of slavery because slaves could count on the help of abolitionists and on the goodwill of the urban population.

Insurrections, crimes, work badly done, orders not fulfilled, lies, negligence were the many ways slaves fought oppression. But most of all, they ran away. The newspapers of the period are filled with advertisements dealing with escaped slaves and promising rewards to anyone who captured them. In 1855, up to 30$000 was offered. Twenty

FIG. 12. Punishment in the public square

years later, when slave prices had risen to two and a half *contos*
(2:500$000) or even more, some owners would offer up to 400$000
for the capture of a runaway slave.

The profession of *capitão do mato* (hunter of runaway slaves) had
existed since the colonial period. In the nineteenth century, *capitães do
mato* did not hesitate to put advertisements in the newspapers offering
their services. But with the spread of abolitionist ideas they gradually
became targets of popular satire and sometimes even of physical attacks.

The slaves' potential for rebellion was contained not only by repression, but also by the rivalries and enmities that divided the slave
community. In rural areas, the household servants often considered
themselves better than slaves who worked in the fields. Maids, cooks,
seamstresses, coachmen, pages, washerwomen, and nursemaids received special treatment and had greater opportunities to gain their
freedom through manumission than did fieldhands. The household
servants often lived more or less separated from their fellow slaves.
Their apparent superior status tended to separate them from their
natural group and imposed on them a code of etiquette full of prohibitions. They did not belong to the slave quarter, but they were not accepted in the world of the masters. Their position was not without am-

biguities, and ambiguous was their behavior. Some were bound by ties of affection to the master's family; others hated their masters to such an extent that they did not hesitate to eliminate them. The accounts of crimes committed by household slaves kept the master class apprehensive and watchful as long as slavery lasted.[17]

Many other forms of rivalry further divided the slave population. In the cities blacks often organized themselves by "nations" (their places

Fig. 13. Capitão do Mato

of origin). And sometimes they kept old hierarchies. Some African princes are said to have maintained the respect of their subjects in slavery. To the traditional African hierarchical positions, new distinctions were added based on occupation. As one traveler noted at midcentury, "A well-dressed and well-turned out high-class female slave feels no compassion or sympathy for her ragged and dirty fellow." The master's position also reflected on the slave, and one who belonged to a plantation owner felt himself superior to another who worked for a modest official—even though he might be subject to a more rigorous discipline. In spite of these divisions, feelings of solidarity also developed among slaves. And in the second half of the nineteenth century the activities of the abolitionists were important not only in spurring the slaves to join together in winning their freedom but in providing them with the means to do so.

African traditions had an important role to play in keeping the slave community united. Cultural traditions were apparently more easily retained in the cities than in the countryside. In urban areas, blacks from the same parts of Africa had at least the possibility of seeing one another and forming groups. On the plantations, where masters tried to prevent the formation of homogeneous groups, such contacts were more difficult. People of different cultural traditions were mixed together. The family or kin that had constituted the basis of the social structure in Africa fell apart. The traditional collective symbolic systems took on new meanings. Cults and rituals brought from Africa underwent a process of interpretation based on new circumstances imposed by slavery.

Music, religion, and magic were intimately related and played an immense part in the life of the slaves. Some masters permitted their slaves to dance and sing on Saturdays, Sundays, or holidays. In the cities and towns, African songs and dances were usually prohibited, out of a fear that any gathering of slaves could degenerate into a subversive movement. The only authorized celebrations were those of a Christian character, such as that of Nossa Senhora do Rosário, patron saint of blacks, and a few dances, such as the *congadas*.[18]

For the most part, however, Christianity was little more than a veneer over African traditions and practices. Few masters made much effort at Christianizing their slaves. Although most plantations had chapels, mass was rarely celebrated. Priests were in short supply, and the few who appeared from time to time had no opportunity to initiate the slaves in the real practices of Christianity. Household rites and family prayers prevailed. The master would lead prayers, aided by the slaves, who repeated them mechanically often without understanding their meaning. In practice, African and Christian traditions became thoroughly mixed, and African deities survived under Christian guise. The inclusion of African cultural elements in Catholicism made possible their preservation under a Christian exterior. But in this process, many African deities acquired a sinister character and often the warlike ones came to be preferred. The Muslim slaves, who were heavily concentrated in the Northeast, were the most resistant to Christianity, and some even managed to maintain their own places of worship. Nevertheless, slavery often made it impossible to observe religious requirements strictly, and it was mainly among free blacks that African traditions survived, however modified.

The fate of the slave actually depended as much on the prosperity of the master as on his benevolence and humanity. And it varied from region to region, from one plantation to another. It was said that Rio was better than Maranhão and that the worst masters were to be found in Campinas. "I will sell you to Campinas," said masters in western São Paulo to rebellious or lazy slaves. In Bahía, unruly blacks were threatened with being sent to the south. In Pernambuco the threat was to sell them to Maranhão. There was considerable mystification in this insinuation, but slave treatment did vary with the productivity of the various regions. In areas suffering from soil exhaustion—but still productive—such as the Paraiba Valley after 1870, the planter demanded longer hours and the care of a larger number of trees from his slaves to compensate for the decline in productivity of the coffee trees. In totally decadent areas, poverty sometimes brought slave and master closer together, and when slaves were not sold, master and slave relations became somewhat more civilized as they both struggled for survival. In the most prosperous areas, where productivity was higher and labor abundant, living conditions for the slaves were usually better.[19]

On the whole, living conditions seem to have improved after the abolition of the slave trade in 1850, when the price of slaves increased and slaveowners became more concerned with keeping their slaves in good health. In the twenty years from 1855 to 1875, slave prices almost trebled, going from one *conto* to two and a half and even three. While slave prices in Rio and São Paulo (in the coffee areas) maintained an upward trend from mid-century to about 1880, rising abruptly in the 1850s and then more gradually during the next decades, in the sugar areas prices began to decrease from the late 1850s on, reaching their lowest point in the 1870s. The fall of slave prices was related to changes in commodity prices; while sugar prices tended to decline, coffee prices reached their highest levels during the 1870s.[20] The difference between slave prices in the Northeast and in the South and the higher demand for slaves in the South led to a dislocation of the slave population from the Northeast to the South. The majority of bondsmen sold in the southern provinces, however, seem to have come not from plantations but from urban areas or small farms less dependent on slave labor.

During the first years after the interruption of the slave trade, there was a movement of slaves from the less productive regions to the more productive, from the cities to the countryside. Intra- and interprovincial trade replaced the external trade. Slave traders scoured the Northeast, offering high prices for slaves whom they then sold to the coffee planters of the South. Concerned about this loss of labor, the governments of the northeastern provinces tried to limit departures by imposing high taxes on them. A report by the president of the province of Maranhão in 1853 noted that the tax on the export of slaves had brought in more than in prior years because of the high slave prices prevailing in the Rio de Janeiro market. In Pernambuco, the tax on slaves leaving the province, which was 5$000 in 1842, reached 200$000 in 1859. In 1866 the provincial president reported that from 1855 to 1864, 4,023 slaves had been transferred to other provinces. In Bahía in 1860, over 200:000$000 was collected in taxes on slaves leaving the province. The situation was similar in Alagoas, where the largest source of revenue in 1862 was the tax on the export of slaves. Wanderley, representing the planters of Bahía, tried unsuccessfully in 1854 to secure approval in the House of Representatives for a bill prohibiting the interprovincial slave trade. The interests of large-scale agriculture in the South were stronger. The northeastern provinces, suffering from chronic crisis, thus lost much of their slave population.

It is impossible to calculate the exact number of slaves transferred to the coffee-growing areas from other provinces. Ferreira Soares provides data that permit an estimate of slightly over 5,000 slaves imported annually from the Northeast to Rio. Tavares Bastos writes of around 37,000 slaves entering Rio between 1850 and 1862. Recent scholarship has evaluated the internal slave trade at between 6,000 (Klein) and 9,000 (Slenes) a year.[21] Using port records of Rio de Janeiro and Santos, Slenes arrived at the conclusion that between 1873 and 1881, 71,000 bondsmen entered the coffee areas. This does not include slaves brought through other ways or to other ports.

Internal trade followed the pattern of external trade. More men than women were traded and more young men than adults. The majority of slaves traded were below forty years of age. Males were more prized than females. Many were registered as African-born, having originally come from Cabinda, Congo, Benguela, and Mozambique.

Whatever the precise numbers and qualifications, the fact is that intra- and interprovincial trade led to a concentration of slaves in the coffee-growing provinces. In 1823, Minas Gerais, Rio de Janeiro, and São Paulo contained approximately 386,000 slaves while Bahía, Pernambuco, and Maranhão reported around 484,000. Fifty years later the situation was reversed, and the latter provinces held 346,000 while the coffee-growing provinces contained almost 800,000 slaves.

The growing disproportion between the slave population of the North and that of the South finally alarmed southern politicians who saw this imbalance as a threat to the maintenance of the slave system. In 1874 the president of São Paulo requested a new tax on slaves entering the province. To emphasize the risks that would result from the transfer of slaves from North to South, he recalled what had happened in the United States. Some years later, a São Paulo deputy, Moreira Barros, presented a bill to the Chamber prohibiting the sale and trans-

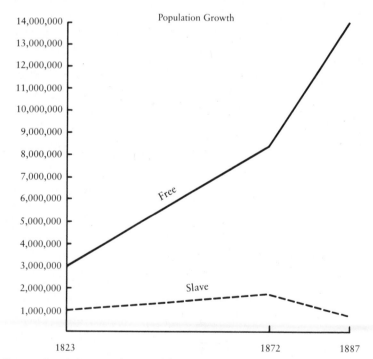

FIG. 14. Population growth in Brazil from 1823 to 1887

fer of slaves from one province to another. He said that this measure would end the antagonism that was developing between the two parts of the empire over slavery and would put all provinces on an even footing to resolve the question of slavery when that might be opportune. All these men feared, not unreasonably, that the North, after exporting its slaves to the South, would come to view the plans of the abolitionists with greater complacency.

What was happening in the cities showed that they were right. Abolitionists had more success in urban centers, where free labor had made progress. While slaves were increasingly concentrated in the coffee-growing areas, free labor made headway in the cities where free blacks and immigrants replaced the slaves. In 1860 Ferreira Soares noted that in Rio de Janeiro the number of slaves on the street had fallen noticeably: most peddling and selling, transportation, and other tasks previously done by slaves were done by freemen. The number of foreigners employed in these occupations was also growing.

As this was happening in the cities, high prices received for coffee seduced the planters, who expanded their coffee fields. Plantations spread westward in search of virgin land and their owners complained

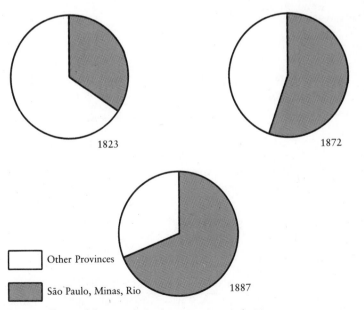

1823   1872

Other Provinces

São Paulo, Minas, Rio   1887

FIG. 15. Slave and free population in 1823, 1872, and 1887

of the shortage of labor and the high price of slaves. The demand for labor required a search for new solutions.

The lack of success with sharecropping, the failure of most of the immigrant settlements based on independent small farming in the coffee areas, and the difficulties involved in other sorts of contracts for agricultural labor had temporarily discredited attempts to promote immigration. The planters then turned to possible means of forcing the Brazilian rural population to work on plantations. Some argued, however, that Brazilian workers were lazy and shiftless and blamed the backwardness and ignorance in which workers lived as well as the ease with which people could support themselves in a country where nature was so generous. Sometimes it seemed that laziness was a "natural tendency of the Brazilian people, a trait of its national character." There were, however, a few observers who gave somewhat more objective explanations. Millet, a sugar planter in Pernambuco, wrote that

> whoever travels through the interior notes, along with the extraordinarily rich and uncultivated vegetation, the miserable huts which this class inhabits, the frugality, privation, and poverty in which they live. . . . Some attribute their idleness partly to the fact that they are settled on land which does not belong to them, the owners of which refuse to sell it even though they cannot cultivate it, and one cannot expect a man to acquire habits of work in a place where work provides no profits at all.[22]

André Rebouças voiced a similar opinion in 1883 in *Agricultura Nacional*, a book in which he analyzed the problems of Brazilian agriculture. Rebouças denied the charges of idleness leveled against the rural population and insisted that the empire needed profound reforms in order to permit the utilization of the thousands of individuals living a vegetative existence in the interior. Some years later, A. Taunay, trying to promote colonization, pointed out that "The obstacles to laying claim to a bit of land of their own provide good arguments for idleness and make it difficult for tenants [*agregados*], though free, to move very far from the lowly and submissive state peculiar to the condition of slaves.[23]

In spite of these opinions, the majority continued to believe that Brazilians were not much inclined to work and needed to be forced to it. The more profound reasons for the reluctance of the free population to work on plantations escaped them: the existence of slavery, the extremely low wages, and the easy access to land, although not to landownership. In such circumstances, it was unreasonable to expect that men who lived on subsistence agriculture would submit themselves, in exchange for meager salaries, to the extremely hard work on the plantations, not to mention that such work on plantations meant, for them, to be reduced to the level of slaves. Nevertheless, in those regions in which slave labor declined, free workers increasingly came to be used on plantations. This was particularly true in the Northeast, where droughts in the 1870s forced the population of the backlands to move to the sugar cane areas for employment on plantations. A study of the sugar economy in Pernambuco has shown that, by the middle of the century, slaves outnumbered free laborers by a ratio of over three to one. But by 1872 free workers already outnumbered slaves both in skilled and unskilled labor.[24]

In the new coffee areas, however, the planters struggled with the problem of labor supply. Faced with growing labor needs, some of the coffee planters most affected by the shortage of slaves considered importing Chinese coolies. Those who advocated such a solution claimed that in other areas coolies constituted the basis of wealth and prosperity, as in some of the French and British colonies, in some parts of the United States, and in such Latin American countries as Cuba, and in Peru. During the Sinimbu cabinet (1878–79), Chinese immigration was seriously considered. In the agricultural congress that met in Rio de Janeiro in 1878, representatives of the most important coffee-growing areas recommended the importation of coolies.[25]

Most planters seemed convinced that the thousands of *contos* spent on European immigration had brought no benefits at all to the great estates. They wanted cheap, hardworking, and submissive labor. Coolies seemed to be the only workers capable of adapting to the low standard of living offered in Brazilian agriculture. Pamphlets and articles favoring and opposing Chinese immigration appeared, but the advocates of Chinese immigration met considerable resistance both in Brazil and abroad. In Parliament the dangers of "mongolizing" the country were discussed, and frightening charges were made against the Chinese: they were drug addicts, naturally corrupt, weak, and indolent. The Brazilian Immigration Society and the Central Immigration Society, both involved in encouraging European immigration, lobbied against the proposal. In the Chamber of Deputies, Martinho Prado, representing some of the most dynamic coffee-growing sectors, attacked the supporters of coolie immigration.

The company founded to promote the importation of Chinese workers encountered difficulties in carrying out its mission. The British and Portuguese prohibited the enlistment of such workers from Hong Kong and Macáo. Unable to fulfill its commitments, the Company for Commerce and Chinese Immigration was dissolved on 14 November

1883, a few days after the hasty departure of the Chinese envoy Ti-Kung-Sing, mediator of the negotiations. Thus vanished the hopes of those who had expected to be able to replace blacks with coolies, slaves with serfs.

While the old and least productive coffee plantations continued to use slaves, in some of the more productive frontier areas, more in need of labor, planters expressed interest again in promoting European immigration.[26] Free labor, some began to argue, was more productive than slave labor. In the Northeast also, those planters who had managed to modernize their methods of production came to view free labor more favorably. This tendency had grown more marked as the transportation system expanded with the building of railroads, ports were improved, sugar and coffee processing advanced, and the opening of new possibilities for investment in banks and railroads and industries made immobilization of capital in slaves less attractive than before.

The precarious means of transportation had always been an obstacle to economic development. During the rainy season, transport

*lavoura! já não bastava o preto, vaes ter o amarello!
com o auxilio de duas raças tão intelligentes, ella ha de progredir
um modo espantoso!*

*O Sr. ministro dos Estrangeiros e todos os apologistas dos
Chins, acreditarão realmente que o Chicote é o principal
motor dos nossos trabalhos agricolas?!*

FIG. 16. Caricature of Chinese immigrants, published in the *Revista Illustrada* in 1879

Technology as factor in free vs
slave labor productivity debate

was interrupted by landslides, flash floods tore up roads, and bridges, usually wooden, were wrecked by high water. In many places, mule drivers were forced to ford rivers because of the lack of bridges. Many of the economically important routes, such as that from São Paulo to Santos, were dirt roads, and until midcentury roads that could be used by even simple wheeled vehicles were rare. Oxcarts tore up the roads and constant use by mule trains turned them often into impassable quagmires.[27]

The conditions of such vital roads as that from São Paulo to Santos were so bad in the 1860s that carts could not carry more than forty to forty-five *arrobas*, and a round trip that today would take less than two hours took a minimum of ten to twelve days. The problems of transportation were so serious that often the merchandise deteriorated in storage bins before the muleteer came to pick it up. Even when coffee was shipped in time, spoilage in transit damaged its quality. The inadequacy of the communication routes retarded distribution, raised transportation costs, diverted a considerable part of the labor force to transport, and limited the expansion of the coffee plantations beyond a certain point, after which the costs of transportation were too high to make the enterprise viable. Most of all, the difficult means of transportation inhibited the development of an internal market.

Conditions in the Northeast were not better. A large number of sugar mills had to use river transportation because transportation by land was quite difficult. The animals got bogged down in mud, their loads were lost, and trips dragged on endlessly in obligatory stops and in long waits for rain to end, a bridge to be repaired, or a road to be made passable again.

In the coffee-growing areas the problem became increasingly pressing with the expansion of production and the growing traffic of mules carrying their loads to the ports. Planters were quite aware of the losses resulting from this state of affairs and pressured the government for improvements. They put their hopes on the construction of railroads, which would allow them to ship their goods rapidly, and more cheaply.[28]

Railroads changed the economy profoundly, benefiting some regions and ruining others. In the sugar-growing areas, the mills far from the tracks could not compete with those directly served by railroads. They continued to export their products by the traditional means—boat or muletrain—and to suffer the economic disadvantages of this type of transportation. But railroads quickly multiplied and by 1881 Millet could say that the cars of the Palmares railroad alone transported half the sugar exported from the port of Recife and two-thirds of the entire production of the province of Pernambuco. Some years later, in 1882, 12,421,172 kilos of sugar and 318,295 of cotton were carried on the Pernambuco railways.

In the coffee-growing areas of the South, the rail network began to develop in the 1860s. The Santos-Jundiaí line was inaugurated in 1867 and extended to Campinas in 1872. The railway between São Paulo and Rio de Janeiro was completed, and elsewhere branch lines extended into the interior of the province, tying the plantations to the port cities. In Minas Gerais, progress was slower, in part because mountainous terrain made construction more difficult and expensive. In 1882 the province had 441 kilometers constructed, while São Paulo and Rio de Janeiro had 1,400 and 1,634 kilometers, respectively. All the other provinces had a total of 1,451 kilometers.

The construction of the railroads caused profound changes in the economic structure of the country: capital invested in the acquisition and maintenance of mule teams was freed and to some extent labor previously tied up in transportation could now be utilized in agriculture. Predictably, transport capacity and the speed of distribution increased enormously, and costs were reduced. Products shipped by rail were in better condition and so commanded higher prices on the world market. The possibilities for profit increased. On the other hand, the railroads furthered the process of urbanization and made it easier for planters and slaves to move about. The railroads offered, in short, new perspectives for free labor, new areas of investment, and new possibilities for the creation of a market economy.

Equally important in the transition from slavery to free labor were the steady improvements in the technology of sugar production and coffee processing.[29] In the coffee-growing areas, drying yards were now made of brick or macadam, and primitive mortars and grinders were widely replaced in western São Paulo during the second half of the nineteenth century with modern machinery for drying and hulling coffee. The importance of such improvements was striking. New machines could do in an hour what took primitive devices a day. Plantation owners from western São Paulo were the most receptive to innovation because of the higher productivity of these plantations. Heavy yields from new lands and high coffee prices facilitated the purchase of processing machinery. The growing labor problems encouraged those changes, since mechanizing production meant reducing the number of workers required. In 1883 a traveler noted that on many plantations in central and western São Paulo coffee was transported to the processing machinery, hulled, sorted, polished, bagged, and weighed mechanically.[30]

The acquisition of machinery, however, required investments so substantial that they were beyond the economic capabilities of the planters whose plantations were in decline. For this reason, the planters of the Paraíba Valley generally failed to adopt most of the improvements, with the exception of those whose plantations showed higher productivity. Relying on slaves they had bought in a period when slaves were plentiful, and facing the declining productivity of their coffee trees, these planters had difficulties in modernizing their plantations.

Something similar to what happened in the South occurred in the Northeast but with a difference. While the coffee economy was expanding rapidly, the sugar-growing areas lived in a state of constant crisis interrupted by brief moments of euphoria triggered by an increase in sugar prices in the international market. The international situation had been favorable to Brazil during the Napoleonic Wars and the social upheaval in the West Indies, but when that period ended, matters worsened considerably. Competition from beet sugar and the protection given by European countries to their colonies hampered Brazilian sugar production. This fact was aggravated by the introduction in the West Indies of mechanical processes that substantially raised productivity, making Brazilian sugar production even less competitive. The small size of the internal market reinforced Brazil's dependence on the fluctuations of the international market. During the second half of the nineteenth century, as a consequence of the unfavorable international conjuncture, Brazilian producers received less and less for their products and planters had difficulties in improving methods of manufacturing sugar. There was no shortage of attempts to publicize the most recent developments in the sugar industry. Books and pamphlets were published on the subject, and the Society for the Advancement of Brazilian Industry promoted expositions with the aim of informing planters about processes used in other countries. Moreover, the government attempted to stimulate improvements in the methods of production. It ordered plant cuttings from abroad, provided information about systems of production, subsidized the purchase of machinery, gave tax exemptions to planters who introduced new techniques, awarded prizes for new inventions, and established commissions to study improvements in the cultivation of cane and the production of sugar in other centers of production. The government also attempted to develop technical training and even created training centers with the objective of spreading new techniques. None of these attempts succeeded. Great economic changes do not arise from technical knowledge alone, but from the possibility of applying this knowledge. An economy in a state of crisis does not provide capital enough for costly technological innovations.

In spite of the difficulties, some of the wealthiest plantation owners struggled successfully against the backward methods that hindered production, and a few sugar mills in particularly favorable situations, such as those located on good land, well served by means of communication, and close to ports, were able to change their methods of production. In the beginning of the nineteenth century, the first steam-powered mills appeared: one in Bahía in 1815 and another in Pernambuco two years later. Steam-powered mills spread only slowly. In 1857, out of a total of 1,106 mills in Pernambuco, only 18 were run by steam and 346 by water power; the rest were all driven by animals.[31] Most of the machinery used in these mills was imported from England. In 1829 a factory that made parts had been set up in Recife and in 1836 it had been able to assemble a completely Brazilian-made steam mill. However, English competition had finished off the attempt, and machinery continued to be imported.

In 1834, furnaces with grates came into use. Toward midcentury the use of horizontal grindstones was recommended, and kettles with flat bottoms were found to be better than those with curved bottoms. Another improvement introduced was the use of cane pulp to heat the kettles. French technicians were commissioned by the government to improve methods of sugar production, and a new technique, known as the Derosne system, was introduced. With this method, it was possible to increase yields by 40 percent and to make them of higher quality.

In 1853, a commission sent by the authorities of Bahía to study production techniques used in Europe, the United States, and Cuba came to the conclusion that *massapé* and *salmorão* soil would produce much better harvests if plows and other agricultural implements were used, following a system employed in Louisiana. Using this method, as well as improved techniques in the manufacture of sugar, slaves could produce ten boxes of superior sugar each, whereas they were able to produce only two and a half or three boxes of inferior sugar using traditional methods. But the machinery necessary for this improvement cost 1$000 to 1$500 per *arroba* during a year, roughly 50 *contos* for the manufacture of 50,000 *arrobas*—a sum that many planters could not afford.

Despite the efforts of the government and others, progress was slow. In 1859, a report on the state of agriculture, manufacturing, industry, and mining in the various districts of Pernambuco noted that in some areas the processes of planting cane and refining sugar were the same as those employed thirty or forty years earlier. The usual method for grinding cane wasted power, and the regulation of rates for cooking and purifying the cane juice was inefficient. The system of purification was limited to placing a little clay on the sugar and then throwing water over it—a system that removed some impurities but produced dark and inferior sugar.

Almost twenty years later in a congress held under the auspices of the Agricultural Assistance Society, it was clear that the processes of preparing sugar were still rudimentary on most plantations. In many of them, the Labat method was still used, in which purification, evaporation, and cooking were done wastefully over an open fire. Only a few mills had installed improved machinery using steam, pressure cooking, and centrifugal force to process the pulp. This method was quite superior, providing 30 or 40 percent higher yields from each harvest. Such improvements, however, required investments that only planters who produced large harvests could make. Nine-tenths of the mills were small and in a critical state. Often the owners could not pay their dealers and had to turn their slaves over. Shortages of labor and cane supplies paralyzed the mill. And in certain periods, the price received for sugar did not even cover the costs of production, taxes, and transportation. Sugar production was profitable only in well-equipped mills where more rational methods of operation generated higher productivity.

The chronic need for capital—interest ranged from 12 to 74 percent a year—and the deficits of most of the small mills made the modernization of production methods impossible. A majority of the mills produced less than 1,000 loaves of sugar, and many under 600. Production in such small quantities resulted in high costs. In the larger sugar mills—even those using old methods—the cost of production was lower. With the prices of sugar declining, the smaller mills were forced into bankruptcy and many closed down or started manufacturing only rum.

The central mills, which began to spread in the 1870s, brought about a true revolution in the process of sugar production. Law 2689 of 6 January 1875 sought to encourage central mills like those in Egypt, Java, Martinique, and Cuba through guaranteed interest rates and other benefits. The imperial government fostered the creation of these undertakings and guaranteed returns ranging from 6.5 to 7 percent. But until 1880 the results of the central mills did not seem very encouraging. Some concessionaires were incompetent, while others did not comply with their obligations and so lost their contracts. In addition, resistance to the establishment of the central mills was very strong on the part of the planters.

The report of the Ministry of Agriculture in 1880 provides a list of the concessions made by the government as of that date: ten for Minas Gerais, São Paulo, and Rio de Janeiro; thirteen for Maranhão, Rio

Grande do Norte, Pernambuco, Sergipe, and Bahía; two for Pará. The
capital employed varied from three hundred to a thousand *contos*, and
the quantity of cane to be ground daily was calculated at between
150,000 and 250,000 kilos.[32]

There was, however, considerable speculation, and some concessionaires sold their charters on the London market for a few *contos de
reis*. The weakness of Brazilian capitalism encouraged a veritable invasion of foreign capital, largely British, in this sector. Some powerful
companies monopolized the construction of central sugar mills in the
Northeast: the Central Sugar Factories of Brazil, Ltd., the North Brazilian Sugar Factories, and the General Sugar Factories, Ltd., were
some of the factories built with foreign capital. The first was organized
in London in December 1881 under the concessions granted by the imperial government and the guaranteed interest of 8.5 percent a year on
4,200:000$000. The firm assumed responsibility for the construction
of sugar mills in the counties of Cabo, Escada, Ribeirão, Água Preta,
Jaboatão, and Goiana. By 1884, four sugar mills were already in
operation. In the harvest of 1885–86, four mills ground 46,510,330
kilos of cane, producing 2,975,370 kilos of sugar and 573,250 liters of
rum. Up to 1887, thirteen concessions had been issued for the construction of central mills in Pernambuco: six to Central Sugar and
seven to North Brazilian Sugar Factories. The same rush to build sugar
mills took place in Bahía. In 1880, the Central Factory of Bom Jardim
was established, employing the most recent technology and with a
daily capacity of 200,000 kilos of cane. In the same period, a mill with
a capacity of 250 tons of cane a day was being set up in Joazeiro, and in
the following years several new undertakings were begun. The same
phenomenon occurred elsewhere. In Maranhão, for example, cotton
was abandoned in favor of sugar cane. New mills were constructed and
equipped with modern machinery. The principle of state-sponsored
central sugar mills failed, but *usinas* (sugar factories) equipped with
modern machinery appeared everywhere.

The revolution in the system of production proceeded slowly but
irreversibly, creating conflict between the new entrepreneurs and the
traditional planters. Some of the new entrepreneurs in the Northeast
lost interest in the maintenance of slavery. It was the backward sector,
unable to adapt to new forms of production, that remained tied to the
slave system.

Low productivity explains why some sugar producers clung tena-
ciously to the use of slaves and why it was impossible for them to
adopt free labor. Even when repeated droughts devastated the backlands and sent substantial numbers of refugees fleeing toward the

coast, thus increasing the labor supply, many plantation owners remained pessimistic about the possibility of replacing slaves with wage
laborers.

In 1876 it seemed to Millet, a planter in Pernambuco, that even
those sugar mills capable of producing 1,000 or 1,500 loaves of sugar
would continue in operation only as long as slavery existed, since they
could not count on using free workers. Only the large sugar mills with
modern equipment, he argued, could do without slaves. The expectation that a sugar mill could function with free workers exclusively
seemed utopian to him.

In the coffee plantation areas, the situation was very similar to the
one in the Northeast. The areas that continued to use slave labor almost entirely were those where the concentration of slaves was highest,
productivity lowest, and traditional methods of production were retained. The more productive sectors, which modernized their methods
of production, evolved more easily toward free labor. In São Paulo,
many plantation owners of the western parts of the state began to use
coffee-processing machines on their plantations and to experiment with
free labor, making every effort to encourage immigration. Martinho
Prado, representing the opinion of the most advanced planter group,
told the Chamber of Deputies that a *colono* (immigrant) was worth
three slaves. Nevertheless, the majority of plantation owners in areas
affected by the declining productivity of their coffee trees continued
to prefer slaves. In 1884, Louis Couty claimed that outside of São
Paulo—where the number of immigrants was sufficient to replace
in part the slaves who died or were freed—plantation owners had
done nothing to replace their slaves. In most of the plantations of the
Paraíba Valley, it was still a common belief that coffee could not be
produced without slaves, and most planters still stubbornly asserted
that immigrants were an impractical labor force for the plantations.[33]

The planters of the Paraíba Valley, whose declining estates produced
20 to 30 *arrobas* per 1,000 trees compared to the 80 to 100 in western
São Paulo, were unable to replace slaves who died. Moreover, most of
them failed to improve their machinery or spend the sums necessary to
secure immigrants for their estates. They were unable to compete in
the labor market with the areas paying higher wages. Thus they remained tied to their slaves who, in the 1880s, represented the greater
part of their patrimony. The Paraíba Valley plantation owners were in-
dignant at the behavior of those Paulista planters who seemed to have
lost interest in the slave system and who regarded the advance of abolition almost with indifference.

In a letter to Francisco de Paula Rodrigues Alves a year before abolition, Rodrigues de Azevedo, a coffee planter in Lorena, expressed quite bitterly his opinion about the situation of agriculture. He represented very clearly the viewpoint of most planters in the Paraíba Valley (the North, as it was called at the time), who felt threatened by the prospect of abolition:

> Unfortunately, the North is not equal to the West, where the fertility of the soil and the high production invite free labor and provide it with remuneration. Here we do not have, nor will we soon be able to have, foreign immigration. As long as there is no fundamental change in agriculture, we cannot do without slaves or free Brazilian workers. What immigrant would want to care for 1,000 coffee trees to harvest 20 *arrobas*? But for this very reason, we cannot be ignored or sacrificed to our rich brothers; on the contrary, it would be good policy to sacrifice them. . . . I see no reason to want to impose on us an opinion which we do not share, and a course of action identical to that followed by those who are rich and can dispense with certain services, which we are in no condition to do without. If they find that at the present time slave labor is no longer profitable for the producer, and that it is a burden for those who use it, let those who think this way free their slaves, regardless of the law; but they should not require others, who out of necessity understand the matter differently, to follow the same course of action. . . . Northern São Paulo and the province of Rio de Janeiro are, unfortunately, in the same situation: for us, immigration is a dream difficult to put into practice and the measures which the government takes in regard to it do not benefit us.[34]

In fact, immigrants who arrived in 1885, destined for the Paraíba Valley, refused to sign contracts with planters of the region and were returned to the Hospedaría de Imigrantes (Reception Center for Immigrants) in São Paulo, from where they went on to the western part of the province, where they were sure to get better pay. Rodriges Alves, president of the province, commented in 1888 on the situation of the Paraíba Valley planters and the preference the immigrants showed for the western part of the province: "In fact, the plantation owners with their vast landholdings cannot give immigrants the advantages which they find in the more fertile areas, where work is easier and better paid. Even if settled on depleted land, the immigrants certainly will not remain there if they learn of more favorable possibilities."[35]

While the slaveholders of the Paraíba Valley protested, planters of the frontier areas found in Italian immigration the definitive solution for the labor question.

Overall conditions became more favorable to immigration, as the demand for coffee grew and the area under cultivation continued to expand. Slaves had become increasingly difficult to acquire. Slave prices rose steadily, reaching their highest levels between 1876 and 1880. By this time slavery had been abolished in other parts of the world and was universally condemned. Slaves no longer existed in the United States and in the French West Indies there had been no slavery since the middle of the century. Slavery had been abolished in 1873 in Puerto Rico and in 1880 in Cuba. At the same time abolitionist pressure had grown in Brazil. Meanwhile, improvements in the transportation system along with advances in coffee processing and sugar manufacture, the growth of the free population, and the expansion of the market economy—all had modified the conditions of the economy, creating greater possibilities for free labor. More important, in some areas slave labor became less productive when compared to free labor.[36] This happened in plantations in which, thanks to changes in the process of production and in the means of transportation, it became possible to reduce the permanent labor force and hire additional workers at the time of harvest. Hiring slaves, however, was difficult because all planters needed extra labor at the same time. The solution was to resort to free laborers and to employ their families whenever extra work was needed. By doing this planters could avoid investing capital in slaves—capital which in any case was condemned to disappear in the long run. This solution became increasingly attractive at a time when new opportunities for investments in railroads, banks, insurance companies, and factories were multiplying. Not that investments in slaves paid lower interest than capital invested in other sectors,[37] but by diversifying their investments, planters could minimize capital risks. All this made free labor gradually more attractive than slave labor. Slaveowners, however, did not give up their slaves, mainly because they continued to represent capital, and most plantation owners were still skeptical about the possibility of using free labor. Gradually, however, more people—particularly in the frontier areas more in need of labor—started giving more thought to the idea of replacing slaves by immigrants. The need to do so became even more urgent when abolitionists intensified their campaign. By the 1880s slaveowners had become convinced that slavery was an institution condemned to disappear. At the same time conditions abroad had become more propitious for immigration to Brazil. The political and economic transformations that followed the Italian unification forced thousands of people to leave their homes and to migrate to the New World. Be-

tween 1873 and 1887 more than 60,000 small holdings were confiscated by Italian authorities for nonpayment of taxes and between 1881
and 1901, the number of holdings lost by peasants rose to more than
200,000. Destitution reached rural areas, which became centers of emigration, and many Italians emigrated to Brazil. Italian immigrants
adapted better to coffee cultivation in São Paulo than had the Swiss
and Germans of the 1850s. One factor that contributed to the success
of Italian immigration were the subsidies given by the government.[38]

The authorities of the province of São Paulo, identifying themselves
with the interests of the planters, sought to stimulate immigration by
all possible means. As early as 1871, a law had been passed authorizing the government to issue bonds up to 600 *contos* to aid in the payment of immigrant passages. Each person would be assigned 20$000.
By a contract with the imperial government, this sum was raised to
100$000. The period of subsidized immigration thus began. On 9 Au-
gust 1871, the Association to Aid Colonization was established, bringing together important planters and entrepreneurs of São Paulo. In
1874, the association received 100 *contos* as a subsidy for the financing of immigrant passages. In the 1880s several special credits were
granted by the provincial government to aid immigration. Between
1881 and 1891, the expenditures of São Paulo on immigration and
colonization came to 9,244:226$000. The planters concerned with
immigration found means of moving the administration in the direction of their objectives.[39]

The agencies interested in immigration grew. The naming of the
baron of Paraíba, Antonio de Queiroz Telles—a coffee planter himself
and one of the pioneers of immigration in the early eighties—as president of the province of São Paulo favored the movement considerably.
More immigrants entered the province of São Paulo in the 1880s than
during the previous twenty-five years. Between 1871 and 1886, slightly
over 40,000 arrived. In the next two years the figure rose to 122,000.

Until then, work on most coffee plantations had continued to be
carried out largely by slaves. There were about 400,000 slaves occupied in growing coffee and 800,000 employed in cultivating other
crops and in raising livestock in the country as a whole. The participation of free workers was still small in coffee-growing areas, and only a
few plantations employed them exclusively. But at this point slavery
had come to be seen by many as one of the obstacles to the promotion of
immigration. By 1875, João Elisário Carvalho Monte Negro, owner of
the Nova Louzã and Nova Colombia colonies—considered model
ones in the period—said that as long as "this black stain called slavery" existed in Brazil, there could be no immigration. He remarked

that foreigners were reluctant to work side by side with slaves, and he claimed in addition that the maintenance of the slave system provided a pretext in Europe for spreading a series of notions discrediting Brazil. He concluded by affirming that the shortage of labor derived in part from slavery.[40] Gradually, the number of planters who thought as he did grew, particularly when slaves started abandoning the plantations, disrupting their economy. By then the landowners not only lost their interest in maintaining the slave system but set out to eliminate it.

The adherence of this group to the idea of free labor made the final victory of abolition possible in Parliament and explains in great part the relatively peaceful character of the movement. In general, however, planters in traditional large-scale agriculture—that is, the more backward or less productive sectors—continued to be hostile to abolition, sometimes even to the point of armed resistance. To the very end they opposed abolition, which implied not only modification of the labor system but also abandonment of a traditional world view and the relinquishing of a series of values related to it. For many, particularly those whose properties were mortgaged and whose slaves represented a great part of their collateral, abolition would represent the loss of economic and social status.[41]

Abolitionist ideas found greater support in urban areas, among the social groups least tied to slavery. But even in the cities there were supporters of slavery. These contradictory attitudes can be explained by the peculiarities of the Brazilian middle classes. In nineteenth-century Brazil there was no clear dividing line between the urban bourgeoisie and the rural aristocracy. Many of the lawyers, doctors, engineers, teachers, and government functionaries came directly from the rural oligarchies, and when they were not linked to it by family ties, their economic and financial interests operated within its clientele. Thus they too were often spokesmen for the interests of the agrarian groups. Among the urban middle class there were many, however, who were not directly dependent on slave labor and who could therefore be more receptive to abolitionist propaganda. Thus, in general, abolition was favored by these representatives of the urban classes, which were gaining importance because of economic changes taking place in Brazil, such as the development of the railroads, the appearance of the first industrial enterprises, insurance companies, and credit organizations, the increase in retail commerce, and the growing numbers of schools, newspapers, and magazines. Equally favorable to the liberation of the slaves were the free workers, Brazilian or foreign, whose number was growing in the cities. Their collaboration was decisive in the revolutionary action unleashed in the 1880s with the creation of an "underground railroad system." The followers of Antonio Bento, who was active in São Paulo—inciting slaves to flee from the plantations, threatening the overseers, and beating the men sent out to catch runaway slaves—were recruited primarily among printers, coachmen, railroad workers, lawyers, journalists, doctors, and businessmen.[42]

The rural population remained, in general, indifferent to the fate of the slaves. Joaquim Nabuco, the leader of the abolitionist movement in Parliament, bitterly criticized in 1884 the attitude of those classes which did not know their own interests: "It is not with us, who raise the cry of abolition, that these impassive victims of the monopoly of land by the few join, but with the others who raise the cry of slavery—slavery which oppresses them without their realizing it because it has crushed them from the cradle."[43] Among the rural groups immigrants seem to have been the most receptive to abolitionism. Many of them were caught indoctrinating slaves, inciting them to insurrection, holding forth on the injustices of captivity. With the exception of some Portuguese merchants and a small number of North Americans (Confederate exiles) in São Paulo, the greater part of the foreigners living in Brazil favored abolition.

Free blacks also played an important role in the abolitionist movement. Despite the indifference of many former slaves toward the fate of those still in bondage, many were attracted to the movement, particularly those who like Luiz Gama, a lawyer in São Paulo, José do Patrocínio, a journalist in Rio, and André Rebouças, an engineer also in Rio, had climbed the social ladder. But even among those there were many like Machado de Assis, the famous novelist, who kept a much more discreet attitude in regard to abolition and a few would go as far as to oppose it. If there was sometimes ambivalence on the part of the free blacks, slaves were not ambivalent. They were ready to fight for their own emancipation. Rebellion in the slave quarters during the last years of slavery was a decisive factor in the final disintegration of the system.[44]

Abolitionist propaganda and the prospect of liberation made captivity more difficult to endure. The existence of free labor alongside slavery only served to emphasize the injustice of the institution. The abolitionist campaign supplied the slaves with arguments to justify their rebellion while at the same time it generated among other social groups more sympathy for the plight of the slave. Travelers in the provinces of São Paulo and Rio de Janeiro in 1883 often had the impression that a social revolution was imminent. There were signs of unrest everywhere; escapes, revolts, and crimes committed by slaves increased the tension. Slaves were refusing to obey orders and were frequently finding aid and sympathy among the free population.

As the economic bases of the slave system weakened, the abolitionists' arguments gained influence and as their arguments gained influence the economic basis of the slave system was undermined even further.[45] Contrary to what happened in the United States, no one dared to make an outright doctrinaire defense of slavery in the second half of the nineteenth century. But in Brazil as in the U.S., the slaveowners' spokesmen insisted that the slaves' living conditions were superior to those of European laborers. They also made a point of stressing that in Brazil slavery was milder than in other countries, masters were more benevolent, and relations between masters and slaves were paternal in tone. Proslavery spokesmen even argued that the slaves had been happy up to the moment that subversive ideas spread by the abolitionists had created discontent. Theoretically, planters were all in favor of gradual emancipation—provided that property rights were safeguarded. But whenever any measure aiming at emancipation was suggested, slaveowners invoked the right of property and accused the abolitionists of being "communists" and agitators who had nothing to lose and who by their actions jeopardized public security and national prosperity. In Parliament representatives of the slaveowners argued that abolitionism had no support from the public, that it was a campaign promoted by "anarchists" preaching illegal and subversive doctrines, threatening the highest national interests, which had been created and maintained under the protection of the law. And they always considered premature any emancipatory measure, which had not been prepared for by prior studies, statistics, and far-reaching reforms, such as immigration, the construction of railroads and canals, and the development of the credit system.

In 1871 the bill designed to free the children born of slave mothers was labeled a crime, robbery, theft, and a communist plot. One deputy affirmed—in a style much to the taste of the period—that the proposal "unfurled its sails on an ocean also navigated by the pirate ship International."[46] The government was accused of seriously compromising the future of the nation by permitting the question to be debated in Parliament. Some politicians in Parliament talked of the social agitation and the economic disaster that would result if slavery were abolished.

The abolitionists were no less vehement. They said that slavery created obstacles to the economic development of the country, impeded immigration, inhibited the mechanization of agriculture, and generated a false wealth well described by the proverb "Rich father, noble

son, poor grandson." Abolitionists of the 1870s and 1880s repeated
the arguments that had been heard so many times since independence:
Slavery corrupted society and the family, encouraged laziness and
wastefulness, degraded the masters, debased the slaves, corrupted the
language, religion, and mores, and violated natural law. To the traditional arguments provided by the Enlightenment and by the doctrines
of romanticism and classical economics, arguments derived from positivism were now added. Slavery, said the positivists, was an anach-
ronistic and transitory state which was destined to be eliminated.

Ideology, however, often bowed to personal interests. The positivist
group, for example, was divided. There were some like Miguel Lemos,
who favored abolition with indemnification, while others like Pereira
Barreto and Ribeiro de Mendonça, who were tied to agrarian interests, urged gradual emancipation. All of them invoked the fathers of
positivism to justify their positions.[47]

Until the 1860s antislavery ideas had had little influence on public
opinion. Bills introduced in Parliament seeking to improve the living
conditions of slaves had aroused strong opposition. But gradually the
situation changed. Writers who had presented a conventional picture
of the black man, rather than of the slave, slowly became more aware of
the problems created by slavery. Among the poets, Castro Alves best
exemplifies this new tendency. In prose, Macedo in *Vítimas e Algozes*
is the best example of militant literature during the period. Beginning
with the Paraguayan War (1864–70), the number of works in this
genre increased; short stories, novels, plays, feuilletons, and pamphlets
were written with the purpose of fighting slavery. The number of abolitionist newspapers also grew. The press prepared public opinion to accept abolitionist ideas. It chastised slaveowners and praised those who
were emancipating their slaves. Predictably, manumissions increased in
number. Masters freed slaves at baptisms, weddings, graduations, and
other celebratory events. All over the country abolitionists organized
clubs with the purpose of promoting manumission and campaigning
for abolition. Citing the 1831 law that had prohibited the importation
of blacks, the abolitionists argued that most of the slaves were kept illegally and on this ground mounted an intense campaign in favor of
slave emancipation. In São Paulo, the ex-slave Luíz Gama became famous for his legal battles on behalf of abolition and his defense of the
cause of the illegally enslaved Africans.[48]

Unearthing this law, whose effects had been annulled by custom,
threatened slaveownership, since most of the slave population was
composed of people who either had entered Brazil after 1831 or were
the descendants of those who had. When the cases were brought to the

courts, some ruled in favor of the slaves. This generated panic among slaveholders. The specter of the 1831 law terrified the defenders of the status quo who feared that if this principle was accepted by the courts, the majority of their slaves would be freed.

The Free Birth Law was voted under this climate of apprehension on the part of the landowning groups. Despite the reluctance of many politicians to discuss the slavery question in Parliament, it could not be avoided. It had become a widely debated public issue and since 1869 the Liberal party—then in the opposition—included gradual abolition in its platform. Politicians had turned the idea of emancipation into an instrument of political action, and each party tried to make the best of it. Abolitionist ideas had come from the streets to Parliament and would return reinforced by the heat of the parliamentary debates. The public followed with great interest the debates in the press. The law was finally approved after an intense campaign that profoundly stirred public opinion and contributed to the radicalization of both sides.

The slavery question transcended partisan interests. In Parliament, Conservatives and Liberals, forgetting partisan rivalries, often joined in opposing the bill. The opposition to the bill was led largely by the representatives of those coffee-growing regions where slaveholding interests still prevailed.[49]

Despite the vehemence of those opposing the 1871 bill, it represented merely a delaying tactic, a concession to more radical demands. The measure provided that the children of slave mothers born in the empire after the date of the law were to be free. It further stipulated that the owner had to raise such children until they were eight years old, at which time he could either turn them over to the government and receive a compensation of 600$000, or keep them until they were twenty-one, using their services as payment for the cost of their upkeep. Thus the principle of indemnification was established and slave status maintained for all those born before the date of the law.

Most slaveholders chose to make use of the labor of the children of their slaves, who, though legally free, continued to live as slaves until they were twenty-one. An emancipation fund created by the law with the purpose of liberating a certain number of slaves annually in each province did not have much effect. Up to 1885 slightly more than 23,000 had been freed in the entire empire, while spontaneous manumission during the same period had reached more than 170,000. And these numbers tended to increase while the slaves emancipated by the manumission fund in 1888 amounted to not many more than 32,000—obviously a very disappointing result when compared to the total slave population, which at the time of final abolition was around 750,000.

After the approval of the Free Birth law, slaveowners hoped that the parliamentary campaign for abolition would end. They argued that nothing else needed to be done on that matter since with the passage of years slavery would eventually end. Thus, as soon as the Free Birth law was passed, its most bitter opponents became its most ardent defenders and opposed any new measures to further abolition. The antislavery forces, however, were far from satisfied. Ruy Barbosa, one of the most enthusiastic defenders of abolition in the Chamber, soon raised his voice to declare that if the country were to await the effects of the law, slavery would end only in the middle of the twentieth century. Something had to be done to accelerate the process.

For a while, however, abolitionism seems to have lost its drive in Parliament. Politicians seemed to be more concerned with the economic crisis which had reached the country in 1875 and with electoral reform. But the abolitionist campaign continued in the streets and at the beginning of the eighties, after the approval of a new electoral law, the abolitionist campaign found resonance in Parliament again. From this period onward a conflict clearly developed in the Chamber between the majority of representatives from the Northeastern provinces, who favored discussion of the slavery question, and the representatives of the coffee-growing provinces, the majority of whom favored the maintenance of the status quo.

Outside Parliament the abolitionist campaign continued to gain strength. Abolitionists organized conferences, bazaars, fund-raising parties, and public meetings. More violent and effective were the activities of groups of abolitionists who promoted the escape of the slaves. Helped by abolitionists, an increasing number of slaves ran away from plantations, causing serious losses to their owners.[50]

Although abolitionists were more active in the coffee-growing provinces, particularly in the urban centers, it was in the provinces of the North and Northeast, least dependent on slave labor, that emancipation advanced most rapidly. In 1883–84 slavery was abolished in Amazonas, a province which had very few slaves, and Ceará, where small farming was the usual form of agriculture. Abolitionists in Rio celebrated with great alacrity these two events. And in 1884 because of abolitionist pressure the question of emancipation was brought back to Parliament. Opinion among abolitionists was divided. Some still believed gradual emancipation to be the most advisable course, others wanted immediate and total abolition. For some such as Nabuco, the cause had to be won in Parliament; for others such as Patrocínio, a mulatto journalist, and Lopes Trovão, one of the few socialists in Brazil at the time, it had to be fought in the streets and in the slave quarters. In spite of their divergence, the activities of the agitators prepared for and strengthened the action of Parliament.

In the areas of greatest concentration of slaves, such as the sugar-growing region of Campos and the coffee-growing parts of Rio de Janeiro and São Paulo, tension between slaveowners and abolitionists led to harsh confrontations. Plantation owners, with weapons in their hands, sought to defend their threatened property and attacked the abolitionists. They established secret clubs and created private militias. In the small towns of the backland, judges and functionaries who favored the slaves were threatened and abolitionists were persecuted and expelled. Parliament was flooded with petitions against the abolitionist movement. And representatives of the landowners spoke in favor of repressive measures:

> This group of agitators who have now gotten together in this country to propagandize in favor of the abolition of slavery are the same who make up the nihilist party in Russia, the socialist party in Germany, and the communist party elsewhere in Europe. Let us therefore be forewarned against this rabble who prefer sanguinary struggles and rivers of blood to having the question regularly channeled and peacefully resolved,

said one representative, and his words were supported by others who blamed the government for not restraining the abolitionists.[51]

In this atmosphere of agitation, a new cabinet was called to form a government. The head of the cabinet, Manuel Pinto de Souza Dantas, presented himself to Parliament as firmly committed to raising the question of slavery once more. The cabinet's program was moderate and could be summed up in a single phrase, which Dantas used in Parliament: "Neither retreat, nor halt, nor undue haste." His program, however, provoked an immediate reaction both within the Chamber and outside it. The climate of tension created in the capital spread to the countryside.

The bill presented to the Chamber of Deputies by the government merely proposed the emancipation of slaves over sixty years of age. The only aspect that could be considered revolutionary was that freedom was granted without compensation. The bill required newly freed slaves who chose to remain on the plantations to work in accordance with their abilities. It established a progressive tax on the transfer of slaves, increased the emancipation fund, and provided for new registration of all slaves. Those freed under the terms of the bill were required to live for five years after emancipation in the county in which they had previously resided.

Rui Barbosa defended the bill and prophetically warned those who opposed it: "Your apparent victories will turn against you. After each one, the spirit of freedom becomes more powerful, more demanding, more audacious, and reemerges on a wider scale. The moderate concessions which you refuse today will tomorrow satisfy no one." His warning had no effect. The cabinet received a vote of confidence by a small margin. Once again it became clear that the slavery question transcended parties. The delegations from São Paulo, Rio de Janeiro, and Minas Gerais, three coffee-growing provinces, voted almost en masse against the new cabinet, with the Liberals among them voting against their own party. Of the representatives of these three provinces, only seven voted in favor.[52]

Protests against the bill grew. The coffee, agricultural, and commercial associations all were firmly opposed. And all the rhetorical devices of the period were mobilized in the declamation of impassioned and vacuous speeches for or against the bill. The newspapers in the pay of the slaveholders assailed the bill and the abolitionists. The opponents of the law argued that since the Free Birth law would lead naturally to an end of slavery, nothing else needed to be done in that direction. And their slogan was "No concession without compensation."

The opposition was such that the cabinet was finally defeated. The bill was reformulated by the cabinet that followed and was approved only after another Liberal cabinet fell and was replaced by a Conservative one. By that time one important change had been introduced in the bill: the period for the freeing of slaves was extended and severe penalties were imposed on those who aided runaway slaves, a measure conceived to placate slaveowners. Among the supporters of the law there had been many who, afraid of agitation, intended to make a concession which, without going very far, would deter the march of subversion.

The discussion of the bill made clear the existence of a new division within the coffee-growing group. The representatives of the western São Paulo region, the most productive, voted in favor of the bill. This shift in their earlier position provoked discontent among the others who were still tied to slavery and trusted that the government could free slaves only by means of compensation.[53]

Slavery, however, was doomed. From this point onward the disintegration of the slave system proceeded rapidly. An important factor in this process was the mass escape of slaves from the plantations—often observed with indifference by the troops called to recapture them.

Clashes increased whenever the authorities tried to guarantee order and capture runaways. The plantation owners, unable to prevent the slaves from running away, granted them freedom on the condition that they continue working on the plantations for a number of years. Even so, many were still unable to retain their workers. The slaves, encouraged and led by abolitionists, continued to leave their work and go to other plantations where they were hired as salaried laborers. Even the most reluctant plantation owners were forced to accept these arrangements, which had been imposed upon them by the tumult that had spread through the rural areas. In São Paulo, the Republican party—largely made up of coffee plantation owners from the western part of the province—which since its foundation in 1870 had not committed itself on the slavery question, ended up by approving in 1887 a report deciding that the Republicans would free their slaves by 14 July 1889.[54]

The abolitionist campaign had never been so intense and so successful. In Parliament in 1887, Nabuco urged the army to refuse to catch runaway slaves. Shortly thereafter the military decided to request of Princess Isabel that they be relieved of such dishonorable tasks. Slavery was losing its last basis of support. Unrest had reached such a point that the São Paulo provincial assembly requested Parliament to carry out abolition. Disorder and turmoil had created a dangerous and unbearable situation.

Upon reopening in 1888, Parliament was faced with a de facto situation: João Alfredo, who had organized a new cabinet at the request of the princess regent, proposed the immediate and unconditional abolition of slavery.[55]

Only nine deputies voted against the bill, eight of whom represented the province of Rio de Janeiro. This was the last protest by the agricultural interests of that province, which would be the most affected by abolition. The law of 13 May 1888 abolishing slavery without compensation was the death blow to an area already in crisis and meant the loss of status for many coffee plantation owners from this region as well as for a large number of northeastern sugar growers who were operating with a small margin of profit.

With abolition came a shift in political power. The collapse of the traditional oligarchies that had held power during the empire and had identified themselves with the monarchy was accelerated. In the following year the monarchy was overthrown and the republic proclaimed. Political power shifted from the sugar cane areas to the new coffee-growing areas. In western São Paulo coffee grown in the *terras roxas* produced harvests never equalled before. A new oligarchy emerged which would rule the country during the first republic (1889–1930).

After abolition, the dreary prophecies of national catastrophe were not fulfilled. Despite the temporary disorganization of labor, the rapid decline of some areas, and the impoverishment of some planters, the pace of economic development in Brazil accelerated. Immigrants flowed in large numbers to the coffee areas. They served the needs of an expanding agriculture and made possible the organization of plantations along more modern and rational lines. However, the living conditions of the rural workers did not change substantially. And many of the prejudices developed during the period of slavery remained unchanged.

In spite of these limitations, new possibilities for upward social mobility were opened. The beginning of the urbanization process and the attempts to develop industry, the construction of the railroads, the organization of credit institutions, and the increase in commerce had all opened up new horizons. The expansion of coffee plantations and the westward movement of the frontier also favored social mobility.

Immigrants took advantage of these new opportunities. The former slaves, because of racial discrimination, were, with few exceptions, unable to compete with foreigners. The majority continued at their hoes, in a style of life not different from the one they had had before abolition. Some, attracted by the mirage of the cities, gathered in the urban centers, where they came to live by their wits, taking on the lowest tasks. Others left the plantations and went into subsistence agriculture.[56]

Since abolition had been the result more of a desire to free Brazil from the problems of slavery than of a wish to emancipate the slaves, the dominant classes did not concern themselves with the black man and his integration into a class society. The ex-slave was left to his own devices. His difficulties in adjusting to new conditions were taken by the elites as proof of his racial inferiority. Many ex-slaveholders went as far as to say that the blacks had been happier as slaves than they were as free men since they were incapable of leading their own lives.[57]

Contemporaries differed in interpreting abolition. Some identified with the abolitionist movement and considered it the result of the actions of a handful of idealists. Others, more identified with the rural classes, saw abolition as the will of the emperor and of Princess Isabel. Some said that the 1888 law had been wise and opportune, others that it had driven the rural classes into bankruptcy. Those subjective impressions interfered with the evaluation of the process. Basing their studies on the testimony of contemporaries and relying primarily on parliamentary evidence, historians of the first generation after abolition saw it mainly as a political phenomenon. The ties between the disintegration of the slave system and the economic and social changes at work in Brazil during the second half of the century passed unnoticed. It was only later, when starting from viewpoints less compromised by the seigneurial view of the world, that historians and social scientists began revising the myths that society had elaborated to justify the slave system. Only then was it possible to analyze slavery and the abolitionist movement in a new light.

Abolition represented a stage in the process of the liquidation of Brazil's colonial structures, involving an extensive revision of the lifestyles and values of Brazilian society. It did not, however, mean a definitive break with the past. Rationalization of production methods, the improvement in the living standards of rural workers, and the struggle against racial discrimination are all parts of a process still under way.

7 TOWN AND COUNTRY

The study of Brazilian history has been plagued by the use of models of interpretation that derive from the analysis of historical processes which took place in the "central" areas of the capitalist world. From this perspective, Brazilian history has gone two ways: either it has become an exercise in identifying the similarities between what has happened elsewhere and what happens in Brazil, or it has become a desperate search for the "Brazilian specificity." But whether historians stress similarities or differences, their point of reference is in fact the same conception of what "normal" patterns of historical change or development are—that idealized picture of what took place in the central areas of the capitalist system, defined mostly as Britain and France. However "useful" those models may have been in the past (and perhaps we should ask, useful for whom?), today they seem to have a counterproductive effect: they blind Brazilians to the reality of their own historical experience.

Following European and North American models, historians who study nineteenth-century Brazil have usually equated urbanization with modernization. They have depicted urban middle classes as the primary—sometimes even exclusive—carriers of progress. To the middle classes goes most of the credit for the campaigns in favor of abolition, universal suffrage, separation of Church and State, the proclamation of the republic, intellectual movements like positivism, and new literary styles.

Underlying these perceptions is a conviction that rural societies are inherently traditional: aristocratic, patriarchal, conservative, committed to an elitist education that is rhetorical and ornamental, given to leisure and ostentation, and held inert by massive illiteracy and limited social mobility. The city, on the other hand, is conceived as, inherently, the locus of modernity. It is bourgeois, individualistic, and democratic; it generates and thrives on mobility instead of fixed status; it promotes literacy, science, and experimentation; and it values work and thrift. According to this model, in modern cities there is a breakdown of traditional social structures that were based on family ties and other forms of kinship; human relations become more contractual and less personalized. Status is not ascribed, as it is in the agrarian and traditional countryside; it is acquired. The historians who have worked with this model, in one of its variants or another, have usually assumed that in the long run the modernizing influence of urbanization would overtake the traditional world and transform it.

Although this conceptual model of urbanization has come under criticism from a variety of angles, it has shown remarkable resilience, and we continue to see young scholars repeating its old mistakes. This resilience is probably explained by the fact that whenever empirical evidence contradicts the theoretical model, the evidence is simply dismissed as atypical. But merely to designate something atypical is not to understand it. For this, we need to develop new models of interpretation, and this essay is intended as a contribution to that task.[1]

At the beginning of the nineteenth century, Brazil's population was predominantly rural. The few important cities were located primarily along the coast, where they functioned as centers for the export of colonial products and the import of manufactured goods. The only areas of the interior with an appreciable number of urban centers were the mining regions, but none of the mining towns compared to the major port cities. Except for a few places that had acquired significance from their location at the intersection of trade routes, settlements were insignificant and the population was dispersed in the rural areas.

Data for the late eighteenth century show that Rio de Janeiro, seat of the viceroyalty since 1763 and the port through which gold had been leaving Brazil since the beginning of the century, had a population of about 50,000. Next in importance was Salvador, the capital city of the colony from 1548 to 1763. An important port for sugar and tobacco, Salvador had a population close to 45,000. The third city was Recife, an important port for the sugar cane area, with 30,000. São Luiz do Maranhão, a port for the export of cotton, was next with 22,000 people. The only relatively important urban center that was not a port city was São Paulo, with 15,000. Located on a plateau, miles away from the coast, São Paulo had benefited since the beginning of the colonial period from its strategic geographic position as gateway to the hinterland; it had become the point of departure of routes leading to western, central and southern Brazil.[2]

The relative insignificance of the urban centers as well as their pattern of distribution along the coast can be explained by colonial policies and by the system of production prevalent during the colonial period. Originally, coastal cities had served as outposts from which explorers and pioneers had departed for the backlands. Colonial cities were military posts for the defense of the colony as well as seats of civil and religious authority and centers of culture and trade. Soon, however, the direction taken by the colonial economy led to a predominantly rural pattern of settlement, undercutting the cities' hegemony over the life of the colony.

Initially the colony was organized to produce tropical products for the world market. A rigid system of monopolies and privileges obliged the colonists to export and import everything through the mother country. During the first two centuries, Brazil specialized in the production of sugar, a highly profitable commodity in great demand in the international market. Sugar production, requiring heavy initial investments, led to the concentration of land, labor, and wealth in the hands of a few. This tendency was facilitated by the land policies of the Portuguese Crown, which stipulated that land would be given to those who had means to use the land productively—in other words to those with capital.

Millowners seeking to secure the necessary supply of cane to their mills incorporated more and more land into their estates. They also discovered that by owning more land they could increase the number of tenants and sharecroppers living under their control and dependent on their patronage. These men would help them protect their property from Indian attacks and could work on the plantation whenever extra labor was needed. In spite of legal restrictions limiting the size of grants given to a single person, millowners gradually managed to increase their estates. They evaded royal prohibitions by requesting grants in the names of different people within their families. And they acquired land through purchase, squatting, and marriage. In one way or another landowners in the sugar areas of the Northeast succeeded in monopolizing large tracts of land where they produced sugar for export as well as most of the things necessary for their own subsistence. Of course their monopoly over land and labor was never absolute. Smaller planters—those who owned land but did not have capital enough to build mills—supplied millowners with cane. And the great majority of the population, unable to participate directly in the export economy, cultivated small plots of land for their own subsistence, provided occasional services to the plantation, and sold their own produce in the small local markets. Outside the sugar areas, colonists who had access to the market economy either grew staples like cotton or tobacco or raised cattle.[3]

Everywhere, but more in the export sectors of the economy, the main problem confronting the colonists was the supply of labor. The colonists were few and access to the land was relatively easy. Thus, it was difficult to recruit people to work on plantations. The native population, living at the neolithic stage and unadapted to patterns of the commercial economy, resisted—at times violently—the settlers' attempts to force them to work on their plantations and farms. The Jesuits' opposition to Indian enslavement and the Crown's restrictions on the use of Indian labor complicated the colonists' problem of getting an adequate labor force. The solution they adopted was to use African slaves.[4] Of course, this was only possible in areas where capital accumulated and colonists had resources to buy African slaves. Elsewhere they continued to resort to Indian labor. By the end of the sixteenth century, black slaves had replaced the Indians on most of the plantations in the Northeast. The use of slave labor reinforced the tendency for wealth to become concentrated in the hands of a small minority. The acquisition of land and slaves became the major form of reinvestment of capital and the natural mechanism for expanding the economy. Land and labor also became symbols of status. The use of slave labor and the concentration of land and wealth in the hands of a minority were important factors in shaping the social structure and the system of values of colonial Brazil.

To extract maximum profit from their investments in slaves, the owners had to keep them busy throughout the year, but commercial crops had a seasonal character. If the conditions of the internal or international market had been different, the planters could have diversified their production. But in the early centuries, the internal market was insignificant, methods of transportation precarious, and the international market not ready to absorb a great variety of products. Thus sugar planters, in order to extract the maximum from their slaves, employed them in the production of crops for their own subsistence, selling the surplus in the cities or to the neighboring population. Although primarily devoted to the commercial economy, plantations functioned as semiautonomous entities producing most of what was necessary for their subsistence and importing only metal products, gunpowder, and luxury goods.[5]

The self-sufficiency of the large estates and their control of the internal market made it difficult for the small landholder to enter the commercial economy. Restricted in their participation in the internal market, small landowners were also shut off from the export economy by lack of capital and labor. With the exception of those located near towns, who gained some benefit from the existence of small local markets, most of the free population remained at or near the subsistence level.

The same system was responsible for the large number of vagrants that worried colonial authorities and chroniclers. These dispossessed, most of them free blacks, mulattos, or mestizos, were often blamed for the climate of insecurity in the colony. Ironically, however, the same men were given the task of defending the colony against maroons and Indians. They were jacks of all trades, always ready to join in protests against the colonial regime.

Whether as sharecroppers, tenants, or small proprietors, the rural population was almost totally dependent on the landlord, whom they served and from whom they expected protection. Millowners ground their cane, bought their produce, occasionally hired their services, often controlled their access to the land, and mediated between them and the royal bureaucracy. The small farmers do not seem to have developed any awareness of their own common interests. There was nothing similar in colonial Brazil to the Indian peasant communities in other Latin American countries. The Brazilian small proprietors, tenants, and sharecroppers tended to be isolated from each other, although always conscious of their dependency on the landlord to whom they were linked by bonds of patronage. Ethnically, they were a mixed lot of Portuguese, Indians, free blacks, mulattos, and mestizos. They came from different parts of the world and from a bewildering variety of cultural traditions. They shared only their poverty and dependence. As African slaves became the principal labor force, the small landholders were left undisturbed, except for occasional pressure from landlords to work or fight for them. In fact, their communities were essentially artificial arrangements centering on their shared relationship to landlords and millowners. God-parental relationships helped lend some cultural legitimacy to these artificial communities but could scarcely eliminate the conflicts and tensions that riddled them. In a seigneurial society, based on slave labor, where the maintenance of order depends on constant surveillance and repression, violence and arbitrariness are the real essence of life. So it is not surprising that popular versions of the medieval chansons de geste, exalting personal courage and violence, continued to be sung in Brazil even into the twentieth century.

In such a setting, the great landowners of the backlands exercised a control over society that was practically uncontested. And the backland towns were extensions of their domain. The landlords' hegemony was reinforced by the way municipal councils were organized. According to the traditional custom, all manual laborers as well as all those who could not prove the "purity of their blood" (that is, mestizos, mulattos, blacks, and Jews) were denied the right to participate in municipal councils. Women were also excluded. Most of the population was thus formally barred from political participation.[6]

In this circumstance, political struggles in the backlands were often more a matter of rivalries between important families and their clienteles than between different classes with contradictory goals. Municipal councils could occasionally become the stage for other types of conflict: resistance against royal authority and disputes between merchants and planters or between colonists and Jesuits. But until gold was discovered and the pattern of settlement changed from one essentially rural to one more urban and until the internal market began to develop, municipal councils in Brazil lacked the dynamism one finds in analogous institutions in other parts of the world. Those institutions, which had a long tradition in the Iberian Peninsula, gradually lost their power in the colony. The peasant and urban communities that had given strength to those institutions in Europe had been replaced in the colony by the artificial communities of the big estates and their clients. In the backlands, the plantation, not the peasant burg, constituted the cell of the society. And municipal arrangements tended to mirror the realities of surrounding plantations.

The power of the big landowners in the backlands was enhanced by the attitude of the royal bureaucracy, which tended to leave them very much on their own. The bureaucrats' attitude is easy to understand, for the bureaucracy's main functions were to supervise tax collection, to guarantee or enforce royal monopolies and privileges, and to defend the territory against foreigners' attacks. Since Brazil's economy relied almost exclusively on imports and exports and since internal trade was scarce, most of those supervisory functions could be accomplished in the port cities. For the maintenance of internal order—fighting against Indians and keeping slaves under control—the colonial bureaucracy could gladly rely on the large landowners who often kept their own private militia. Only when things got out of hand did the government send colonial troops to their support. The landowners also asserted their right to dispense justice to their clients, thus saving the royal government much of the nuisance of maintaining an elaborate court system in the backlands. And so royal officials tended to stay in the coastal cities, leaving the rural population more or less at the mercy of the planters.[7]

Lacking the commercial, industrial, political, judicial, and administrative functions that gave life to European and North American cities, the towns of the backlands were reduced to mere points of periodic gathering for the rural population to participate in religious rituals and exchange the surplus produce of their farms. But the self-sufficiency of the plantations—including even the construction of chapels on many of them—severely limited these periodic ritual and economic functions of the towns.

Nor could the backland towns develop any sort of manufacturing base. Defending the interests of merchants at home, Portugal restricted manufacturing in the colony. These regulations worked only because the internal market in Brazil for manufactured goods was so limited. Thus, with the exception of a few industries like shipbuilding—located obviously in port cities—most of what was not manufactured on the big estates by slaves or other craftsmen during the colonial period was imported from Europe.[8]

Education, another function usually associated with urban life, also had little import in this agrarian society, where most of the work was done by slaves and the predominant religion was Catholicism. Contrary to Protestantism or Judaism, which tended to require literacy on the part of the believer, Catholicism was based on oral communication of doctrine and did not encourage the critical reading of religious texts. Indifference toward education was reinforced by political practices that excluded most of the population from participation. Thus, since there were no economic, political, or religious reasons for the population to be instructed, culture became a privilege of the clergy and the elites. The great majority of the population remained illiterate. Unlike the Spaniards, who had to confront the problem of controlling massive Indian populations showing great cultural sophistication, the Portuguese met with a scattered, stone-age native population. This limited the missionary work in the colony and reduced the role of religious education. Spiritual assistance to African slaves, such as it was, came either from chaplains residing on plantations or from itinerant priests.

Portugal, again unlike Spain, preferred to retain a monopoly on higher education and did not create a single university in Brazil throughout the entire colonial period. The sons of the elite had to go to Portugal for a university education. It was left to the religious orders to fill the other cultural needs in the colony. The ordaining of priests and nuns, the preparation of small bureaucrats, the education of the sons and daughters of the elite remained throughout the colonial period the main purpose of education.[9] In a society predominantly rural, in which opportunities were limited and patronage controlled social mobility, education was seen more often as a badge of status than as an instrument for social improvement; it was a tool for preserving the social order, not for changing it. Medieval scholasticism accomplished this purpose better than modern empiricism. Education stressed rhetorical skill and erudition rather than science and experimentation. Within this context, the survival of medieval notions in colonial Brazil, the elitist tone of the educational system and the high degree of illiteracy of the colonial population were not mere "legacies" of the Iberian world, or products of the Thomistic "tradition"—as they have sometimes been seen. They were as much products of Brazil's economic, social, and political structure as they were impositions of the mother country.

Within the framework of a slave society, in which there was little opportunity for social mobility, the idea of work and thrift characteristic of what has been called the "capitalist ethos" could have little meaning. In place of these values the Brazilian elite cultivated ostentation, luxury, and leisure. Such values, usually considered typical of "aristocratic" or "precapitalist" societies, tended to permeate the whole of Brazilian society, not just its elite. The first action of a freedman when he succeeded in accumulating a little capital was to buy a slave and not to work anymore. During the colonial period all chroniclers complained about the laziness of the population, its tendency to live in an aristocratic way, to abhor manual labor, to be concerned with fancy clothes, and to display manners typical of the nobility. To believe those chroniclers, white and black, poor and rich were all guilty of the same sin. Even if we discount such remarks as products of an exacerbated moral zeal, we cannot but believe that some of it was true.

"Aristocratic" tendencies were not new, and they had not been invented in Brazil. They had already been the subject of complaints in Portugal in the sixteenth century. The Portuguese playwright Gil Vicente had ridiculed them in his plays. And the Crown had tried without success to curtail vagrancy and to prevent commoners from adopting the ways of the nobility. But the situation does seem to have been aggravated in the colony. As one historian remarked, "even those who had earned their living by wielding the mattock and the hoe in Portugal and the Azores had no intention of doing so in Brazil if they could possibly avoid it." [10] The perpetuation in the colony of legislation that granted so many privileges to the nobility—exemption from taxes, special justice, access to certain positions from which other social groups were barred—made noble status most desirable. And since to live as a noble a man could not work with his hands or get involved in commerce and trade (at least until the eighteenth century, when the legislation changed), it should not be surprising to find that many people avoided those activities. This aristocratic ethic was clearly reinforced by the system of property and labor, a system that allowed the elite to live in a noble way and demoralized labor.

The control of the means of production by a few also created conditions for the survival among the elites of the extended family organized on paternal lines. Following the Iberian legal tradition, in colonial Brazil the head of the family had supreme authority over his family. He decided the fate of his children, who were his dependents and owed him obedience in return for his protection and support. The system of inheritance and the institution of the dowry did give relative autonomy to some upper-class women. And during the colonial period many were heads of plantations after their husbands died. But, in general, upper-class women played a subordinate role, supervising the domestic economy and bearing children.[11]

Alongside the monogamous family, sanctified by the church and strengthened by concerns with the preservation of property, slavery created particularly favorable conditions for the development of illicit sexual relations, those relations involving upper-class males and lower-classes females, slave and free. Although condemned by the Church, such liaisons were more or less accepted by society, as the frequent recognition in wills of illegitimate children testifies. Within this context, moral tolerance and laxity prevailed. The secular clergy, always mindful of its ties with the plantation, accommodated. The prohibition against the marriage of priests—often disregarded—only reinforced this tendency toward moral tolerance.

Economic structures and traditional institutions and values were thus intimately related in such a way that they not only contributed to the perpetuation in the colony of an "aristocratic ethos" but reinforced it. In spite of being directly involved in the production of commodities for the international market and being moved by profit the Brazilian plantation owner, surrounded by his family, his slaves, and his clientele of free men, could pretend to recreate in the New World a seigneurial style of life.[12] Merchants and other social groups modeled their behavior upon that of the landlords. Thus Brazilian colonial society was scarcely receptive to the values of the urban petite-bourgeoisie, which in Europe was laying the foundation for a capitalist ethos.

In short, the conditions of production that prevailed in the sugar cane areas of the northeast in the early centuries of colonization did not favor the proliferation of urban centers, or the emergence of bourgeois values commonly associated with the process of urbanization in Europe. Although conditions in other areas of the country where plantations did not develop were different, in the first two centuries of Brazilian history the sugar elites set the tone and established the limits of adequate behavior.

The cattle economy originally developed in the Northeast and in

Bahía as a complement to the sugar plantations. But it, too, led to the concentration of large tracts of land in a few hands. And, although the tobacco economy favored small farms, its social patterns were not radically different, for the owners gravitated toward the port cities. In areas where sugar, cattle, or tobacco did not thrive, colonists tended to recreate a style of life which seemed to their chroniclers to be reminiscent of Portuguese villages. This was the case for São Paulo during the sixteenth century. Located on a 2,400-foot plateau, with only difficult access to the sea and its trade, São Paulo grew as a gateway to the *sertão* (backland), the point of origin for expeditions in search of gold, silver, and Indian labor. A study of Paulista wills for this early period does not show the extraordinary concentration of wealth that was typical of the sugar areas and suggests that the local government was more democratic in structure. The farming economy was one of subsistence for the most part, and there were few black slaves. But the large numbers of Indians (mostly women) recruited to work on São Paulo's farms, and the wealth that resulted from trade with sugar areas and later with the mines, led to the development of a seigneurial mentality, with its preoccupation with genealogy and family struggles.

The discovery of gold in the late seventeenth century forced a reorientation of colonial policies. To avoid gold smuggling, the Portuguese Crown was forced to extend its control to the countryside. Roads were built to link the coast to the mining areas, which became a point of attraction for people coming from different areas in the colony. The news that gold had been discovered in Brazil led thousands of Portuguese to emigrate in search of fortune. In the mining areas towns grew at a rapid pace. The mining towns became thriving commercial, political, administrative, cultural, and religious centers. Their growth induced other areas to grow crops and raise cattle to supply the miners. The expansion of the internal market created new opportunities for social mobility. And it was not by chance that it was in the mining areas that the first conspiracy for independence took place.

In an 1804 census of the captaincy of Minas Gerais and Vila Rica, a total of 8,180 people were surveyed, 6,087 free and 2,893 slaves. Wealth, as measured by the ownership of slaves, was still mostly concentrated in the hands of a white elite. Mineowners, merchants, and high civil or military bureaucrats were at the top of the social ladder. But the census also registered a number of free blacks and mulattos in a wide variety of occupations—prospectors, grocers, tailors, shoemakers, tinsmiths, carpenters, saddlers, wood-vendors, masons, musicians, cabinetmakers, sculptors, peddlers, soldiers, carters, bakers, and so on. Many owned one or two slaves.[13]

If gold led toward the creation of a more fluid society, the overwhelming presence of the royal bureaucracy, the restrictive policies of the Portuguese Crown, and the use of slave labor in the mines tended to perpetuate some of the traditional structures characteristic of the earlier settlements. The royal bureaucracy continued to be a source of patronage. Royal monopolies and prohibitions continued to limit the expansion of free trade and the development of manufactures. Land still accumulated in the hands of those who had capital (since the size of land grants depended on the number of slaves the applicants owned). And, although there were more opportunities for free laborers, slaves remained the principal work force. Finally, even though gold stimulated the development of an internal market, part of the wealth produced was pumped out by the fiscal policies of the Portuguese Crown. And so, at the end of the century, when the placer deposits were already exhausted, the mining towns, deprived of the wealth that had given them life, lost their impetus. The coastal cities continued to be hegemonic, and most of the population continued to live in the rural areas.

In 1808, forced to flee to Brazil because of Portugal's invasion by Napoleonic troops, Prince João, regent of Portugal, opened the Brazilian ports to all nations, allowed the development of manufactures

FIG. 17. View of Rio de Janeiro about 1860

and took other measures to liberate the colony from the restrictions that had inhibited its development. Prince João's policies—which were justified in terms of liberal ideas—inaugurated a new period in Brazilian history. A few years later, in 1822, when the regent returned to Portugal, Brazil became an independent nation. This gave a new impulse to the port cities where most of the provincial capitals were located. These cities benefited from the expansion of international trade and became important political, administrative, and cultural centers. First among them was Rio de Janeiro, the capital of the new empire.

The change in legal status favored a somewhat more rapid accumulation of capital in the newly emancipated colony, but it did not alter the structure of the economy. The country continued to export tropical products. The large estate continued to be the standard unit of production and slaves were still the main source of labor. The development of manufactures was blocked not only by the competition of other countries, particularly England, but by the lack of interest of the entrepreneurial groups that already derived large profits from plantations and trade. Stressing the "agrarian vocation" of the country, they refused to support the projects to develop manufactures suggested by a few visionaries who argued in favor of protectionist tariffs.

Under these conditions, the social structure of Brazilian society and the patterns of urbanization remained substantially the same until after the middle of the nineteenth century. The only new trends were the emergence of a group of politicians, bureaucrats, and other professionals—coming out of schools created with the purpose of forming a ruling elite—and the increasing importance of local merchants who profited from the expansion of the export-import economy. These new groups, however, did not constitute a new class. They were integrated into the clientele of the agrarian elite, to whom they were often tied by links of family and patronage, and whose world view they shared. Among them, however, there were always a number of dissidents, mostly merchants and artisans who were being hurt by the new foreign competition that resulted from independence. But these dissidents could be easily crushed (see chap. 3).

Although exports and imports increased, subsistence farming continued to be an important activity for most of the population and internal trade was still limited. The rural population had little power for consumption and the few who had it, the big planters, usually bought what they needed through their agents in the ports. Such transactions stimulated commercial activities in the coastal cities, but did little to improve the dismal state of commerce in local towns.

Many travelers visiting Brazil in the nineteenth century commented on the profound contrast between the busier, more modern and Euro-peanized port cities and the sleepy towns of the interior, which with few exceptions seemed to exist on the edges of civilization.[14] In the backlands, the boundaries between rural and urban were imprecise. Farm lands reached right into the town. Cows, goats, pigs, chickens, and horses were frequently seen grazing in the streets, feeding on the grass that grew in the plazas or sprouted up between the coarse paving stones. Town houses were constructed of wattle and daub, following the colonial tradition, and many remained closed during the week since their occupants came to the city only on Sundays and holidays to participate in religious ceremonies and local fairs.

In these backland towns the most conspicuous buildings were the church, the town hall, and the jail. The church continued to be the center of public activities. In the church the dead were buried and elections took place. The church bells tolled the hour. Holidays and festivals promoted by the church marked the pace of life. Lacking modern facilities, the residents remained dependent on public fountains and wells. Waste was emptied into streams and sometimes drained down the middle of the streets. Public lighting was rare, and wherever it did exist the usual source of illumination was fish oil. Most towns had no hospitals or doctors. Some hospital service was provided by the santa casas, philanthropic religious institutions supported by lay brother-hoods. As during the colonial period, these brotherhoods gathered leading members of the community, who assisted the santa casa with both personal donations and state subsidies they were able to obtain through their political influence. In return, the santa casa's patrons used the institution to provide medical assistance for their innumer-able clients and slaves.[15] But the santa casas operated in only a few towns. Little wonder that many foreigners visiting the backlands dur-ing the first half of the century were mistaken for doctors and found themselves besieged by town dwellers with questions about symptoms and treatments.

With the exception of the rich planters, most of the backland popu-lation lived in isolation, ignorant of the outside world. In the absence of other methods of communication, peddlers and muleteers carried news and gossip from one place to the other. At the time of independ-ence, a French traveler in the province of São Paulo found that the inhabitants knew nothing about important events only a few miles away.[16] The general ignorance and apparent apathy of the rural and ur-ban population in the backlands was not just the result of illiteracy or of the lack of an adequate postal service or newspapers. It was also a consequence of the absence of a tradition of political participation. Paternalistic practices inherited from the colonial period left the town dwellers of the backlands with a political vision no broader than that of their rural neighbors. Like them, the urban population often belonged to the clienteles of the important planters.

Considering the isolation in which they lived, it is not surprising that most of the people in the backlands received travelers with a great deal of curiosity and excitement, gladly opening their doors to them. But in the backlands, hospitality was more than the product of curiosity; it was a necessity. Since hotels and inns were rare, travelers depended on the good will of the local population for shelter, and usually a letter of recommendation was all that was needed to solve the problem. Because the urban centers were small and most people knew each other, the population felt safe and doors were never locked. Except for petty thefts, crimes against property were still uncommon in this society not yet permeated by capitalist values. Much more common were crimes of passion, usually resulting from family rivalries or offenses against personal honor.

While life in most backland towns seemed to continue without fundamental changes, in the port cities things were changing more rapidly. It was in these cities that business deals were made and political schemes were plotted. Wealthy planters visited them regularly, to take care of their business, to find entertainment, or to satisfy their desire "to take a bath of civilization." In these cities, artisanry, small business, and services flourished. Even for slaves life seemed to be easier. They could walk through the streets and meet with fellow countrymen, come in contact with free blacks and mulattos, join fraternities and religious brotherhoods and even earn some money with which they could buy their freedom.

Upper-class women also enjoyed more freedom in the cities. In the backlands they still lived a very cloistered life, subordinated to strict patriarchal discipline, participating only in family or church-sponsored events, rarely being seen in public places alone. In Rio de Janeiro, Recife, Salvador, São Paulo, and other big cities, they were allowed to attend the theater, balls, and other public events. At the court, where the cream of society gathered, Maria Graham, an English traveler who visited Brazil at the time of independence, met women who, in her opinion, could have felt at home in the most sophisticated salons in Europe.[17] But those were exceptional women. Since most women were still restricted to domestic functions and interacted primarily with slaves, the education provided them continued to be poor, and travelers still marveled at the Brazilian custom of segregating wives and daughters. Life was freer for lower-class women. In spite of the ordeals they faced, they enjoyed a freedom of movement and a degree of independence unknown to most upper-class women.

Generally speaking, class and color lines seem to have coincided in the urban as well as in the rural areas. Burmeister, traveling through Brazil in 1853, observed that he rarely found an estate or mine owned by a person of color. The further he penetrated the interior, however, the greater the number of colored persons he found holding high positions. In towns far from the coast blacks and mulattos were police officers, judges, schoolmasters, and priests—something rarely seen in the port cities. Everywhere, however, whites monopolized positions of influence.[18]

Whether in rural or urban areas, mulattos as a whole were more upwardly mobile than their darker-skinned brethren. The opportunities for social elevation increased in proportion to the lightness of a freedman's skin. And as the nineteenth century progressed, the situation of the mulatto improved. The expansion of administrative and bureaucratic services, the proliferation of cultural institutions, increased commercial activity, the gradual elimination of slavery from the cities and the consequent growth of opportunities for free laborers, all opened new avenues for social mobility. But the path upward was still open only to a few outstanding blacks and mulattos, either the illegitimate sons of white men or members of their clienteles. They rose in society through the patronage of their fathers, godfathers, or friends. Illustrious blacks and mulattos, such as Tôrres Homem, José do Patrocínio, Luiz Gama, André Rebouças, Gonçalves Dias, Natividade Saldanha, Machado de Assis, José Maurício, Tobias Barreto, occupied important positions in the Council of State, the Chamber of Deputies, the Senate, the diplomatic service, or stood out in the field of arts and letters. But they were still exceptions to the rule.

Although the cities were growing, the new urban groups did not acquire enough autonomy to develop an independent political view. The political system based on income qualification barred most of the population from political participation. In fact one could argue that immediately after independence, the oligarchies acquired even more power than they had had before. Now they, or their representatives, were the government. They controlled the bureaucracy and monopolized positions in the Parliament, the Council of State, the ministries, and other government offices. Legislation that followed independence did not grant much autonomy to the city populations. City governments were dependent on the provincial government for the approval of municipal regulations and for the appointment of local function-

FIG. 18. The white woman at home

aries. Even decisions concerning the local budget had to be approved
by the provincial assembly. Moreover, because of the extreme centralization characteristic of the Brazilian political system, the cities were
left with very little resources. In 1868, the central government received
80 percent of all revenues. The provinces collected just over 16 percent, and the municipalities just under 3 percent. These political, administrative, and financial constraints subordinated urban groups to
the rural oligarchies that controlled politics and administration at the
provincial and national levels.[19]

In the important coastal centers the rural oligarchies did have to
share power with urban groups—including importers, exporters, merchants, and professionals. But since their interests were often comple-
mentary, it was not difficult for them to reach some sort of compromise. In the backlands, however, the rural oligarchies' domination was
uncontested. The patriarchal structure, the system of clientele, and traditional mores all remained in place. Landowners built mansions in
the cities that followed the plans of their houses in the countryside and
bought to the countryside some urban amenities. Their plantation
houses were sometimes even more elegant than the houses they built in
the cities. But in the backland cities, as well as in the rural areas, the
landowners ruled. They had political power, controlled the administration and set the tone for public life. They resisted with success the

FIG. 19. Supper time at the master's house

occasional attempts on the part of the central government to curtail their power.

In one typical instance, a royal functionary was sent to São Paulo by the imperial government to investigate a case of slave contraband. He was forced to stop his inquiry because of pressure from the powerful people involved in this illicit transaction. The unfortunate functionary could not find a single witness willing to testify against those powerful men, even though many people were aware of their wrongdoings. Equally suggestive is the case of another functionary who could not enforce the law in a small town in São Paulo because all the public offices were controlled by one family which was not willing to cooperate.[20]

Considering the obstacles faced by the royal bureaucrats whenever they tried to implement the law in the backlands, it is not surprising that they left the local bosses very much on their own. Thus, the local population was forced to seek the support of the local bosses to whom they gave their ballots in exchange for "aid and protection." As a consequence, even as late as the 1870s, local politics in the cities of the backlands consisted mainly of squabbles between clienteles.

Everywhere, in the backlands as well as in the coastal cities, the boundaries between public and private were not clear. Civic improve-

ments were often the result of donations made by large landowners
who, in return, used municipal funds to further their personal interests. Politicians did not act as representatives of the people but as their
benefactors. And constitutional rights were often perceived as personal privileges granted to a few by those in power. Because of the system of clientele and patronage, civic matters rarely attained the level of
impersonality necessary to insure administrative efficiency. Bureaucratic appointments depended much more on friendship than on merit.
The number of bureaucrats increased arbitrarily and often unneces-

Fig. 20. Black woman selling goods

sarily because patrons had to provide enough jobs to insure the loyalty of their clients. And whenever a political party took power, it dismissed or persecuted functionaries appointed by the party that had fallen from grace. As a consequence of these practices the bureaucracy was inefficient and unstable. And while the multiplicity of posts and pensions may have enhanced the political power and prestige of the rural oligarchies, it also drained municipal finances and blocked attempts to make administration more modern and efficient.

Political patronage was also a precondition for success at the national level. Politicians did not succeed in their careers, writers did not become famous, generals were not promoted, bishops were not appointed, entrepreneurs were not successful without the help of a patron. As the novelist José de Alencar wrote, "Industrial enterprises, commercial associations, banks, public works, financial operations, privileges . . . all these abundant sources of wealth issue from the heights of Power . . . Everything depends on patronage, even the press, which needs State subsidies to survive."[21] Trapped in a system that devalued personal initiative and intensified dependence, urban people—particularly in the backlands—had no real choice. They had to assimilate to the landed oligarchy's clienteles. In this milieu liberal political institutions imported from Europe and the United States were put at the service of a minority, and the typical "bourgeois" values did not thrive.

During the second half of the nineteenth century several changes contributed to the expansion of the internal market, stimulated the process of urbanization, and created opportunities for the emergence of new groups that made a critique of the social and political order, in the name of liberal ideas and bourgeois notions. At the same time rural elites, bowing to external economic and political pressures, were forced to "modernize" the structures of production. They abolished the slave trade in 1850, made experiments with free labor, promoted immigration, introduced new systems of processing sugar and coffee, and invested money in industries and banks. All these initiatives were financed either with foreign capital or with capital accumulated in exports and imports.

After 1850, when the slave trade ended, the scarcity of bondsmen and the rapid expansion of coffee plantations combined to stimulate the transfer of slaves from the cities to the rural areas. The same pressures accelerated planters' efforts to substitute immigrants for slaves. The gradual change from slave to free labor contributed to the growth of the internal market and created new bases for industrial development. From mid-century on, and especially between 1870 and 1900, European immigrants arrived in Brazil in increasing numbers. In a little over ten years (1890–1901) the province of São Paulo alone received about 800,000 Italian, Portuguese, Spanish, and Austrian immigrants, along with others from other nations.[22] Most of these immigrants headed for the coffee estates, where they took on work previously done by slaves. In contrast, further south, in the provinces of Paraná, Santa Catarina, and Rio Grande do Sul, a different type of immigrant settlement developed. There, immigrants received plots of land and created communities devoted to their own subsistence. Gradually, however, they were incorporated into the market economy. The demographic growth of Blumenau, a German town founded in 1850 in the Itajaí Valley in Santa Catarina typifies this process, but it also shows how slow this process was. Although Blumenau was founded by the middle of the nineteenth century, it continued to be a small town until the turn of the century, when the area was integrated into the national economy. Whatever they devoted themselves to, immigrants contributed to the development of the internal market and to urban growth. Even those who remained on the coffee plantations managed sometimes to grow foodstuffs between the rows of coffee trees and sold their surplus in nearby cities in exchange for other goods, bringing more life to the backland towns.[23]

As soon as immigrants managed to amass some capital, they moved to towns where they worked as artisans or small merchants. Those who had arrived with some capital or had connections in the cities went straight to the cities. As a consequence, the immigrant population grew very rapidly in the urban centers. By 1872, Rio de Janeiro had a total of 275,000 inhabitants, 84,000 of whom were foreign-born. In 1890, its population reached approximately 522,000, of whom 124,000 were foreigner, about one-fourth of the total. In 1872, the foreign-born accounted for 12 percent of the population in Porto Alegre, 12 percent in Curitiba, and almost 8 percent in São Paulo. In 1890, 22 percent of the people in the city of São Paulo were foreign-born. Immigrants tended to concentrate in the southern provinces. Very few went to live in the North or the Northeast. By 1890, São Paulo, Minas, the Federal District, and Rio Grande do Sul had almost 90 percent of the foreign-born population. In 1900, 50 percent of the immigrant population lived in the province of São Paulo.[24]

In *The Mansions and the Shanties*, Gilberto Freyre claimed that because immigrants did not share the traditional Brazilian prejudice against manual labor, they came to control artisanry and most of the retail trade in the important urban centers. Brazilians—even those of the poorest families—preferred bureaucratic positions. Later research showed, however, that immigrants coming from areas in which negative attitudes toward manual labor prevailed, particularly Spain, Italy, and Portugal—countries that provided the bulk of the immigrant population in Brazil—behaved very much as Brazilians did. The second generation aspired to bachelor's degrees and coveted "respectable" positions.[25] Although these findings may have held true for some immigrant groups, the fact remains that immigrants did monopolize manual labor in the cities. It is not clear whether this was a result of their lack of prejudice against manual labor or of the lack of alternatives, but there is no doubt that immigrants played an important role in the development of urban activities and contributed much to the growth of the internal market.

A precondition for the expansion of the internal market was the improvement of transportation. Until the middle of the nineteenth century most produce continued to be transported by oxcarts, mule trains, and barges, or by sail boats navigating along the coast. After the 1850s the construction of railroads contributed to the expansion of the internal market and to the development of urban centers. By the end of the century there were 9,000 kilometers of track completed and another 15,000 under construction. The repercussions of this new method of transportation, however, were far from uniform. The railroads had been built primarily to facilitate the flow of Brazilian products to the international market. Because of this they tended to be concentrated in coffee and sugar areas. Railroads gave birth to some cities but doomed others to extinction. Once-thriving urban centers not reached by the railroad tracks went into rapid decline, while new settlements cropped up around train stations. With the building of railroads, planters were able not only to increase their production for exports but to diminish the area devoted to subsistence, since many things could be easily brought from the outside. Trains also allowed planters to take up residence in the major cities. As a consequence, while these cities grew rapidly and modernized their appearance, the small towns of the interior gradually lost the little prestige they had gained when planters built their town houses there.

When planters started building their houses in the capital cities, they became more concerned with urban improvements. Hotels, public gardens, theaters, coffeehouses, and stores mushroomed. Concentration of capital, foreign and local, made it possible for a few to enjoy some of the most modern inventions. Street paving improved, as did lighting, water supply, sewage, and urban transportation. The first urban trolley system was installed in Recife in 1868. Between 1872 and

1895 others were built in Salvador, Rio de Janeiro, São Luiz, Campinas, and São Paulo. In the 1880s telephone service began in São Paulo, Salvador, Rio, and Campinas. In the 1870s a telegraph line connected Brazil to Europe, and most Brazilian cities were linked to each other. In the largest cities public lighting was also improved: gas came into use in Rio by 1854 and in São Paulo by 1872.[26] Public instruction improved and the big cities also became lively cultural centers. In the city of São Paulo in 1835, only 5 percent of the population could read and write. By 1872, this number had reached 35 percent, and in 1887, 47 percent, while the figure for the province as a whole was only 29 percent.[27] Urban commerce developed, as did artisanry and industry. In the wealthier districts of the big cities the old adobe houses gave way to brick European-style mansions, and English or French furniture replaced the heavier colonial pieces. Imported wallpaper and lamps decorated the interiors, and the facades were done over with glass windows and metalwork. In the poorer neighborhoods tenement houses multiplied.[28]

With schools and increasing literacy, newspapers and magazines also grew in number. Artistic and musical societies were formed. The pace of life became more intense. The rigid patriarchal discipline that had in the past dictated the seclusion of middle- and upper-class women began to weaken. They were seen with more frequency on the streets, and it became fashionable for them to participate in public events. There was a growing concern with women's education, and the first feminist journals and women's magazines were founded. Still, such publications had a small audience, more or less restricted to a minority of cultivated middle-class women. And in spite of their new rhetoric of equal rights, they continued to stress women's "natural vocation" as mothers and wives.[29]

This period also witnessed the first large outdoor political rallies. Politics, so long confined to the theaters and salons, spilled into the streets and public squares. In the 1880s abolitionists and republicans promoted great public rallies in the streets. A cabinet fell because of an urban riot triggered by the increasing streetcar prices. In 1889, rallies promoted in Rio de Janeiro by Lopes Trovão in support of the Republican party drew a large number of people who voiced their demands for urban improvements and political change. In the last decade of the empire, workers' strikes and popular demonstrations were becoming part of the urban scene.[30] Although politicians were for the first time courting the urban masses, all these changes were still very circumscribed and superficial. Most people could not vote, and this left politicians vulnerable to the whims of the system of patronage. In 1881, Taunay, a famous publicist and politician describing his political campaign stressed that the support of local political leaders counted more than the candidate's platform. He added, ruefully, that "knowing how to dance the polka" was sometimes more decisive in earning the support of the local elites than political eloquence or ideological consistency.[31]

Most of these changes, limited as they were, were confined to the important urban centers. Although progress in communications allowed news to circulate more rapidly and helped to break down the isolation and apathy that had plagued the towns of the backlands, the contrast between the big urban centers and the small towns of the interior only grew. And in those regions located outside the reach of railroads, telephones, and telegraphs, the rhythm of life hardly changed.

Industries helped to accentuate these differences. Predictably, most of the factories were located in the main urban centers, particularly in Rio, São Paulo, Minas Gerais, and Rio Grande do Sul. In these areas, availability of labor and capital, the existence of a relatively developed market, and an infrastructure of credit and transportation all created conditions for industrial development. In 1880, there were 18,100 persons registered as factory workers. By 1907, the industrial labor force amounted to 136,420 workers distributed among 2,983 establishments. According to a 1907 census, industry in the Federal District employed nearly one quarter of these industrial workers, about 35,000. São Paulo had 22,000, Rio Grande do Sul 15,000, and Rio 12,000. Industrial growth was still hampered, however, by the small size of the market and by foreign competition, not to mention the lack of adequate credit facilities. Most of the industries were consumer-goods industries. Textiles and beverages represented the great bulk of industrial production, and many industries like those that produced machines for processing coffee, sugar, or meat were really agricultural subsidiaries.[32]

In spite of their visible growth, industries were not the main factor in the growth of the cities, as they were in other parts of the world. Urbanization in Brazil during the second half of the nineteenth century was primarily the product of the commercial expansion resulting from Brazil's increasing integration into the world market and the resulting increase in exports. That is why São Paulo and Rio de Janeiro, located in the expanding coffee areas, grew faster than Recife, whose fortunes were tied to the faltering sugar economy. City growth reflected the vitality of the export economy much more than the expansion of the internal market. Between 1840 and 1880 the total income generated by exports grew almost 400 percent. It was capital accumulated in foreign trade that helped to create the infrastructure necessary for further development.[33] This accounts for the contrast between the interior towns and the port cities. It also explains why the cities that did prosper in the interior were those linked in one way or another to the export economy (Campinas or São Paulo, for example, both important centers in the coffee areas). It is their dependence on the international market that explains the "exotic" character of Brazil's cities, their tendency to form links with Europe rather than with their own hinterlands, and their resultant inability to exert a modernizing influence on the countryside. Moreover, it is their vulnerability to the fluctuations of the international market that explains the instability of the Brazilian urban network and the phenomenon of the "ghost town" so common in Brazil—towns that went into decline as soon as local participation in the export economy waned.

In many European countries, where urbanization was associated with industrialization, life in the cities was often shaken by conflicts between the new entrepreneurial bourgeoisie and the established agrarian aristocracy, between the urban middle classes and the traditional rural oligarchies, or between industrial workers and entrepreneurs. Brazilian historians looking for analogous tensions and conflicts in the Brazilian reality have often thought they found in Brazil the same types of conflicts, particularly between industrialists and the rural elites.[34] And it is quite true that as late as the mid-nineteenth century, a progressive entrepreneur like Barão de Mauá found it difficult to overcome the opposition of some of the representatives of traditional oligarchies who looked with suspicion on his industrial ventures. As late as 1881, the Industrial Association still complained that the government not only ignored industrialists' efforts but also created obstacles by adopting a free trade policy that hampered industrial development.

After mid-century, however, industrial development began to be seen in a more positive light. Many planters whose plantations were doing well and who were accumulating large profits not only started introducing technological improvements on their own estates but invested their money in industries, railroads, and banks.[35] Many of them also adopted a critical attitude toward monarchical institutions and joined the Republican party. The counterpart of these landowners-turned-entrepreneurs was the entrepreneur-turned-landowner—the man who originally earned his fortune in commerce or industry but reinvested part of his profits in agricultural enterprises. Aside from the similarity of their interests these groups were also tied by links of family and friendship. As a result, the opposition between rural and urban elites that has often been attributed to other societies did not manifest itself sharply in Brazil.[36] There, the conflict was between representatives of decadent agrarian sectors—with their mortgaged properties, forced by the lack of capital to hold on to slave labor and traditional forms of production—and the newer, more capital-rich groups, linked both to agriculture and industry.

The conflicts between industrialists and workers characteristic of industrial societies was just beginning in nineteenth-century Brazil. Workers were making their first attempts to develop an autonomous political movement. In the last decades of the nineteenth century, the rhetoric of class struggle was used with increasing frequency. The number of workers' organizations grew and socialist groups appeared. But the numerical and structural insignificance of the working class in the nation's economy, and the obstacles workers had to face whenever they tried to organize themselves, diminished their impact. In spite of the new rhetoric of class struggle and the occasional workers' demonstrations that were changing the tone of life in cities like São Paulo and Rio, workers did not yet constitute a serious threat to the social order. Some of the workers' manifestos actually echoed the demands of the industrialists, asking for exemptions from import taxes on industrial machinery and property taxes on factories, or demanding protective tariffs and credit facilities for industrial enterprises.[37]

Like the workers, the new urban "middle classes" were not a serious threat to the traditional elites. In the last years of the empire, middle-class dissatisfaction with the system of clientele and patronage had increased and had given energy to reformist movements. Yet for every one in the middle classes who supported abolition or who joined the Republican party, there was another who sided with the traditional oligarchies. The truth is that the urban middle class did not assume a truly autonomous position. This was due in part to the fact that even though the job market had improved in the cities and there were more opportunities than before, most middle-class individuals continued to depend on patronage for finding jobs. The middle class was composed mostly of bureaucrats, professionals, and people working in the service sector. They were directly dependent on either the export-import sector of the economy or on the state. Thus, the role attributed to professionals in the crisis of Brazilian patriarchalism by Gilberto Freyre and others seems exaggerated. The Brazilian patriarch and oligarch survived until the twentieth century, as did Brazilian reliance on the agrarian export economy and on the great estate. The professionals, those whom Freyre called *bacharéis*, frequently acted as the planters' urban representatives rather than as their opponents, and even when they assumed a critical posture, they could not hide their ambivalence.

Perhaps the best evidence of this attitude can be found among the

Intellectuals ambivalence

intellectuals. Some, like Sylvio Romero, came from families whose background was or had been rural. Others were second-generation urbanites. Whatever their social or geographical background, intellectuals living in the cities in close contact with a cosmopolitan and European culture became increasingly alienated from the rural areas and sometimes critical of the traditional oligarchies. They denounced the oppression of the urban and rural population, the big estate, and slave labor. They often criticized traditional philosophy (eclecticism), condemned traditional literary conventions (romanticism), and ridiculed the bookish system of education. They adopted instead new philosophical fashions, particularly positivism and Spencerism, and new forms of expression, such as realism and naturalism. They proposed a new system of education more oriented toward science and technology. But in spite of their critique of the traditional society, these intellectuals continued to depend on the patronage of the elites—the same elites that constituted the intellectuals' main audience. So it is not surprising that when intellectuals criticized the system of patronage, what they seemed to be asking for was not that patronage be abolished, but that it be replaced by an enlightened patronage that would reward only merit and talent.[38]

Living in cities that were rapidly undergoing a process of modernization, and fascinated by European literary, political and philosophical fashions, these intellectuals often felt exiled in their own country. They idealized European institutions, creating an ideal model which they used to judge the reality around them. They turned to European modes of interpretation for an explanation of what they perceived to be the "anomaly" and the "backwardness" of Brazilian society. In Gobineau's and Lapouge's racist theories and in Ratzel's determinism they found their answers.[39] Very often the intellectuals' commitment to reform was more an expression of their wish to "elevate" Brazil to the category of a civilized nation, than of their recognition of the structural needs of Brazilian society. The dilemmas faced by this type of intellectual were starkly revealed in the attitudes of a man like Tobias Barreto. Although living in Escada, a small town of the backlands, he published a newspaper in German, for which there were probably no local readers, and he made speeches attacking the local oligarchies, before a public most likely composed of their relatives, friends, and clients. Tobias Barreto's alienation was so complete, his identification with German culture so compelling, that he once wrote to one of his correspondents "I live in Escada, but this does not matter. Let it be for you as if I lived in Berlin."[40]

Intellectuals frequently advertised their sympathy for "the people,"

a mulatto

the "unprotected," and "the exploited." But, for the most part, they found it impossible to ally themselves with "the people," whom they saw as ignorant and backward, those rural or urban masses of ex-slaves and their descendants, or recently arrived immigrants who could barely speak Portuguese. It was equally difficult for them to ally with the emerging urban proletariat, whose demands frequently impressed intellectuals as utopian or irrelevant. As a result, they adopted a paternalistic and enlightened tone, speaking in the name of the people but not to the people. These elitist attitudes account not only for the intellectuals' widespread acceptance of positivism and their high regard for the motto "order and progress," but also for the sympathy some of them even displayed for military intervention in the nation's political life. The armed forces seemed to be the only group capable of "modernizing" the country without popular mobilization.

The intellectuals' position in society set limits to their ideological commitment to reform. Their program rarely went beyond the program of the most "progressive" industrial, agricultural, and commercial elites. And when they did venture beyond these limits—criticizing, for example, the monopoly of land by a few or the tyranny of foreign capital—their isolation from the masses rendered their protests innocuous and ineffective. For all these reasons the most important reforms of this period, such as abolition, electoral reform, and the overthrow of the monarchy, were results of the joint actions of urban groups, segments of the rural elites, and elements within the army. A tacit compromise was reached between the men who frequented Rio de Janeiro's salons and cafes, wore European clothes, and quoted foreign writers in their speeches, and the leaders of the hinterland who modernized their estate houses and introduced technological innovations on their plantations.

As a product of these alliances, "modernization" of the country was little more than a facade, confined mostly to the large cities and to the privileged groups of Brazilian society, whether rural or urban. Often, only a few miles beyond a thriving city, people lived a life reminiscent of colonial times. Although the urban population grew markedly from the early nineteenth century on, this growth was not accompanied by fundamental changes. New cities more oriented toward the internal market did appear in the backlands, in the rural frontier, and along the newly built railroads. But the cities linked to the export-import economy continued to be the major urban centers just as they had been since the colonial period. Even as late as 1912, four of the five leading cities were leading ports for foreign trade: Rio de Janeiro, Salvador, Recife, and Belem. The only exception was São Paulo, which relied on Santos as a port for coffee exports. The growth of these cities remained intimately tied to the expansion of exports. The population of São Paulo rose from 31,820 inhabitants in 1872 to 239,820 in 1900. And the city of Rio de Janeiro went from 274,972 to 811,443 in the same period. Belem the main exporter of rubber—a commodity that entered a boom period near the turn of the century—increased from 61,977 to 95,560. Between 1872 and 1890 Salvador experienced a similar growth, going from 129,109 to 205,813. Only Recife exhibited a slight reduction in population with a drop from 116,617 to 113,106.[41]

Despite this trend toward urbanization most Brazilians continued to live in rural areas. In 1890 only about 10 percent of the total population was living in the capital cities. In 1900, only four cities had over 100,000 inhabitants, and two of those had between 200,000 and 240,000. Only one reached more than 800,000, and that was Rio de Janeiro, capital first of the empire and then of the republic, commercial, industrial, political, administrative, and cultural center, the most important Brazilian city in the nineteenth century.

The process of development itself, by preserving the underlying structures of the Brazilian economy almost intact throughout the nineteenth century, was responsible for the rural population's preponderance over the urban and for the survival of structures of domination, values, and forms of behavior compatible with what has been often defined as a "traditional" society. Independence did not alter Brazil's position as a supplier of agricultural goods and a buyer of manufactured products in the world market. Brazil's position in the developing international division of labor explains the agrarian nature of the Brazilian economy, the preponderance of vast landholdings and slave or semiservile forms of labor. This in turn not only limited capital accumulation but inhibited the internal division of labor and the formation of a domestic market. As a consequence of this type of development, most of the urban functions tended to be performed in the principal export centers, which underwent a relative process of modernization and Europeanization. Meanwhile those inland cities that were outside the circuit of the international economy remained the carriers of tradition.

The transformations that occurred in the second half of the nineteenth century—the abolition of slavery, the construction of a transportation network, immigration, and industrialization—did not alter the nation's economic orientation but did contribute to the formation of an incipient internal market and stimulated urbanization. These changes, however, did not generate any fundamental conflict between industrialists and the representatives of the agrarian sectors. Land-owners often became entrepreneurs, and many businessmen invested in land. The fundamental conflict during the nineteenth century was between the representatives of the decadent rural sectors who, because of the decline in the productivity of their plantations and their lack of capital, were unable to make the leap toward new forms of production and the spokesmen for the expanding sectors who were ready to adopt all the innovations necessary to guarantee profit accumulation. The tensions between these two groups took the place of the classic struggle between bourgeoisie and aristocracy. The technological and scientific revolution that was associated with industrialization and urbanization in other parts of the world did not take place in Brazil, mostly because of its dependent position in the international market, the fragility of the internal market, the availability of cheap labor, and the importation of technology.

Since their destinies were intrinsically linked to international trade, the cities did not become vehicles for the modernization of the interior, nor did the urban middle classes struggle against the privileges of the landed elites. The coastal cities served as a stage for the conciliation of rural and commercial interests, while the inland towns continued with few exceptions to be extension of the landowners' dominion. The inhabitants of these towns continued to live under the patronage of the rural elites.

Even those segments of the population that one would expect to be a source of opposition to the established system failed to develop any tangible alternative to the patriarchal order. The newborn labor movement tended to be isolated, disorganized, inarticulate, and incapable of creating a base for antiestablishment struggles. The intellectuals of the period, whenever they ventured beyond accepted boundaries in their social critique, proved incapable of forming alliances with the masses. Most intellectuals operated within the oligarchy's orbit and limited themselves to interpreting the points of view expressed by the more "progressive" members of the elite.

In spite of all these limitations the development of cities in the nineteenth century did contribute to changing, in some parts of the country, the quality if not the foundations of Brazilian life. The cities created new forms of social interaction, increased opportunities for social mobility, contributed to the rise in literacy, and made the "benefits of civilization" available to a broader cross section of society. Although the urban middle classes were unable or unwilling to become an autonomous political force, it was among them that the main supporters for reformist movements were recruited.

The process of urbanization as it occurred in nineteenth century Brazil accentuated the distance separating inhabitants of the interior from residents of the capital cities, and city dwellers from rural "hicks." The extent of the contrast justifies the imagery used by Sylvio Romero to condemn government expenditures on modernization of the capital: "a system of illusion that reduces us to an impoverished and divided land, a Janus head with two faces, one of true misery and the other of phony and deceptive prosperity." [42]

8 THE FALL OF THE MONARCHY

The fall of the empire in 1889 is usually attributed to the alienation of the monarchy's three important sources of support—the Church, the planters, and the military. Conflict between Church and State, culminating in the imprisonment of the bishops of Pará and Pernambuco, tarnished the Crown's image among the general population; abolition turned the planters against the regime, encouraging them to adopt republican ideas; and the military's dissatisfaction with the government, which had grown steadily since the Paraguayan War, finally drove them, in the coup of 15 November 1889, to overthrow the monarchy and establish a republic in Brazil.[1]

To prove that Brazilians showed limited enthusiasm for republican ideals, historians often pointed to the insignificant numbers actually registered in the Republican party and the scarcity of Republican representatives in Parliament. In their view the proclamation of the republic was a product, not of republican sentiment and agitation, but of dissatisfaction on the part of monarchists themselves. Their complaints had discredited the monarchy so totally that a military parade was enough to overthrow the regime. This, in brief, is the argument presented by Oliveira Vianna in *O Ocaso do Império* (*The Fall of the Empire*), an interpretation that continues to appear in most textbooks.[2]

Not all historians, however, accept his version. Some feel that the monarchy, from the beginning, was an exotic plant in America; it was only by chance that a republican regime was not adopted in Brazil at the time of independence. As the revolutionary movements that developed both before and after independence proved, the republic had always been a national aspiration. It was therefore natural that the actions of the Republican party, which was founded in 1870, would ultimately bear fruit. The incompetence and the excesses of the Crown merely hastened the advent of the republic by discrediting the monarchical system.

These two explanations of the fall of the monarchy, which are sometimes combined, merely reproduce contemporary opinions about the events of November 15. Relying exclusively on eyewitness accounts, historians have endorsed the participants' perceptions of the complex process that culminated in the proclamation of the republic. Soon after that event, a monarchist and a republican version of the fall of the monarchy emerged.

The monarchists idealized the monarchy and considered the overthrow of the regime an infelicitous accident. Unable to perceive any flaws in monarchical institutions, they could not understand that the system had been undermined by growing tensions since 1870. Because of their inability to evaluate the regime, they refused to admit that the republican movement could have been based on rational demands. In their opinion the republic was the product of a military coup motivated by petty personal interests. The Republicans, an insignificant minority with no popular support, had fought against the monarchy for their own benefit. At the last minute they were joined by an unruly and discontented army and by slaveowners who resented abolition.[3]

The republican version was in some ways more objective, although still inexact and incomplete. For the Republicans, a change in government was the only way to eliminate the vices of the monarchical regime—abuse of the emperor's personal power, election of senators for life, excessive centralization, and electoral fraud that gave the government total control over the ballot. The republican movement had answered national aspirations; together the Republican party and the military had carried out the will of the people. Under the widespread influence of positivism, some chroniclers portrayed the monarchy as an institution condemned by history—an institution that had to give way to the republic.[4]

Both the republican and the monarchist accounts gave great importance to individuals in the political arena and considered their actions crucial in explaining the events that culminated in the fall of the monarchy. Benjamin Constant, Quintino Bocaiuva, Silva Jardim, Deodoro da Fonseca, Floriano Peixoto, the viscount of Ouro Preto, the princess Isabel, her husband, the conde d'Eu, and the emperor Pedro II were the main actors in the historical drama. Writers took great pleasure in analyzing their ability or ineptitude, their inclinations, and their idiosyncrasies. Since monarchist and republican writers had been personally involved in the events they described, they had difficulties in understanding the process as a whole, and they drew diverse and contradictory pictures of what they witnessed.

These early versions were repeated by historians in the decades that followed the proclamation of the republic and are still to be found in most textbooks. But after the 1930s there was a shift. Some historians began to see the fall of the monarchy in an entirely different light. Many factors combined to change this perspective. The process of urbanization and industrialization that occurred in the first three decades of the twentieth century brought new groups to the political scene. The Brazilian population doubled and the new urban middle classes and the growing urban proletariat could not be absorbed by the system of clientele and patronage that had regulated the relationship of the elites to the masses for more than a century. Although many industrialists were still linked by family to the traditional agrarian elites and continued to invest money in both the agrarian and the industrial sectors, there were many newcomers, particularly immigrants, who did not always agree with policies adopted by the government, which was controlled by the rural oligarchies. Besides the tensions between new and traditional groups, the struggle for power at the local and national levels during the First Republic (1889–1930) had caused conflict among the traditional elites themselves.

The increasing dissatisfaction of those who had no control over the state apparatus was expressed in a series of workers' strikes, middle-class conspiracies, and military uprisings. Finally the 1929 economic depression, which reduced coffee exports catastrophically, weakened the rural oligarchies that had controlled the government since 1889, and in 1930 a revolution brought new groups to power under the leadership of Getúlio Vargas. The Vargas era inaugurated a period of intense industrialization and a new political style characterized by appeals to the urban masses. When Vargas was cast out of power in 1945, his "populist" strategies were adopted by many politicians. A new ideology, growing out of the Vargas era, placed high value on economic development and social harmony, emphasizing the commonality of interests among workers, the middle classes, and the industrialists—all of whom, according to the new ideology, were interested in modernizing Brazilian society. At the same time the rural oligarchies were portrayed as conservative and "reactionary."

Thus it is not surprising that historians who wrote between 1930 and 1960—facing a new Brazil and looking at the past from a new perspective—became more attentive to economic and institutional factors and more sensitive to the political roles of socioeconomic groups.[5] As a consequence, they offered a new interpretation of the 1889 movement, deemphasizing the personalities and anecdotes that had so impressed the early chroniclers and historians. Projecting backwards the experience of their time, they portrayed the events that led to the proclamation of the republic as confrontations between progressive and conservative groups. And they attributed the fall of the monarchy to the inadequacy of existing institutions in the face of new social and economic realities. This was the interpretation suggested by Caio Prado, Jr., a Marxist historian, and it was endorsed by Nelson Werneck Sodré.[6] According to these authors, the proclamation of the republic was the result of profound economic and social transformations during the second half of the nineteenth century. Immigration, industrialization, and urbanization combined to weaken the monarchy and ignite the sparks of subversion. The most progressive groups—the middle classes and dynamic segments of the landowning elite—were eager for reforms: abolition, electoral reform, federalism, and the republic. They opposed the stagnating and backward groups, the traditional rural oligarchies who supported and were supported by the Crown. The army, identified with the interests of the middle class, had the final hand in ousting a regime that had paid little attention to the needs of important segments of the population, a regime whose institutions stood in the way of progress.

If the traditional historians had incorporated and endorsed the myths of the past and overemphasized the role of individuals in historical events, the new historians tended to portray men as puppets of impersonal historical forces. Despite this limitation, their interpretation represented an advance. It called attention to problems that had not previously been recognized. Oddly enough, however, the traditional versions continued to appear in most textbooks; Prado and Sodré's new directions were not developed.[7]

Both the traditional and the Marxist interpretations can of course be criticized. The newer version often reifies the historical process and projects onto the past the myths of the present; the traditional version, on the other hand, is naively voluntaristic and relies much too heavily on the myths of the past. In some way both were right and may even complement one another. Traditional historians rightly perceived the actions and thoughts of those who participated in the republican movement as important. In analyzing past events, however, the historian must go beyond the surface phenomena seen and registered by contemporary observers to the transformations of social and economic structures and their larger political consequences, which are sometimes invisible to those living through them. What appears relevant to contemporaries is what is most easily observed: individual actions, discovered conspiracies, the most notorious episodes and intrigues. Even when it is clear and accurate, the eyewitness account tends to personalize social occurrences and to ignore the larger social context in which people live. The chronicler often forgets that, in order to

— Não vos aproximeis de mim! Vossas mãos ainda tintas do sangue dos e[...]

FIG. 21. This caricature, published in the *Revista Illustrada*, shows Brazilian farmers abandoning the monarchy after abolition and following the republic.

...riam as minhas vestes! Retirae-vos, eu não vos quero...

understand the actions of an individual, we must take into account not only his personal motives but also his opportunities and the limitations imposed on him by circumstances. It is the historian's task to analyze events in the context of this larger reality; for while individual behavior is in part a matter of personal ideas, sympathies, and idiosyncrasies, it can be understood only by considering the entire process within which it occurs. In studying the proclamation of the republic in Brazil, it is less important to know the personal inclinations of Marshall Deodoro da Fonseca and Benjamin Constant than to analyze the social contradictions that facilitated the diffusion of republican ideas among the groups who would conspire against the monarchy.

Most of the sources used by early historians on the fall of the monarchy do not, however, offer enough data for such analysis. We must therefore shift our angle of observation and look to other sources for insight into the social and economic tensions at the end of the empire. This will help us to understand the political arena. Equally important is to examine both the political structures which defined those who had power and those who had not, and the political mythology that inspired their actions.

The idea that abolition provoked the fall of the monarchy because the landowners, former supporters of the Crown, showed their resentment of the new law by supporting the Republican party, began to circulate even before the law was signed. Supporters of slavery, who warned that unimaginable catastrophes would follow closely upon abolition, prophesied that the monarchy would fall if slavery was abolished. The day the law was passed (13 May 1888) several politicians predicted that by decreeing slave emancipation the princess would lose the throne. And indeed the monarchy fell the following year, which seemed to confirm these grim predictions. In July of 1889, a few months before the proclamation of the republic, Joaquim Nabuco, an important abolitionist leader, commented in the Chamber of Deputies that the strength of the Republicans was based on the discontent engendered by abolition. Other chroniclers of the time agreed with him. This interpretation, born of a superficial and hurried appreciation of the facts, was later endorsed by many historians.

In fact, the Lei Áurea merely dealt the final blow to a colonial structure of production and labor that had barely managed to survive the changes occurring in Brazil since 1850.[8] The segments of the landowning class most dependent on the traditional system of production were already weak; modernization had left them far behind. Many had given away their slaves and were indifferent to abolition.[9] The new elites that had appeared in the dynamic frontier areas, facing increasing opposition on the part of abolitionists and unable to put down slave insurrection, had finally accepted the idea of free labor, and by 1888 most of them supported the law. Only a few representatives voted against it in 1888; they expressed the interests of a minority of coffee planters whose plantations were mortgaged and who hoped that slavery would not be abolished without compensation. If some of these landowners supported the Republican party out of vengeance (something which has not yet been shown to be true), they were isolated cases that cannot explain the fall of the monarchy. The most that can be said is that abolition, by dealing the final blow to rural sectors that had traditionally supported the Crown, precipitated its fall. Abolition was not the cause of the republic; it would be more correct to say that abolition and the proclamation of the republic were repercussions, at the institutional level, of changes in the economic and social structure, and in people's perceptions.

If the role played by abolition in the fall of the monarchy has been exaggerated, so has the impact of the conflict between Church and State (the "questão religiosa").[10] This conflict had started when the bishops of Pará and Pernambuco, in accordance with the pope's new guidelines, had barred Freemasons from participating in church activities and had forbidden Catholics to join the Masonry. When Masons protested and appealed to the government, the Crown invoked the right of royal patronage—which subordinated the Church to the State—and supported the Masons. The bishops stubbornly resisted, challenging the state's authority. In response the government had the bishops arrested, a decision that caused a great uproar and was hotly debated in Parliament and the press.

The bishops were finally released but many observers felt that the incident had alienated Catholics from the monarchy. On closer examination, however, it becomes clear that the Church itself was divided; a number of priests and Catholics were themselves Freemasons, and it was precisely this fact that had created the trouble in the first place. Thus the incident was primarily a conflict within the Church complicated by the interference of the State. State interference in Church matters was nothing new. It had a long tradition in the colonial period, and it had legal support.

During the conflict between the cabinet and the bishops there was no unanimity within the ranks of the Conservative and Liberal parties. Republicans too were divided on the issue. Some were inclined toward the Freemasons and others toward the bishops. Those who supported the Freemasons found themselves in the awkward position of back-

S. M. — Parece incrivel que este desgraçado não accorde á minha chamada! Será possivel q
Q. B. — Meu amigo, se elle não accordou com todos esses males que o devem affligir e que tenho com

FIG. 22. This caricature, published in the O *Polichinello* in 1876, shows the Vatican (the snake) threatening Brazil who sleeps surrounded by frogs (a choir of flattering voices). On the ground lies popular sovereignty.

ro do Vaticano consiga devoral'o?!

e, como podemos esperar que elle se levante á nossa voz?!

ing the government. Many of the Republicans called themselves "free thinkers," an expression that suggests their hostility to anything that smacked of Church or clergy. The Republican party program[11] included complete freedom of religious practice, equality of all religions before the law, and consequent abolition of the Catholic church's official position. This would imply the separation of secular and religious education, the institution of secular marriage, the creation of a civil register for births and deaths, and the secularization of the cemeteries and their administration by the municipalities. Considering this program it is tempting to conclude that Republicans were more concerned to emancipate society from the Church than to emancipate the Church from the State. And, on the whole, they would hardly be inclined to protect the Church's prerogatives.

In fact the Brazilian elite as a whole was not known for its deeply clerical spirit. On the contrary, the most educated sectors of the male population often assumed an indifferent and somewhat anticlerical, almost Voltairian posture, even in Catholic circles. Brazilian politicians frequently boasted about their independence in spiritual matters and looked with distaste on what they saw as the Church's manipulations. This explains why Princess Isabel's well-known religiosity served as ammunition in the Republicans' campaign against her.[12] They knew that emphasizing her devotion was an effective way of alienating from her the most enlightened and politically active segments of the population.

Given these facts, the *questão religiosa*, which generated a split between Church and State, could not have been a primary cause for the fall of the monarchy. At most, by revealing the potential conflict between secular and religious powers, the crisis could have increased the number of people on both sides who saw a need for the separation of Church and State, thus indirectly feeding the republican cause.

The role of the army in establishing the republic is also misrepresented by traditional historians.[13] Certainly the proclamation of the republic was not the unexpected result of a military parade, nor was the army a mere tool of the Republicans.[14] Several military leaders possessed solid republican convictions bolstered by positivist ideas. Under the tutelage of positivists like Benjamin Constant, Serzedelo Correia, Solon, and other officers they had been conspiring for some time. Convinced that the dissolution of the monarchy and the installation of the republic would solve all of Brazil's problems, they were inspired to action by a profound belief that only the military could save the country.[15]

This opinion had become increasingly widespread since the Paraguayan War and gained adherents as the army became more institutionalized. The military had many grievances. They complained about their low wages and accused the government of neglecting the needs of the army. They resented the interference of politicians in cases of promotions and transfers. They also condemned the politicians' use of the draft during elections, when those in power drafted—or threatened to

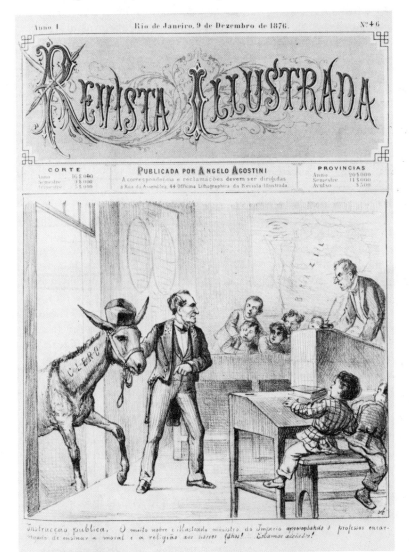

FIG. 23. This caricature, published in the *Revista Illustrada* in 1876, criticized those who wanted to increase the influence of the clergy over education.

draft—their political adversaries' clients to keep them from voting. Military draft deferments distributed by politicians to their friends were another source of discontent among the officers. Political interference in army affairs ended by alienating young officers who, after the demoralizing experience of the Paraguayan War, had grown aware of the need to modernize the army. Their resentment and their commitment to reorganize the army on more efficient terms made them receptive to positivist and republican ideas. This tendency was reinforced when the army started recruiting a larger number of officers among the new middle classes. Lacking personal contact with the political elite, these young officers felt even more hostile to the regime. But it would be a great mistake to portray the army as a political monolith. On the contrary, the military was divided on the best course of action. Republican ideas had a wider following among the lower-ranked officers and recent graduates of the military school; officers at the higher levels continued in general to give their support to the monarchy. Thus although the support of the military was essential to the Republican cause, its role should not be exaggerated. If the army had not been courted by members of the Republican party, it would hardly have taken the initiative in overthrowing the monarchical regime.

While emphasizing the role of the military and the impact of abolition and religious controversy, historians who adopted the monarchist perspective have probably underestimated the role of Republican ideas. This misperception becomes understandable when one examines the sources they use. Looking at the membership of the Republican party and election results, one could conclude that the majority of the Brazilian population was indifferent if not hostile to the Republican program.[16] In fact, although there were Republican clubs throughout the country, Republican nuclei tended to be small except in São Paulo, Minas Gerais, Rio de Janeiro, and Rio Grande do Sul. Moreover, Republicans encountered difficulty in presenting their list of candidates and in winning elections. Yet these facts taken by themselves are not an accurate index of the penetration of Republican ideas. The existing electoral system, based on income qualification criteria, denied the right to vote to the majority of the population. On the eve of the declaration of the republic, the Brazilian electorate represented little more than 1.5 percent of the nation's total population. More important, widespread electoral fraud always favored the government party. In the face of these obstacles, the São Paulo Republican party was remarkably successful. In 1889 it controlled one-fourth of the state's electorate.

Though the Republican party members still constituted an insignifi-

cant minority, the party's use of meetings, conferences, and above all
the press as channels of propaganda had helped to create favorable
sentiment toward republicanism, particularly among the urban segments of the population.[17] Besides, the fact that Republicans constituted a minority did not necessarily mean that they were an insignificant force in the overthrow of the empire. Active and organized
minorities have always been important participants in revolutionary
movements, as long as conditions favor the initiation of revolutionary
action.

What needs to be explained, then, is not, as the monarchists suggest, the limited appeal of Republican ideas, but their greater appeal in
the final years of the empire, especially since we know that these ideas
had existed in Brazil since the late eighteenth century, if not before.

By stressing the significance of Republican ideas, Republican historians saw their role more objectively than historians in the monarchist
tradition did, but they in their turn tended to exaggerate the role of
monarchical abuses in toppling the regime.[18] Criticism of the Crown
and of the emperor had existed since independence without bringing
down the system. Many times during the empire monarchist politicians had accused the emperor of abusing his prerogatives.[19] These
criticisms had issued from the conflict over what was defined in the
constitution as the "moderating power" (*poder moderador*).[20] Granted
to the emperor by the constitution of 1824 in addition to executive
power, moderating power gave him, as we have seen, the right to intervene in both the judiciary and the legislature. The emperor could
choose his ministers and councillors of state freely; he could dissolve
the Chamber of Deputies and call new elections; he could also choose
senators from among the three men with the most votes in each state;
and he was empowered to appoint judges to the higher courts. All this
could be a source of irritation for candidates and parties who were
passed over.

One party or the other would oppose the emperor whenever he
exerted his prerogative to appoint a senator. If he chose a Conservative
to fill a senate seat, the Liberals would protest the "exorbitant abuses"
of his powers; the Conservatives would protest if the situation was reversed. Because prime ministers were freely appointed by the emperor
independent of parliamentary majority, their errors fell on his shoul-
ders, despite the fact that the parliamentary system had been created
to avoid such problems. When he dissolved the Chamber of Deputies,
appointed a new prime minister, and called for new elections, the new
cabinet manipulated the election to insure their party's victory, thus
exacerbating the defeated party's discontent and animosity toward the

Crown. This was exactly what happened in 1868. Liberals had a technical majority. The emperor dissolved the Chamber of Deputies and appointed a Conservative prime minister. The new cabinet then succeeded in manipulating the elections and achieved a Conservative majority, provoking rage among liberals. This triggered the greatest political crisis of the empire. Two years later a group of discontented Liberals founded the Republican party. Ironically, the moderating power, which had been created with the intention of protecting the emperor, had placed him at the center of the political arena, the target of all criticism. This constant tension gave rise to the myth of personal power (*poder pessoal*), the myth of the emperor as an abusive and authoritarian monarch.

A more thorough analysis of the functioning of the empire's political system, however, reveals that in matters of national importance, the emperor was rarely able to enforce his will. Imperial policies were actually controlled by the rural oligarchies and their allies, acting through the Council of State, the Chamber of Deputies, the Senate, the ministries, the provincial assemblies, and the bureaucracy.

Given the way in which the political system functioned under the empire, it seems ridiculous to blame the emperor for the fruits of the regime. He was not responsible for the agrarian orientation of Brazil's economy, for electoral fraud, or for the survival of a patriarchal and slave society. Nor was it the emperor who promoted abolition, electoral reform, or any other important change that took place under his rule. The social and economic structure of Brazilian society gave immense power to the regional oligarchies, and the emperor, though exhibiting a certain amount of intransigence on small issues, always yielded to the oligarchies on questions of national importance.

The dynamics of the moderating power do not sufficiently explain the advent of the republic. The emperor's use of this power could of course have generated hostility toward him. But criticism of the Crown had a long history. Why then was the republic proclaimed in 1889 and not before? There seems to be only one plausible answer to the question. It was only then that republican ideas, which had circulated in the country for over a century, found propitious conditions for their realization. What were the transformations occurring in Brazilian society that allowed this change? Which social groups served as support for the monarchy? How were they affected by social and economic change? What new groups were rising at the time, and what were their needs and aspirations? Could those needs be satisfied by the monarchical system? Finally, which segments of society made up the Republican party? Those are some of the questions that we have to answer in order to understand the origins of the republic in Brazil.

During the long reign of Pedro II, there were profound changes in Brazil's economy and society. The railroads slowly began to replace the more traditional modes of transportation such as muleback, oxcarts, and river barge. This network, while admittedly limited, was sufficient to revolutionize the system of transportation and production in the most dynamic regions of the country. Equally important was the gradual replacement of sailing vessels by steamships in the coastal trade.

In the second half of the nineteenth century, new techniques were gradually introduced in the sugar industry, and sugar "factories" (*usinas, engenhos centrais*) began to appear side by side with the more traditional mills (*banguês*).[21] On the coffee plantations of the Paulista west, a pioneering and dynamic frontier zone, new coffee-processing methods were introduced to increase productivity. These changes in agricultural technology were accompanied by a change in the system of labor. Slavery as a system came into crisis, both because of the changing international conditions brought about by the industrial revolution and because of transformations occurring within the national borders. Free labor began to replace slave labor, especially in the more dynamic coffee areas, where immigration became, in the 1880s, a remedy for the labor shortage.[22]

Industrial capitalism also made progress in this period. In the decade between 1874 and 1884, the number of industrial establishments rose from 175 to over 600. Although these establishments were as a rule small and modestly capitalized, they presaged a profound transformation in the economy and the society.[23] In conjunction with this growing industrial complexity and diversification, the Brazilian economy saw the multiplication of credit institutions, insurance companies, and public facilities.

As both the economy and the population expanded, certain areas of the country became more urbanized.[24] With the growth of the urban population and the amelioration of the transportation system, the internal market expanded a bit. Agriculture was no longer viewed as the only sector for capital investment: railroad construction, urban facilities, credit institutions, and industrial establishments began to lay a rival claim for available funds.

These economic transformations profoundly affected the society. New groups appeared, whose interests frequently diverged from those of the traditional elites. Those connected to the fledgling industrial sector, for example, petitioned the government for protection. In 1881 the Industrial Association, organized in Rio de Janeiro, issued a manifesto written by Felício dos Santos asserting that the country could free itself from the instability of a monoculture economy by developing its industry. Only thus could the nation diminish imports, improve the balance of trade, and move toward economic independence. For such a policy to succeed, however, it needed government support, and the agrarian interests, who were more than amply represented in Parliament, were not always supportive of the industrialists—a situation which of course created tensions.

In addition to the ascendancy of groups tied to industry, the empire witnessed the rise of sectors of the middle class.[25] These classes were made up primarily of people linked to mercantile activity, the professions, public administration, transportation, and banking. Most of these middle class groups, though living in the cities, moved in the orbit of the rural elite. They were linked to the landowners by economic interest and family ties and some were the "prodigal sons" of important families, who had left the plantations to try their luck in the cities. Others belonged to declining sectors of the rural elite and had brought with them nostalgia for their lost status.[26] There were also members of the lower classes who had climbed to higher positions through patronage. Yet, despite its economic and cultural links with the rural oligarchies, the emerging urban bourgeoisie developed, on certain issues, a perspective of its own. Life in the city was different from rural life and the urbanized generation was often tempted to abandon traditional values.[27]

As we have seen, it is difficult to set firm boundaries between urban and rural sectors, for while certain urban elements came from the landowning class, many members of the urban middle classes "ruralized" themselves as soon as they accumulated capital, buying plantations, marrying into plantation families, and becoming slaveowners. But even if frequent crossovers make rigid classification impossible, it would be a mistake to overlook the growth of an urban population whose behavior and values did not completely coincide with those of the seigneurial group. The response of new urban groups to abolition, to direct elections, and finally to the republic reveal the novelty of their position in Brazilian society.

As one might imagine, the economic changes of the late nineteenth century also affected the traditional elite. While landowners in the frontier areas adopted new techniques on their plantations and gradually substituted free labor for slave labor, those in the older zones,

argument contradict preceding chapter?

Divisions in S.P. (handwritten)

threatened with ultimate ruin due to declining productivity, were forced to cling to outmoded systems of production and to slave labor.

Coffee planters in the Paraíba Valley, in dramatic decline during the 1870s,[28] were unable to compete for immigrant labor in the 1880s and therefore could not replace their slave labor force.[29] Coffee plantations that had once yielded two hundred or more *arrobas* per thousand trees were yielding a maximum of fifty. In 1883 the total debt of Brazil's coffee plantations was calculated at 300,000 *contos*, most of it owed by the Paraíba Valley planters. Fifty percent of the landowners of that area were operating at a loss, with little hope of recovery.[30] At the level of provincial politics, there were violent conflicts between the Paraíba planters and those of the frontier areas of the Paulista West. The *fazendeiros* of the Paulista West advocated subsidies for immigration programs and for the construction of railroads in their region, while those of the Paraíba Valley argued that such projects would put an unnecessary burden on provincial coffers.[31]

SUGAR (handwritten)

Although a general crisis in the sugar economy during the nineteenth century made modernization of sugar production quite difficult, a milder version of the same battle was fought between more productive and less productive sectors in the sugar cane areas. The owners of mills close to the railroad lines managed to improve their processing system, thereby expanding their productive capacity. Their new prosperity contrasted sharply with the decline and ruin of the *banguês*. And the same contrast between old and new created conflict in the cattle ranching areas of Rio Grande do Sul, where the *xarqueadas* (producers of jerked beef) were superseded by modern beef producers.[32]

CATTLE (handwritten)

Conflicts between the various elite groups became intensified as the contrast between the more and less capitalized sectors grew ever more apparent. The weakening of traditional sectors, the groups that had formed the monarchy's strongest base of support, eroded the foundations of the throne. Abolition was a cruel blow for these groups and vitiated whatever strength the monarchy had continued to draw from them. Economic and social transformations not only weakened the groups who had once monopolized political power in the empire, they also brought to the political arena the aspirations of new groups. Industrial interests fought for protectionist policies. Planters in the Paulista West demanded policies favorable to immigration. And very often those interested in furthering immigration argued for the separation of Church and State, since this seemed to be a precondition for attracting immigrants from Protestant countries. Urban groups committed to the destruction of the slave system campaigned for abolition and called for greater political representation, demanding that the system of indirect elections, which insured disproportionate representation to the traditional agrarian elites, be replaced by direct elections, which would presumably favor the urban populations. The growth of the urban population created demands for urban utilities such as water, gas, and electricity, as well as transportation and sewage systems.[33]

These demands could not easily be satisfied, and very often they led to conflict between the new groups and the power elite and to confrontations in the parliament and in the press. Contradictory interests sometimes took the form of conflicts between provincial and central governments since different provinces were affected in different ways by economic growth. In time, many people began to see federation as the only solution to political bottlenecks. The excessive centralization of the imperial system, which allowed an oligarchy to interfere in every aspect of the country's life, was often identified as an obstacle to the development of the nation and to the solution of the country's most urgent problems.

Federalism was not a new idea in Brazil. At the time of independence, several groups were convinced that a federal system was better than a centralized one. Though during the colonial period each region was theoretically subordinate to the viceroy, the provinces had always established direct contact with the Portuguese Crown. After independence nothing seemed more natural than to follow this tradition and to respect the autonomy of the different provinces, particularly in view of the extreme regional variety and diversity of interests. Nevertheless, unitarian tendencies prevailed in 1822. The example of other South American states, which had been unable to maintain their territorial unity after independence and were constantly menaced by agitation and internal struggles, served to buttress the argument of Brazilians who considered a centralized state the best form of government.

In the years that followed independence, the issue of federalism cropped up whenever the policies of the central government came into conflict with regional interests.[34] But from 1848, when the last rebellion against the central government was repressed, until the beginning of the seventies, Brazilian politicians appear to have forgotten federalism. For twenty years the congruence between political and economic power, and the absence of fundamental conflict within the elite, made it possible for a centralized state to survive unchallenged. In the last decades of the century, however, conflicts and contradictions generated by structural change and the growing disequilibrium between economic power and political power brought the efficacy of the system into question once again. In 1870, the newly created Republican party presented itself to the nation with a manifesto supporting a federal system. "We adopt the principle of a federalist regime," said the manifesto, "based on the reciprocal independence of the various provinces, elevating them to the level of independent states linked only by their common nationality and their common interest in representation and national defense."[35]

From then on, the federalist ideal gained increasing support. In 1885, in a famous speech to the Chamber of Deputies, Joaquim Nabuco urged the monarchy to put into practice an ideal that had existed since independence. He argued that federalism was necessitated by the great distances between regions in Brazil, which made it impossible for the center to administer the provinces effectively. Vast regional differences were another argument in favor of the idea: the problems of the Northeast differed greatly from those of the central provinces, and the important issues in the South were so far removed from those in the rest of the country that a single, centralized administration could not hope to cope with them all. Moreover, he continued, since regional diversity dictated diverse interests, a centralized government, far away and unable to solve local problems, could not hope to remain legitimate. The urgent need for greater local autonomy was obvious. The tight control of the provinces by the central government did not contribute to the prosperity of the country. In fact the national debt grew each year, placing an unnecessary burden on the provinces. Nabuco expressed his concern that such trends would give rise to secessionist feelings, concluding that only federalism could save the country from this "ultimate disaster."

The occasion for Nabuco's speech was the presentation in the Chamber of Deputies of a proposition signed by 39 Liberal representatives. This proposition suggested that the electorate decide whether the constitution should be amended to give the country a federalist system. The proposed constitutional amendment read: "The government of Brazil shall be a federalist monarchy. The provincial governments shall be completely independent of the central government insofar as this does not interfere with the internal and external defense of the Empire, its representation abroad, the collection of general taxes, and the institutions needed to guarantee national unity and protect the constitutional rights of Brazilian citizens." During the empire, however, the proposed amendment never became law, and only with the republic was a federal system adopted.

Nabuco's apprehensions about secessionist tendencies were not totally unfounded. When he made his statement, he was most probably thinking about declarations made in São Paulo by prestigious poli-

ticians who had publicized their resentment of the central government
and their dreams of secession. Separatist ideas were born of the profound imbalance between political and economic power that existed at
the end of the empire. This imbalance, generating so much discontent
among new groups who felt they were insufficiently represented in the
government, derived primarily from the organization of the political
system. Since appointments to the Senate and the Council of State, two
important political organs, were for life, the traditional groups continued to wield political power long after they had lost their economic
power. Moreover, the number of representatives that each province
could send to the chamber and the Senate had not been adjusted to
adequately reflect demographic and economic changes.

An examination of the empire's political rolls[36] shows that, in 1889,
only 4 out of 59 senators came from São Paulo, the richest province in
the country—the Baron of Souza Queiroz, appointed in 1848; Joaquim Floriano de Godói, named in 1872; and Antonio da Silva Prado,
who became a senator in 1887, two years before the fall of the empire;
the fourth place was vacant. Pará, the main center of the booming rubber economy, also had 3 senators, while Sergipe, Alagoas, and Paraíba,
three small and rather poor provinces, each had 2; Bahía, 6; Minas
Gerais, 10; Pernambuco, 6; and Rio de Janeiro, 5. São Paulo had only
9 representatives in the Chamber of Deputies while Ceará, one of the
poorest provinces in the country, had 8; Pernambuco had 13; Bahía,
14; the Province of Rio de Janeiro and the capital city (Côrte), 12; and
Minas Gerais, 20. It was rare to see a Paulista from the West—the
most progressive area in the country after 1870—in the ministry or as
a member of the Council of State, which was dominated by men from
Minas Gerais, Bahía, Pernambuco, and Rio de Janeiro. With a few exceptions, most of the Paulistas who gained such positions represented
the Paraíba Valley, where coffee plantations had been steadily declining
since 1870, rather than the new thriving areas of the São Paulo West.
To aggravate the situation the provincial presidents, appointed by the
government, were most often from outside the province. Thus Paulistas
often had politicians from Bahía, Rio de Janeiro, or other areas presiding over their provincial government. Faced with these realities
Paulistas of the West became increasingly sympathetic to federalism as
well as republicanism. They were proud of their achievements, their
plantations, their railroads, their banks. Yet they felt that their interests were neglected and their initiatives thwarted by excessive centralization. It is not surprising, then, that the Republican movement found
many followers among them. Although the more extreme voices called

for secession, the majority considered a federal republic an ideal solution to their problem.

The total number of separatists was small during this period, but the mere fact that they existed indicated the level of tension during the last years of the empire. In 1877, on the opening of the railroad line from São Paulo to Rio, Ferreira de Menezes commented in the *Gazeta de Noticias* that:

> The Paulista . . . is a poet, a poet of progress, a practical poet. His verses are: good roads, machines, agriculture, improvements. He loves himself and is therefore more chauvinist [regionalist] than other people. In his eyes, the greatest grace that God can give a man is to make him a Paulista. . . . The Paulista's self-esteem has grown enough to make him dream of independence. . . . Every year, the Paulists sum up what they have received from the central government and compare it to what they have given. And since they are giving more than they are receiving, being positive men, practical poets, they already murmur: Why should we not be independent? [37]

This was an early expression of the "Paulista mystique" and of the separatist tendencies of the Paulistas, tendencies that would become more visible in the following years. One of the principal advocates of separatism was Martim Francisco, who in a speech to the Provincial Assembly in 1879 lamented the fate of São Paulo. "So much wealth is wasted in a province which alone could constitute a State," he said, "and which in less than ten years of peace and work would be the first power in South America," but which instead, because of bad government, could look forward to nothing but "discredit and bankruptcy." Two years later, in a circular to the Paulista electorate, Martim Francisco boasted that he was prouder to be a Paulista than to be a Brazilian. And in 1884 he complained that the needs of his province were never considered by the national government. "When we want to progress," he remarked bitterly, "the centralization web envelops us; our political offices are filled with people alien to our way of life, to our interests, and to our customs." On that occasion, Lourenço de Albuquerque asked him to what he attributed the unhappiness of São Paulo. Martim Francisco was quick to answer: to our insufficient representation. Every Paulista representative stood for at least 1,500 voters, he said, while the number represented by those from the northern provinces was at most 800. Martim Francisco's figures were slightly exaggerated. In fact, if we believe Santana Nery's figures, São Paulo representatives in the Chamber of Deputies represented about 1300 voters while the representative for Sergipe, Alagoas, Ceará, Paraiba represented between 700 and 900 voters. In spite of his lack of precision Martim Francisco was right in pointing to the fact that São Paulo was underrepresented in the Chamber of Deputies.

Years later in an article entitled "Bitter Truths," Martim Francisco returned to the same theme, commenting that each of São Paulo's nine representatives stood for more than 166,000 people. This was almost double the entire population of Espírito Santo, a province that elected two representatives, and nearly three times the population of Amazonas, which also elected two. Moreover, calculating representation by electoral districts, each Paulista senator represented 375,000 inhabitants, more than any other senator in the country.

Martim Francisco did not stop there in his condemnation of the political system. He complained that São Paulo contributed 20:000,000$000 to the national treasury each year but received a mere 3:000,000$000. The customs duties collected during three months in Santos (the principal port for coffee exports) were equivalent to the sum paid annually to the Paulistas by the central government. São Paulo contributed one-sixth of the entire national revenue. Furthermore, the levies gathered by the municipal councils in São Paulo, taken together, were greater than the average revenue of almost any one of the northern provinces. The income of the *município* (county) of São Paulo alone was greater than the total revenue for the whole province of Piauí.

These facts—right or wrong—seemed to Martim Francisco sufficient justification for the separatist language he began to use in 1887. Both under the pseudonym of Nemo and under his own name, he wrote articles insisting that São Paulo was the victim of grave injustice. "I sometimes believe," he once wrote, "that my fellow Paulistas and I descend in a straight line from Jesus Christ. He paid the price for all the sins of humanity, whereas we pay for all the North's embezzlements and all the consequences of the imperial minister's incompetence." His ironic style reached its peak in a comedy he published later that year. In this dramatic parable, São Paulo is the rich brother, exploited by his siblings. Exasperated and exhausted, he finally decides to leave his family, to the dismay and protest of all. Used to living at São Paulo's expense, they cannot accept the decision of the "Breadwinner of the Empire" to abandon them and live his own life.[38]

Martim Francisco's feelings were not unfounded. In fact, the province of Minas Gerais, which in 1883 had 20 representatives and 10 senators, had a budget of 1:932$828; while São Paulo, which had only 9 representatives and 4 senators, had a budget of 9:164$757, five times greater. This imbalance would be accentuated toward the end of the empire because of the rapid growth of the Paulista population and its increasing prosperity. And with this increasing political disequilibrium the Paulista's dissatisfaction grew.

Martim Francisco was not the only one to feel bitter about the situation and to harbor separatist ideas. Other Paulistas started writing books and newspaper articles expressing the same point of view. The Republican newspaper *Província de São Paulo* began a series of separatist articles in February 1887, and several books were published that year under the suggestive title *The Paulista Nation* (*Patria Paulista*). In one of them, Alberto Salles,[39] a positivist and a Republican journalist, wrote that "secession had become a deep Paulista aspiration." In another, J. F. de Barros wrote: "As to my nationality, I am a Paulista; as to my politics, I am a militant Republican and separatist at all costs." Under the title "Cartas a Feps" (letters to Feps, the pseudonym of Pacheco e Silva), Fernando de Barros published several articles in the *Província de São Paulo* advocating secession. On one occasion he commented:

> It will be marvellous when São Paulo is able to announce in the *Times* or the New York *Herald*, and in other newspapers in the Old and New World, the following: "The province of São Paulo, having finished off its business relationship with the old firm Brazil Bragantino Corruptions and Co., declares that it is now a free nation with its own private firm. It promises to maintain its business relations with other nations, and to substitute integrity, pride and dignity for the duplicity, deceit, and cowardice of the old firm.[40]

In an article published in the *Diário Popular*, Pacheco e Silva, a man of property and standing and a member of the Republican party since its formation, wrote that São Paulo would progress enormously if it were able to apply its revenue to material improvements and practical education, thus raising the intellectual and moral level of its inhabitants instead of subsidizing the central government. Similar thoughts were expressed in Campinas by Ubaldino do Amaral.

Yet the separatist ideal was ultimately rejected at the Republican party congress. Although several politicians spoke in favor of secession, most notably Horácio de Carvalho, Campos Salles, Alberto Salles, and Jesuino Cardoso, other equally important members of the party, such as Glicério and Júlio de Mesquita, the owner of the newspaper *Província de São Paulo*, opposed the idea.[41] Separation or federation, the latter understood as complete political and economic autonomy for the provinces, became the dilemma facing the Paulista Republicans, a dilemma that not even the proclamation of the republic could resolve completely.

Visiting Brazil shortly after the republic was proclaimed, Max Leclerc,[42] a French journalist, noted that the inhabitants of São Paulo still claimed to prefer secession to participation in a centralized government. During the first republican presidency, Campo Salles, a Paulista who was minister of justice, dissolved the commission appointed to draw up the civil code because he considered this a function of the state rather than the federal government. The strong desire for autonomy that had prompted some Paulistas to suggest secession continued into the early years of the republic, during the period when Paulistas were securing for themselves a greater control over the nation's government. Once they were in control, they seemed to have forgotten the issue. Separation would be resurrected in 1932, when they thought they had lost their political control.

In 1889, the call for secession was clearly not so strong as the Republican party's federalist leanings. On the eve of the proclamation of the republic, the majority of the Paulistas chose a federalist republican solution because they hoped it would resolve the major problems of political imbalance without endangering national unity. Thus the idea of overthrowing the monarchy and organizing a republican regime prevailed in the end.

As we have seen, the republican ideal was not new in Brazil but had a long history in the country's political life. At the end of the colonial period Brazilian colonists in rebellion against the mother country intended to create an independent republic. After independence those who conspired and rose against the government continued to assert their commitment to republican ideals. But it was only in 1870 that a Republican party with a program of its own was organized in Brazil.

From 1870 to 1889 the Republican party broadened its influence. Republican clubs were created in many areas, and Republican newspapers appeared all over the country. But these Republican organizations tended to be concentrated in the South. As Oliveira Viana has demonstrated, 79 percent of the newspapers and 89 percent of the clubs existing in 1889 were located in São Paulo, Rio de Janeiro, and Rio Grande do Sul.[43]

The Republican party in São Paulo was somewhat different from the party in other parts of the country, where it recruited most of its supporters among the urban population. In São Paulo, in addition to members of urban groups such as doctors, engineers, lawyers, journalists, and merchants, the Republican party also recruited many landowners, mostly from the Paulista West. Of the 133 delegates to the 1873 Republican convention in Itu, 76 declared agriculture their profession, not to mention those who identified themselves as lawyers or businessmen who had invested in plantations.[44] The same can be said of the subscribers to *Província de São Paulo*, the most important organ of the Paulista Republican party: they were mainly landowners from Campinas and Itu.

The preponderance of planters in the Paulista Republican party helps to explain its reticence to deal with the abolition of slavery.[45] Although the party included among its members such renowned abolitionists as the practitioner-lawyer Luiz Gama, Republican leaders in São Paulo made it clear from the beginning that they did not want to discuss abolition. By avoiding the issue the party leadership hoped to maintain the support of the rural sectors, which despite some experiments with free labor continued to depend mainly on slaves.

It is also interesting to note the almost complete absence of Paraíba Valley planters in the Republican party and the predominance of those from the West.[46] This seems to confirm the hypothesis raised earlier that the landowners from the São Paulo West joined the Republican party because they resented lack of representation in the political system and hoped that in a republican system they could have more political control. Planters in the Paraíba Valley who already had sufficient representation in the government did not become Republicans.

It should be emphasized, however, that the landowners of the Paulista West were in many ways a unique group. They were planters in a frontier zone that had recently become the country's wealthiest region, a region where the almost unlimited possibilities stimulated experimentation. The western planter distinguished himself by his capacity to be innovative. He perfected the methods of coffee processing and tried to replace slave labor with immigrant labor. He also invested his capital in railroads and banks. The Paulista of the West was an active and enterprising pioneer.[47] This was not merely a question of mentality, but of means. Located in virgin lands his plantation was more productive and he had capital enough to be experimental. Besides, in the West, the great social mobility typical of frontier areas blurred the distinction between rural and urban men. The Paulista West attracted people from extremely diverse origins and professions, often with no previous agricultural experience. Among these planters were men who had begun their careers as merchants, doctors, and lawyers—men of the city who brought with them their urban experiences and perceptions. After the railroads made it easier to travel, the planters spent a good part of each year in the city. All these factors made the Paulista planter of the West more susceptible to the new ideas and more willing to join the Republican party than other planters, and helps to explain why in São Paulo the majority of the Republicans came from rural areas, while in Rio de Janeiro and other provinces they came mainly from urban groups.

In the 1880s the party intensified its campaign, trying to enlarge its base and define new strategies. The leadership was divided. One group recommended the adoption of a revolutionary strategy and called for popular revolution; the other was convinced that the republic could be achieved through the electoral process. Silva Jardim and Quintino Bocaiuva represented these two positions, respectively.[48]

At a congress held in São Paulo in May 1888, the "evolutionist" strategy was officially sanctioned through the appointment of Quintino Bocayuva as national leader of the party. This event generated a crisis within the party. Silva Jardim published a manifesto on 28 May violently attacking the moderate faction, but his protest had little effect. In the end the pacific wing prevailed. One year later, however, the monarchy would be overthrown by a military coup.[49]

In fact, by 1887 the leadership of the Republican party had already begun to consider the possibility of asking the military for help. That year a series of incidents involving military men and civilian politicians created increasing hostility toward the regime within the army. Rangel Pestana, a member of the Republican party in São Paulo, suggested to the permanent committee of the party that it come to terms with the military in order to carry out a revolution. When he attended the national party congress in Rio, he continued to express this point of view and, despite the disapproval of the committee, approached certain individuals in the military, including Sena Madureira, Serzedelo Correia, and the viscount of Pelotas. This tactic was favored by Glicério, another Republican leader from São Paulo, who in March 1888 wrote to Bocaiuva and insisted that he make contact with the military. Américo Werneck, a leader of the party in Rio de Janeiro, also argued that the triumph of the republican revolution would come about only through the use of military force. And the republican hierarchy in Rio Grande do Sul came out at the same time in favor of a militarist solution.

Once they agreed on the importance of obtaining military support, the Republicans started courting the army in several different ways. Republican leaders made contact with sympathetic officers. And the Republican press gave widespread coverage to the conflict between the army and the government, never missing an opportunity to turn the military against the monarchy, while assuring them of Republican support.

The first attempt at conspiracy took place two years before the proclamation of the republic. It failed, apparently because of the intervention of Tomás Coelho, minister of war and a personal friend of the Republican leader Quintino Bocaiuva. In 1888 there was a second attempt, when Silva Jardim contacted the military officer Sena Madureira—the pivot in the conflict between the army and the imperial government—to plan an uprising. As we have seen, Silva Jardim had difficulty in finding support for his project among some of the principal Republican leaders, who were still reluctant to resort to a military coup. Yet all events seemed to point in this direction. The sharpening of the conflict between the military and the government and the impatience of the Republican leaders led to new meetings between the two groups.

Republicans found great receptivity in the army, where dissatisfaction had been growing since the Paraguayan War.[50] The increasing professionalization of the army had aggravated rather than reduced its conflict with the government. Military men had acquired a keen sense of their importance; they complained that they were badly paid and that the government did not treat them with the consideration they deserved. Most of all they resented the fact that politicians were constantly interfering in matters of military interest and the army was often subordinated to civilian ministers who did not understand the needs of the military. All these feelings tended to encourage insubordination and even rebellion. Pelotas, one of the military's most prestigious leaders, confessed in 1886 that out of 13,500 men in the army, 7,526 had been imprisoned for disobedience.

In spite of this lack of discipline the military was a cohesive body. When military men became involved in social or political issues, they never lost their esprit de corps. As a result, what would be a minor incident if it involved two civilians could become a grave menace to national security when it involved an officer and a civilian, since other officers would leap to the defense of their comrade. This is not to say that all military men shared the same opinions on politics. On the contrary, there were deep disagreements within the army; but whenever military men felt offended by civilians, they reacted as one.

What facilitated the alliance between the Republicans and the military was the military's conviction that it was their duty to improve their country's social and political organization. The belief that men in uniform were pure and patriotic while civilians or *casacas*—as they were called by the military—were venal, corrupt, and unpatriotic was then widespread in the army. From this conviction derived a missionary spirit that is clearly manifested in a famous letter to General Neiva on 10 July 1887 from Floriano Peixoto, an important leader in the army, and later president of the republic. Commenting on the conflict between military and civilians Peixoto wrote:

> I have seen the solution given to our class problem, which has most certainly surpassed the expectations of all. This very fact proves conclusively that our poor country is in an advanced state of moral corruption, and needs a military dictatorship to cleanse it. As a liberal, I cannot wish for my country a dictatorship by the sword, yet everyone knows—and examples abound—that only this type of government knows how to purify the blood of a social organism, such as ours, which is in such a corrupt state.[51]

It was this state of mind that made the military available to those conspiring against the regime.

When civilians approached these dissatisfied officers with the intention of planning a coup, they were extremely well received, since both groups shared a desire to change existing institutions. From the moment they were approached by the Republicans, groups within the army started plotting the overthrow of the monarchy. Military clubs became the main organs of the conspiracy.

The agitation created by military protests, the abolitionist propaganda, and the republican campaign generated strong apprehensions among monarchists about the future of the Brazilian monarchy. The feeling became widespread that the empire was undergoing a dangerous crisis and that the republic would soon be proclaimed if something was not done. In December 1888, Silva Jardim met the baron of Cotegipe, an influential supporter of the monarchy, in the Paineiras Hotel and attempted to sound him out. Cotegipe, an old and experienced politician who was a senator, a member of the council of state, and had been several times a minister, uttered prophetic words:

> Do not run hurriedly toward her [the Republic] for she is running toward us. My ministry fell because of a palace conspiracy, and my successor will leave at the point of a bayonet, and perhaps with him, the monarchy. Our ministries do not last long now, and therefore you do not have long to wait.[52]

Ouro Preto, a Liberal, assumed the position of prime minister on 7 June 1889, perfectly conscious of the risks he confronted. When the emperor appointed him, Ouro Preto had told him most clearly:

> Your majesty has certainly noticed that in some of the provinces there is agitated and active propaganda for a change in the form

of government. This propaganda bodes no good for the future, for it wishes to expose the country to institutions for which the country is not prepared, institutions that do no fit existing conditions and cannot bring happiness.

In my humble opinion, it is important not to underestimate this torrent of false and imprudent ideas, but instead to weaken and incapacitate it, not allowing its strength to increase. The way to achieve this is not through violence and repression, but rather by demonstrating practically that the present system of government has sufficient elasticity to recognize the most progressive principles, satisfy all the demands of enlightened public opinion, consolidate liberty, and realize the prosperity and greatness of our nation, without disturbing the internal peace in which we have lived for so many years.

We will reach this goal, Sir, by initiating, with strength and courage, wide political, social, and economic reforms, inspired by democratic ideals. These reforms should not be postponed, for otherwise they may become futile. That which today is enough may perhaps be too little by tomorrow.[53]

Ouro Preto was proposing a program of reforms designed to neutralize criticism and realize the frustrated aspirations of the opposition.

At the parliamentary session of 11 June, he presented his program— actually a version of the Liberal program of 1869. It contained suggestions for political, economic, and social reforms: limitation of the senate term; reduction of the Council of State to a mere administrative body with no political power; election of municipal administrators and nomination of provincial presidents and vice presidents from a list selected by the electorate; and extension of representation to all male citizens who were literate, engaged in legitimate professions, and in possession of their civil and political rights. Ouro Preto suggested that freedom of worship be granted to all as well as freedom of education. He also proposed that the existing system of education be reformed. In regard to economic questions he recommended the reduction of export duties; the enactment of a law facilitating acquisition of land; the reduction of freight rates and the development of rapid means of communication; the conversion of the foreign debt and amortization of the paper currency; the achievement of a balanced federal budget; and the creation of credit institutions to issue paper currency. He did not, however, include any provision for adopting a federal system.[54]

In sum, Ouro Preto proposed a program which he expected would please those who seemed most dissatisfied with the regime and who were drifting toward a republican system. When the cabinet president presented these proposals, Pedro Luiz Soares de Souza, a representative from Rio de Janeiro, could not repress an exclamation that certainly expressed the feeling of most of those present. "It is the beginning of the Republic," he said—to which Ouro Preto responded, "No, it is the defeat of the Republic."

Ouro Preto's program was based on the assumption that these reforms, if not instituted under the monarchical regime, would be brought about by a republican revolution. From his point of view, the best way to neutralize the effect of republicanism was to satisfy republican demands. But his approach had a serious limitation. He felt that it was impossible under existing conditions to propose a federalist system, one of the crucial Republican goals.

To some, Ouro Preto's reforms were not enough; to others they were far too much. And the latter constituted the majority in the Chamber of Deputies, which recoiled when faced with his suggestions. After the minister had presented his program, the Conservatives proposed a motion of no confidence, which was approved by a vote of seventy-nine to twenty. The vote was preceded by a heated discussion, during which the representatives Cesário Alvim and Father João Manuel stated their commitment to the republican ideal. But the vote made it clear that the dominant elite was incapable of accepting the necessary changes and reforms. To the opposition it seemed that it was impossible to realize progressive goals within the context of the monarchy. A few days later, on 17 June, the Chamber of Deputies was dissolved and the government promoted elections to organize a new one, which would be called for an extraordinary session on 20 November of the same year.

The dominant oligarchy had proven too inflexible to accept the institutional changes necessitated by the new economic and social realities of the 1880s. Their reluctance was understandable, since these reforms—taken to their logical conclusions—meant the destruction of the traditional oligarchy's base of power. But the consequence of their reluctance was a military coup.

After the Chamber of Deputies was dissolved, the situation became increasingly tense. Ouro Preto took measures that displeased the army and provided ammunition for the Republicans.[55] Predictions of the government's retaliation against the military ran wild. Taking advantage of the turbulent atmosphere, segments of the Paulista and Rio de Janeiro Republican parties renewed their efforts to convince the military to lead a movement against the established government. Benjamin Constant, Frederico Solon, Bernardo Vasques, and Lieutenants Antonio Adolfo, Mena Barreto, Carlos de Alencar, Sebastião Barreto, and Joaquim Ignácio, all members of the army, helped to circulate Republican propaganda within their ranks. Major Antonio Bezerra de

Tenentes

Cavalcanti, Celestino Alves Bastos, and Antonio Batista da Costa, Jr., also became outspoken in the republican cause.[56]

On 11 November, Rui Barbosa, Benjamin Constant, Aristides Lobo, Bocaiuva, Glicério, and Colonel Solon (some Republicans, others military men) met at the house of the Marshall Deodoro da Fonseca to convince him to lead the movement, something he reluctantly agreed to. On 15 November, the monarchy was overthrown by a military coup and the republic was declared.

The movement had resulted from the concerted action of three groups: a military faction, plantation owners from the Paulista West, and members of the urban middle classes. They were indirectly aided in the attainment of their goal by the declining prestige of the monarchy and of the traditional oligarchies which had supported the Crown. Although the revolutionaries were momentarily united around the republican ideal, profound disagreements among them would surface during the first attempts to organize the new regime. In the first years of the republic, latent contradictions exploded into conflict contributing on several occasions to the instability of the new regime.

Ultimately, however, 1889 did not mark a significant break in the Brazilian historical process. The urban middle classes and emerging proletariat were not strong enough to undermine the power of the new rural oligarchies during the First Republic (until 1930).

The system of production and the colonial character of the economy survived unchanged, and the country continued to depend on foreign markets and foreign capital as it always had. The main difference was that the traditional rural oligarchy had been supplanted by a new one: the coffee planters of the West and their allies, who, once in power, promoted only those institutional changes that were necessary to satisfy their own needs. November 15 was thus a *journée des dupes* for all the other social groups who had hoped that the republic would represent a break with tradition.

9 THE MYTH OF RACIAL DEMOCRACY
A Legacy of the Empire'

40 ?

In a series of talks given more than thirty years ago in the United States and later published under the title *Brazil: An Interpretation*, the Brazilian sociologist Gilberto Freyre described the idyllic scene of Brazilian racial democracy. Although he acknowledged that Brazilians were not entirely free of racial prejudice, he argued that in Brazil social distance was the result of class difference rather than prejudices about race or color.[1] Because Brazilian blacks enjoyed social mobility and opportunities for cultural expression, they did not develop a consciousness of being black as their American counterparts did. Freyre also pointed to the fact that in Brazil anyone who was not obviously black was considered white. He expressed the conviction that blacks were rapidly disappearing in Brazil and merging into the white group.[2] He went further. He rebuked those who were concerned about the possible negative effects of ethnic amalgamation. He reaffirmed confidence in the social and intellectual capacity of the mulatto. It was precisely in the process of miscegenation, Freyre thought, that Brazilians had found the way of avoiding the racial problems that tormented Americans.

Some twenty years later, a new generation of social scientists studying race relations in Brazil arrived at very different conclusions. They piled up a new harvest of evidence that Brazilian whites were prejudiced. Blacks were not legally discriminated against but were "naturally" and informally segregated. The majority of the black population remained at the bottom of society with no chance to move up. Possibilities for social mobility were severely limited for blacks, and whenever blacks competed with whites, they were discriminated against. The prevailing orthodox characterization of Brazil as a racial democracy

A version of this essay was first published in English in *The African Dispersal*, Afro-American Studies Program, Boston University (Boston, 1979).

234

was a mere myth for the revisionists, who talked about the "intolerable contradiction between the myth of racial democracy and the actual prevalence of discrimination against Negroes and Mulattoes."[3] They accused Brazilians of having the ultimate prejudice: to believe they were not prejudiced.

Gilberto Freyre's picture of race relations in Brazil expressed, however, a widespread opinion, shared not only by the majority of the white elite but, surprisingly enough, by many blacks. Both these groups received the work done by the revisionists as they had received the attempts to organize a black movement in Brazil: with suspicion, if not resentment, and sometimes with indignation. The revisionists were accused of inventing a racial problem that did not exist in Brazil.

The study of Brazil's changing racial ideologies gives us an excellent opportunity to analyze the dynamics of social mythology. Social myths, as we all know, are constantly being created and destroyed. They are an integral part of social reality and should not be seen merely as epiphenomena. In daily life, myth and reality are inextricably interrelated. Social scientists and historians operate at the level of social mythology. Willy-nilly, they themselves help to destroy and to create myths. In the process, the "truth" of one generation very often becomes the myth of the next. American scholars might talk today about the myth of the self-made man.[4] However, for many who lived in the United States in the nineteenth century (and perhaps even for many today) the myth corresponded to their life experience and was not simply a dream that helped the common man to confront his daily frustrations. The myth helped reduce social conflict, to be sure, but it also drove men to great undertakings, some successes and some failures. It was part of American reality, as real in people's experience as money, work, or hunger.

The myth of the self-made man, so pervasive in American society, did not have the same appeal in nineteenth-century Brazil. It made sense perhaps to some "petit-bourgeois" groups, mainly immigrants who were involved in a feverish struggle for social ascension, but it remained alien to the experience of most Brazilians, upper and lower class alike, who believed instead in the myth of racial democracy. In the United States the myth of the self-made man helped to blind Americans to class differences. In Brazil the myth of racial democracy obscured racial differences. In both cases the "truth" of past generations became the myth of today.

In the United States as well as in Brazil intellectuals helped both to create and to destroy those myths. We might hope that more familiarity with the dynamics of social mythology will not only improve our knowledge of society and history but also contribute to a better understanding of the predicaments of our work.

In outline, the facts are clear enough: A powerful myth, the idea of racial democracy, which controlled the perception and to some extent the lives of Freyre's generation of Brazilians, became, for the next generation of social scientists, broken and discredited. Several obvious questions are suggested by these facts. How could white Brazilians of Freyre's generation have been unaware of their own prejudices? How could Brazilian blacks of that period have been blind to the discrimination that was such a large and stubborn fact of life for most of them? How could alert and articulate Brazilians, white or black, have closed their eyes to the realities of racial discrimination, when those realities were made starkly plain in official and well-publicized figures? Any Brazilian who could read and do simple arithmetic, for example, could have learned the lessons of the official figures of 1950. These figures classified about 60 percent of the total population as technically white, about one-fourth as mulatto and 11 percent as black. But the population of the elementary schools had a dramatically different distribution. Only 10 percent of the pupils were mulatto, and only 4 percent were black. And as one moved up the educational ladder, the warping along racial lines became even more marked. Only 4 percent of the students in secondary schools were mulatto and less than 1 percent were black; in the universities, just over 2 percent were mulattos, and only about one-quarter of 1 percent were blacks. The figures were not secret, and they were not difficult to understand. But they were ignored. And there were many other figures like these to demonstrate white predominance and discrimination against blacks to which nobody in Brazil paid any attention.[5]

It is important to explain not only how Brazilians could have been blind to such social realities but also why they made a point of defining Brazil as a racial democracy. What made them deny that they were prejudiced? What functions did this myth have? How was it used? Who benefited from it? Finally, why was the new generation of social scientists sensitive to the manifestations of prejudice ignored by the former generation? Why were the new social scientists not impressed with the lack of *apparent* racial conflict, or with the absence of legal discrimination, or with the presence of numerous blacks among the elite—facts, all of which had served as evidence for the Brazilian racial-democracy myth? Why did they feel the need to reveal the existence of subtle forms of discrimination unnoticed before? Why were they driven to "unmask" the reality behind the myth?

For somebody who thinks that ideologies merely reflect the "real" world, an easy way out would be to say that objective changes occurring in Brazilian society—industrialization, urbanization, capitalist development—aggravated social conflicts and increased competition, making Brazilians racists. Thus it would not be surprising that social scientists, merely registering changing racial attitudes, became after the fifties more aware of prejudice and discrimination. This would be to say that both Gilberto Freyre and Florestan Fernandes (the leader of the revisionist school in Brazil) were correct.[6] One expressed the social reality of traditional Brazil, the other characterized the modern trends in Brazilian society.

A second easy way out would be to argue that ideologies are actually nothing but inverted images of the real world and are artifacts that dominant groups manufacture to disguise forms of oppression or to create political hegemony. On such a premise, one might say that prejudice and discrimination had always existed in Brazilian society and that the myth of racial democracy was a distortion—either deliberate or involuntary—of the real pattern of race relations in Brazil. Following this argument to its logical conclusion, someone always ready to believe in the conspiratorial capacities and Machiavellian behavior of the ruling classes could see the myth of racial democracy as a manipulative device used by the white upper classes (for whom Gilberto Freyre and other intellectuals of his generation were the spokesmen) to mask the oppressive reality of race relations. Only the new generation of social analysts, not identified with the traditional elite, could finally reveal the "real" nature of race relations in Brazil.

There is a third way of dealing with the problem. We might attribute to external circumstances the creation and destruction of the myth, locating the sources of the Brazilian racial ideology in events occurring in Europe or the United States. The myth of racial democracy would then appear as an attempt to accommodate racist ideas, which became fashionable in Europe in the second half of the nineteenth century, to Brazilian reality. Infected with theories that stressed the superiority of the white population and the inferiority of mestizos and blacks, the Brazilian elite—a minority of whites, few of whom could be sure of the "purity" of their blood, surrounded by a majority of mestizos—found no better solution than to put its hopes in the process of "whitening." Brazil would overcome its racial problems, its inferiority—through miscegenation. The population *would become* increasingly white. To a segregationist ideology characteristic of the United States, where any offspring of a black and a white was considered black, the Brazilian elite opposed an ideology based on integration and assimilation, which implied the repression of prejudiced attitudes against blacks and assumed that mulattos were halfway between blacks and whites. Instead of a prejudice of origins (any amount of black blood makes a man black) Brazilians had a prejudice of color (a person is white or black depending on his or her appearance).[7]

After the Second World War these external points of reference changed dramatically. With the Allied victory over the Nazis, racism was "defeated" on the battlefield. Within a few years the United States moved toward integration; Brazilians could no longer point to the odious institution of segregation or to the horrors of lynching in the United States.[8] These changes led to a growing interest in the study of race relations. On the assumption that Brazilians' experience might offer the rest of the world a unique lesson in "harmonious" relations among races, UNESCO promoted a series of research projects on the theme of race relations in Brazil.[9] Contrary to the expected outcome this research revealed the existence of prejudice and discrimination. The new generation of social scientists launched an attack on the traditional racial mythology.

One could argue that what I have presented is a caricature of the three types of interpretation, that I have built these straw men just to knock them down. I must admit that I deliberately exaggerated common trends in the history of social mythology in order to prove some points, but a careful analysis of the works published about race relations in Brazil will show that many authors have adopted one or more of the three approaches. The use of these interpretations has led to distortions that we should be aware of in order to avoid their traps. They are reductionist, establish false correlations, and omit important mediations. Moreover, in spite of being fundamentally different these three approaches have one thing in common: the assumption that those who wrote and talked about race and prejudice were concerned only or even primarily with race and prejudice. We know, however, that very often what seems to be the main theme of a generation is nothing but a metaphor to express other realities or concerns. This is what George Fredrickson has shown in *The Black Image in the White Mind* and Leonard Richards has demonstrated in *Gentlemen of Property and Standing*.[10] Anxieties Americans experienced about changing family patterns, about the political system, about the new forms of social stratification and authority led them to become abolitionists or antiabolitionists. The lesson is clear: In order to explain people's perceptions of racial patterns one would have to look outside the narrow frame of race relations.

In spite of being limited and insufficient, the three interpretations mentioned above carry some truth. There is no doubt, for instance, that Brazilian intellectuals of the nineteenth and early twentieth centuries were very influenced by Lapouge, Gobineau, and other European writers who talked about the inferiority of the mixed people and the superiority of the white race.[11] But this does not explain the myth of racial democracy—not even a minor and subsidiary aspect of it like the idea of "whitening." In fact, Brazilian intellectuals were not merely responding to outside ideas. They chose the ideas that would allow them to deal better with contemporary Brazilian reality. Without this understanding how can we explain their indifference to other ideas (Marxism, for example) during that same period? It is obvious that Brazilian intellectuals picked up certain European ideologies and left others aside. The question is: Why did they select racist ideas that stressed white superiority when in Brazil only 40 percent of the population around 1870 could be considered white, and when some members of the elite could not be sure of their racial "purity"?

When we look closer at what they did with European racial ideas, it becomes clear that Brazilians were not passive recipients of ideas produced outside, mere victims of a colonial mentality trying to view their reality through ideas coming from abroad. It would perhaps be as correct to say that they viewed those ideas through their reality. The Brazilian white elite already had in their own society the elements they needed to forge their racial ideology. They had learned since the colonial period to see blacks as inferiors. They also had learned to make exceptions for some *individual* blacks or mulattos. Any European or American who postulated white superiority would be welcome. He would bring the authority and prestige of a superior culture to ideas Brazilians already had. They would have only to make some adjustments. And they did. In order to formulate the "negro problem" in their own terms, they "discarded two of the European racist theories' main assumptions: the innateness of racial differences and the degeneracy of mixed bloods."[12] Thus, while asserting the superiority of whites over blacks, they could afford to accept blacks among their ranks. And they could hope to eliminate the black "stigma" in the future through miscegenation.

One can see that the influence of foreign ideas should be taken into consideration in an analysis of the Brazilian racial ideology, but that influence is not a sufficient explanation for the origin and destruction of the myth of racial democracy. Equally insufficient is the "realist" approach. It would be correct to say that industrialization, urbanization, and the development of capitalist relations of production did create profound dislocations in Brazilian society, as they did everywhere. And one could argue, following Van den Berghe's analysis in *Race and Racism*, that the patterns of race in Brazil changed from a paternalistic to a competitive model—from racial accommodation to racial conflict, from a system of race relations in which prejudice, though present, is "not needed," to a system in which prejudice is "needed." [13] But even if we admit that there was an objective change in racial patterns, we still have not explained how the myth was created and destroyed. We still must ask why Gilberto Freyre's generation needed to proclaim the existence of a racial democracy and why it became important for the next generation to fight this particular myth.

Just as insufficient are those approaches that postulate the manipulative character of social myths and would characterize the myth of racial democracy as a creation of the white upper classes to disguise prejudice and discrimination. Granted, the myth masked the real nature of race relations in Brazil and hid prejudice and discrimination. It made the development of black consciousness more difficult and racial confrontation less likely. It also excused the white upper classes from doing anything for the deprived black majority.[14] But this is not to say that it had been created purposefully by the white elite to perform these functions. We cannot infer intentions and purposes from effects or functions. Only after the myth was identified and exposed would an attempt to deny racial prejudice raise the suspicion of being an act of bad faith.

It was obvious that whites benefited from the myth, but some blacks benefited as well, although in a more limited and contradictory way. The denial of prejudice, the belief in the "whitening process," the identification of the mulatto as a special category, the acceptance of individual blacks among the ranks of the white elite made it difficult for blacks to develop a sense of identity as a group. On the other hand, it created opportunities for some *individual* blacks or mulattos to move up in the social scale. Socially mobile blacks had to pay a price for their mobility: they had to adopt the whites' perception of the racial problem and of themselves. They had to pretend they were whites. They were "special" blacks, "blacks of white soul," a common expression used by white upper-class Brazilians in referring to their black friends. But the stakes were high enough for many blacks and mulattos to be willing to accept the rules of the game. If some of them were painfully conscious of subtle forms of prejudice and discrimination, they made a point of not mentioning it, sometimes not even to themselves. And they often shared with whites the myth of racial democracy. For society in general their success served as vivid testimony to the myth's reality, as evidence of the lack of prejudice and the possibilities for social mobility enjoyed by blacks in Brazil.

An anecdote about Machado de Assis illustrates well the dilemma of the upper-class mulatto in Brazil during the nineteenth century and will, I hope, set us on our way to explaining the life and "death" of the myth of racial democracy in Brazil. When Machado de Assis died, one of his friends, José Veríssimo, wrote an article in his honor. In an outburst of admiration for the man of modest origins and black ancestors who had become one of the greatest novelists of the century, Veríssimo—a mulatto himself—violated a social convention and referred to Machado as the mulatto Machado de Assis. Joaquim Nabuco, who read the article, quickly perceived the faux-pas and recommended the suppression of the word, insisting that Machado would not have been pleased by it. "Your article," he wrote to Veríssimo,

> is very beautiful but there is one sentence that caused me chills: "Mulatto, he was indeed a Greek. . . ." I would not have called Machado mulatto and I think that nothing would have hurt him more. . . . I beg you to omit this remark when you convert your article into permanent form. The word is not literary, it is derogatory. . . . For me Machado was a white and I believe he thought so about himself.[15]

This story tells a lot about the social and racial tensions and forms of accommodation characteristic of Brazilian society in the nineteenth and twentieth centuries. Nabuco was white, from a family of important politicians, himself a distinguished figure in the Parliament. He was also the leader of the abolitionist movement in the Chamber of Deputies and the author of the most famous indictment of slavery published in Brazil.[16] Like many other members of the Brazilian elite, he had blacks and mulattos among his friends. He knew what was expected from him as a white person whenever he addressed a black or a mulatto. He would treat his black friends as equals, conveying in subtle ways that he was not prejudiced against blacks—a strong conviction he had not only about himself but about white Brazilians in general.[17] He would carefully avoid any situation that could make blacks feel embarrassed or ashamed, conscious of being black. He would treat them as if they were whites.

Everybody knew Machado was a mulatto but to acknowledge it publicly would be a *gaffe*. And it would have been considered so by Machado himself. Nabuco was right. All his life, Machado had been haunted by three nightmares: his epileptic seizures, his modest origins, and his color—three sources of fear, anxiety, and shame. He seems to have become more reconciled to his epilepsy than to his origins and color. He visited his family at hours when he could not be seen; he married a white woman and maintained a discrete and reserved attitude toward abolition. In his novels he dealt with the personal tragedies of white individuals and rarely and only marginally referred to slaves and blacks.[18] He never confronted the issue of "blackness." Instead Machado did what many other blacks of his generation who climbed to important positions did. He lived with the ambiguity of his situation and performed conscientiously the role he was supposed to play in the community of whites of which he had become a part. Machado would not have liked to be called a mulatto, an expression which would uncover the fiction of his public self.

Nabuco's attitude corresponded to the ideal of gentility cultivated by the white elite. He knew and respected protocol, as did the emperor, who, when he noticed at a court ball that the black engineer André Rebouças had not danced at all, asked his own daughter, Princess Isabel, to dance with him.[19] But all the paternalism of the emperor, all of Nabuco's respect for social etiquette, all the social prestige of men like Machado and Rebouças, all the display of equality by members of the Brazilian elite in their relationships with their black friends—all this care and discretion—could not finally erase the reality of racial prejudice and racial discrimination in Brazilian society. Machado, whose most remarkable quality as a writer was his sense of irony and who spent most of his life as a novelist revealing the contradictions between people's images and the hidden realities of their lives, would probably have sensed it better than his white friend. Nabuco, from his white upper-class position, could be oblivious to his own prejudices. After all, did he not have among his friends many illustrious mulattos? Like many other Brazilians, however, he hoped that European immigration would bring to the tropics the "flow of lively, energetic, and healthy Caucasian blood."[20] The same form of delusion and the same ambiguity in race relations made it possible for the mulatto Nina Rodrigues, the famous Brazilian anthropologist of the 1930s, to propagate ideas about the inferiority of blacks.

Naturally men like Machado and Rebouças were used as evidence of black social mobility and the lack of prejudice and racial discrimination, a set of beliefs which constituted the core of what the generation of the 1960s called the myth of racial democracy. The myth was nothing but the formalization at the theoretical level of experiences shared by whites like Nabuco and blacks like Machado. The key for understanding the racial pattern, the process of formalizing the myth and its criticism can be found in the system of clientele and patronage and its breakdown.

Since the colonial period, the monopoly of the means of production by the white minority (plantation owners, merchants, bureaucrats) and the limited opportunities for economic, social, and political participation of the masses created the basis for a system of clientele and patronage.[21] Within this system poor whites, free blacks, and mulattos (the majority of the population) functioned as the clientele of the white elite. Social mobility was not acquired through a direct competition in the market, but through a system of patronage in which the decisive word belonged to the white elite. Sure of its position, controlling social mobility, imbued with a hierarchical concept of social organization[22]—which sanctified social inequalities and emphasized reciprocal obligations, rather than personal freedom and individual rights—the Brazilian elite did not fear the population of free blacks as their American counterparts did. Blacks could move up in the social scale only when permitted by the white elite. Thus, the Brazilian slaveowner, who shared with slaveowners everywhere negative stereotypes about blacks, never translated them into open racism or legal discrimination. Slaveowners could even afford to break the discriminatory rules against blacks embodied in the Portuguese legal tradition.[23] They could accept from time to time within their own ranks a light-skinned mulatto who, like Machado, would automatically acquire the status of white.[24] Blacks occupying an upper-class position identified themselves with the white community. They represented a model for the majority of blacks, who remained at the bottom of society. The fact that some blacks had apparently gotten rid of their "stigma" and had joined the white community induced blacks and whites to see the deprivation under which the majority of blacks lived as a consequence of class rather than racial differences or of black inferiority rather than white discrimination. On the other hand, the black and white lower classes, equally dependent on the patronage of the white elite, could live in the illusion of solidarity created by shared poverty and common helplessness and dependence on the white elite.

After independence, with the creation of representative forms of government, the elite's need to control the electorate gave new strength to the system of clientele and patronage. The relative expansion of the internal market and the opening of new careers in the bureaucracy, law, journalism, and engineering had the same effect. The internal market was still limited and the elite could continue to use traditional forms of control over the process of social mobility. In the twentieth century, however, there were new opportunities for social mobility. With increasing urbanization, the jump in population from 14,000,000 to more than 100,000,000 since 1890, and slightly better distribution of wealth, it became difficult for the traditional elite to maintain its position. There were splits within the elite. New sectors opposed traditional groups. The emergent urban middle classes had a chance to choose between being clients of the traditional oligarchies and following the new groups. Some could even dream of developing an autonomous worldview and independent political action.[25] In the 1920s the word "oligarchy" was often used critically in analyses of Brazilian society.[26] It was also during this period that a series of upheavals and conspiracies involving the military, middle-class sectors, and workers threatened the political order, culminating in the revolution of 1930, which put an end to the political hegemony of the traditional oligarchies.[27]

Gilberto Freyre's generation was caught in this process of rapid change. Men and women of his generation saw the growth of the new factories that replaced the traditional sugar mills and watched a great number of other factories being built in the South. They discovered a new social problem—the working class—and saw the sons of immigrants becoming entrepreneurs while members of the traditional "aristocracy" occupied meaningless positions.[28] They confronted a new style of life and politics and they were not quite sure they liked it. Although the scenario was changing more rapidly in the South than in the Northeast, change could be felt everywhere and people responded differently to it. In the 1920s, while the Paulista intellectuals organized Modern Art Week and signed the Modernist Manifesto, Gilberto Freyre and his friends responded with the Regionalist Manifesto, which emphasized tradition.[29] Paulistas (the Brazilian version of Yankees) seemed to have committed themselves to progress; they seemed to mock their tradition, to have cut loose from the past. Gilberto Freyre would write the epic *Masters and Slaves*. He would reveal in a sympathetic way the seignorial tradition. He would engage in a "Proustian" search for the lost past.[30] He would show to the Brazilian Yankee and to the Americans the positive aspects of his tradition. Nothing seemed more opportune—especially in a moment when blacks organized a Black Front to fight for the improvement of their conditions[31]—than talking about Brazilian racial democracy.

The problem was that with the gradual breaking down of the system of clientele and patronage and the development of a competitive system, it was becoming more difficult for blacks and whites to avoid situations in which prejudice and discrimination would become apparent. Although the display of prejudice was basically incompatible with the old system of clientele and patronage, it was a natural instrument for whites to use against blacks in the new competitive society. Whites became more aware of their prejudiced attitudes once they had to confront blacks where they had rarely been seen before, in clubs, theaters, universities, and upper-class hotels, or when they had to deal face to face with an "aggressive," "uppity" black who did not play his traditional role of humility and meekness. Blacks themselves realized when they had to fight for positions in the job market, without the support of a white patron, that they were the subjects of discrimination.

Social scientists of the sixties, however, were not merely responding to these new realities. To be sure, there were more opportunities for perceiving prejudice and discrimination than before, but it is not because prejudice and discrimination had become more obvious that social scientists picked the myth of racial democracy as the target of criticism. The attack on the myth came out of the political struggle against the traditional oligarchies which reached its climax in the sixties. The denunciation of traditional mythologies can be understood only within the context of class (or segments of class) confrontation.

Intellectuals, of course, had their way of explaining what they were trying to do. Octávio Ianni, one of the important figures among the revisionists, explained that what motivated them was the belief that in some way the "advance of Brazilian civilization depended upon the scientific study of the nature and direction of race relations." He argued that it was important to destroy false social images since "the dominant myths in a society were always those which would help to maintain the prevailing structure of vested interests and social conventions." He expressed his conviction that the new studies on race, adopting a new perspective, constituted "an important contribution to the development of democracy in Brazil." Ianni stressed his confidence in scientific methods as techniques for developing a rational consciousness of social reality. And he predicted social science would have an important role to play in creating conditions for social progress, and consequently in destroying myths which, in his words, "were of value only to the dominant groups in an agrarian export society," an opinion he shared with Florestan Fernandes, the leading scholar in the modern study of race relations in Brazil.[32]

The revisionists were products of the University of São Paulo and analogous institutions, which had been created in the thirties with the purpose of forming a new elite of professionals and bureaucrats relatively independent from the traditional oligarchies. Many of the social scientists trained in these new institutions had come from middle-class and a few from lower-class families. Some were mulattos. They did not, however, feel the same embarrassment that Machado did when they talked about their modest origins. They did not depend on the traditional system of clientele and patronage. They acquired their status through their affiliations with the new institutions. Their audience was also different. As part of the process of creating a new cultural elite, university teaching had been democratized. Night courses had started in 1946, immediately after the fall of Vargas. The new students, like their teachers, represented a new social stratum, and they, too, were ready to participate in criticizing the traditional myths.[33]

Fighting myths that are still alive in a society, however, has always been a difficult and risky task. In Brazil the myth of racial democracy is not completely dead. Although profoundly weakened in the urban centers, the system of clientele and patronage still survives in Brazil—almost intact in some areas of the backland or remodeled to fit the modern society. This will explain why until now it has been difficult in Brazil to organize a successful black movement. It also explains, at least in part, why Professors Ianni and Fernandes, like hundreds of others who considered it their task to destroy traditional myths that inhibited the process of democratization in Brazilian society, were forced to retire from the University of São Paulo in 1969.

EPILOGUE

All in all, throughout the history of the Brazilian empire there was the invisible hand of the market forces, limiting choices and defining possibilities. In the nineteenth century, when the international division of labor between industrial and nonindustrialized nations took place, Brazil continued to occupy the position it had in the colonial period. It continued to supply the world market with tropical products and raw material. This would have important consequences for years to come.

Driven by the notion of profit Brazilian elites concentrated their investments in the agricultural sector and imported most industrial products from the outside. They lagged behind in the Industrial Revolution. The Brazilian internal market was slow to develop. While a great many people in other parts of the world lost control of their means of production and were thrown in the labor market, many people in Brazil continued to live in the subsistence economy.

Since the elites were reluctant to tax themselves (there was no land tax or income tax during the empire), most of the population was poor, and the tasks of the state were overwhelming, the Brazilian government had to borrow heavily in the international market, particularly from England. Brazilian foreign debt increased steadily during the second half of the century. In the last decades of the empire the servicing of the debt consumed an average of 40 percent of the surplus left from the balance of trade.

Thus, although between 1840 and 1880 there was a growth of almost 400 percent in the total income generated by exports, particularly coffee, rubber, cotton, and cacau, there was a permanent drain of capital to pay for the debts. But that was not the only way in which capital disappeared. Profit remittance was another. In the second half of the nineteenth century British capitalists started investing in Brazil as they did in other Latin American countries. They enjoyed privileges granted to them by the government and made handsome profits. The history of where those profits went is still to be written, but there is little evidence that they were reinvested in Brazil.

Brazil's dependence on the international market made a growing number of people vulnerable to the frequent crises that struck the capitalist world in the nineteenth century. When banks in London and New York withdrew credit and the prices of products fell in the international market, the Brazilian economy would be hurt, and when prices went up and credit was easy, the economy would boom.

The subordination of the Brazilian economy to the international market had other effects as well. European institutions and European ideas and fashions (particularly English, French, and more rarely German) became the necessary point of reference for the Brazilian elites. Europe and by the end of the century the United States represented progress and development. The Brazilian imperial elites wanted to emulate them and looked down on their own traditions. In this process, however, there was a basic irony. By promoting capitalist development, they undermined in the long run the basis of their own power and contributed to the fall of the empire.

NOTES

AALPSP	*Anais da Assembléia Legislativa da Província de São Paulo*
AESP	Arquivo do Estado de São Paulo
APB	*Anais do Parlamento Brasileiro*
APBCD	*Anais do Parlamento Brasileiro, Câmara dos Deputados*
APUH	Associação dos Professores Universitários de História
CG	*Congressional Globe*
Cebrap	Centro Brasileiro de Pesquisas
FFCL	Faculdade de Filosofía Ciências e Letras
FFCH	Faculdade de Filosofía e Ciências Humanas
HAHR	*Hispanic American Historical Review*
IFCH	Instituto de Filosofía e Ciências Humanas
IHGB	Instituto Histórico e Geográfico Brasileiro
ILAS	Institute of Latin American Studies
LARR	*Latin American Research Review*
SH	Secção Histórica (Brazilian National Archive classification)
UMG	Universidade de Minas Gerais
USP	Universidade de São Paulo

CHAPTER ONE

1. Adam Smith, *An Inquiry into the Nature and Causes of the Wealth of Nations* (New York, 1937), vol. 4, chaps. 2, 3, 7.

2. Jean Baptiste Say, *Traité d'économie politique ou simple exposition de la manière dont se forment, se distribuent et se consomment les richesses*, 3d ed. (Paris, 1817).

3. Myriam Ellis, *O Monopólio do Sal no Estado do Brasil, 1631–1801* (São Paulo, 1955); idem, "As Feitorias Baleeiras Meridionais do Brasil Colonial" (Ph.D. diss., FFCL, USP, 1958).

4. Charles Boxer, *The Golden Age of Brazil, 1695–1750: Growing Pains of a Colonial Society* (Berkeley, 1969), 112–25; B. Fernandes Gama, *Memórias Históricas da Província de Pernambuco* (4 vols.; Recife, 1844–48), 4:54–330; Manuel dos Santos, "Narração Histórica das Calamidades de Pernambuco desde o Ano de 1707 até o de 1715," *Revista do IHGB* 53:1–307; F. A. Pereira da Costa, *Anais Pernambucanos* (7 vols.; Recife, 1951–54), 5:85–

178; Mario Melo, *A Guerra dos Mascates como Afirmação Nacionalista* (Pernambuco, 1941).

5. Sérgio Buarque de Holanda, ed., *História Geral da Civilização Brasileira* (7 vol.; São Paulo, 1960–69), 1(2):386; Bernardo Pereira de Berredo, *Annaes Históricos do Estado do Maranhão*, 2d ed. (Maranhão, 1840).

6. A. E. Taunay, *História Geral das Bandeiras Paulistas* (11 vols.; São Paulo, 1924–50), 9:487–518; Manuel Cardozo, "The Guerra dos Emboabas, Civil War in Minas Gerais, 1708–1709," *HAHR* 22 (August 1942): 470–92; José Soares de Melo, *Emboabas, Chronicas de uma Revolucão Nativista: Documentos Inéditos*, quoted by Boxer, *The Golden Age of Brazil* (1962 ed.), 386.

7. Traslado do Auto de Sequestro feito nos bens que se acharam na Casa do Cônego Luis Vieira da Silva, *Autos da Devassa da Inconfidência Mineira* (7 vols.; Rio de Janeiro, 1936–38), 1:279; E. Bradford Burns, "The Enlightenment in Two Colonial Brazilian Libraries," *Journal of the History of Ideas* 25 (July–September 1964): 430–38; Eduardo Frieiro, *O Diabo na Livraria do Cônego* (Belo Horizonte, 1957); Silvio Gabriel Diniz, "Biblioteca Setecentista nas Minas Gerais," *Revista do Instituto Histórico e Geográfico de Minas Gerais* 6 (1959): 33–334; A. J. R. Russel-Wood, ed., *From Colony to Nation: Essays on the Independence of Brazil* (Baltimore, 1975); Carlos Guilherme Mota, *Atitudes de Inovação no Brasil, 1789–1801* (Lisbon, 1970); idem, *Nordeste, 1817: Estruturas e Argumentos* (São Paulo, 1972). On the influence of the American Revolution, see *Autos da Devassa da Inconfidência Mineira* 1:108, 137, 142–43, 159. On the influence of the French Revolution, see also "Autos da Devassa do Levantamento e Sedição Intentados na Bahía em 1798," *Anais do Arquivo Público da Bahía*, vols. 35–36 (1959–61); and "A Inconfidência da Bahía em 1798," *Anais da Biblioteca Nacional do Rio de Janeiro* 45 (1922–23): 3–421; "Devassa Ordenada pelo Vice-Rei Conde de Rezende, 1794," *Anais da Biblioteca Nacional do Rio de Janeiro* 61 (1939): 243–51, 308–9, 248–85, 280.

8. *Autos da Devassa da Inconfidência Mineira* 1:108, 111, 137, 142, 161, 170.

9. "Devassa . . . Conde de Rezende," *Anais da Biblioteca Nacional do Rio de Janeiro* 61:284–85, 302–3, 308–9.

10. "Autos da Devassa do Levantamento e Sedição na Bahía," *Anais do Arquivo Público da Bahía*, vols. 35–36. See Manuel Faustino's deposition. For a study of the Tailors' Rebellion, see Mota, *Atitudes de Inovação*, and Donald Ramos, "Social Revolution Frustrated: The Conspiracy of the Tailors in Bahía, 1798," *Luso-Brazilian Review* 13 (Summer 1976): 74–90.

11. "Devassa . . . Conde de Rezende," *Anais da Biblioteca Nacional do Rio de Janeiro* 61:243.

12. L. F. de Tollenare, *Notas Dominicais Tomadas Durante uma Residência em Portugal e no Brasil nos Anos de 1816, 1817, 1818, Parte Relativa a Pernambuco*, trans. by Alfredo de Carvalho, preface by M. de Oliveira Lima (Recife, 1905). On the 1817 revolution, see also Francisco Muniz Tavares, *A Revolução de Pernambuco em 1917*, 3d ed. (Recife, 1917); Mota, *Nordeste*.

13. Carlos Rizzini, *O Livro, o Jornal e a Typografia no Brasil* (São Paulo, 1945); Célia de Barros, "A Ação das Sociedades Secretas," in Holanda, *História Geral* 2(1):191.

14. Carlos Guilherme Mota, *Idéia de Revolução no Brasil no Final do Século XVIII* (São Paulo, 1967).

15. Augusto de Lima, Jr., *Pequena História da Inconfidência de Minas Gerais*, 3d ed. (Belo Horizonte, 1968). See also Kenneth Maxwell, *Conflicts and Conspiracies: Brazil and Portugal, 1750–1808* (Cambridge, 1973). As late as 1822, José Joaquim Carneiro de Campos, writing to his friend Francisco Saraiva, expressed his fear that the example of Santo Domingo would be followed in Brazil; see *Documentos para a História de Independência* (Rio de Janeiro, 1923), 360–64.

16. Francisco Muniz Tavares, *História da Revolução de Pernambuco em 1817*, 3d ed. (Recife, 1917); Mota, *Nordeste*, 154.

17. About priests' participation in the 1817 revolution, see Maria Graham, *Journal of a Voyage to Brazil and Residence There During Part of the Years 1821, 1822, 1823* (London, 1824), translated into Portuguese *Diário de uma Viagem ao Brasil e de uma Estada Nesse País Durante Parte dos Anos 1821, 1822, 1823* (São Paulo, 1956), 121; John Armitage, *The History of Brazil, from the Period of the Arrival of the Bragança Family in 1808 to the Abdication of Don Pedro the First in 1831* (2 vols.; London, 1836), translated into Portuguese, *A História do Brasil Desde o Período da Chegada da Família de Bragança em 1808, Até a Abdicação de D. Pedro I em 1831* (São Paulo, 1914), 25. See also Biblioteca Nacional, *Revolução de 1817* (9 vols.), *Documentos Históricos*, vols. 101–9 (Rio de Janeiro, 1953–55), 106:154, 187, 190, 206, 216, 219.

18. Holanda, "A Herança Colonial, sua Desagregação," in *História Geral* 2(1):16.

19. See, for example, the document issued by Thomaz Antonio de Villanova Portugal, published in *Documentos para a História da Independência* (Lisbon and Rio de Janeiro, 1923), 108–13.

20. *Autos da Devassa de Inconfidência Mineira*, 7:181.

21. José Honório Rodrigues, *Conciliação e Reforma no Brasil, um Desafío Histórico Cultural* (Rio de Janeiro, 1965), 38.

22. "A Inconfidência da Bahía em 1798," *Anais da Biblioteca Nacional* 45:55.

23. See "Devassa . . . Conde de Rezende," *Anais da Biblioteca Nacional* 61:243–51.

24. Also "Autos da Devassa do Levantamento e Sedição Intentados na Bahía," *Anais do Arquivo Público da Bahía*, vols. 35–36. On popular participation see Mota, *Nordeste*. On the rural oligarchy and its participation in the 1817 revolution, Biblioteca Nacional, *Documentos Históricos* 103:91, 107:8, 14, 109:193.

25. Biblioteca Nacional, *Documentos Históricos* 102:12.

26. Roberto Simonsen, *História Econômica do Brasil, 1500–1800*, 3d ed. (São Paulo, 1957), 389–90.

27. A law of October 1808 exempted from custom taxes textiles manufactured in Portugal. A decree exempted Chinese merchandise from customs whenever it belonged to Portuguese subjects. Another decree of January 1813 went even further, exempting all Portuguese merchandise from customs taxes. A decree of November 1811 prohibited any ship which did not belong to a Portuguese or to a Brazilian or have a crew three-quarters Portuguese from unloading products from Asia in Brazil. A decree of November 1814 prohibited foreigners from navigating along the Brazilian coast. See *Coleção das Leis do Brasil, 1810–1822* (Rio de Janeiro, 1887–90).

28. José Antonio de Miranda, *Memória Constitucional e Política sobre o Estado Presente de Portugal e do Brasil, Dirigido a El Rey Senhor D. João VI e Oferecido a Sua Alteza o Principe Real do Reino Unido de Portugal, Brasil e Algarves, Regente do Brasil* (Rio de Janeiro, 1821); Informação Verbal do Ministro dos Negócios Estrangeiros, *Revista do Instituto Histórico e Geográfico Brasileiro* 51 (1888): 369–77.

29. "Exame Analítico Crítico da Solução da Questão: O Rei e a Família Real de Bragança Devem, nas Circunstancias Presentes Voltar à Portugal ou Ficar no Brasil?" in *Documentos para a História da Independência*, 208.

30. *Reflexões sobre a Necessidade de Promover a Uniáo dos Estados de que Consta o Reino Unido de Portugal, Brasil e Algarve nas Quatro Partes do Mundo* (Lisbon, 1822).

31. Francisco Sierra y Mariscal, "Idéias Gerais Sôbre a Revolução do Brasil e suas Consequências," *Anais da Biblioteca Nacional do Rio de Janeiro* 42–44 (1920–21): 51–81.

32. *Memória sôbre as Principais Causas Porque Deve o Brasil Reassumir os seus Direitos e Reunir as suas Provincias, Oferecida ao Principe Real por R.J.G.* (Rio de Janeiro, 1822).

33. Tollenare, *Notas Dominicais.*

34. J. Friedrich von Weech, *Reise über England und Portugal nach Brasilien und den Vereinigten Staaten das La-Plata strömes wahrend den Jahren 1823 bis 1827* (Munich, 1835), quoted by Manuel de Oliveira Lima, *O Movimento da Independência, 1821–1822* (São Paulo, 1922), 36.

35. Carlos Guilherme Mota, ed., *1822: Dimensões* (São Paulo, 1972).

36. Augustin de Saint Hilaire, *Segunda Viagem à São Paulo e Quadro Histórico da Província de São Paulo* (São Paulo, 1953), 100.

37. Ibid., 103–6.

38. Maria Isaura Pereira de Queiroz, "O Mandonismo Local na Vida Política Brasileira, da Colonia à Primeira República," *Estudos de Sociología e História* (São Paulo, 1957), 216.

39. *Documentos para a História da Independência*, 361.

40. Ibid., 378–81, 383.

41. *Reforço Patriótico ao Censor Lusitano na Interessante Tarefa que se Propôs de Combater os Periódicos* (Bahía, 1822).

42. *Coleção das Leis do Brasil*, decree of 19 June 1822.

43. Pedro Octávio Carneiro da Cunha, "A Fundação de um Império Liberal," in Holanda, *História Geral*, vol. 2(1); de Oliveira Lima, *O Movimento da Independência, 1821–1822.*

44. Brazil, National Archives, SH, box 295.

45. *Documentos para a História da Independência.* See also Charles K. Webster, *Britain and the Independence of Latin America, 1812–1830: Select Documents from the Foreign Office Archives* (2 vols.; London, 1938), and Brazil, Ministerio das Relações Exteriores, *Archivo Diplomatico da Independência* (6 vols.; Rio de Janeiro, 1922–25).

46. Barão de Vasconcelos e Barão Smith de Vasconcelos, *Arquivo Nobiliárquico* (Lausanne, 1968).

47. Augustin de Saint Hilaire, *Segunda Viagem do Rio de Janeiro à Minas Gerais e à São Paulo, 1822,* 2d ed. (São Paulo, 1938), 180.

Chapter Two

1. *Refôrço Patriótico ao Censor Lusitano na Interessante Tarefa que se Propôs de Combater os Periódicos* (Bahía, 1822).

2. About the historiography and the legend of José Bonifácio and of the independence movement in Brazil, see Emília Viotti da Costa, "José Bonifácio: Mito e Histórias," *Anais do Museu Paulista* 21 (1967): 291–350; reprinted in *Da Monarquia à Republica,* 2d ed. (São Paulo, 1979), 53–108. See also José Honório Rodrigues, *Independência Revolução e contra Revolução* (São Paulo, 1975–77); idem, *Vida e História* (Rio de Janeiro, 1966), 24–47; and the introduction to Edgard Cerqueira Falcão, ed., *Obras Científicas, Políticas e Sociais de José Bonifácio de Andrada e Silva* (3 vols.; São Paulo, 1963).

3. *Documentos para a História de Independência* (Lisbon, and Rio de Janeiro, 1923), 402.

4. *O Tamoio,* 26 August 1823 and 2 September 1823 (Facsimile; Rio de Janeiro, 1944).

5. José da Silva Lisboa, *História dos Principais Sucessos Políticos do Império do Brasil* (1830).

6. Divaldo Gaspar de Freitas, *Paulistas na Universidade de Coimbra* (Coimbra, 1958).

7. Melo Franco, *No Reino da Estupidez* (Paris, 1818), xi, 62.

8. *Revista da Academia Real de Ciências de Lisboa* (June 1816).

9. Falcão, *Obras . . . de José Bonifácio.*

10. José Bonifácio, Manuscript, IHGB.

11. For details about events that led to independence, see Emília Viotti da Costa, "Introdução ao Estudo da Emancipação Política do Brasil," in Manuel Nunes Dias, ed., *Brasil em Perspectiva* (São Paulo, 1968), 73–141, translated into English in A. J. R. Russell-Wood, ed., *From Independence to Nation* (Baltimore, 1975), 43–88. See also chap. 1.

12. Octávio Tarquínio de Souza, *José Bonifácio, 1763–1838: O Pensamento Vivo de José Bonifácio* (Rio de Janeiro, 1944), 84.

13. Ibid., 2d ed. (1961), 131.

14. "Viagem Mineralógica na Província de São Paulo," *Arquivo do Museu Nacional do Rio de Janeiro* 24 (1823): 217–36.

15. Falcão, *Obras . . . de José Bonifácio* 2: 93–102.

16. Venancio Neiva, *Resumo Biográfico de José Bonifácio de Andrada e Silva, o Patriarca da Independência do Brasil* (Rio de Janeiro, 1936), 249.

17. Atas do Conselho de Estado, Manuscripts, Arquivo Nacional, SH, box 295.

18. J. Avelar Figueira de Melo, "Correspondência do Barão Wenzel de Mareschall, Agente Diplomático da Austria no Brasil de 1821 a 1831," *Revista do Instituto Histórico e Geográfico Brasileiro* 80 (1916): 65.

19. Neiva, *Resumo Biográfico*, 117–18.

20. Manuscripts, Arquivo Nacional, SH, box 295.

21. Manuscripts, Arquivo Nacional, SH, boxes 309, 740, 753.

22. See the newspapers *Nova Luz Brasileira* and *Jurujuba dos Farroupilhas*.

23. Falcão, *Obras . . . de José Bonifácio* 3: 15.

24. Tarquínio de Souza, *José Bonifácio*, 128. See also Afranio Peixoto and Constancio Alves, eds., *Antología Brasileira* (Rio de Janeiro, 1920), 175.

25. Tarquínio de Souza, *José Bonifácio*, 117.

26. Neiva, *Resumo Biográfico*, 215.

27. Manuscripts, IHGB, box 191, doc. 4864. Also José Bonifácio, Manuscripts, Museu Paulista.

28. Tarquínio de Souza, *José Bonifácio*, 131–32.

29. Neiva, *Resumo Biográfico*, 61; Tarquínio de Souza, *José Bonifácio*, 133.

30. *Anais do Parlamento Brasileiro, Assembléia Constituinte, 1823* (Rio de Janeiro, 1874), 1:26.

31. Cartas Andradinas, *Anais da Biblioteca Nacional do Rio de Janeiro* 14 (1890): 14, 22; Neiva, *Resumo Biográfico*, 204.

32. José Bonifácio de Andrada e Silva, *Representação à Assembléia Geral Constituinte e Legislativa do Império do Brasil sôbre a Escravatura* (Paris, 1825); republished in Falcão, *Obras . . . de José Bonifácio*, vol. 2; see also Neiva, *Resumo Biográfico*, 213.

33. See João Severiano Maciel da Costa, *Memória sobre a Necessidade de Abolir a Introdução de Escravos Africanos no Brasil, sobre o Modo e Condições Com que essa Abolição Deve se Fazer e sobre os Meios de Remediar a Falta de Braços que ela Pode Ocasionar* (Coimbra, 1821); and Jose Elóy Pessoa da Silva, *Memórias sobre a Escravatura a Projeto de Colonização dos Europeus e Pretos da África no Império do Brasil* (Rio de Janeiro, 1826).

34. Joaquim Nabuco, *O Abolicionismo* (São Paulo, 1938), 35.

35. Falcão, *Obras . . . de José Bonifácio*, 2:99–100.

36. *Anais . . . Assembléia Constituinte, 1823*, 7–9, 29–30 October and 6 November. Also José Bonifácio, Manuscripts, Museu Paulista.

37. Cartas Andradinas, *Anais da Biblioteca Nacional do Rio de Janeiro* 14:11.

38. *A Malagueta*, 5 June 1823, Coleção Fac-Similar de Jornais Antigos (Rio de Janeiro, 1945).

39. *Anais . . . Assembléia Constituinte* 4:231.

40. *Poesias Avulsas de Américo Elísio* (Bordeus, 1825).

41. José Bonifácio, Manuscripts, Museu Paulista. Also Neiva, *Resumo Biográfico*, 257.

42. Tarquínio de Souza, *José Bonifácio*, 328.

43. José Bonifácio, Manuscripts, Museu Paulista.

44. Tarquínio de Souza, *José Bonifácio*, 332, 335, 337.

45. Neiva, *Resumo Biográfico*, 257.

46. Cândido Ladisláu Japí-Assú, *Defesa do Ilustríssimo e Excelentíssimo Sr. José Bonifácio de Andrada e Silva* (Rio de Janeiro, 1835).

47. "Brazilian politicians want Brazil to become like England or France; I wish Brazil would always keep its simple and natural uses and customs and rather remain backward than corrupted," wrote José Bonifácio; quoted by Tarquínio de Souza, *José Bonifácio*, 137.

48. Gondin da Fonseca, *José Bonifácio, Nacionalista, Republicano, Homem de Esquerda* (São Paulo, 1963).

CHAPTER THREE

1. Nelson Saldanha, *História das Idéias Políticas no Brasil* (Rio de Janeiro, 1968); Maria Stella Bresciani, "Liberalismo, Ideologia e Controle Social" (Ph.D. diss., FFCH, USP, 1976); José Honório Rodrigues, *Conciliação e Reforma no Brasil* (Rio de Janeiro, 1965). Paulo Mercadante, *Consciência Conservadora no Brasil* (Rio de Janeiro, 1965). For an analysis of the relationship between patronage and liberalism, see Roberto Schwarz, "As Idéias Fora do Lugar," *Estudos Cebrap* 3 (São Paulo, 1973), 151–61; Maria Sylvia Carvalho Franco, "As Idéias Estão no Lugar," *Debates* (São Paulo, 1976), 61–64; Carlos Nelson Coutinho, "Cultura Brasileira: um Intimismo Deslocado à Sombra do Poder," *Debates* (São Paulo, 1976), 65–67.

2. Roberto Schwarz, *Ao Vencedor as Batatas: Formas Literárias e Processo Social nos Inícios do Romance Brasileiro* (São Paulo, 1977).

3. Hipólito da Costa, *Antologia do Correio Braziliense*, ed. Barbosa Lima Sobrinho (Rio de Janeiro, 1977); Antonio Joaquim de Mello, ed., *Typhis Pernambucano: Obras Políticas e Literárias de Frei Joaquim do Amor Divino Canéca* (Recife, 1878).

4. "Notícia de uma Revolução entre os Pretos no Ano de 1821 em Minas Gerais," *Revista do Arquivo Público Mineiro* 5 (1900): 158.

5. *Coleção das Leis do Brasil*, 1822, 125.

6. For an analysis of the conflicts between the National Convention and the emperor, see *Anais do Parlamento Brasileiro, Assembléia Constituinte, 1823* (Rio de Janeiro, 1874).

7. Beatriz Westin Cerqueira Leite, *O Senado nos Anos Finais do Império, 1870–1889* (Brasília, 1978); Fernando Machado, *O Conselho de Estado e sua História no Brasil* (São Paulo, 1972); João Camillo de Oliveira Tôrres, *O Conselho de Estado* (Rio de Janeiro, 1965); A. E. Taunay, *A Câmara dos Deputados* (São Paulo, 1950); Waldemar de Almeida Barbosa, *A Câmara dos Deputados e o Sistema Parlamentar do Govêrno no Brasil* (Brasília, 1977).

8. Raymundo Faoro, *Os Donos do Poder: Formação do Patronato Político Brasileiro*, 2d ed. (2 vols., São Paulo, 1975); Maria Isaura Pereira de Queiroz, *O Mandonismo Local na Vida Política Brasileira* (São Paulo, 1969); Afonso de E. Taunay, *Memórias* (Rio de Janeiro, 1960); João Camillo de Oliveira Tôrres, *Os Construtores do Império: Idéias e Lutas do Partido Conservador Brasileiro* (São Paulo, 1968); Luís Eul Soo-Pang and Ron Seckinger, "The

Mandarins of Imperial Brazil," *Comparative Studies in Society and History* 9, 2 (1972): 215–44.

9. *Anais do Parlamento Brasileiro, Assembléia Constituinte*, 1823, 1, 94.

10. Augustin de Saint Hilaire, *Segunda Viagem ao Rio de Janeiro e Minas Gerais e São Paulo*, 2d ed. (São Paulo, 1938), 180.

11. Raymundo de Magalhães, Jr., *Três Panfletários do Segundo Reinado* (São Paulo, 1956).

12. Sérgio Buarque de Holanda, ed. *História Geral da Civilização Brasileira: O Brasil Monárquico* (São Paulo, 1969–75), vol. 1; Felisbelo Freire, *História de Sergipe*, 2d ed. (Rio de Janeiro, 1977); Odilon Nunes, *Pesquisas para a História do Piauí: Confederação do Equador* (Petrópolis, 1977); Gilberto Vilar de Carvalho, *A Liderança do Clero nas Revoluções Republicanas, 1817–1824* (Petrópolis, 1980); Horácio de Almeida, *História da Paraíba*, 2 vols. (João Pessoa, 1978); João Alfredo de Souza Montenegro, *O Liberalismo Radical de Frei Canéca* (Rio de Janeiro, 1978).

13. De Mello, *Typhis Pernambucano*.

14. Octávio Tarquínio de Souza, *Evaristo da Veiga* (Rio de Janeiro, 1957); idem, *Bernardo Pereira de Vasconcelos* (Rio de Janeiro, 1957).

15. Tarquínio de Souza, *Evaristo da Veiga*, 122.

16. Ibid. 161.

17. Robert Walsh, *Notices of Brazil in 1828 and 1829* (2 vols., London, 1830), 2:445–46.

18. *APBCD* (1828), 4:131–32.

19. Bernardo Pereira de Vasconcelos, *Carta aos Senhores Eleitores da Província de Minas Gerais*, 2d ed. (Rio de Janeiro, n.d.).

20. Tarquínio de Souza, *Bernardo Pereira de Vasconcelos*, 79.

21. Ibid. 202.

22. For a listing of other radical newspapers published during this period, see Nelson Werneck Sodré, *A História da Imprensa no Brasil* (São Paulo, 1956); for an analysis of the newspaper *Nova Luz Brasileira*, see Octávio Tarquínio de Souza, *Fatos e Personagens em torno de um Regime* (Rio de Janeiro, 1957), 243.

23. *Nova Luz Brasileira*, 27 Sept. 1831.

24. Ibid. 246, 697, 911. See also *O Jurujuba dos Farroupilhas*, August 1831.

25. *Nova Luz Brasileira*, 207, 428, 651, 807, 957.

26. *O Jurujuba dos Farroupilhas*, 12 Sept. 1831; *Nova Luz Brasileira*, 30 July 1831.

27. *Nova Luz Brasileira*, Jan. 1831.

28. Octávio Tarquínio de Souza, *Diogo Antonio Feijó* (Rio de Janeiro, 1957), 166; Paulo Pereira de Castro, "A Experiência Republicana, 1831–40," in Sérgio Buarque de Holanda, ed., *História Geral da Civilização Brasileira: O Brasil Monárquico*, 2:16; Alcir Lenharo, *As Tropas da Moderação* (São Paulo, 1979).

29. Paulo Pereira de Castro, "A Experiência Republicana," 20.

30. See *Coleção das Leis do Brasil* for the years 1840 and 1841. An inter-

esting account of the events that preceded the coup of 1840 can be found in Tristão de Alencar Araripe and Aurelino Leal, *O Golpe Parlamentar da Maioridade* (Brasília, 1978). For the meaning of judicial reforms, see Thomas Holmes Flory, "Judge and Jury in Imperial Brazil: The Social and Political Dimensions of Judicial Reforms, 1822–1848," (Ph.D. diss., University of Texas, Austin, 1975); Jeanne Berrence de Castro, *A Milícia Cidadã: A Guarda Nacional de 1831 à 1850* (São Paulo, 1977).

31. *Autos dos Inquéritos da Revolução de 1842 em Minas Gerais* (Brasilia, 1979); Odilon Nunes, *Pesquisas para a História do Piauí* (8 vols.; Rio de Janeiro, 1975), vol. 3; Manuel Correia de Andrade, *Movimentos Nativistas em Pernambuco: Setembrizada e Novembrada* (Recife, 1971); Felisbelo Freire, *História de Sergipe*, 2d ed. (Petrópolis, 1977); F. A. Pereira da Costa, *Cronología Histórica do Estado do Piauí*, 2d ed. (Rio de Janeiro, 1974); Moacyr Flores, *Modêlo Político dos Farrapos: As Idéias Políticas da Revolução Farroupilha* (Porto Alegre, 1978); Izabel Andrade Marson, *Movimento Praieiro: Imprensa, Ideología e Poder Político* (São Paulo, 1980).

32. Américo Braziliense d'Almeida e Mello, *Os Programas dos Partidos e o Segundo Império* (São Paulo, 1878); José Murilo de Carvalho, "Elite and State Building in Imperial Brazil" (Ph.D. diss., Stanford University, 1974), published in Portuguese under the title *A Construção da Ordem: A Política Imperial* (Rio de Janeiro, 1980).

33. Magalhães, *Três Panfletários*, 218–75.

34. About the conflict between Church and State, see George Boehrer, "The Church in the Second Reign, 1840–1889," in Henry Keith and S. F. Edwards, eds., *Conflict and Continuity in Brazilian Society* (Columbia, S.C., 1969), 113–40; Mary C. Thornton, *The Church and Freemasonry in Brazil, 1872–1875* (Washington, 1948); Antonio Carlos Villaça, *A História da Questão Religiosa no Brasil* (Rio de Janeiro, 1974); Nilo Pereira, *Conflito entre Igreja e Estado* (Recife, 1976).

35. For vote patterns, see Robert Conrad, *The Destruction of Brazilian Slavery, 1850–1888* (Berkeley, 1972), 301.

36. Barão de Javarí, *Organizações e Programas Ministeriais*, 2d ed. (Rio de Janeiro, 1962), 196.

37. Magalhães, *Três Panfletários*, 247.

38. Machado de Assis, *Esaú e Jacó*, 181.

39. Magalhães, *Três Panfletários*, 252.

40. Ibid., 42.

41. José Murilo de Carvalho, "A Composição Social dos Partidos Políticos Imperiais," *Cadernos do Departamento de Ciências Políticas da Universidade de Minas Gerais* 2 (Dec. 1974): 1–34.

42. Barão do Javarí, *Organização e Programas Ministeriais*, 84.

43. For details, see Joaquim Nabuco, *Um Estadista do Império: Nabuco de Araujo, sua Vida, suas Opiniões e sua Época* (3 vols.; São Paulo, 1936); João Camillo de Oliveira Tôrres, *A Democracia Coroada* (Rio de Janeiro, 1957); Faoro, *Os Donos do Poder*.

44. Reynaldo Carneiro Pessoa, *A Idéia Republicana no Brasil Através dos*

Documentos (São Paulo, 1973), 37–62; for a study of the Republican party, see George Boehrer, *Da Monarquia à República: História do Partido Republicano no Brasil, 1870–1889* (Rio de Janeiro, 1954); José Maria dos Santos, *Bernardino de Campos e o Partido Republicano Paulista: Subsídios para a História da República* (Rio de Janeiro, 1960); José Murilo de Carvalho, "Elite and State Building in Imperial Brazil."

45. D. Pedro II, *Conselhos à Regente*, introduction by J. C. de Oliveira Torres (Rio de Janeiro, 1958); *Falas do Trono desde o Ano de 1823 até o Ano de 1889* (São Paulo, 1977).

46. Barão do Javarí, *Organizações e Programas Ministeriais*; see also *APBCD*, 11 June 1889.

47. João Camillo de Oliveira Tôrres, *O Positivismo no Brasil* (Petrópolis, 1964); Joao Cruz Costa, *A History of Ideas in Brazil* (Berkeley, 1964); idem, *O Positivismo na República: Notas sobre a História do Positivismo no Brasil* (São Paulo, 1956); Robert Nachman, "Positivism, Modernization and the Brazilian Middle-Class," *HAHR* 57 (Feb. 1977): 1–23; Ivan Lins, *História do Positivismo no Brasil* (São Paulo, 1964).

48. Machado de Assis, *Crônicas (1878–1888)*, in *Obras Completas*, 4:10.

CHAPTER FOUR

1. Eric Foner, *Free Soil, Free Labor, Free Men: The Ideology of the Republican Party before the Civil War* (New York, 1970); Malcolm J. Rohrbough, *The Land Office Business: The Settlement and Administration of American Public Lands, 1789–1837* (New York, 1968); Howard W. Ottoson, ed., *Land Use Policy and Problems in the United States* (Lincoln, Neb., 1963); Roy M. Robbins, *Our Landed Heritage: The Public Domain, 1776–1936* (Lincoln, Neb., 1962); Harry N. Scheiber, ed., *United States Economic History: Selected Readings* (New York, 1964); Henry Nash Smith, *Virgin Land: The American West as Symbol and Myth* (New York, 1950).

2. Warren Dean, "Latifundia and Land Policy in Nineteenth-Century Brazil," *HAHR* 51 (Nov. 1971): 606–25; Ruy Cirne Lima, *Pequena História Territorial do Brasil: Sesmarías e Terras Devolutas*, 2d ed. (Porto Alegre, 1954); Brasil Bandecchi, *Origem do Latifúndio no Brasil* (São Paulo, 1963); Alberto Passos Guimarães, *Quatro Séculos de Latifúndio* (São Paulo, 1964); José Marcelino Pereira de Vasconcelos, *Livro de Terras* (Rio de Janeiro, 1860); José Murilo de Carvalho, "A Modernização Frustrada. A Política de Terras no Império," *Revista Brasileira de História*, March 1981, pp. 39–58.

3. *APBCD*, 1843, 2:348 ff.

4. Manuel Diegues, Jr., *População e Propriedade da Terra no Brasil* (Washington, D.C., 1959), 14.

5. *APBCD*, 1843, 2:349, 380, 389–90, 401, 664, 669, 709, 716, 742, 745–47, 801, 829, 840, 853, 862, 871.

6. Ibid., 390, 401.

7. Ibid., 390.

8. Ibid., 380–90.

9. Ibid., 380, 389.

10. Ibid., 390.

11. Ibid., 349, 742, 746.

12. Murilo de Carvalho, "A Modernização Frustrada," 39–58.

13. *APBCD*, 2:390.

14. *APBCD*, 2:857, 863, 868.

15. Foner, *Free Soil*.

16. CG, 37 Cong. 2 sess., 1862.

17. CG, 32 Cong. 1 sess., 1852, 1183.

18. CG, 37 Cong. 2 sess., 1862, 1031.

19. Ibid., 1033.

20. Ibid., 1034.

21. CG, 32 Cong. 2 sess., 1852, 1022.

22. CG, 37 Cong. 2 sess., 1862, 1034.

23. Ibid.

24. CG, 32 Cong. 2 sess., 1852, 1280, 1858.

25. Ibid., 1313.

26. Robbins, *Our Landed Heritage*, 176.

27. CG, 32 Cong. 2 sess., 1852, 1277.

28. Ibid.

29. Ibid.

30. Smith, *Virgin Land*, 227 ff.

31. Foner, *Free Soil*, 37.

32. Ibid., 27.

33. Smith, *Virgin Land*, 221 ff.

34. Paul Wallace Gates, "The Homestead Act in an Incongruous Land System," in Scheiber, ed., *United States Economic History*, 242.

35. Robbins, *Our Landed Heritage*, 209.

36. United States Department of Commerce, Bureau of the Census, *Historical Statistics of the United States, Colonial Times to 1957* (Washington, D.C., 1960). For Brazil, T. Lynn Smith, *Brazil, People and Institutions*, rev. ed. (Baton Rouge, 1964).

37. Several newspapers of the regency express the point of view of these groups. See, for instance, *Nova Luz Brasileira* (Rio de Janeiro) 1831. For the study of Brazilian intellectuals who wrote against the latifundio and in favor of the abolition of slavery in the first half of the nineteenth century, see in particular Edgard Cerqueira Falcão, ed., *Obras Científicas, Políticas e Sociais de José Bonifácio de Andrada e Silva*, 3 vols. (São Paulo, 1965); Frederico Leopoldo Cesar Burlamaque, *Memória Analítica Acerca do Comércio de Escravos e Acerca dos Males da Escravidão Doméstica* (1837); João Severiano Maciel da Costa, *Memória Sobre a Necessidade de Abolir a Introdução dos Escravos Africanos no Brasil* (Coimbra, 1821).

38. Richard Morse has suggested, with intelligence and wit, that the Brazilians attempted to use land policy as a "safety belt" much as America used it as a "safety valve."

39. Warren Dean considers the Land Law of 1850 essentially a political issue which divided liberals and conservatives. See Warren Dean, "Latifundia and Land Policy," 606–25.

40. Like the Homestead Act the Brazilian Land Law of 1850 was in some respects simply disregarded. The coffee planters soon realized that even after the interruption of the slave trade, they could obtain manpower by buying slaves from economically decadent areas of the country. The internal slave trade was substituted for the external trade. It was only in the eighties that immigrants were introduced on plantations in larger numbers, and this was done essentially through private initiative. See the analysis of the transition from slavery to free labor in Emilia Viotti da Costa, *Da Senzala à Colonia*, 2d ed. (São Paulo, 1982). On the other hand, land continued to be acquired by squatting under the cover of forged documents. It was only after the proclamation of the republic that the land policy was revised.

CHAPTER FIVE

1. Djalma Forjaz, *O Senador Vergueiro, sua Vida, sua Época, 1778–1835* (São Paulo, 1924), 34. For a study of labor policies during the empire, see Emília Viotti da Costa, "Colonias de Parceria na Lavoura de Café: Primeiras Experiências," in *Anais do II Simpósio de Professores Universitários de História* (Paraná, 1963), 275–309, reprinted in *Da Monarquia à Republica*, 2d ed. (São Paulo, 1979), 149–78; Thomas Davatz, *Memórias de um Colono no Brasil* (1850), 2d ed. (São Paulo, 1941); Warren Dean, *Rio Claro: A Brazilian Plantation System, 1820–1920* (Stanford, 1976); José Sebastião Witter, "Um Estabelecimento Agrícola no Estado de São Paulo mos Meados do Século XIX," *Revista de História* 98 (1974); José de Souza Martins, *A Imigração e a Crise no Brasil Agrário* (São Paulo, 1973); idem, *O Cativeiro da Terra* (São Paulo, 1979); Thomas H. Holloway, "The Coffee Colono of São Paulo, Brazil, Migration and Mobility, 1880–1930" in Kenneth Duncan and Ian Rutledge, eds., *Land and Labor in Latin America* (Cambridge, 1977), 301–21; Sylvia Bassetto, "Política de Mão de Obra na Economia Cafeeira do Oeste Paulista" (Ph.D. diss., FFCL, USP, 1982); Maria Stella Bresciani, "Suprimento de Mão de Obra para a Agricultura; um dos Aspectos do Fenônemo Histórico da Abolição," *Revista de História* 53 (1976): 333–53; Verena Stolcke and Michael M. Hall, "The Introduction of Free Labour on São Paulo Coffee Plantations," *Journal of Peasant Studies* 10 (Jan.–April 1983): 170–200; Michael Hall, "The Origins of Mass Immigration in Brazil, 1871–1914" (Ph.D. diss., Columbia University, 1969); Lucy Maffei Hutter, *Imigração Italiana em São Paulo, 1880–1889* (São Paulo, 1972); Jean Roche, *La colonization allemande et le Rio Grande do Sul* (Paris, 1959).

2. MSS, Arquivo do Estado de São Paulo (hereafter, AESP), Império, Colonias, box 1, December 1847.

3. *AALPSP*, 1854, 363.

4. *AALPSP*, 1852, 29.

5. *AALPSP*, 1856, 256.

6. *AALPSP*, 1854, 367.

7. Auguste von der Straten Ponthoz, *Le Budget du Brésil* (3 vols.; Brussels, 1859), 3:5.

8. MSS, AESP, Império, Colonias, box 2.

9. Charles Expilly, *La traîte, l'immigration et la colonisation au Brésil* (Paris, 1865).

10. Luis Couty, *Pequena Propriedade e Imigração Européia* (Rio de Janeiro, 1887), 69.

11. Relatório de 1870 do Dr. José Maria Correa de Sá e Benevides a Assembléia Legislativa do Rio de Janeiro, 55.

12. MSS, Arquivo Público Mineiro, books 569 and 1379.

13. Charles Reybaud, *La colonisation au Brésil* (Paris, 1958), 17; Charles Expilly, *La traîte*, 59.

14. *AALPSP*, 1848–49 and 1852–54.

15. Davats, *Memórias de um Colono*; Forjaz, *O Senador Vergueiro*; Carlos Perret Gentil, *A Colonia Senador Vergueiro* (Santos, 1851).

16. MSS, AESP, Império, Colonias box 1, letter written in January 1853, signed by Vergueiro and addressed to the provincial president.

17. *Discurso com que o Sr. José Antonio Saraiva, Presidente da Província de São Paulo, Abriu a Assembléia Legislativa da Província de São Paulo, no Dia 15 de Fevereiro de 1855.* See also Relação das Colonias Existentes em 1860, MSS, AESP, Império, Colonias, box 2.

18. Johan Jakob von Tschudi, *Viagem às Províncias do Rio de Janeiro e São Paulo* (São Paulo, 1953), 131.

19. MSS, AESP, Império, Colonias, box 1.

20. MSS, AESP, Império, Colonias, box 2.

21. All the documents quoted here can be found in MSS, AESP, Império, Colonias, box 2.

22. Von Tschudi, *Viagem às Províncias*, 46, 163.

23. Davatz, *Memórias de um Colono*, is the best testimony for the colonists' point of view. The sharecroppers' perception that they were treated as if they were slaves was not totally unfounded. Examining a justice of the peace book in Amparo, Sylvia Bassetto found that an immigrant was arrested because he was "insubordinate and insisted on keeping his hat on while he talked to his boss." Four others were in jail for having received in their homes for more than three days families from other plantations; Sylvia Bassetto "Política de Mão de Obra," 167.

24. MSS, AESP, Império, Colonias, box 1. For a study of a rebellion years later see Sylvia Bassetto, "Política de Mão de Obra." See also Stolcke and Hall, "The Introduction of Free Labour."

25. The law of 11 September 1861 tried to remedy the situation by legalizing marriages of non-Catholics. See Aureliano Candido Tavares Bastos, "Memória sobre Imigração," in *Os Males do Presente e as Esperanças do Futuro* (São Paulo, 1939), 115.

26. MSS, AESP, Império, Colonias, box 1 and box 2.

27. Tavares Bastos, *Os Males do Presente*, 74.

28. MSS, AESP, Império, Colonias, box 1.

29. MSS, AESP, Império, Colonias, box 1 and 2.

30. Charles Expilly quotes J. U. Sturz's letter of 5 December 1857 in which he says: "Si vous pouviez parvenir à sacrifier assez de vos compatriotes allemandes pour que leur travail peut revenir au Brésilien à aussi bon marché que celui des nègres, vous seriez certes hautement loué, bien payé et même distingué"; Expilly, *La traîte*, 27.

31. MSS, AESP, Império, Colonias, box 1.

32. Von Tschudi, *Viagem*, 152.

33. About the colonist's social mobility, see MSS, AESP, Império, Colonias, box 1; Sylvia Bassetto, "Política de Mão de Obra," 135; Holloway, "The Coffee Colono of São Paulo." See also Thomas Holloway, *Immigrants on the Land: Coffee and Society in São Paulo, 1886–1934* (Chapel Hill, 1980).

34. Barão Patí do Alferes, *Fundação e Custeio de uma Fazenda na Província do Rio de Janeiro* (Rio de Janeiro, 1963).

35. MSS, AESP, Império, Colonias, box 1.

36. Stanley Stein, *Grandeza e Decadência do Café no Vale do Paraiba* (São Paulo, 1961), 353.

37. Patí do Alferes, *Fundação e Custeio*, 245–46, 262–67; Augusto Ramos, "Máquinas Primitivas para Beneficiar Café," in *O Café no Segundo Centenário de sua Introdução no Brasil* (Rio de Janeiro, 1934), 1:75.

38. C. F. van Delden Laërne, *Brazil and Java Report on Coffee Culture in América, Ásia, and África* (London, 1885).

39. AALPSP, 1854–55, 47.

40. MSS, AESP, Império, Colonias, box 2.

41. Ibid.

42. Ibid., letter from the municipal judge Antonio Peixoto, Campinas, 30 May 1858, to the provincial president.

43. Ibid.

44. Ibid., box 1.

45. Ibid., box 2, letter dated Campinas, 23 December 1865, signed G. H. Krug.

46. Von Tschudi, *Viagem*, 131.

47. Davatz, *Memórias de um Colono*, 29–30. According to José de Souza Martins, 67 colonies had been founded between 1851 and 1860, whereas only 18 were founded between 1861 and 1870; *A Imigração e a Crise do Brasil Agrário*, 53.

48. MSS, Arquivo Nacional, SH Códice 544, Relatório do Inspetor Geral de Terras e Colonização José Cupertino Coelho Cintra ao Sr. Cansanção de Sinimbu. See also Thomas Holloway, "Condições do Mercado de Trabalho e Organização do Trabalho nas Plantações na Economia Cafeeira de São Paulo, 1885–1915, Uma Análise Preliminar," *Estudos Econômicos* 2, 6 (1972): 145–77.

49. Expilly, *La traîte*, 93.

50. João E. Carvalho Monte Negro, *Colonias Nova Lousã e Nova Colombia* (São Paulo, 1875).

51. Johan Jakob von Tschudi talks about 400 *reis*, Sérgio Buarque de

Holanda in his preface to Davatz mentions 500 and even 600 *reis*. This difference between these authors can probably be explained by difference in chronology.

52. MSS, AESP, Impérios, Colonias, box 1 and 2.

53. *Relatório apresentado ao Ilmo. Sr. Dr. Jorge Tibiriçá . . . pelo Inspetor de Engenharia, Leandro Dupré* (1893). See also José Francisco Camargo, *Crescimento da População no Estado de São Paulo e seus Aspectos Econômicos* (3 vols.; São Paulo, 1952).

54. For a different interpretation of the failures of the sharecropping system, see Dean, *Rio Claro*, 106.

CHAPTER SIX

1. Hipólito da Costa, *Correio Braziliense* (29 vols.; London, 1808–22), 7:608–9. For an abridged edition, see Barbosa Lima Sobrinho, *Antologia do Correio Brasiliense* (Rio de Janeiro, 1977), 103, 107, 132, 605, 607.

2. João Severiano Maciel da Costa, *Memória sôbre a Necessidade de Abolir a Introdução dos Escravos Africanos no Brasil: sôbre o Modo e Condições com que esta Abolição se Deve Fazer e sôbre os Modos de Remediar a Falta de Braços que Ela Pode Ocasionar* (Coimbra, 1821); José Bonifácio de Andrada e Silva, *Representação à Assembléia Geral Constituinte e Legislativa do Império do Brasil sôbre a Escravatura* (Paris, 1825); José Eloy Pessoa da Silva, *Memória sôbre a Escravatura e Projeto de Colonização dos Europeus e Pretos da África no Império do Brasil* (Rio de Janeiro, 1826); and Frederico L. Cesar de Burlamaque, *Memória Analítica Acerca do Comércio de Escravos e Acerca dos Males da Escravidão Doméstica por F.L.C.B.* (Rio de Janeiro, 1837).

3. M. F. J. Santanna Nery, *Le Brésil en 1889* (Paris, 1889); A. Balbi, *Essai statistique sur le royaume du Portugal et d'Algarve, comparé aux autres états de l'Europe* (2 vols.; Paris, 1822); Malte Brum, *Tableau statistique du Brésil* (Paris, 1830).

4. Emília Viotti da Costa, *Da Senzala à Colonia*, 2d ed. (São Paulo, 1982).

5. *Relatório apresentado à Assembléia Legislativa da Província do Rio de Janeiro Pelo Conselheiro Antonio Nicoláu Tolentino* (Rio de Janeiro, 1858); Maria Sylvia de Carvalho Franco, *Homens Livres na Ordem Escravocrata* (São Paulo, 1969); Eny Mesquita, "O papel do Agregado em Itú" (Master's thesis, FFCH, USP, 1975).

6. Many travelers gave detailed descriptions of slaves' living conditions. See Jean Baptiste Debret, *Viagem Pitoresca e Histórica ao Brasil*, 2d ed. (3 vols.; São Paulo, 1941); Charles Ribeyrolles, *Brasil Pitoresco*, 2d ed. (2 vols.; São Paulo, 1941); Henry Chamberlain, *Views and Costumes of the City and Neighborhood of Rio de Janeiro* (London, 1822); Daniel Kidder, *Sketches of Residence and Travels in Brazil* (2 vols.; Philadelphia, 1845); Ferdinand Denis, *Le Brésil: Histoire, moeurs, usages et costumes des habitants de ce royaume* (2 vols.; Paris, 1822); Maria Graham, *Journal of a Voyage to Brazil and Residence There during the Years 1821, 1822, 1823* (London, 1824); Henry Koster, *Travels in Brazil* (2 vols.; Philadelphia, 1817); Johan Moritz Rugendas, *Viagem Pitoresca através do Brasil*, 3d ed. (São Paulo, 1941); Carl Seid-

ler, *Dez Anos no Brasil*, 2d ed. (São Paulo, 1941). See also farmers' guides such as those published by Luis Peixoto Lacerda Werneck, *Memória Sôbre a Fundação e Custeio de uma Fazenda na Província do Rio de Janeiro* (Rio de Janeiro, 1878); João Baptista A. Imbert, *Manual dos Fazendeiros ou Tratado Doméstico Sobre as Enfermidades dos Negros* (Rio de Janeiro, 1839); Antonio Caetano da Fonseca, *Manual do Agricultor e dos Gêneros Alimentícios* (Rio de Janeiro, 1863). Particularly informative are Katya Queiroz Mattoso, *Etre esclave au Brésil* (Paris, 1979); Mary C. Karash, "Slave Life in Rio de Janeiro, 1808–1850," (Ph.D. diss., University of Wisconsin, 1972); Francisco Vidal Luna, *Minas Gerais: Escravos e Senhores* (São Paulo, 1981).

7. Leslie Bethell, *The Abolition of the Brazilian Slave Trade: Britain, Brazil, and the Slave Trade Question, 1807–1869* (Cambridge, 1970); idem, "The Independence of Brazil and the Abolition of the Slave Trade: Anglo-Brazilian Relations, 1822–26," *Journal of Latin American Studies* 1 (November 1969): 115–47; Robert Conrad, "The Contraband Slave Trade to Brazil, 1831–1845," *HAHR* 49 (November 1969): 618–38.

8. *AALPSP*, 1855, 101, 266, (1856), 182; MSS, Arquivo do Estado de São Paulo, Império, Escravos, box 1.

9. Philip Curtin, *The Atlantic Slave Trade: A Census* (Madison, Wis., 1969); Herbert Klein, *The Middle Passage: Comparative Studies in the Atlantic Slave Trade* (Princeton, 1978); W. P. Christie, *Notes on Brazilian Questions* (London, 1865), 83–86; Robert Slenes, "The Demography and Economics of Brazilian Slavery, 1850–1888" (Ph.D. diss., Stanford University, 1976); Maurício Goulart, *Escravidão Africana no Brasil: Das Origens à Extinção do Tráfico* (São Paulo, 1949).

10. *Coleção Das Leis do Império do Brasil* (1850).

11. Rumors of contraband were heard from time to time until as late as 1870; see MSS, Arquivo do Estado de São Paulo, Império, Escravos, box 1 and MSS, Arquivo Nacional, Ij. 525, Ij. 522.

12. See below, n. 14.

13. Slenes, "The Demography and Economics of Brazilian Slavery"; Warren Dean, *Rio Claro: A Brazilian Plantation System, 1820–1920* (Stanford, 1976); Maria Luiza Marcílio, *La ville de São Paulo: Peuplement et population, 1780–1850, d'après les registres paroissiaux* (Rouen, 1968).

14. Viotti da Costa, *Da Senzala à Colonia*, xliii–xliv; Evaristo de Moraes, *A Escravidão Africana no Brasil: Das Origens à Extinção* (São Paulo, 1933), 174; about slaves' marriage, see Francisco Vidal Luna and Irací del Nero, "Vila Rica: Nota sobre Casamentos de Escravos, 1727–1826," *África* 4 (1981): 3–6; idem, "Devassa nas Minas Gerais: Observações Sôbre Casos de Consubinato," *Anais do Museu Paulista* 31 (1982): 3–15.

15. For a discussion of paternalism, see Eugene Genovese, *Roll, Jordan, Roll* (New York, 1979).

16. Clovis Moura, *Rebeliões das Senzales* (São Paulo, 1959); Stuart Schwartz, "The Mocambo: Slave Resistance in Colonial Bahia," *Journal of Social History* 3 (Summer 1970): 313–33; idem, "Resistance and Accommodation in Eighteenth Century Brazil," *HAHR* 57 (1977): 69–81.

17. Debret, *Viagem Pitoresca* 2:185; Ribeyrolles, *Brasil Pitoresco* 1:36; Adolphe d'Assier, *Le Brésil contemporain* (Paris, 1867), 98.

18. MSS, Arquivo Público Mineiro, Livro 573; Debret, *Viagem Pitoresca* 2:225; Roger Bastide, *Les religions africaines aux Brésil* (Paris, 1960); idem, *Sociologia do Folclore Brasileiro* (São Paulo, 1959).

19. Viotti da Costa, *Da Senzala à Colonia*, 274.

20. Pedro Carvalho de Mello, "The Economics of Slavery in Brazilian Coffee Plantations, 1850–1888," (Ph.D. diss., University of Chicago, 1977); idem, "Aspectos Econômicos da Organização do Trabalho na Economia Cafeeira do Rio de Janeiro, 1850–1888," *Revista Brasileira de Economia* 32 (January–March, 1978): 19–67; Peter Eisenberg, *Sugar in Pernambuco: Modernization without Change, 1840–1910* (Berkeley, 1974).

21. Klein, *The Middle Passage*, 97–98; Slenes, "The Demography and Economics of Slavery," 123.

22. *Trabalhos do Congresso Agrícola do Recife, Outubro de 1878* (Recife, 1978); see also Eisenberg, *Sugar in Pernambuco*, 154–55.

23. André Rebouças, *A Agricultura Nacional: Estudos Econômicos, Propaganda Abolicionista e Democrática* (Rio de Janeiro, 1883); Luis Peixoto Lacerda Werneck, *Idéias sôbre Colonização* (Rio de Janeiro, 1855), 62; Quintino Bocaiuva, *A Crise da Grande Lavoura e da Grande Propiendade no Brasil* (Rio de Janeiro, 1878), 10; C. A. Taunay, *Algumas Considerações sobre a Colonização como Meio de Coadjuvar a Substituição do Trabalho Cativo pelo Trabalho Livre no Brasil* (Rio de Janeiro, 1834).

24. Eisenberg, *Sugar in Pernambuco*, 181.

25. Viotti da Costa, *Da Senzala à Colonia*, 124–28.

26. Sylvia Bassetto, "Política de Mão de Obra na Economia Cafeeira do Oeste Paulista" (Ph.D. diss., FFCH, USP, 1982); see also Viotti da Costa, *Da Senzala à Colonia*, and Thomas H. Holloway, *Immigrants on the Land: Coffee and Society in São Paulo, 1886–1934* (Chapel Hill, 1980).

27. Viotti da Costa, *Da Senzala à Colonia*, 138–57; Augusto Emílio Zaluar, *Peregrinação pela Província de São Paulo, 1860–1861* (São Paulo, 1953), 191; AALPSP, 1863, 372, 396.

28. Flávio Saes, "A Grande Emprêsa de Serviços Públicos na Economia Cafeeira" (Ph.D. diss., FFCH, USP, 1979);

29. Cheywa R. Spindel, *Homens e Máquinas na Transição de uma Economia Cafeeira* (Rio de Janeiro, 1979); Eduardo Perez de Souza, "A Evolução das Técnicas Produtivas no Século XIX: O Engenho de Açucar e a Fazenda de Café" (Master's thesis, IFCH, Universidade de Campinas, 1978).

30. Louis Couty, *Etude de biologie industrielle sur le café* (Rio de Janeiro, 1883); C. F. Van Delden Laërne, *Brazil and Java: Report on Coffee Culture in America, Asia, and Africa* (London, 1885).

31. Eisenberg, *Sugar in Pernambuco*.

32. Ibid.

33. Louis Couty, *Le Brésil en 1884* (Rio de Janeiro, 1884); idem, *Pequena Propriedade e Imigração Européia, 1883–1884* (Rio de Janeiro, 1887).

34. Aroldo de Azevedo, "Última Etapa na Vida do Barão de Santa Eulália," *Revista de História* 10; 3 (1952): 417–30.

35. Rodrigues Alves, *Relatório Apresentado à Assembléia Legislativa Provincial de São Paulo* (1888).

36. The debate over slave productivity is still very much alive. For Warren Dean (*Rio Claro*) free labor is more productive than slave labor. This is also the opinion of Fernando Henrique Cardoso (*Capitalismo e Escravidão no Brasil Meridional* [São Paulo, 1962]) and Octavio Ianni ("O Progresso Econômico e o Trabalhador Livre" in Sérgio Buarque de Hollanda, ed., *História Geral da Civilização Brasileira* [1969], 2[3]:297–319). Both Jacob Gorender (*O Escravismo Colonial* [São Paulo, 1978]) and Pedro Carvalho de Mello ("Aspectos Econômicos"), consider slave labor more productive than free labor. Jaime Reis (*Abolition and the Economics of Slaveholding in Northeast Brazil*, Glasgow University, Institute of Latin American Studies, Occasional Papers [Glasgow, 1979], argues that slave labor is sometimes more and sometimes less productive than free labor. For discussions of this problem, see also Sylvia Bassetto, "Política de Mão de Obra," 68; Odilon Nogueira de Matos, "O Visconde de Indaiatuba e o Trabalho Livre em São Paulo," *Anais do VI Simpósio da APUH* (São Paulo, 1973), 69.

37. Carvalho de Mello, "Aspectos Econômicos."

38. Hall, "The Origins of Mass Immigration in Brazil"; Thomas Holloway, "Immigration and Abolition: The Transition from Slave to Free Labor in the São Paulo Coffee Zone," in *Essays concerning the Socio-Economic History of Brazil and Portuguese India*, ed. Dauril Alden and Warren Dean (Gainesville, Florida, 1977).

39. Viotti da Costa, *Da Senzala à Colonia*, 172–79.

40. João Elisário Carvalho Monte Negro, *Colonias Nova Lousã e Nova Colombia* (São Paulo, 1875); see also Bassetto, "Política de Mão de Obra," 72–75.

41. João Pedro da Veiga, *Estudo Econômico e Financeiro sôbre o Estado de São Paulo* (São Paulo, 1896), 63; Francisco de Paula Ferreira de Rezende, *Minhas Recordações* (Rio de Janeiro, 1944), 27, 438, 442, 498.

42. Alice Barros Fontes, "Os Caifazes, 1882–1889" (Master's thesis, FFCH, USP, 1976); Viotti da Costa, *Da Senzala à Colonia*, 421; see also Evaristo de Moraes, *A Campanha Abolicionista, 1876–1888* (Rio de Janeiro, 1924); Osório Duque Estrada, *A Abolição, 1831–1888* (Rio de Janeiro, 1918); Suely Robles Reis de Queirós, *Escravidão Negra em São Paulo: Um Estudo das Tensões Provocadas pelo Escravismo no Século XIX* (Rio de Janeiro, 1977).

43. Joaquim Nabuco, *Campanha Abolicionista no Recife: Eleições de 1884* (Rio de Janeiro, 1885), 10.

44. Viotti da Costa, *Da Senzala à Colonia*, 290–319. See also Robert B. Toplin, *The Abolition of Slavery in Brazil* (New York, 1972).

45. For a different point of view, see Pedro Carvalho de Mello, "The Economics of Slavery"; Robert Slenes, "The Demography and Economics of Bra-

zilian Slavery"; Robert Conrad, *The Destruction of Brazilian Slavery, 1850–1888* (Berkeley, 1972).

46. *APBCD*, 1871, 4, 26.

47. F. A. Brandão, Jr., *A Escravatura no Brasil* (Brussels, 1865). See the articles published in the newspaper *A Província de São Paulo*, 24 Nov. 1880, 23 Dec. 1880, 15 Jan. 1881. See also João Cruz Costa, *O Desenvolvimento da Filosofia no Brasil no Século XIX e a Evolução Histórica Nacional* (São Paulo, 1950), 227–365.

48. Sud Menucci, *O Precursor do Abolicionismo no Brasil: Luiz Gama* (São Paulo, 1938).

49. For a detailed analysis of the pattern of voting, see Viotti da Costa, *Da Senzala à Colonia*, 384, and Conrad, *Destruction of Brazilian Slavery*, 301, 303.

50. Viotti da Costa, *Da Senzala à Colonia*, 290–319; Robert Toplin, *The Abolition of Slavery in Brazil* (New York, 1972).

51. *APBCD*, 1884, 4, 121.

52. *APBCD*, 1885; *Anais do Senado* (1885).

53. Viotti da Costa, *Da Senzala à Colonia*, 418.

54. José Maria dos Santos, *Republicanos Paulistas e a Abolição* (São Paulo, 1942). See also Emília Costa Nogueira, "O Movimento Republicano em Itú: Os Fazendeiros do Oeste Paulista e os Pródromos do Movimento Republicano," *Revista de História* 20 (1954): 379–405.

55. Barão do Javari, *Organização e Programas Ministeriais*, 2d ed. (Rio de Janeiro, 1962).

56. Florestan Fernandes, *A Integração do Negro na Sociedade de Classes* (São Paulo, 1964). See also José Bento de Araujo, *Relatório Apresentado a Assembléia Legislativa Provincial do Rio de Janeiro* (1888).

57. Amélia de Rezende Martins, *Um Idealista Realizador, Barão Geraldo de Rezende* (Rio de Janeiro, 1939), 289, 358.

CHAPTER SEVEN

1. Gilberto Freyre, *The Mansions and the Shanties (Sobrados e Mucambos): The Making of Modern Brazil* (New York, 1963); Pedro Pinchas Geiger, *Evolução da Rede Urbana Brasileira* (Rio de Janeiro, 1963); Richard Morse, "Cities and Societies in Nineteenth Century Latin America: The Illustrative Case of Brazil," in Jorge Hardoy and Richard Schaedel, eds., *The Urbanization Process in America from Its Origins to the Present Day* (Buenos Aires, 1969); José Arthur Rios, "The Cities of Brazil," in T. Lynn Smith and A. Marchant, eds., *Portrait of Half a Continent* (New York, 1951), 108–208; Stuart Schwartz, "Cities of Empire: Mexico and Bahia in the Sixteenth Century," *Journal of Inter-American Studies and World Affairs* 11 (October 1969): 616–37; Richard Morse, "Brazil's Urban Development: Colony and Empire," in A. J. R. Russell-Wood, ed., *From Colony to Nation* (Baltimore and London, 1975); Katya Queiroz Mattoso, *A Cidade do Salvador e seu Mercado no Século XIX* (São Paulo, 1978).

2. Geiger, *Evolução da Rede Urbana*, 70.

3. João Antonio Andreoni, *Cultura e Opulência do Brasil* (Texto da Edição de 1711), Introduction by A. P. Canabrava (São Paulo, 1967); Stuart Schwartz, "Free Labor in a Slave Economy: The Lavradores de Cana of Colonial Bahia," in Dauril Alden, ed., *Colonial Roots of Modern Brazil* (Berkeley, 1973), 147–97; idem, "Elite Politics and the Growth of a Peasantry in Late Colonial Brazil," in Russell-Wood, *From Colony to Nation*, 133–54; Catherine Lugar, "The Portuguese Tobacco Trade and Tobacco Growers of Bahia in the Late Colonial Period," in Dauril Alden and Warren Dean, eds., *Essays Concerning the Socio-Economic History of Brazil and Portuguese India* (Gainesville, Fla., 1977), 26–70; Rae J. D. Flory, "Bahian Society in the Mid-Colonial Period: The Sugar Planters, Tobacco Growers, Merchants and Artisans of Salvador and the Reconcavo, 1680–1725" (Ph.D. diss., University of Texas, 1978); Rae Flory and David Smith, "Bahian Merchants and Planters in the Seventeenth and Early Eighteenth Centuries," *HAHR* 58 (November 1978): 571–94.

4. Alexander Marchant, *From Barter to Slavery: The Economic Relations of Portuguese and Indians in the Settlement of Brazil, 1500–1580* (Baltimore, 1942).

5. William Dampier, *Voyage aux Terres Australes, a la Nouvelle Hollande etc. . . . fait en 1699* (Rouen, 1715). Among the things imported Dampier lists hats, silk stockings, wines, olive oil, butter, cheese, salted meat, iron, metal tools, pewter lattes and silverware, and mirrors. A very similar list can be found in Adriaen Van der Düssen, *Relatório sôbre as Capitanias Conquistadas no Brasil pelos Holandeses, 1639: suas Condições Econômicas e Sociais*, translated into Portuguese by J. A. Gonçalves de Mello Neto (Rio de Janeiro, 1947).

6. Charles Boxer, *Portuguese Society in the Tropics: The Municipal Council of Goa, Macáo, Bahia and Luanda, 1500–1800* (Madison, 1965); A. J. R. Russell-Wood, "Local Government in Portuguese America: A Study in Cultural Divergence," *Comparative Studies in Society and History* 16 (March 1974): 187–231. For race relations in the colony see Charles Boxer, *Race Relations in the Portuguese Colonial Empire, 1415–1825* (Oxford, 1963); idem, *The Golden Age of Brazil, 1695–1750: Growing Pains of Colonial Society* (Berkeley, 1962); about vagrants see Laura de Mello e Souza, "Notas Sôbre os Vadios na Literatura Colonial do Século XVIII," in Roberto Schwarz, ed., *Os Pobres na Literatura Brasileira* (São Paulo, 1983).

7. Stuart Schwartz, *Sovereignty and Society in Colonial Brazil: The High Court of Bahia and Its Judges, 1609–1751* (Berkeley, 1973); idem, "Magistracy and Society in Colonial Brazil," *HAHR* 50 (November 1970): 715–30.

8. Van der Düssen noticed that blacksmiths, carpenters, masons, tailors, shoemakers, saddle-makers, and other craftsmen were very much in need in the colony in spite of the large number of slaves occupied in those crafts. This seems to indicate that slaves never had complete monopoly of the trades; Van der Düssen, *Relatório*.

9. Susan Soeiro, "The Social and Economic Role of the Convent: Women and Nuns in Colonial Bahia, 1677–1800," *HAHR* 54 (May 1974): 209–32;

idem, "The Feminine Orders in Colonial Bahia, Brazil: Economic, Social and Demographic Implications, 1677–1800," in Asuncion Lavrin, ed., *Latin American Women: Historical Perspectives* (Westport, Conn., 1978); Francisco de Morais, "Estudantes Brasileiros na Universidade de Coimbra," *Anais da Biblioteca Nacional do Rio de Janeiro* 67 (1940): 137–335.

10. Boxer, *The Golden Age of Brazil*, 11.

11. A. J. R. Russell-Wood, "Women and Society in Colonial Brazil," *Journal of Latin American Studies* 9 (May 1977): 1–34; idem, "Females and Family in the Economy and Society of Colonial Brazil," in Lavrin, *Latin American Women*, 60–100; Charles Boxer, *Women in Iberian Expansion Overseas: Some Facts, Fancies and Personalities* (New York, 1975); Elizabeth Kuznesof, "Household Composition and Headship as Related to Changes in Modes of Production, São Paulo, 1756–1836," *Comparative Studies in Society and History* 22 (January 1980): 78–108.

12. For a description of the seigneurial style of life in the Northeast see Andreoni, *Cultura e Opulência do Brasil*; for São Paulo, see John D. French, "Riqueza, Poder e Mão de Obra Numa Economia de Subsistência: São Paulo, 1596–1625," *Revista do Arquivo Municipal* 45, 195 (São Paulo, 1982): 79–107.

13. Donald Ramos, "A Social History of Ouro Preto: Stresses of Dynamic Urbanization in Colonial Brazil, 1695–1726" (Ph.D. diss., University of Florida, 1972); Boxer, *The Golden Age of Brazil*; Kenneth Maxwell, *Conflicts and Conspiracies: Brazil and Portugal, 1750–1800* (Cambridge, 1973). The 1804 census was published in Ministério da Justiça, Arquivo Nacional, *Um Recenseamento na Capitania de Minas Gerais: Vila Rica, 1804.* For an analysis of this census, see Donald Ramos, "Vila Rica, Profile of a Colonial Urban Center," *The Americas* 35 (April 1979): 495–526; Francisco Vidal Luna and Iraci del Nero da Costa, "A Presença do Elemento Fôrro no Conjunto de Proprietário de Escravos," *Ciência e Cultura* 32 (July 1980): 836–41.

14. The description of the backland towns and the port cities is based on a great number of travelers. Particularly useful were: Adolphe d'Assier, *Le Brésil Contemporain* (Paris, 1867); R. C. B. Avé-Lallemant, *Viagem pelo Sul do Brasil no Ano de 1858* (Paris, 1862); Karl Burmeister, *Viagens ao Brasil através das Províncias do Rio de Janeiro e Minas Gerais, Visando Especialmente a História Natural dos Districtos Auridiamantíferos* (São Paulo, 1952); Henry Chamberlain, *Views and Costumes of the City and Neighborhood of Rio de Janeiro* (London, 1822); John Codman, *Ten Months in Brazil* (Boston, 1867); Oskar Constatt, *Das Republikanische Brazilien in Vergangeheit und Gezenwart* (Leipzig, 1898); Louis Couty, *Le Brésil en 1884* (Rio de Janeiro, 1884); Jean Baptiste Debret, *Viagem Pitoresca e Histórica ao Brasil*, 2d ed. (3 vols.; São Paulo, 1940); Ferdinand Denis, *Le Brésil* (Paris, 1822); Charles Expilly, *Mulheres e Costumes no Brasil* (São Paulo, 1935); Maria Graham, *Journal of a Voyage to Brazil and Residence There During the Years 1821, 1822, 1823* (London, 1824); Daniel Kidder, *Sketches of a Residence and Travels in Brazil* (2 vols.; Philadelphia, 1845); Henry Koster, *Travels in Brazil* (2 vols.; Philadelphia, 1817); John Luccock, *Notas sôbre o Rio de Janeiro e Partes Me-*

ridionais do Brasil, 2d ed. (São Paulo, 1942); Pierre Emile Levasseur, *Le Brésil* (Paris, 1889); Charles Reybaud, *Le Brésil* (Paris, 1856); Charles Ribeyrolles, *Brasil Pitoresco*, 2d ed. (São Paulo, 1941); Johan Moritz Rugendas, *Viagem Pitoresca Através do Brasil*, 2d ed. (São Paulo, 1940); Augustin F. C. de Saint-Hilaire, *Segunda Viagem ao Rio de Janeiro e Minas Gerais e São Paulo, 1822*, 2d ed. (São Paulo, 1940); idem, *Segunda Viagem à São Paulo: Quadro Histór-ico da Província de São Paulo*; idem, *Viagem à Província de São Paulo*, 2d ed. (São Paulo, 1940); idem *Voyage dans les Provinces de Rio de Janeiro et Minas Gerais* (Paris, 1830); M. F. Santanna Nery, *Le Brésil en 1889* (Paris, 1890); Adèle Toussaint-Samson, *Une Parisienne au Brésil* (Paris, 1883); Carl Seidler, *Dez Anos no Brasil* (São Paulo, 1941); Maximilian A. Philip Neue-Wied, *Voyage au Brésil dans les Années 1815, 1816, 1817* (Paris, 1821–22); Augusto Emílio Zaluar, *Peregrinação Pela Província de São Paulo, 1860–1861* (São Paulo, 1953). For a description of the backland towns and rural culture the best book still is Antonio Cândido Mello e Souza, *Os Parceiros do Rio Bonito*, 4th ed. (São Paulo, 1977).

15. A. J. R. Russell-Wood, *Fidalgos and Philanthropists: The Santa Casa de Misericordia of Bahia, 1550–1755* (Berkeley, 1968); Laima Mesgravis, *A Santa Casa de Misericórdia de São Paulo* (São Paulo, 1978).

16. Saint-Hilaire, *Segunda Viagem à São Paulo: Quadro Histórico*, 116–17.

17. Graham, *Journal of a Voyage to Brazil.*

18. Burmeister, *Viagem ao Brasil*, 146; see also Lucila Herman, "Evolução da Estrutura Social de Guaratinguetá num Período de Trezentos Anos," *Revista de Administração* 2 (1948): 3–396.

19. Donald Carr Lowe, "The Brazilian Município: The Myth of Local Self-Government" (Ann Arbor, University Microfilms, 1959); Raymundo Faoro, *Os Donos do Poder: Formação do Patronato Político Brasileiro*, 2d ed. (2 vols.; São Paulo, 1975); Maria Isaura Pereira de Queiroz, *O Mandonismo Local na Vida Política Brasileira* (São Paulo, 1969).

20. Emília Viotti da Costa, *Da Senzala à Colonia*, 2d ed. (São Paulo, 1982).

21. José de Alencar, *Obras Completas* (Rio de Janeiro, 1960), 1097; for his comments on patronage, see also pp. 1074 and 1080.

22. Michael Hall, "The Origins of Mass Immigration in Brazil, 1871–1914" (Ph.D. diss., Columbia University, 1969); Paul Singer, *Desenvolvimento Econômico e Evolução Urbana* (São Paulo, 1968), 37; Geiger, *Evolução da Rede Urbana*, 152; José Francisco de Camargo, *Crescimento da População no Estado de São Paulo e Seus aspectos Econômicos: Ensaio sôbre as Relações entre a Demografia e a Economia* (3 vols.; São Paulo, 1952), 1:149.

23. Singer, *Desenvolvimento Econômico e Evolução Urbana.*

24. Camargo, *Crescimento da População*, 149. See also Singer, *Desenvolvimento Econômico e Evolução Urbana*, and Pedro Pinchas Geiger, *Evolução da Redé Urbana.*

25. Freyre, *The Mansions and the Shanties*; Carlos Castaldi, "O Ajustamento do Imigrante à Comunidade Paulistana: Estudo de um Grupo de Imigrantes Italianos e de Seus Descendentes," in Bertram Hutchinson, ed. *Mobi-*

lidade e Trabalho: Um Estudo da Cidade de São Paulo (Rio de Janeiro, 1960), 181-342.

26. Geiger, *Evolução da Rede Urbana*, 96.

27. Richard Morse, *From Community to Metropolis: A Biography of São Paulo, Brazil* (Gainesville, Fla., 1958), 215.

28. Nestor Goular Reis Filho, *Quadro da Arquitetura no Brasil* (São Paulo, 1970); Luis Saia, *Morada Paulista* (São Paulo, 1972).

29. June Hahner, "Feminism, Women's Rights and the Suffrage Movement in Brazil, 1850-1932, *LARR* 15 (1980): 65-111; idem, "The Nineteenth Century Feminist Press and Women's Rights in Brazil," in Lavrin, *Latin American Women*, 254-85; idem, "Women and Work in Brazil, 1850-1920," in Alden and Dean, *Essays Concerning the Socio-Economic History of Brazil*; Maria Odila Leite da Silva Dias, *Quotidiano e Poder em São Paulo no Século XIX: Ana Gertrudes de Jesus* (São Paulo, 1984); Sandra Lauderdale Graham, "Protection and Obedience: The Paternalist World of Female Domestic Servants, Rio de Janeiro, 1860-1910" (Ph.D. diss., University of Texas, 1982).

30. Sandra Lauderdale Graham, "The Vintem Riot and Political Culture, Rio de Janeiro, 1880," *HAHR* 60 (August 1980): 431-50; Edgard Carone, *Movimento Operário no Brasil, 1877-1944* (São Paulo, 1979).

31. Alfredo d'Escragnolle Taunay, *Memórias* (Rio de Janeiro, 1960).

32. Simon Schwartzman, "Urbanizacion y Desarollo en Brasil," in Jorge Henrique Hardoy and Carlos Tobar, eds., *La Urbanizacion en America Latina* (Buenos Aires, 1969); Stanley Stein, *The Brazilian Cotton Manufacture: Textile Enterprise in an Underdeveloped Area, 1850-1950* (Cambridge, 1957); Richard Graham, *Britain and the Onset of Modernization in Brazil, 1850-1914* London, 1968); Celso Furtado, *Formação Econômica do Brasil* (São Paulo, 1977); F. R. Versiani and J. R. Mendonça de Barros, eds., *Formação Econômica do Brasil e a Experiencia da Industrialização* (São Paulo, 1977); Flavio Versiani, "Industrial Investment in an Export Economy: The Brazilian Experience before 1914," University of London, ILAS, Working Papers (1977); Wilson Cano, *Raízes da Concentração Industrial em São Paulo* (Rio de Janeiro, 1977); Warren Dean, *The Industrialization of São Paulo, 1880-1945* (Austin, 1969); Nathaniel Leff, "Long Term Brazilian Economic Development," *Journal of Political Economy* 81 (May-June 1973); Singer, *Desenvolvimento Econômico e Evolução Urbana*; Brasil, Ministerio da Agricultura, Indústria e Comércio, *Recenseamento do Brasil, 1920* (Rio de Janeiro, 1923).

33. Singer, *Desenvolvimento Econômico e Evolução Urbana*, 287; Rui Guilherme Granziera, *A Guerra do Paraguai e o Capitalismo no Brasil* (São Paulo, 1979), argues differently. For him commercial capital prevailed until the Paraguyan War, but after the 1870s industrial capital became increasingly important in determining the growth of the cities.

34. Nícia Vilela Luz, *A Luta Pela Industrialização no Brasil, 1808-1930*, 2d ed. (São Paulo, 1971).

35. Flávio Azevedo Marques Saes, "A Grande Emprêsa de Serviços Públicos na Economia Cafeeira: Um Estudo sôbre o Desenvolvimento do Grande Capital em São Paulo," (Ph.D. diss., FFCH, USP, 1979).

36. Emília Costa Nogueira, "O Movimento Republicano em Itú: Os

Fazendeiros do Oeste Paulista e os Pródromos do Movimento Republicano," *Revista de História* 20 (1954): 379, 399, 405.

37. Carone, *Movimento Operário no Brasil*, 189.

38. Sylvio Romero, *O Castilhismo no Rio Grande do Sul* (n.p., 1912).

39. Thomas Skidmore, *Black into White: Race and Nationality in Brazilian Thought* (New York, 1974).

40. Tobias Barreto, *A Questão do Poder Moderador e Outros Ensaios Brasileiros* (Petrópolis, 1977), 38.

41. Singer, *Desenvolvimento Econômico e Evolução Urbana*, 302.

42. Sylvio Romero, *Provocações e Debates* (n.p., 1910), 179.

CHAPTER EIGHT

1. Emília Viotti da Costa, "Sôbre as Origens da República," *Anais do Museu Paulista* 18 (1964): 63–120; George Boehrer, "The Brazilian Republican Revolution: Old and New Views," *Luso-Brazilian Review* 3, 2 (Winter 1966): 43–57; Stanley Stein, "A Historiografia do Brasil, 1808–1889," *Revista de História* 29 (September 1964): 81–133.

2. Francisco José de Oliveira Viana, *O Ocaso do Império* (São Paulo, 1925).

3. Visconde de Ouro Preto, *Advento da Ditadura Militar no Brasil* (Paris, 1891); José Francisco da Rocha Pombo, *História do Brasil*, vol. 10 (Rio de Janeiro, 1906); Joaquim Nabuco, *Um Estadista do Império: Nabuco de Araújo, sua Vida, suas Opiniões, sua Época* (3 vols.; Rio de Janeiro, 1898–1900); Manuel de Oliveira Lima, *O Império Brasileiro, 1822–1889* (São Paulo, 1927). For a modern monarchist version, see João Camillo de Oliveira Tôrres, *A Democracia Coroada. Teoría Política do Império do Brasil* (Rio de Janeiro, 1967).

4. Suetonio, *O Antigo Regimen: Homens e Coisas* (Rio de Janeiro, 1896); Oscar Araujo, *L'idée republicaine au Brésil* (Paris, 1893); Felício Buarque, *Origens Republicanas: Estudos de Gênese Política*, 2d ed. (São Paulo, 1962); Euclydes da Cunha, *À Margem da História* (Pôrto, 1896).

5. Caio Prado, Jr., *A Evolução Política do Brasil* (São Paulo, 1933).

6. Nelson Werneck Sodré, *Panorama do Segundo Império* (São Paulo, 1935); idem, *Formação da Sociedade Brasileira* (Rio de Janeiro, 1944); idem, *Formação Histórica do Brasil* (São Paulo, 1962; new ed., Rio de Janeiro, 1976).

7. See, for example, Leoncio Basbaum, *História Sincera da República* (Rio de Janeiro, 1957; 4th ed., São Paulo, 1976); Heitor Lyra, *História da Queda do Império* (2 vols.; São Paulo, 1964). For a different interpretation, see Richard Graham, "Landowners and the Overthrow of the Empire," *Luzo Brazilian Review* 7, 2 (December 1970): 44–56.

8. Emília Viotti da Costa, *Da Senzala à Colonia*, 2d ed. (São Paulo, 1982).

9. On the abolition of slavery, see also Robert Conrad, *The Destruction of Brazilian Slavery, 1850–1888* (Berkeley, 1972), Robert Toplin, *The Abolition of Slavery in Brazil* (New York, 1972), and Richard Graham, "Brazilian Slav-

ery Reexamined: A Review Article," *Journal of Social History* 3 (1970): 431–53.

10. Percy Alvin Martin, "Causes of the Collapse of the Brazilian Empire," *HAHR* 4 (February 1921): 4–48; C. H. Haring, *Empire in Brazil* (Cambridge, Mass., 1959); George Boehrer, "The Church in the Second Reign, 1840–1889," in Henry H. Keith, and S. F. Edwards, eds., *Conflict and Continuity in Brazilian Society* (Columbia, S.C., 1969), 115–43; George Boehrer, "The Church and the Overthrow of the Brazilian Monarchy," *HAHR* 48 (August 1968): 380–401. For a study of the conflict between Church and State, see also Antonio Carlos Villaça, *A História da Questão Religiosa no Brasil* (Rio de Janeiro, 1974); Nilo Pereira, *Conflitos entre a Igreja e o Estado no Brasil* (Recife, 1976); David Queirós Vieira, "Protestantism and the Religious Question in Brazil, 1855–1875" (Ph.D. diss., American University, 1972).

11. Américo Braziliense de Almeida e Mello, *Os Programmas dos Partidos e o Segundo Império* (São Paulo, 1878).

12. See, for example, Silva Jardim, *A Pátria em Perigo* (Santos, 1885).

13. Oliveira Viana, *O Ocaso do Império*, 7.

14. Tobias Monteiro, *Pesquisas e Depoimentos para a História* (Rio de Janeiro, 1913), 112–13.

15. June G. Hahner, *Civilian Military Relations in Brazil, 1889–1898* (Columbia, S.C., 1969); José Murilo de Carvalho, "As Forças Armadas na Primeira República: O poder Desestabilizador," in Boris Fausto, ed., *História Geral da Civilização Brasileira* (São Paulo, 1971), 3 (2):181–234; John Schulz, "The Brazilian Army in Politics, 1850–1854" (Ph.D. diss., Princeton University, 1973); idem, "O Exército e o Império," in Sérgio Buarque de Holanda, ed., *História Geral da Civilização Brasileira* (São Paulo, 1971), 2 (4):235–58; W. S. Dudley, "Institutional Sources of Officer Discontent in the Brazilian Army, 1870–1889," *HAHR* 55 (February 1975): 44–65; June Hahner, "The Brazilian Armed Forces and the Overthrow of the Monarchy: Another Perspective," *The Americas* 26, 2 (October 1969): 171–82. Very informative is Nelson Werneck Sodré, *História Militar do Brasil* (Rio de Janeiro, 1968). About positivism, see João Camillo de Oliveira Tôrres, *O Positivismo no Brasil* (Petrópolis, 1957); Ivan Lins, *História do Positivismo no Brasil* (São Paulo, 1964); Robert Nachman, "Positivism, Modernization and the Brazilian Middle Class," *HAHR* 57 (February 1977): 1–23; Raimundo Teixeira Mendes, *Benjamin Constant*, 2d ed. (Rio de Janeiro, 1913); Umberto Peregrino, *História e Projeção das Instituições Culturais do Exército* (Rio de Janeiro, 1967).

16. Oliveira Viana, *O Ocaso do Imperio*.

17. On the Republican party, see George Boehrer, *Da Monarquia à República: História do Partido Republicano no Brasil, 1870–1889* (Rio de Janeiro, 1954); José Murilo de Carvalho, "Elite and State Building in Imperial Brazil" (Ph.D. diss., Stanford University, 1974).

18. Suetonio, *O Antigo Regimen*; Araujo, *L'idée republicaine*; Buarque, *Origens Republicanas*.

19. See, for example, Afonso d'Albuquerque Mello, *A Liberdade no*

Brasil, seu Nascimento, Vida, Morte e Sepultura (Recife, 1864); Timandro, "Libélo do Povo" in R. Magalhães, Jr., ed., *Tres Panfletários do Segundo Reinado* (São Paulo, 1946), 61.

20. Antonio Manuel Fernandes, *Índice Cronológico, Explicativo e Remissivo da Legislação Brasileira de 1822 até 1848* (Niteroi, 1848).

21. Peter Eisenberg, *The Sugar Industry in Pernambuco: Modernization without Change, 1810–1910* (Berkeley, 1974).

22. Viotti da Costa, *Da Senzala à Colonia*, 188–202; Stanley Stein, *Vassouras: A Brazilian Coffee County, 1850–1900: The Roles of Planter and Slave in a Changing Plantation Society* (New York, 1970); Eduardo Perez de Souza, "A Evolução das Técnicas Produtivas no Século XIX, o Engenho de Açucar e a Fazenda de Café" (M.A. thesis, University of Campinas, 1978); Michael Hall, "The Origins of Mass Immigration in Brazil, 1871–1914" (Ph.D. diss., Columbia University, 1969); Lucy Maffei Hutter, "Imigração Italiana em São Paulo, 1880–1889: Os Primeiros Contactos do Imigrante com o Brasil" (Ph.D. diss., University of São Paulo, 1972). See also chap. 5, n. 1, above.

23. Warren Dean, *The Industrialization of São Paulo, 1880–1945* (Austin, 1969); Nícia Vilela Luz, *A Luta pela Industrialização do Brasil* (São Paulo, 1961; 2d ed., São Paulo, 1971); Wilson Cano, *Raízes da Concentração Industrial em São Paulo* (Rio de Janeiro, 1977; 2d ed. São Paulo, 1979); Flavio Versiani, "Industrial Investment in an Export Economy: The Brazilian Experience before 1914," University of London, Institute of Latin American Studies Working Papers (London, 1977); Stanley Stein, *The Brazilian Cotton Manufacture: Textile Enterprise in an Underdeveloped Area, 1850–1950* (Cambridge, 1957).

24. Richard Morse, *From Community to Metropolis* (Gainesville, Fla., 1958); Paul Singer, *Desenvolvimento Econômico e Evolução Urbana* (São Paulo, 1968).

25. About the role of middle classes in the republican movement, see Nícia Vilela Luz, "O Papel das Classes Médias Brasileiras no Movimento Republicano," *Revista de História* 57 (1964): 13–28.

26. For an opposite opinion, see Charles Wagley, *A Revolução Brasileira; uma Análise da Mundança Social desde 1930* (Salvador, 1967).

27. Richard Graham, *Britain and the Onset of Modernization in Brazil, 1850–1914* (London, 1971).

28. Sérgio Milliet, *Roteiro do Café e Outros Ensaios* (São Paulo, 1941), 19–20. See also chap. 7.

29. Stein, *Vassouras: A Brazilian Coffee County*.

30. C. F. van Delden Läerne, *Brazil and Java: Report on Coffee Culture in America, Asia, and Africa with Plates, Maps, and Diagrams* (London, 1885), 212–24.

31. Emília Costa Nogueira, "O Movimento Republicano em Itú: Os Fazendeiros do Oeste Paulista e os Pródromos do Movimento Republicano," *Revista de História* 20 (1954): 384–85. For a different opinion, see Peter Eisenberg, "A Mentalidade dos Fazendeiros no Congresso Agrícola de 1878," in

Joseí Amaral Lapa, ed., *Modos de Produção da Realidade Brasileira* (Petropólis, 1980), 167–95.

32. Fernando Henrique Cardoso, *Capitalismo e Escravidão* (São Paulo, 1961); Peter Eisenberg, *The Sugar Industry in Pernambuco*.

33. *Revista Illustrada*, March 1889 and August 1889.

34. See the opinions of Frei Canéca in Antonio José de Melo, ed., *Typhis Pernambucano. Obras Literárias de Frei Joaquim do Amor Divino Canéca* (Recife, 1875), 1 July 1824.

35. Américo Braziliense, de Almeida Mello, *Os Programas dos Partidos e o Segundo Império*.

36. Barão do Javarí, *Organização e Programas Ministeriais: Regime Parlamentar no Império*, 2d ed. (Rio de Janeiro, 1962); Santanna Nery, *Le Brésil en 1889* (Paris, 1889), 202.

37. Tácito de Almeida, *O Movimento de 1887* (São Paulo, 1934), 17.

38. Martim Francisco, *São Paulo Independente: Propaganda Separatista* (São Paulo, 1887).

39. Alberto Salles, *A Pátria Paulista* (Campinas, 1887).

40. J. F. de Barros, *A Pátria Paulista* (São Paulo, 1887).

41. Boehrer, *Da Monarquia à República*, 275. See also José Maria dos Santos, *Bernardino de Campos e o Partido Republicano Paulista: Subsídios para a História da República* (Rio de Janeiro, 1960).

42. Max Leclerc, *Cartas do Brasil* (São Paulo, 1942), 131.

43. Oliveira Viana, *O Ocaso do Império*.

44. Costa Nogueira, "O Movimento Republicano em Itu", 391.

45. José Maria dos Santos, *Os Republicanos Paulistas e a Abolição* (São Paulo, 1943).

46. Costa Nogueira, "O Movimento Republicano em Itu," 387–95.

47. Ibid., 396–97. See also Pierre Mombeig, *Pionniers et Planteurs* (Paris, 1952); Richard Morse, *From Community to Metropolis*.

48. Santos, *Bernardino de Campos e o Partido Republicano Paulista*, 40.

49. Boehrer, *Da Monarquia à República*.

50. See Tobias Barreto, *Pesquisas e Depoimentos para a História* (Rio de Janeiro, 1913); José Soares de Souza, *O Militarismo na República* (São Paulo, 1925); Sérgio Buarque de Holanda, ed., *História Geral da Civilização Brasileira* (São Paulo, 1972), 2 (5):316–60; Ximeno de Villeroy, *Benjamin Constant e a Política Republicana* (Rio de Janeiro, 1928). See note 15 above.

51. Oliveira Viana, *O Ocaso do Império*, 127.

52. José Maria dos Santos, *Política Geral do Brasil* (São Paulo, 1930), 181.

53. The argument that the country is not prepared for change and that those who speak for reforms are threatening the social order is always used by conservative elements, and it was one of the favorite arguments used against republicans by the monarchists. See, for example, an article published in *A Província de Minas* on 11 October 1888: "Forgetting the lessons of the past, the experience of generations, the uncontested strength of the instinctive genius, habits, and traditions of the Brazilian people, the republican propaganda

raises the red banner of war against the monarchy above the clamors of resentment, despair, and blind passions."

54. Javarí, *Organização e Programas Miniseriais*, 245.

55. *Revista Ilustrada*, June 1889.

56. Villeroy, *Benjamin Constant*.

CHAPTER NINE

1. Gilberto Freyre, *Brazil: An Interpretation* (New York, 1945), 126, 97.

2. Ibid., 154, 96.

3. Octávio Ianni, "Research on Race Relations in Brazil," in *Race and Class in Latin America*, ed. Magnus Morner (New York, 1970), 267. The most important revisionists are L. A. Costa Pinto, *O Negro no Rio de Janeiro* (São Paulo, 1952); Florestan Fernandes and Roger Bastide, *Relaçóes Raciais entre Brancos e Negros em São Paulo* (São Paulo, 1955); Thales de Azevedo, *As Elites de Côr: um Estudo da Ascensão Social* (São Paulo, 1955); Guerreiro Ramos, *Introdução Crítica à Sociología Brasileira* (Rio de Janeiro, 1957); Fernando Henrique Cardoso e Octávio Ianni, *Côr e Mobilidade em Florianópolis* (São Paulo, 1960); Fernando Henrique Cardoso, *Capitalismo e Escravidão: o Negro na Sociedade Escravocrata do Rio Grande do Sul* (São Paulo, 1962); Octavio Ianni, *As Metamorfoses do Escravo* (São Paulo, 1962); Florestan Fernandes, *A Integração do Negro na Sociedade de Classes*, 2 vols. (São Paulo, 1964), translated into English as *The Negro in Brazilian Society* (New York, 1969); Thales de Azevedo, *Cultura e Situação Racial no Brasil* (Rio de Janeiro, 1966); Octávio Ianni, *Raças e Classes Sociais no Brasil* (Rio, 1966); Florestan Fernandes, *O Negro no Mundo dos Brancos* (São Paulo, 1972).

Among the American authors: *Race and Class in Rural Brazil*, ed. Charles Wagley (Paris, 1952); Richard Morse, "The Negro in São Paulo, Brazil," *Journal of Negro History* 38 (July 1953): 290–306; Marvin Harris, *Town and Country in Brazil* (New York, 1956); Bertram Hutchinson, *Village and Plantation Life in Northeastern Brazil* (New York, 1963; new ed., 1971); Carl Degler, *Neither Black nor White: Slavery and Race Relations in Brazil and the United States* (New York, 1971).

As representatives of the traditional school in the United States: Frank Tannembaum, *Slave and Citizen: The Negro in the Americas* (New York, 1946); Donald Pierson, *Negroes in Brazil* (Washington, D.C., 1959); new ed., Chicago, 1967); Stanley Elkins, *Slavery: A Problem in American Institutional and Intellectual Life* (Chicago, 1959).

4. Irwin G. Wyllie, *The Self-Made Man in America: The Myth of Rags to Riches* (New York, 1966).

5. Richard Morse had already registered racial discrimination. See his "Negro in São Paulo, Brazil," 290–306.

6. Pierre Van den Berghe, *Race and Racism* (New York, 1967); Thomas Skidmore, *Black into White: Race and Nationality in Brazilian Thought* (New York, 1974).

7. Oracy Nogueira, "Skin Color and Social Class," in *Plantation Systems in the New World*, ed. Vera Rubin (Washington, D.C., 1959), 164–79.

8. Skidmore, *Black into White*, 210–11.

9. The results of this research were published in Wagley, *Race and Class*.

10. George Fredrickson, *The Black Image in the White Mind: The Debate on Afro-American Character and Destiny, 1817–1914* (New York, 1971); Leonard L. Richards, *Gentlemen of Property and Standing: Anti-Abolition Mobs in Jacksonian America* (New York, 1970).

11. Skidmore, *Black into White*, 48–53.

12. Ibid., 77.

13. Van den Berghe, *Race and Racism*, 32.

14. Skidmore, *Black into White*, 218; Fernandes, *The Negro in Brazilian Society*, 134–38.

15. *Revista do Livro* 5, 2 (March 1957): 164, quoted by Eduardo de Oliveira e Oliveira, "O Mulato um Obstáculo Epistemológico," *Argumento*, July 1974, p. 70.

16. Joaquim Nabuco, *O Abolicionismo* (London, 1883). On Nabuco, see Carolina Nabuco, *The Life of Joaquim Nabuco* (Stanford, 1950); Luis Viana Filho, *A Vida de Joaquim Nabuco* (São Paulo, 1952).

17. Skidmore, *Black into White*, 23.

18. Raymundo Faoro, *Machado de Assis, A Piramide e o Trapézio* (São Paulo, 1974). See also Miécio Tati, *O Mundo de Machado de Assis* (Rio, 1961); Roberto Schwarz, *Ao Vencedor as Batatas* (São Paulo, 1977).

19. On the emperor, see Heitor Lyra, *História de D. Pedro II* (3 vols.; São Paulo, 1939–40); Mary Wilhelmine Williams, *D. Pedro the Magnanimous* (Chapel Hill, 1937).

20. Skidmore, *Black into White*, 24.

21. About the system of clientele and patronage, see Victor Nunes Leal, *Coronelismo Enxada e Voto* (Rio de Janeiro, 1948; new ed. São Paulo, 1975); Raymundo Faoro, *Os Donos do Poder: Formação do Patronato Brasileiro*, 2d ed. (2 vols.; São Paulo, 1975); Maria Isaura Pereira de Queiroz, *O Mandonismo Local na Vida Política Brasileira* (São Paulo, 1969); idem, "O Coronelismo numa Interpretação Sociológica," in Boris Fausto, ed., *História Geral da Civilização Brasileira* (São Paulo, 1975–), 3(1):175–90; Marcos Vilaça e Roberto Cavalcanti e Albuquerque, *Coronel Coronéis* (Rio de Janeiro, 1965); Simon Schwartzman, "Regional Cleavages and Political Patriarchalism in Brazil" (Ph.D. diss., University of California, Berkeley, 1973).

22. Richard Morse, "The Heritage of Latin America," in *Politics and Social Change in Latin America: The Distinct Tradition*, ed. Howard J. Wiarda (Amherst, Mass., 1974), 25–70.

23. Charles Boxer, *The Golden Age of Brazil, 1695–1750* (Berkeley, 1969), 166; idem, *Race Relations in the Portuguese Colonial Empire, 1415–1825* (Oxford, 1963), 117.

24. On the mulatto in Brazilian society, see Degler, *Neither Black nor White*. For a different point of view, see the review of Degler's book by Oliveira, "O Mulato: um Obstáculo Epistemológico." For an analysis of the ways in which the mulatto embraced the ideology of the whites; see A. Preto-Rodas, *Negritude as a Theme in the Poetry of the Portuguese Speaking World*, Univer-

sity of Florida, Humanities Monograph, vol. 31 (Gainesville, Fla., 1970). See also Roger Bastide, *A Poesia Afro-Brasileira* (São Paulo, 1943); idem, "A Imprensa Negra no Estado de São Paulo," in Roger Bastide, ed., *Estudos Afro-Brasileiros* (São Paulo, 1973), 129–50.

25. Edgard Carone, *A República Velha. Evolução Política* (São Paulo, 1971); idem, *A República Velha Instituições e Classes Sociais* (São Paulo, 1970); Décio Azevedo Marques de Sales, *O Civilismo e as Camadas Médias Urbanas na Primeira República Brasileira, 1889–1930*, Cadernos Universidade Estadual de Campinas IFCH (n.d.), 1.

26. Emília Viotti da Costa, "Sobre as Origins da República," *Anais do Museu Paulista* 18 (São Paulo, 1964): 76–77, reprinted Emília Viotti da Costa, *Da Monarquia à República* (São Paulo, 1977), 243–90.

27. Boris Fausto, *Pequenos Ensaios de História da República, 1889–1945*, Cadernos Cebrap (São Paulo, 1972), 10.

28. Rui Barbosa, *A Questão Social e Política no Brasil* (Rio de Janeiro, 1958). Very expressive of these anxieties are José Lins do Rêgo's novels which belong to the "sugar cane cycle."

29. On modernism, see Wilson Martins, *The Modernist Idea* (New York, 1970); John Nist, *The Modernist Movement in Brazil* (Austin, 1967); Mário da Silva Brito, *História do Modernismo Brasileiro*, vol. 1, *Antecedentes da Semana de Arte Moderna*, 2d ed. (Rio de Janeiro, 1964); Afranio Coutinho, *An Introduction to Literature in Brazil* (New York, 1969). On the regionalist manifesto see José Alderaldo Castello, *José Lins do Rego: Modernismo e Regionalismo* (São Paulo, 1961); Gilberto Freyre, *Região e Tradição* (Rio de Janeiro, 1941).

30. Gilberto Freyre, *The Masters and the Slaves: A Study in the Development of Brazilian Civilization*, abridged (New York, 1964), 11.

31. Fernandes, *The Negro in Brazilian Society*, 189–233.

32. Ianni, "Research on Race Relations," in Morner, *Race and Class*, 257–59.

33. See Octávio Ianni, *Sociologia e Sociedade no Brasil* (São Paulo, 1975), 22.

INDEX